WETLAND ADAPTATIONS IN THE GREAT BASIN

Papers from the Twenty-First Great Basin Anthopological Conference

WETLAND ADAPTATIONS IN THE GREAT BASIN

Papers from the Twenty-First Great Basin Anthopological Conference

Edited by

Joel C. Janetski
Department of Anthropology
Brigham Young University
Provo, Utah

David B. Madsen
Antiquities Section
Utah Division of State History
Salt Lake City, Utah

Museum of Peoples and Cultures
Occasional Papers No. 1

Brigham Young University 1990

Frontspiece: Bone harpoons from Woodard Mound, Utah Valley, Utah

CONTENTS

CONTRIBUTORS

Richard H. Brooks	Department of Anthropology, University of Nevada, Las Vegas, Nevada
Sheilagh Brooks	Department of Anthropology, University of Nevada, Las Vegas, Nevada
William J. Cannon	Bureau of Land Management, Lakeview District, Lakeview, Oregon
C. Cliff Creger	Department of Anthropology, University of Nevada, Reno, Nevada
Amy Dansie	Nevada State Museum, Carson City, Nevada
Michael P. Drews	Intermountain Research, Silver City, Nevada
Catherine S. Fowler	Department of Anthropology, University of Nevada, Reno, Nevada
Don D. Fowler	Department of Anthropology, University of Nevada, Reno, Nevada
Ruth L. Greenspan	Heritage Research Associates, Inc., Eugene, Oregon
Michele B. Haldeman	Department of Education, University of Kansas, Lawrence, Kansas
Eugene M. Hattori	Department of Anthropology, California Academy of Sciences, San Francisco, California
Joel C. Janetski	Department of Anthropology, Brigham Young University, Provo, Utah
Robert L. Kelly	Department of Anthropology, University of Louisville, Louisville, Kentucky
David B. Madsen	Antiquities Section, Utah Division of State History, Salt Lake City, Utah
Albert C. Oetting	Heritage Research Associates, Inc., Eugene, Oregon
Virginia M. Parks	U.S. Fish and Wildlife Service, Stillwater Wildlife Refuge, Nevada
Anan W. Raymond	U.S. Fish and Wildlife Service, Portland, Oregon

David Rhode   Desert Research Institute, Reno, Nevada

Mary J. Ricks   Department of Anthropology, Portland State University, Portland, Oregon

Dave N. Schmitt   Intermountain Research, Silver City, Nevada

Nancy D. Sharp   Department of Prehistory, Research School of Pacific Studies, The Australian National University, Canberra

David H. Thomas   Department of Anthropology, American Museum of Natural History, New York, New York

Donald R. Tuohy   Nevada State Museum, Carson City, Nevada

PREFACE AND ACKNOWLEDGMENTS

Many of the papers in this volume were presented at the Twenty-First Great Basin Anthropological Conference (GBAC) held in Park City in 1988. The theme (admittedly somewhat informal) of that conference was wetlands studies in the Great Basin. This emphasis was in part due to the research interests of Janetski who acted as program chair for the conference and in part due to the proliferation of work being done in wetlands contexts throughout the Great Basin for various reasons (flooding at Stillwater, for example). Several of the papers included here were not presented at the Twenty-First GBAC, but were invited or offered shortly thereafter; several have been revised substantially from those offered at the meetings. These changes, we feel, give the volume better geographic and topical coverage. Madsen, whose interest in marshes and their use by prehistoric peoples has considerable time-depth, graciously accepted co-editorship at Janetski's request.

The idea of publishing the conference papers focusing on research around lakes and marshes was discussed in appropriate fashion (informally) and a commitment to proceed was reached by whomever happened to be in the smoke-filled room at the time. Funding for the publication came from the coffers of the GBAC and the volume is the first in the Occasional Papers series from the Museum of Peoples and Cultures at Brigham Young University. Numerous publications have been so funded by supporters of the GBAC and have made important contributions to the anthropological literature on the Great Basin. We hope this volume continues that tradition. In the interest of history and ease of reference we have listed the previous GBAC–sponsored publications on the inside front cover (thanks to Don Fowler for supplying the list).

Acknowledgments for a project such as this are many. Major thanks go to the contributors who worked patiently with the editors and who generally responded promptly with papers and refinements requested by reviewers. We also offer sincere thanks to the many reviewers who willingly assisted in reading and commenting on the papers. The Museum of Peoples and Cultures is grateful to the GBAC for providing the wherewithal to initiate the Occasional Papers series. Finally, we owe the greatest debt to Kathy Driggs, the office manager and editorial assistant at the Museum of Peoples and Cultures. Kathy did all the page formatting, put in lots of extra hours, caught innumerable problems that the editors missed, and did it all while expecting her second child.

Joel C. Janetski
David B. Madsen

August 1990

1

INTRODUCTION

David B. Madsen and Joel C. Janetski

The Great Basin is, as many have pointed out, a land of extremes. Lake, river, and marsh environments supplied with "free" water from high mountain ranges, contrast sharply with the desert conditions of intermountain valleys and lower foothills; a contrast made more dramatic by a lack of intervening environmental settings. This physical diversity has long been mirrored in the contrasting nature of Great Basin anthropological debates. Specific arguments and their associated terminology have changed with time, but the structure of the debate has not. Prehistoric and ethnographically known Great Basin groups are argued to be either generalists or specialists; they were either limno–mobile or limno–sedentary; they either lived in a "Garden of Eden" or they lived a life of stress and deprivation. All arguments which can be characterized as "either/or" polemics.

This history of these often contentious debates is covered elsewhere in this volume (Fowler and Fowler this volume) and it is not our purpose to repeat it here. We do want to note, however, that the history of these discourses continues to color our understanding of the way Great Basin peoples lived, reproduced, and died. The pendulum of opinion seems to swing from one extreme to another: either Great Basin wetlands are or are not attractive places to live. Many of the papers included here continue to address issues raised in support of one or the other of these contrasting views, but together suggest that the current swing is towards the view that marshes and lake margins are a wonderful place to live. Since both of us have at one time or another contended that lake, river, and marsh environments were the focus of many prehistoric Basin groups (Madsen 1979, Janetski 1983), it would seem that we should look upon such a swing with some satisfaction. We do not. We view it as merely a continuation of a decades old interpretive dichotomy that is ultimately sterile.

Yet despite this continued focus on extremes, we detect some movement towards a more balanced and integrated view of how Great Basin people lived in and utilized the resources of mountain and valley, desert and lake, marsh and pygmy forest. This integrated view is one we wish to support and in this introduction we want to stress how restricting our efforts to contrasting extremes in Great Basin strategies has tended to obscure our understanding of how many Basin groups actually lived and why they lived that way. In our view, the essential problem with either/or arguments is that they tend to be more descriptive rather than explanatory. That is, they define situations, not explain why they occur; a failure that we believe is the underlying reason why such arguments are gradually being abandoned. They also tend to not be derived from higher–order theory and are not easily subject to test. How and why questions about sedentarism and mobility cannot be answered with simple either/or dichotomies. Such questions are contextual, or, more exactly, they are questions of relative relationships.

We believe that hunter–gatherers (indeed all people) tend towards those behaviors which maximize their reproductive success. That is, we view a natural selection paradigm as the one most likely to be productive in understanding human behavior generally and Great Basin peoples specifically, and, within such a paradigm, either/or arguments are irrelevant. If situations are such that increased mobility will enhance their "fitness," then their behavioral trend will be toward increased mobility. If people can enhance their reproductive success by staying–put in some situations, then the trend will be towards a sedentary existence. People do not "want" to be mobile anymore than they "want" to be sedentary. In short, contrasting foragers with collectors, "limno–mobile" with "limno–sedentary" strategies, and "rich" ecosystems with "poor" ones obscures rather than clarifies our understanding of how and why Great Basin peoples acted in the way they did. Essentially, this is because such contrasts tend to take an absolutist form, while behavior is based primarily on relative comparisons. As a result, we perceive a need in the Great Basin to develop a hierarchically ranked body of theory which allows us to predict human behavior in a **situational** context.

The foundation for pursuing this strategy has been in place for some time. Indeed, O'Connell, Jones and Simms (1982) emphatically called for precisely what we proposed nearly a decade ago. They suggested that investigative approaches grouped under the rubric of "evolutionary ecology" could provide the most comprehensive explanations for human behavior in the Great Basin. In the ten years since they first made that statement, they and a number of other scholars have heeded that advice and a fairly large body of data collected under a natural selection paradigm has begun to accumulate. With this increasingly large research base, Great Basin anthropology has begun to creep out of darkness of either/or. Unfortunately, some of this research has been conducted on the back of the decades–old polarization that has characterized Great Basin anthropology and has occasionally been misused in support of one or another extreme. These newer either/or arguments have changed only in terminology; resources in Basin marshes are now either "low–ranked" and marshes are rotten places to live, or they are "high–ranked" and are the favored focus of hunter–gatherer subsistence systems.

However, from an evolutionary ecological perspective, Great Basin wetlands are neither "good" nor "bad," Basin lakes and marshes are not "better" than Basin uplands and terrestrial resources are not "better" than lacustrine resources. Even the placement of such large categories as "lacustrine" and "terrestrial" in opposition to one another is entirely misleading. Basin wetlands vary in size, composition and reliability, as do adjoining areas of foothill and mountain environments. They vary in productivity and in proximity to other necessary resources. As a result, we should expect marshes to be used in different ways. Even where Great Basin wetlands, and the settings in which they occur, are fundamentally similar, the cultural behavior may differ. Social contexts, as well as the ecological contexts, influence behavioral patterns. In identical physical situations it may be most appropriate for a group of ten to stay–put and for a group of twenty to move about. Whether one is young or old, childless or the parent of several infants, part of a small group of a large one will effect the most appropriate behavior. The over–all context in which people find themselves influences which behaviors will produce the best "fitness." Behavior changes as both the natural and social situation changes. There is no better or worse, no good or bad, no either/or.

The continuing confusion generated by this either/or approach has been exacerbated in the last decade by contrasting foragers with collectors and by associating foragers with residential movement and collectors with logistical movement. This additional either/or contrast seems entirely inappropriate to us since, first, virtually no group of hunter–gatherers depends on only one or the other strategy, and, second, storage rather than movement is the key to distinguishing the two approaches to resource procurement. If the distinction between logical mobility and residential mobility is that in the former you move resources to people and in the latter you move people to resources, then many "collectors" have high residential mobility. That is, in most Basin cases hunter–gatherers move to a patch where they forage (i.e., pick and eat) for current consumption and collect (i.e., pick and store) for future consumption, then move on to the next patch and repeat the process. They then later return and consume these stored resources during the winter months. Depending on the richness and diversity of resources in a "patch," the number of these moves annually may be as few as one or two or as many as ten or fifteen. However, they are still fundamentally similar in that people move to the resources.

In short, the difference between a forager and a collector is the **storage of resources**, while the difference between residential and logistical mobility is the **transport of resources**, and it is east to get into trouble when the two are confused. Foragers **forage** and collectors **collect**, and residential mobility can be associated with either. In some cases they may be related, but they are not necessarily related. Given the high cost of transporting plant foods, hunter–gatherers that depend largely on the collection and storage of vegetal resources, as do most Basin groups, most probably have high residential mobility. That does not mean that they are not "collectors."

In the Basin, our ability to see and understand this fundamental similarity in the way hunter–gatherers collect and store resources and move people to those resources to consume them, is often clouded by our tendency to dichotomize a broad array of environmental settings and the behavioral adaptations to them. By contrasting wetland with upland environments and limno–mobile with limno–sedentary adaptive patterns, it becomes almost impossible to clearly identify the similarities in behavioral processes which underlie them all. Yet, if what we are about as anthropologists is to try to understand the larger issue of why people do what they do, then surely our focus should be on these underlying processes not the contrasts which obscure them.

So why a volume entitled "Wetland Adaptations in the Great Basin?" Does not the title itself suggest more of the either/or syndrome? If the contents promote such a perspective, then the answer is yes, but we do not mean them to. The purpose in presenting this collection of papers is to begin to fill a major void in what we know about those portions of the Great Basin where wetlands are present. As C. Fowler (1977, 1982) has reminded us several times, we do not know very much about these areas, either ethnographically or prehistorically. Part of the problem is that the ecology of the regions containing the most extensive wetlands have been dramatically altered. Ofttimes those were the places where European settlement first occurred. Consequently, not only are we confronted with reconstructing extinct lifeways (a difficult task by itself), we are faced with the even more onerous problem of understanding very complex ecosystems. We hope that this collection of papers can make an important step in rectifying that problem, without adding to the contrastive literature of Great Basin anthropology.

These papers address a wide range of problems from understanding regional material culture (for example, Pinto, Tuohy) to presenting broad overviews (for example, Fowler and Fowler, Oetting, Greenspan) to rather specific analyses of archaeologically recovered data (for example, Brooks et al, Drews) to addressing regional problems of subsistence (Schmitt and Sharp, Dansie) and settlement (Cannon et al., Raymond and Parks, Rhode) or both (Janetski, Kelly). As usual, the western Great Basin wetland systems are the best represented here but papers from the east (Janetski) and northwest (Greenspan, Oetting, Cannon et al.) give the volume a Basin–wide perspective. Only one (C. Fowler) is ethnographic; however, the appearance of this volume seems well timed as two additional ethnographic works for Pyramid and Walker lakes in the west (C. Fowler 1989) and Utah Lake in the east (Janetski n.d.) do much to bolster the existing literature on these regions. Much more is needed, however, especially for eastern Great Basin wetland regions (e.g., Bear Lake, Great Salt Lake marshes, Sevier Lake). This array of papers certainly gives us insights into the range of variability seen in Great Basin wetlands. Perhaps these descriptive papers make the most lasting contribution in elucidating what is needed if we are to understand "how the organism (people) comes to be dynamically integrated with its environment" (Rindos 1985:87).

References

Fowler, Catherine (editor)
   1989   *Willard Z. Park's Ethnographic Notes on the Northern Paiute of Western Nevada, 1933–1934.* University of Utah Anthropological Papers No. 114. Salt Lake City.

Janetski, Joel C.
   1983   *The Western Ute of Utah Valley: An Ethnohistoric Model of Lakeside Adaptation.* Ph.D. dissertation, Department of Anthropology, University of Utah, Salt Lake City. University Microfilms, Ann Arbor.
   n.d.   *The Ute of Utah Lake.* University of Utah Anthropological Papers No. 116. Salt Lake City, in press.

Madsen, David B.
   1979   The Fremont and the Sevier: Defining Prehistoric Agriculturalist North of Anasazi. *American Antiquity* 44(4):711–722.
   1982   Get it Where the Gettin's Good: A Variable Model of Great Basin Subsistence and Settlement Based on Data from the Eastern Great Basin. In *Man and Environment in the Great Basin*, edited by David B. Madsen and James F. O'Connell, pp. 207–226. SAA Papers No. 2. Society for American Archaeology, Washington, D.C.

O'Connell, James F., Kevin T. Jones, and Steven R. Simms
    1982   Some Thoughts on Prehistoric Archaeology in the Great Basin. In *Man and Environment in the Great Basin*, edited by David
            B. Madsen and James F. O'Connell, pp. 227–240. SAA Papers No. 2. Society for American Archaeology, Washington, D.C.
Rindos, David
    1985   Darwinian Selection, Symbolic Variation, and the Evolution of Culture. *Current Anthropology* 26(1):65–88.

2

A HISTORY OF WETLANDS ANTHROPOLOGY IN THE GREAT BASIN

Catherine S. Fowler and Don D. Fowler

Abstract

This paper provides a brief overview of previous studies focussed on or referring to wetlands archaeology and ethnography in the Great Basin region. Although various studies have raised issues regarding subsistence regimes, settlement systems and technological correlates for wetlands adaptations, none have sufficient data to do more than speculate about such matters. Given the state of the data base and the history of its accumulation and use thus far, elucidating the specifics of wetlands adaptations will be a continuing goal and one not soon realized.

Introduction

Although wetlands comprise only a small percentage of the land area of the hydrographic Great Basin, they were, until quite recently, critical loci for prehistoric and historic Indian peoples. Where they existed, wetlands provided important plant, animal, bird and fish resources to the hunter–gatherers who exploited them as part of the seasonal economic round. Since the 1930s, archaeologists and, to some extent, ethnographers have studied native adaptations to Great Basin wetlands. But only in the past two decades has research closely focussed on the complexities of wetlands adaptations and the changes therein over time. The purpose of this paper is to provide a historical perspective for those studies.

To understand wetlands adaptations it is necessary to study present–day wetlands, as well as land–forms on which wetlands formerly existed. Hence, we take "wetlands" in the broadest sense to include lake edges, marshes and stream–side or riparian areas. "Lake edges" include the terraces and beach lines of the some 120 Pleistocene pluvial lakes in the Great Basin (Morrison 1965). Pluvial lakes are now recognized as major features of Pleistocene topography world–wide (Neal 1975). Some of the earliest, and still classic, studies of pluvial lakes were conducted in the Great Basin. These studies also raised two issues of basic importance to all subsequent inquiries into Great Basin prehistory: the relationships of pluvial lake levels to climatic (hence, ecological) fluctuation; and, the question of human occupation of the terraces and beaches when they were lake edges.

Pluvial Lakes Studies

The first description of Great Basin lakes, as well as the first recognition of ancient lake level fluctuation seems to have been by Frey Silvestre de Escalante in 1776. At "Llano Salado," [just south of present–day Deseret, Utah] he observed "some delicate white shells" which suggested to him that "there has been a lake much larger than the present one . . ." at some past time (Bolton 1950:177–187, 192). John C. Fremont, in 1843–44 was the first to recognize and define the Great Basin as a region of internal drainage (Fremont 1988:275–276). Although he noted them, Fremont did not discuss the terraces of the Great Salt Lake nor the tufa formations of Pyramid Lake as evidences of high lake levels (Gilbert 1890:13). Soon after, in 1849, Howard Stansbury (1988:101 and figures facing pages 101 and 208) described and illustrated ancient beach terraces around the perimeter of the Great Salt Lake. Additional significant descriptions and discussions of the Great Salt Lake terraces were made in 1854 by E. G. Beckwith (1855:97n.1), in 1858 by J. H. Simpson (1983:47–56) and in 1871 by F. V. Hayden (1872:17–20). In 1863 J. D. Whitney (1865:451–452) described the terraces at Mono Lake. Between 1867–70 members of the U.S. Geological and Geographical Survey of the Fortieth Parallel, led by Clarence King (1878:488–529), studied and "approximately" mapped the pluvial lakes in northern Nevada and California. King and his colleagues were the first to recognize that the northern reaches of the Great Basin are divided by an uplands region which they called the Nevada Plateau. To the west lay the Nevada Basin containing pluvial Lake Lahontan, as they named it (King 1878:504). To the east was the Utah Basin (Hague and Emmons 1877:311–853). They also recognized a pluvial lake therein, which G. K. Gilbert (1872:49–50, 1875:51) named Lake Bonneville in 1872.

Grove Karl Gilbert focussed his attention on Lake Bonneville from 1872 to 1883. His several papers on the lake, synthesized in his magnum opus, *Lake Bonneville* (Gilbert 1890), are properly regarded as "one of the consummate works of nineteenth–century American geology" (Pyne 1980:134–135). Gilbert's treatise, together with Israel Russell's (1884, 1885, 1895) definitive studies of Lake Lahontan and other western pluvial lakes, are the foundation documents for all subsequent studies of Great Basin Quaternary geology and geoarchaeology (e.g., Antevs 1948, Blackwelder 1948; Davis 1982, 1983; Hubbs and Miller 1948; Mifflin & Wheat 1979; Morrison and Frye 1965; Thompson et al. 1986).

The question of human occupation of Pluvial lake edges was first raised in 1885 by Russell (1885:247, 269 and Figure 33) who reported and illustrated "a[n obsidian] spear head of human workmanship [Figure 1] . . . from upper lacustral clays exposed in the walls of Walker River Canyon, and was associated in such a manner with the bones of an elephant, or mastodon, as to leave no doubt as to their having been buried at approximately the same time. Both are genuine fossils of the upper Lahontan period." The point was found in 1882 by W. J. McGee.[1] In two abstruse and verbose papers, McGee (1888, 1889) discussed the point and other then–suspected North American "Pleistocene" artifactual finds. After much dithering, he concluded that the Walker River find indicated "feebly the contemporaneity of man with the elephant, ox, and camel of the later Pleistocene lake epoch, and almost as feebly (in view of the weight and *a priori* improbability of the conclusion), that this early man was neolithic" (McGee 1889:312).

No further studies of Great Basin pluvial terrace archaeology seem to have been made until the early 1920s. The hiatus was due, in some measure, to a lack of geologically trained archaeologists. But in a larger sense, it was due to what might be called the "Smithsonian Early Man Model" of the peopling of the New World. From ca. 1890 to 1925, William Henry Holmes and Ales Hrdlicka, both of the Smithsonian, stoutly sought to disprove any claims of the antiquity of early man in the New World prior to ca. 3,000 B.C. (e.g., Holmes 1892). Their real aim was not obstructionism (although in later years, Hrdlicka became quite overbearing on the topic), but to instill some rigor into research on the issue. But the result was a chilling effect on the progress of New World Quaternary geoarchaeology for three decades (Willey and Sabloff 1980:47–50).[2] The 1925 find of Pleistocene fauna and projectile points in stratigraphic association at the Folsom Site in New Mexico effectively negated Holmes's and Hrdlicka's conservative time–frame. Suddenly, "Early Man," soon co–named "PaleoIndian" (Roberts 1940), became a respectable topic of archaeological inquiry, and the peopling of the New World in late–Pleistocene times became both probable and a matter of concentrated investigation.

Figure 1. Obsidian "Spear–head of obsidian from Lahontan sediments" in Walker River Canyon Nevada (Russell 1885:Figure 33). Text indicates specimen is four inches long.

Systematic study of Great Basin Pluvial age sites began in 1920 with Malcolm Rogers's (1939) work on the lower Colorado River terraces and adjacent pluvial basins. Elizabeth and William Campbell began their work around Mojave Desert playas in 1925. In the Pinto Basin and subsequently on Lake Mojave terraces, the Campbells (1935; Campbell et al. 1937), like Rogers, found "ancient appearing" lithic assemblages. Among the tool types were some fluted forms and the then—and still—enigmatic crescents.

Rogers (1939:6) defined a putatively early Malpais Industry found "always in relation to the numerous dry water–courses which dissect the great flat expanses of desert pavement lands." On typological and distributional grounds, he also defined three sequential lithic complexes: San Dieguito–Playa, Pinto–Gypsum, and Amargosa (Rogers 1939:27–69).

Rogers's typology has informed, and sometimes bedeviled, all subsequent classifications for the region (Lyneis 1982:174–176; Rozaire 1963; Warren and Crabtree 1986:183–189). But Rogers, the Campbells, and others, were themselves bedeviled by the artifacts and the possible, but directly undemonstrable, ages of the sites. The lithic complexes looked "old," typologically. But the sites were all surface sites and there were no methods of absolute dating. Rogers (1939:3) had to say, in despair, "although the geographic location of the camp–sites which produce the vestiges of the earliest peoples in the California deserts definitely necessitates a climate not believed to have obtained during the past two thousand years, there are few data available to determine where the industries fall in time previous to the era of Christ."

The advent of absolute dating techniques after 1949 did **not** directly resolve the chronological problems of the lithic assemblages on lake terraces. Cross–dating of index artifacts from stratified sites elsewhere with C14 determinations did however partially resolve chronometric issues. But, despite much additional searching, good stratified lake terrace sites remain elusive. Lithic assemblages on lake terraces are now known in many parts of the Great Basin. Finds of "Clovis–like" forms on the terraces conjures up visions of Paleoindians stalking mammoths along lake edges and trapping them in the adjacent marshes. But, no **certain** associations of fluted points and mammoths, or other Pleistocene megafauna, have turned up to date, on lake terraces, or elsewhere (Watters 1979, Tuohy 1968, 1974, Madsen 1982:213, Willig, Aikens and Fagan 1988).

Putative pre–Clovis associations, such as Davis's (1978a, 1978b) China Lake materials, remain equally uncertain and frustratingly enigmatic. As Rogers (1939:1) put it in 1939: "It is universally observable that archaeologic evidence usually diminishes approximately in ratio to time recession; also that the degrees of concentration [of sites] are similarly proportionate." Despite fifty years of subsequent searching along the terraces, and the definition of various, presumably early, lithic assemblages, complexes, traditions, and co–traditions (Bedwell 1973, Davis 1969, Davis & Shutler 1969, Harrington 1957, Warren and Crabtree 1986,

Willig, Aikens and Fagan 1988), Rogers is still essentially correct. "Ancient" sites are few and far between, and they only begrudgingly, if at all, tell us what we want them to about the secrets of the past—particularly why the sites are on the terraces and what type(s) of subsistence regimes they represent.

The Limnosedentary Model

To sum up the previous discussion, although geologists and archaeologists have fretted about late pluvial lake edge occupations for over a century; numerous nagging questions remain. Since the 1950s, they have also worried about similar occupations in later times, periods now glossed as Archaic and Ethnographic. This brings us to the matter of ethnographic analogy, the question of hunter-gatherer mobility, and the "limnosedentary" model. Here, Lovelock Cave assumes an important place in our chronicle. As is well-known, in 1912, A. L. Kroeber, of the University of California, sent a museum guard, L. L. Loud, to Lovelock Cave to salvage what archaeological materials he could from guano mining activities therein (Heizer 1970). In 1924 Loud and M. R. Harrington, of the Museum of the American Indian, conducted further excavations in the cave. They found many wetlands-related artifacts, including fish lines and nets, bags, and mats of tule and the famed cache of duck decoys (Loud & Harrington 1929). Robert Heizer grew up in Lovelock, Nevada. He excavated in Humboldt Cave and Leonard Rockshelter and, with various students, intermittently worked in Lovelock Cave for nearly three decades. The lake-side locale of the cave, and the adjacent pit-house village [26]CH-15, led Heizer (1967:7) to his so-called "limnosedentary hypothesis." The apparent richness of the Humboldt Sink wetlands biome—tules, cattails, fish, waterfowl, etc.—seemed to have "made possible" at least a semi-sedentary lifeway (Napton 1969, Heizer and Napton 1970). By extension, a similar life-way seemed feasible for the Carson Sink, as well as Pyramid Lake, Walker Lake, Utah Lake, and probably other basins with sufficient water at various past times. In their original definition of the Desert Culture, Jennings and Norbeck (1955:3) had called attention to Great Basin wetland areas, and the probability of a higher degree of sedentism thereat due to the "richer resources of the lakes and their shores." Now Heizer and his students drew a more detailed picture of "semi-sedentary occupation of lakeside villages" (Napton 1969:58) in Great Basin lacustrine wetlands areas. However, until Livingston (1986, 1988:36–94) pulled together the still-extant excavation data on [26]Ch-15, it was not possible to adequately judge the basis on which the model was formulated, excepting the data presented in Cowan and Clewlow (1968).

Work at other apparent pit house sites, at Pyramid Lake (Tuohy and Clark 1979), in Surprise Valley (O'Connell 1975), at Lake Abert (Oetting and Pettigrew 1987), and in Warner Valley (Weide 1968, 1974, Cannon et al. this volume) demonstrates a wide-spread pattern of such house types, principally during Mid-Archaic times (Elston 1982:194–96). However, an adequate model of "lake-side villages" in the Western and Northwestern Great Basin remains to be developed. The baseline models provided by O'Connell (1975) and Weide (1968, 1974), together with the Humboldt Sink data and those for Winnemucca Lake (Hattori 1982), provide good starting points for integrating and elaborating more recent work.

In 1979, David Madsen (Madsen 1979, cf. Madsen and Lindsay 1977) suggested that marsh resources, specifically cattails, were the primary subsistence base for sedentism at a number of eastern Great Basin Fremont sites, an assertion subsequently questioned by Binford (1983:201). In a later paper, Madsen (1982:207, 214) broadened his concern to Archaic, as well as Fremont cultures. He pointed to "rich riverine and lacustrine ecosystems, which form oases between areas of much more limited resources. . . . [These] were sufficiently sizeable and productive to support large, stable populations throughout the year." However, Madsen (1982:217) goes on to note that neither Archaic nor Fremont populations **exclusively** exploited wetlands resources, but utilized those in other environmental zones as well, as Jennings and Norbeck (1955:3) had previously suggested.

As Thomas (1985:18–20, 390–391) points out, both Heizer's and Madsen's "limnosedentary" models have served as heuristic devices to trigger an ongoing discussion of the tethering effect of wetlands resources on Great Basin hunter-gatherer populations (e.g., Thomas 1985, Fowler et al. 1989, Cannon et al. this volume). Such discussions in turn contribute to our more general understanding of hunter-gatherer "mobility strategies," as Kelly (1983) calls them (cf. Bettinger 1987:131–138). The application of optimization theory to Great Basin prehistory, promoted by O'Connell, Jones and Simms (1982:231–235; Simms 1987) and others (Jones and

Madsen 1989; Raven and Elston 1988a, 1988b) has caused us to consider in detail just how much food wetlands areas might **in fact** have provided on an annual basis in relation to the costs of their procurement.[3] On the other hand, unresolved problems of applying optimization theory in either ethnographic or archaeological contexts (Ellen 1982:123–176, Jochim 1983, Keene 1983, Smith 1983) warrant continued review of its applications, as O'Connell, Simms and others recognize. As always, much more research is needed. As it is done it is worth recalling what C. Fowler (1982, 1986) Janetski (1983), Thomas (1985:21–28), Wheat (1967) and others have pointed out: Great Basin resources are highly variable, both annually, and long–term, from lake–edge, to dune, to marsh, to riparian area, to sage flats, to uplands. This variability is such that any sweeping generalizations about prehistoric Great Basin sedentism, in wetlands areas or elsewhere, may be fraught with so many exceptions as to approach emptiness. We still do not know enough on a case–by–case basis to do more than continue detailed inquiries at that level. The focus of the present conference on wetlands issues is a major step in that direction.

Ethnographic Studies

It would be pleasing to report that ethnographic data are at hand which might be brought to bear—by analogy—on these archaeological questions. They are not. Indeed, data that allow us to adequately characterize marsh, riverine and lake–side adaptations in immediate pre–contact or early–contact times, are also wanting. Early explorers, such as Escalante (Bolton 1950), and government scientists such as Stansbury (1988), Fremont (1988), and Simpson (1983), called attention to groups practicing fishing and waterfowl hunting in the Great Basin. They seemingly regarded these groups as a cut above the hunting and gathering "diggers" they commonly encountered. Hence, there are hints. But these leads were not systematically developed by the first trained ethnographers who worked in the region.

But the ethnographers were, after all, ethnographers, not ethnohistorians. Most began their studies after the turn of the century, at a time when the major fisheries and even the marshes, had seen heavy impacts from non–Indian users. Most of the early ethnographers were also on very brief trips, and often were principally concerned with making museum collections. Interestingly, their collections speak more eloquently of wetlands adaptations than do their notes. Some who came early **did** note the importance of fishing. For example, Samuel Barrett (1917:8) who visited the Washoe in 1916, remarked:

> Even in the arid section of this area there were fairly large streams fed by melting snows of the high Sierra, and fish of various kinds were abundant. In fact, fishing was a highly important vocation, even of the Paiute living over in the region still farther east, especially about Pyramid, Winnemucca and Walker lakes. In the higher mountain section of the Washoe country, notable at Lake Tahoe, fishing was perhaps the most important phase of this culture."

Barrett (1917:13) regretted that "no opportunity presented itself to go into the details of hunting and fishing," but that "without doubt certain traps and other implements were used for these purposes," and "a more detailed study of Washo culture would bring them out." Regrettably, Barrett did not make the extensive collection of fishing gear for the Washoe that he made for the Pyramid Lake and Walker River Paiute. But then he did not publish notes to go with the Northern Paiute collections, and they went unnoticed until recent times.

Actually, early museum collector J. H. Hudson did make an outstanding collection of fishing gear among the Washoe, including basket traps, harpoons, spears, hooks and lines, nets, etc. But his collection also went unnoticed by a generation of ethnologists who found material culture studies **passe**, and museums dusty and dank and hardly the places for social anthropologists to make theoretical breakthroughs.

Robert Lowie, in his early years a museum collector, between 1912 and 1914 made brief visits to the Pyramid Lake, Lovelock and Fallon Northern Paiute, the Moapa and Shivwits Southern Paiute, the Ute at Navaho Springs and Ignacio, Colorado, and Whiterocks, Utah, and the Wind River Shoshone of Wyoming. His notes, published in 1924 (Lowie 1924), refer in one sentence to "extensive fishing" by the Pyramid Lake, Winnemucca Lake and Humboldt River Northern Paiute; in a paragraph to the use of willow weirs by the Western and Uintah Ute; and in another, but very informative paragraph, to waterfowl hunting from tule balsas by the Fallon Northern Paiute.

There is nothing as grandiose as a seasonal round proposed for any of these groups, nor are there data ony mobility vs. sedentism. These are, after all, *Notes on Shoshonean Ethnography*, not **an** ethnography.

The data presented are excellent, but they are not of the quantity or quality produced by people with longer times in the field, such as Isabel Kelly (1932) for the Surprise Valley Paiute, or Julian Steward (1933) for the Owens Valley Paiute. Lowie **did** collect tule duck decoys, tule sandals, and a model of a cattail house, but no fishing gear. A few of his photographs also illustrate the "tule technology" of the Fallon people. Interestingly, it was L. L. Loud in 1929 (Loud and Harrington 1929) who drew attention to the lake and marsh orientations of the groups in western Nevada through the description of finds in Lovelock Cave. And he referred to Samuel Barrett's (1910) Klamath material culture, not to Lowie's data, for analogies.

As we all know, publication of Steward's (1938) *Basin–Plateau Aboriginal Sociopolitical Groups*, and the model implied in it, of family–based semi–nomadic hunting and gathering, set the stage for most ethnographic—as well as archaeological—interpretations of the Great Basin for many years (Thomas 1983). Later acceptance by anthropologists of Steward's generalized model of Shoshon**ean** culture rather than Western Shoshoni culture, as presented in his *Theory of Culture Change* (Steward 1955), further clouded the issue of lake and marsh oriented subsistence and settlement alternatives.

Regrettably, Steward was not assigned by Kroeber to do the Culture Element Distribution surveys of Western Nevada. If so, he might have been compelled to include in–depth sociocultural and analytical data on these groups in *Basin–Plateau . . .*, as he did for the Western and Northern Shoshone, who were his actual survey assignments (Steward 1943). This is not to say that Omer Stewart's *Element* list for western Nevada is lacking in data, or is somehow less well presented than Steward's, but rather to point out that the first major analytical work on the Basin ended up being biased, perhaps in part as an accident of history. Certainly Stewart (1941) did not overlook fishing and taking waterfowl in his element list: fully 50 elements were used to question about fishing, and a dozen or more about waterfowl. But again, a Culture Element Distribution Survey is not, and was not then, considered to be an ethnography; in the same way that an ethnography is not an ethnological treatise.

Two additional accidents of history had Kelly concentrate on the Surprise Valley Paiute, and Steward on the Owens Valley Paiute, neither noted particularly as fisher folk, or to be lake or marsh–oriented. Isabel Kelly went to Surprise Valley as a college senior because her mentor, A. L. Kroeber, required field work, and her mother knew a woman who ran a boarding house in Cedarville, California; thus she would have a place to stay for the summer. She would have preferred to have done some archaeological work, but Kroeber would not hear of it (I. T. Kelly, personal communication May 1980). Julian Steward worked in Owens Valley because he had attended Deep Springs Preparatory School nearby and formed an attachment for area and its people (Murphy 1977:1–2). Additional accidents of history removed the Utah Lake and Sevier River Ute from their aboriginal homelands long before ethnographers appeared (but see Stewart 1942 for a culture element survey that includes fishing and fowling; Smith 1974 for additional notes on Ute fishing; cf. Janetski n.d.). And, as noted earlier, White exploitation diminished the obvious potential of western Nevada fisheries several decades before they were of any ethnographic concern.

Even the Northern Shoshone, who sat astride one of the major fisheries in the entire west, the Snake River below Salmon Falls, did not fair much better in ethnographic description, given that most of their aboriginal material culture had been altered, and their movements curtailed, before the turn of the century. Although Robert Lowie (1909) was able to collect a few items of fishing gear from the Lemhi Shoshone in 1906 while spending the summer among them, he relied largely on ethnohistoric accounts, rather than ethnography, to describe their fishing technology.

In 1933, Willard Park began field studies in western Nevada among various Northern Paiute groups. He spent most of five summers in the area, between 1933 and 1940. In the process he made some 2,000 pages of ethnographic notes. He concentrated on Pyramid Lake and Walker River, and obtained lesser amounts of data from a former resident of Honey Lake, and from people at Yerington, Lovelock and Fallon. The Fallon data are particularly meager, as he spent very little field time there, due to his inability to find a suitable interpreter. He also made two large, and one small, material culture collections for museums.

Park's notes are again ethnographic, not ethnologic, given that he neither synthesized nor published them. He followed the descriptive paradigm of the day, obtaining data on subsistence, material culture, housing, clothing, social and political organization, the life cycle, religion, mythology, miscellaneous beliefs, etc. (See Kelly 1932 or Steward 1933 for the standard categories). The data he chose to publish in depth, and thus interpret, were those on shamanism: in his doctoral dissertation, published as *Shamanism in Western North America* (Park 1938a). His other, shorter publications dealt mostly with aspects of social organization (Park 1938b).

Although Park did not synthesize the materials he gathered on such topics as fishing and waterfowl hunting, the seasonal round and sedentism, his descriptive data leave little doubt that a considerable amount of time and energy at Pyramid Lake and Walker River were devoted to fishing, and that men, at least, were tethered to lake and stream–side locations (cf. Fowler 1989). Park's data on waterfowl hunting are less complete, with more notes on varying techniques coming from residents at Lovelock. Nonetheless, decoy hunting, coot driving and other activities are documented for all areas. Park's data on large and small mammal hunting are also full, but with some good indications that large game were less important—and perhaps less common—in the larger lake basins. This too may have fostered more dependence on fishing.

Park's brief published statements on the economic cycle, as for example in the "Bands . . ." paper (Park 1938b), generalize for the whole of the Paviotso area, and stress a mixed economy. Perhaps he was influenced to some degree by the newly published Steward model. Had he written an ethnography of either Walker River or Pyramid Lake, and especially one using ethnohistoric sources, we suspect that the characterization would have been different. But then he did not do that, nor did he, in last analysis, publish most of his ethnographic notes. Perhaps if he had, Heizer (Heizer and Krieger 1956), like Loud (Loud and Harrington 1929) would not have had to look to Barrett's Klamath report for analogies for his Humboldt lake–side adaptations and "tule cultures."

But hindsight is never a satisfactory explanation for the present, only an excuse. It is a rare ethnographer who can answer the ethnological questions of other ethnographers fifty years in the future, let alone those of future archaeologists. And given that ethnological and analytical work was even less often attempted, there is even less to cite. For example, in spite of Steward's (1933) use of the term "village" to describe the primary settlements in Owens Valley, we still know precious little about the actual composition and look of them. Steward's only published camp composition data (Steward 1970), are for Fish Lake Valley, not Owens Valley. We do know that the house types are roughly the same as those at Pyramid Lake, Walker River, Fallon, and perhaps elsewhere.

In some senses, on these issues it has been the ethnologists of the Great Basin, not the archaeologists who have been a paradigm behind, since roughly the 1940s. Those ethnologists presently working on issues involving the past, as opposed to current problems, also find the same gaps in the data base, and wish things were different. However, there are living persons who still do know things of value to fill in some of the gaps even though they were born 50 years—some perhaps as many as 75 years—after White settlement. Even though they have never hunted, fished, or taken waterfowl with anything but modern implements, still, aspects of the ways of thinking about resources and about living on the land remain. Perhaps by some additional attention to these persons and what they know, as well as to museum collections and what they represent, we can yet make progress on some of the important issues which affect both ethnological **and** archaeological interpretation. A recent suggestion by Riddington (1982:471), working with Native Americans in Canada, may be applicable:

> Perhaps because our own culture is obsessed with the production, exchange, and possession of artifacts, we inadvertently overlook the artifice behind technology in favour of the artifacts that it produces. . . . I suggest that technology should be seen as a system of knowledge rather than an inventory of objects. . . . The essence of hunting and gathering adaptive strategy is to retain and be able to act upon, information about the possible relationships between people and the natural environment. When realized, these life–giving relationships are as much the artifacts of hunting and gathering technology as are the material objects that are instrumental in bringing them about.

And it is some of these thought patterns that are still retained by Great Basin Native Americans today.

Notes

[1]The point was deposited in the collections of the Smithsonian Institution. Searches by the present authors and others in recent years have failed to find the implement.

[2]Remnants of the Smithsonian Model continued to confuse interpretations of Great Basin prehistory as late as Steward's (1940) overview. See the discussion in D. Fowler (1986:20–22).

[3]The Raven and Elston (1988a, 1988b) papers, and several others cited herein, are part of the "gray literature" and hence extremely difficult of access for many scholars who wish to evaluate the work they report.

References

Antevs, E.
  1948   Climatic Change & Pre-White Man. *University of Utah Bulletin* 38(20):168–191. Salt Lake City.
Barrett, S. A.
  1910   The Material Culture of the Klamath Lake and Modoc Indians of Northeastern California and Southern Oregon. *University of California Publications in American Archaeology and Ethnology* 5(4):239–292. Berkeley.
  1917   The Washo Indians. *Bulletin of the Public Museum of Milwaukee* 2(1):1–52. Milwaukee.
Beckwith, E. G.
  1855   *Report of Explorations for a Route for the Pacific Railroad on the Line of the 41st Parallel of North Latitude.* U.S. Congress. House. 33rd Congress, 2nd Session, House Executive Document 91.
Bedwell, S. F.
  1973   *Fort Rock Basin, Prehistory & Environment.* University of Oregon Books, Eugene.
Bettinger, R. L.
  1987   Archaeological Approaches to Hunter–Gatherers. *Annual Review of Anthropology* 16:121–142.
Binford, L. R.
  1983   *In Pursuit of the Past.* Thames & Hudson, London.
Blackwelder, E.
  1948   The Geological Background. *University of Utah Bulletin* 38(20):3–16. Salt Lake City.
Bolton, H. E. (editor)
  1950   Pageant in the Wilderness: The Story of the Escalante Expedition to the Interior Basin, 1776; Including the Diary and Itinerary of Father Escalante. *Utah Historical Quarterly* 18:1–265.
Campbell, E. W. C., and W. H. Campbell
  1935   *The Pinto Basin Site: An Ancient Aboriginal Camping Ground in the California Desert.* Southwest Museum Papers No. 9. Los Angeles.
Campbell, E. W. C., et. al
  1937   *The Archaeology of Pleistocene Lake Mohave: A Symposium.* Southwest Museum Papers No. 11. Los Angeles.
Cowan, R. A., and C. W. Clewlow
  1968   The Archaeology of Site NV–PE–67. *University of California Archaeological Survey Reports* 73:195–236. Berkeley.
Davis, E. L.
  1969   The Western Lithic Co–Tradition. In *The Western Lithic Co–Tradition*, by E. L. Davis, C. W. Brott, and D. L. Weide, pp. 11–78. San Diego Museum Papers No. 6. San Diego.
  1978a   *The Ancient Californians: Rancholabrean Hunters of the Mojave Lakes Country.* Natural History Museum of Los Angeles County, Science Series No. 29. Los Angeles.
  1978b   Paleoindian Cultural Ecology: China Lake. In *Selected Papers from the 14th Great Basin Anthropological Conference*, edited by D. R. Tuohy, pp. 19–34. Ballena Press Publications in Archaeology, Ethnology and History No. 11. Ramona.
Davis, E. L., and R. Shutler, Jr.
  1969   Recent Discoveries of Fluted Points in California and Nevada. In *Miscellaneous Papers on Nevada Archaeology 1–8*, pp. 154–169. Nevada State Museum Anthropological Papers No. 14. Carson City.
Davis, J. O.
  1982   Bits and Pieces: The Last 35,000 Years in the Lahontan Basin. In *Man and Environment in the Great Basin*, edited by D. B. Madsen and J. F. O'Connell, pp. 53–75. SAA Papers No. 2. Society for American Archaeology, Washington, D.C.
  1983   Level of Lake Lahontan during the Deposition of the Trego Hot Springs Tephra about 35,000 Years Ago. *Quaternary Research* 19:312–324.
Ellen, R.
  1982   *Environment, Subsistence and System. The Ecology of Small–Scale Social Formations.* Cambridge University Press, Cambridge.
Elston, R. G.
  1982   Good Times, Hard Times: Prehistoric Culture Change in the Western Great Basin. In *Man and Environment in the Great Basin*, edited by D. B. Madsen and J. F. O'Connell, pp. 186–206. SAA Papers No. 2. Society for American Archaeology, Washington, D.C.
Fowler, C. S.
  1982   Settlement Patterns and Subsistence Systems in the Great Basin: The Ethnographic Record. In *Man and Environment in the Great Basin*, edited by D. B. Madsen and J. F. O'Connell, pp. 121–138. SAA Papers No. 2. Society for American Archaeology, Washington, D.C.

1986   Subsistence. In *Great Basin*, edited by W. L. D'Azevedo, pp. 64–97. Handbook of North American Indians, vol. 11, W. G. Sturtevant, general editor. Smithsonian Institution, Washington, D.C.

Fowler, D. D.
1986   History of Research. In *Great Basin*, edited by W. L. D'Azevedo, pp. 15–30. Handbook of North American Indians, vol. 11, W. G. Sturtevant, general editor. Smithsonian Institution, Washington, D.C.

Fowler, D. D., E. M. Hattori, and C. C. Creger
1989   *Summary Report of Archaeological Investigations in Warner Valley, Lake County, Oregon, 1987–1988.* Department of Anthropology Research Reports No. 89–1. University of Nevada, Reno.

Fremont, J. C.
1988 [1845]   *Report of the Exploring Expedition to the Rocky Mountains in the Year 1842 and to Oregon and North California in the Years 1843–44.* Smithsonian Institution Press, Washington, D.C.

Gilbert, G. K.
1872   Preliminary Geological Report. *Engineer Dept., U.S. Army. Progress Report Upon Geographical and Geological Explorations and Surveys West of the 100th Meridian in 1872*, Appendix D, pp. 48–52. Washington, D.C.
1875   Report on the Geology of Portions of Nevada, Utah, California and Arizona Examined in the Years 1871 and 1872. *Engineer Dept., U.S. Army. Report Upon Geographical and Geological Explorations and Surveys West of the 100th Meridian . . .* vol. III, *Geology*, Part I, pp. 17–187.
1890   Lake Bonneville. *U.S. Geological Survey Monographs* No. 1. Washington, D.C.

Hague, A., and S. F. Emmons
1877   Report of the Geological Exploration of the Fortieth Parallel. In *Descriptive Geology*, vol. 2. Professional Papers of the Engineer Department, U.S. Army No. 18, Part 2.

Harrington, M. R.
1957   *A Pinto Site at Little Lake, California.* Southwest Museum Papers No. 17. Los Angeles.

Hattori, E. M.
1982   The Archaeology of Falcon Hill, Winnemucca Lake, Washoe County, Nevada. *Nevada State Museum Anthropological Papers* No. 18. Carson City.

Hayden, F. V.
1872   *Preliminary Report of the U.S. Geological Survey of Montana Territory and Portions of Adjacent Territories.* Government Printing Office, Washington, D.C.

Heizer. R. F.
1967   Analysis of Human Coprolites from a Dry Nevada Cave. *University of California Archaeological Survey Report* 70:1–20. Berkeley.

Heizer, R. F. (editor)
1970   *An Anthropological Expedition of 1913, or Get It Through Your Head, or Yours for the Revolution.* Correspondence between A. L. Kroeber and L. L. Loud, July 12, 1913–October 31, 1913. University of California Research Facility, Berkeley.

Heizer, R. F., and A. D. Krieger
1956   The Archaeology of Humboldt Cave, Churchill County, Nevada. *University of California Publications in American Archaeology and Ethnology* 47(1). Berkeley.

Heizer, R. F., and L. K. Napton
1970   Archaeology and the Prehistoric Great Basin Lacustrine Regime as seen from Lovelock Cave, Nevada. *University of California Archaeological Research Facility Contributions* No. 10. Berkeley.

Holmes, W. H.
1892   Modern Quarry Refuse and the Paleolithic Theory. *Science* 20:295–297.

Hubbs, C. L., and R. B. Miller
1948   The Zoological Evidence. *University of Utah Bulletin* 38(20):17–166. Salt Lake City.

Janetski, J. C.
1983   The Western Ute of Utah Valley: An Ethnohistoric Model of Lakeside Adaptation. Ph.D dissertation, University of Utah. University Microfilms, Ann Arbor.
n.d.   *The Ute of Utah Lake.* University of Utah Anthropological Papers No. 116. Salt Lake City, in press.

Jennings, J. D., and E. Norbeck
1955   Great Basin Prehistory: A Review. *American Antiquity* 21(1):1–11.

Jochim, M.
1983   Optimization Models in Context. In *Archaeological Hammers and Theories*, edited by J. A. Moore and A. S. Keene, pp. 157–72. Academic Press, New York.

Jones, K. T., and D. B. Madsen
1989   Calculating the Cost of Resource Transportation: A Great Basin Example. *Current Anthropology* 30:529–34.

Keene, A. S.
1983   Biology, Behavior, and Borrowing: A Critical Examination of Optimal Foraging Theory in Archaeology. In *Archaeological Hammers and Theories*, edited by J. A. Moore and A. S. Keene, pp. 139–55. Academic Press, New York.

Kelly, I. T.
   1932   Ethnography of the Surprise Valley Paiute. *University of California Publications in American Archaeology and Ethnography* 31(3):67–210. Berkely.
Kelly, R. L.
   1983   Hunter–gatherer Mobility Strategies. *Journal of Anthropological Research* 39:277–306.
King, C.
   1878   Report of the Geological Exploration of the Fortieth Parallel, vol. 1. *Systematic Geology*. Professional Papers of the Engineer Department, U.S. Army, No. 18. Washington, D.C.
Livingston, S. D.
   1986   Archaeology of the Humboldt Lakebed Site. *Journal of California and Great Basin Anthropology* 8:99–115.
   1988   *The Avian and Mammalian Faunas from Lovelock Cave and the Humboldt Lakebed Site.* Unpublished Ph.D. dissertation, Department of Anthropology, University of Washington, Seattle.
Loud, L. L., and M. R. Harrington
   1929   Lovelock Cave. *University of California Publications in American Archaeology and Ethnology* 25(1):1–183. Berkeley.
Lowie, R. H.
   1909   The Northern Shoshone. *American Museum of Natural History Anthropological Papers* 2(2):165–306. New York.
   1924   Notes on Shoshonean Ethnography. *American Museum of Natural History Anthropological Papers* 20(3):185–314. New York.
Lyneis, M. L.
   1982   Prehistory in the Southern Great Basin. In *Man and Environment in the Great Basin*, edited by D. B. Madsen and J. F. O'Connell, pp. 172–185. SAA Papers No. 2. Society for American Archaeology, Washington, D.C.
Madsen, D. B.
   1979   The Fremont and the Sevier: Defining Prehistoric Agriculture North of the Anasazi. *American Antiquity* 44:711–722.
   1982   Get It Where the Gettin's Good: A Variable Model of Great Basin Subsistence and Settlement Based on Data from the Eastern Great Basin. In *Man and Environment in the Great Basin*, edited by D. B. Madsen and J. F. O'Connell, pp. 207–226. SAA Papers No. 2. Society for American Archaeology, Washington, D.C.
Madsen, D. B., and L. W. Lindsay
   1977   Backhoe Village. *Antiquities Section Selected Papers* 4(12). Utah State Historical Society, Salt Lake City.
McGee, W J
   1888   Paleolithic Man in America: His Antiquity and Environment. *The Popular Science Monthly* 34:20–36.
   1889   An Obsidian Implement from Pleistocene Deposits in Nevada. *American Anthropologist* o.s. 2:301–312.
Mifflin, M. D., and M. M. Wheat
   1979   Pluvial Lakes and Estimated Pluvial Climates of Nevada. *Nevada Bureau of Mines and Geology Bulletin*, No. 94. Reno.
Morrison, R. B.
   1965   Quaternary Geology of the Great Basin. In *The Quaternary of the United States*, edited by H. E. Wright, Jr., and D. G. Frey, pp. 265–285. Princeton University Press, Princeton.
Morrison, R. B., and J. C. Frye
   1965   Correlation of the Middle and Late Quaternary Successions of the Lake Lahontan, Lake Bonneville, Rocky Mountains (Wasatch Range), Southern Great Plains and Eastern Midwest Areas. *Nevada Bureau of Mines Report* No. 9. Reno.
Murphy, R. F.
   1977   *Julian Steward.* Columbia University Press, New York.
Napton, L. K.
   1969   *Archaeological and Paleobiological Investigations in Lovelock Cave, Nevada: Further Analysis of Human Coprolites.* Kroeber Anthropological Society Special Publications No. 2. Berkely.
Neal, J. T. (editor)
   1975   *Playas and Dried Lakes. Occurrence and Development.* Benchmark Papers in Geology No. 20. Dowden, Hutchison and Ross, Stroudsburg, Pennsylvania.
O'Connell, J. F.
   1975   *The Prehistory of Surprise Valley.* Ballena Press Anthropological Papers No. 4. Ramona.
O'Connell, J. F., K. T. Jones, and S. R. Simms
   1982   Some Thoughts on Prehistoric Archaeology in the Great Basin. In *Man and Environment in the Great Basin*, edited by D. B. Madsen and J. F. O'Connell, pp. 227–240. SAA Papers No. 2. Society for American Archaeology, Washington, D.C.
Oetting, A. C., and R. M. Pettigrew
   1987   *Archaeological Investigations in the Lake Abert–Chewaucan Basin, Lake County, Oregon: The 1986 Survey.* Cultural Heritage Foundation, Portland.
Park, W. Z.
   1938a   Shamanism in Western North America: A Study in Cultural Relationships. *Northwestern University Studies in the Social Sciences* No. 2. Chicago.
   1938b   The Organization and Habitat of Paviotso Bands. *American Anthropologist* 40(4):622–626.
Pyne, T. C.
   1980   *Grove Karl Gilbert.* University of Texas Press, Austin and London.

Raven, C., and R. Elston (editors)
  1988a *Preliminary Investigations in the Stillwater Marsh: Human Prehistory and Geoarchaeology*, 2 vols. U.S. Fish and Wildlife Service Cultural Resources Series No. 1. Portland.
  1988b *Human Geography in the Carson Desert: Part I. Predictive Model of Land Use in the Stillwater Marsh Management Area.* U.S. Fish and Wildlife Service Cultural Resources Series No. 3. Portland.
Riddington, R.
  1982 Technology, World View, and Adaptive Strategies in a Northern Hunting Society. *Canadian Review of Sociology and Anthropology* 19:469–481.
Roberts, F. H. H., Jr.
  1940 Developments in the Problem of the North American Paleo–Indian. *Smithsonian Miscellaneous Collections* 100:51–116. Washington, D.C.
Rogers, M. J.
  1939 *Early Lithic Industries of the Lower Basin of the Colorado River and Adjacent Desert Areas.* San Diego Museum Papers No. 3. San Diego.
Rozaire, C. E.
  1963 Lake–side Cultural Specialization in the Great Basin. In *1962 Great Basin Anthropological Conference*, pp. 72–77. Nevada State Museum Anthropological Papers No. 9. Carson City.
Russell, I. C.
  1884 A Geological Reconnaissance in Southern Oregon. *Fourth Annual Report of the U.S. Geological Survey*:431–464.
  1885 Geological History of Lake Lahontan, A Quaternary Lake of Northwestern Nevada. *U.S. Geological Survey Monographs* 11. Washington, D.C.
  1895 Present and Extinct Lakes of Nevada. *National Geographic Monographs* 4(1):101–132.
Simms, S.
  1987 *Behavioral Ecology and Hunter–Gatherer Foraging: An Example from the Great Basin.* British Archaeological Reports, International Series No. 381. Oxford.
Simpson, J. H.
  1983 *Report of Explorations Across the Great Basin of the Territory of Utah for a Direct Wagon–route from Camp Floyd to Genoa in Carson Valley in 1859.* [1876] U.S. Govt. Printing Office (Reprinted, University of Nevada Press, Reno).
Smith, A. M. C.
  1974 Ethnography of the Northern Ute. *Museum of New Mexico Papers in Anthropology* No. 17. Alburquerque.
Smith, E. A.
  1983 Anthropological Applications of Optimal Foraging Theory: A Critical Review. *Current Anthropology* 24:625–51.
Stansbury, H.
  1988 [1852] *Exploration of the Valley of the Great Salt Lake.* Smithsonian Institution Press, Washington, D.C.
Steward, J. H.
  1933 Ethnography of the Owens Valley Paiute. *University of California Publications in American Archaeology and Ethnology* 33(3):233–350. Berkeley.
  1938 *Basin–Plateau Aboriginal Sociopolitical Groups.* Bureau of American Ethnology Bulletin 120. Washington, D.C.
  1940 Native Cultures of the Intermontane (Great Basin) Area. *Smithsonian Miscellaneous Collections* 100:445–502. Washington, D.C.
  1943 Culture Element Distributions, XXIII: Northern and Gosiute Shoshoni. *University of California Anthropological Records* 8(3):263–392. Berkeley.
  1955 *Theory of Culture Change.* University of Illinois Press, Urbana.
  1970 The Foundations of Basin–Plateau Shoshonean Society. In *Languages and Cultures of Western North America. Essays in Honor of Sven S. Liljeblad*, edited by E. H. Swanson, Jr., pp. 113–151. Idaho State University Press, Pocatello.
Stewart, O. C.
  1941 Culture Element Distributions, XIV: Northern Paiute. *University of California Anthropological Records* 4(3):361–446. Berkeley.
  1942 Culture Element Distributions, XVIII: Ute–Southern Paiute. *University of California Anthropological Records* 6(4):231–356. Berkeley.
Thomas, D. H.
  1983 On Steward's Model of Shoshonean Sociopolitical Organization: A Great Bias in the Basin? In *The Development of Political Organization in Native North America*, edited by E. Tooker and M. H. Fried, pp. 54–68. Proceedings of the American Ethnological Society, 1979. Washington, D.C.
  1985 The Archaeology of Hidden Cave, Nevada. *American Museum of Natural History Anthropological Paper* 61(1). New York.
Thompson, R. S., L. Benson, and E. M. Hattori
  1986 A Revised Chronology for the Last Pleistocene Lake Cycle in the Central Lahontan Basin. *Quaternary Research* 25:1–9.
Tuohy, D. R.
  1968 Some Early Lithic Sites in Western Nevada. *Eastern New Mexico Contributions to Anthropology* 1(4):27–38. Portales.
  1974 A Comparative Study of Late Paleoindian Manifestations in the Great Basin. *Nevada Archaeological Survey Research Papers* 5:91–116. Reno.

Tuohy, D. R., and D. T. Clark
  1979   *Excavations at Marble Bluff Dam and Pyramid Lake Fishway, Nevada.* Submitted to the Bureau of Reclamation, Mid-Pacific
          Office by the Department of Anthropology, Nevada State Museum, Carson City.
Warren, C. N., and R. H. Crabtree
  1986   Prehistory of the Southwestern Area. *In Great Basin*, edited by W. L D'Azevedo, pp. 183–193. Handbook of North American
          Indians, vol. 11, W. G. Sturtevant, general editor. Smithsonian Institution, Washington, D.C.
Watters, D. R.
  1979   On the Hunting of "Big Game" by Great Basin Aboriginal Populations. *Journal of New World Archaeology* 3(3):57–64.
Weide, M. L.
  1968   *Cultural Ecology of Lakeside Adaptations in the Western Great Basin.* Unpublished Ph.D dissertation, Department of
          Anthropology, University of California, Los Angeles.
  1974   North Warner Subsistence Network: A Prehistoric Band Territory. *Nevada Archaeological Survey Research Papers* 5:62–79.
          Reno.
Wheat, M. M.
  1967   *Survival Arts of the Primitive Paiutes*, University of Nevada Press, Reno.
Whitney, J. D.
  1865   Reports of the California Geological Survey, vol. 1, *Geology*. Caxton Press of Sherman and Co., Philadelphia.
Willey, G. R., and J. A. Sabloff
  1980   *A History of American Archaeology.* 2nd ed. W. H. Freeman and Co., San Francisco.
Willig, J. A., C. M. Aikens, and J. L. Fagan (editors)
  1988   *Early Human Occupation in Far Western North America: The Clovis–Archaic Interface.* Nevada State Museum Anthropological
          Papers No. 21. Carson City.

3

ETHNOGRAPHIC PERSPECTIVES ON MARSH–BASED CULTURES IN WESTERN NEVADA

Catherine S. Fowler

Abstract

Originally prepared for a symposium that re–examined various aspects of the Lovelock culture of western Nevada, this paper, (1) brings together data on ethnographic subsistence and settlement systems for lake– and marsh–based Northern Paiute groups in western Nevada; and (2) compares various aspects of Northern Paiute material culture with items recovered archaeologically and often attributed to the Lovelock culture. The latter comparisons suggest certain continuities of general adaptive strategies used by the Northern Paiute and the Lovelock culture as well as discontinuities in technological details that require further investigation.

Introduction

Ethnographic data on pre– and immediately post–contact lake and marsh adaptations in the Great Basin are far from full or complete.[1] Unfortunately, most were also gathered well into this century, a time when aboriginal subsistence and technological systems had ceased to function in anything approaching their pre–contact complexities. However, in spite of these drawbacks, a considerable amount can be gleaned from these sources that is applicable to modeling aspects of lake– and marsh–based cultural systems in the region in the recent past, and perhaps at times of greater antiquity. In this brief paper, I will review some of the data on subsistence and its associated technology for the Northern Paiute of western Nevada, including the Pyramid Lake and Walker River Northern Paiute—both lake– and river-based cultures, and for the Lovelock and Stillwater Northern Paiute—both marsh–oriented groups. In addition, I will look at certain classes of their material culture as contrasted with those of the archaeological Lovelock Culture for similarities and differences. Based on these data, I would like to suggest some lines of research that might be profitably pursued.

Ethnography

The pertinent ethnographic sources on the western Nevada Northern Paiute include the following: brief published accounts by Loud (1929), Curtis (1926), Heizer (1970), and Shimkin and Reid (1970); longer monographs by Kelly (1932), Wheat (1967) and Stewart (1939; 1941), and a cultural overview by Fowler and Liljeblad (1986). Unpublished sources include the miscellaneous notes of John T. Reid (n.d.), a mining engineer from Lovelock, the extensive tape recordings, transcripts and photographs of Margaret Wheat (1950–1981) of Fallon, and the linguistic, ethnobotanical and general cultural notes of Sven Liljeblad and myself of the University of Nevada, Reno. Soon to appear is the first volume of Willard Park's quite extensive ethnographic notes covering Pyramid Lake and Walker River, but unfortunately less extensively Lovelock and Stillwater (Fowler 1989). In addition to these, there are collections of ethnographic material culture from roughly a dozen museums across the country, some with accompanying brief notes. Although not fully analyzed and synthesized, these sources do amount to a sizable, if disparate body of data.

Subsistence data contained in these sources are informative but incomplete. Included are lists of species of plants, mammals, waterfowl, land birds and insects taken, as well as some data on seasonality and mechanisms for taking. Missing is any type of quantitative data, data that could only have been obtained by long–term on–site observations of functioning cultures practicing typical seasonal rounds. Given the scientific paradigms of the day, and the way field work was conducted, it is not surprising to find these missing. A few ethnographic sources, such as J. H. Simpson's (1876) famous comments on Carson Lake, John C. Fremont's (1845) on Pyramid Lake, Dan DeQuille's (1963) wonderful "Washoe Rambles" around the whole of the lower Carson drainage, and Zenas Leonard's (Wagner 1904) comments on nut grass harvesting and bird hunting—wherever he was in the western Basin[2]—are excellent as far as they go—but they do not go nearly far enough. a careful search of additional historical sources adds important anecdotal details, but will not fill the gaps in the record.

Lacking quantitative data, we nonetheless have some idea of the breadth of the diet based on the data at hand. From Wheat's, Liljeblad's and my unpublished notes on the lower Carson, for example, we know that at least 36 species of waterfowl and wading birds were taken for food, as were eggs for most and occasionally young (Table 1).[3] In addition, at least 12 species of marsh/mud flat plants provided food resources (Table 2), as did 30 lower valley plant species (Table 3) and 21 from the uplands (Table 4). Thirty–one species is the minimum food count for mammals, along with 14 land birds and or their eggs, eight named insects and four fishes.[4] These figures are only for subsistence products, and do not count sources of medicines, manufactures, etc.

Although species lists are hardly adequate, note that this marsh habitat was apparently not sufficiently lush that people ignored valley plants and mammals or resources in the uplands and particularly the Stillwater Range. Unique aspects of the lower Carson, however, were the sheer numbers and variety of waterfowl and water plants, and the proximity, because of the extensive alkali flats, of late fall–ripening seeds (*Suaeda, Kochia, Allenrolfea*). These, along with the marsh's alkali bulrush (*Scirpus maritimus*), extended the normal season for seed harvesting well into December, much longer than the season in other areas. The opportunity for resource exploitation was certainly there, even if we cannot assess if the full potential of the region was ever realized. Perhaps it is not by accident, however, that when Agent F. Dodge made his first population count of the western Nevada district in 1859 (Dodge 1860), the lower Carson is listed as having more than double the population of Walker River, Pyramid Lake or any other single district (some 1,600 persons).[5]

The subsistence situation in the Pyramid Lake and Walker River districts differs from that at Stillwater (and perhaps the lower Humboldt where the data are poorest) because of the presence of the extensive fisheries. Both had cutthroat trout (*Salmo clarki henshawi*), suckers (*Catostomus tahoensis*), some whitefish (*Prosopium williamsoni*), tui chub (*Gila bicolor obesus*), dace (*Rhinichthys osculus*) and redsides (*Richardsonius egreqius*). Pyramid lake and Winnemucca Lake had in addition the cui–uis (*Chasmistes cujus*). Park's ethnographic notes for both areas stress the importance of fishing, which for men is described as a year–round pursuit. Park notes, for example, that while the women at Walker River were gathering summer seeds from temporary camps several miles east of the river and lake, or collecting pine nuts in the Wassuk Range, the men continued to go back and forth from their camps to the river to fish. They brought them fresh supplies of fish every few days. Less is made of this for Pyramid Lake, but it may have occurred there as well as the seed collecting grounds are about

Table 1. Stillwater Marsh Waterfowl and Shore Birds used as Food

Birds Eaten	Eggs	Young
Common Loon (*Gavia immer*)	+	
Pied-billed Grebe (*Podilymbus podiceps*)	+	
Eared Grebe (*Podiceps nigricollis*)	+	
Western Grebe (*Aechmophorus occidentalis*)	+	
American White Pelican (*Pelecanus erythrorhynchos*)	+	+
Great Blue Heron (*Ardea herodias*)	+	+
Snowy Egret (*Egretta thula*)	+	
Black-crowned Night-heron (*Nycticorax nycticorax*)	+	+
White-faced Ibis (*Plegadis chihi*)	+	
American Coot (*Fulica americana*)	+	+
Tundra Swan (*Cygnus columbianus*)		
Canada Goose (*Branta canadensis*)	+	+
White-fronted Goose (*Anser albifrons*)		
Snow Goose (*Chen caerulescens*)		
Green-winged Teal (*Anas crecca*)	+	
Mallard (*Anas platyrhynchos*)	+	
Northern Pintail (*Anas acuta*)	+	
Cinnamon Teal (*Anas cyanoptera*)	+	
Northern Shoveler (*Anas clypeata*)	+	
Gadwall (*Anas strepera*)	+	
American Wigeon (*Anas americana*)	+	
Canvasback (*Aythya valisineria*)		
Redhead (*Aythya americana*)	+	
Common Merganser (*Mergus merganser*)		
Common Goldeneye (*Bucephala clangula*)		
Bufflehead (*Bucephala albeola*)		
Ruddy Duck (*Oxyura jamaicensis*)	+	
Killdeer (*Charadrius vociferus*)	+	
Black-necked Stilt (*Himantropus mexicanus*)	+	
American Avocet (*Recurvirostra americana*)	+	
Long-billed Curlew (*Numenius americanus*)	+	
Common Snipe (*Gallinago gallinago*)	+	
Wilson's Phalarope (*Phalaropus tricolor*)	+	
California Gull (*Larus californicus*)	+	+
Caspian Tern (*Sterna caspia*)	+	
Foster's Tern (*Sterna fosteri*)	+	

Table 2. Edible plants of Marsh and Mud Flats, Stillwater

Name	Part Eaten
Tule bulrush (*Scirpus acutus*)	shoots, seeds
Alkali bulrush (*Scirpus maritimus*)	seeds
American Bulrush (*Scirpus americanus*)	seeds
Common cattail (*Typha latifolia*)	pollen, shoots, seeds
Cattail (*Typha domingensis*)	pollen, shoots, seeds
Spikerush (*Eleocharis palustris*)	seeds
Sego pondweed (*Photomageton pectinatus*)	tubers
Chufa fatsedge (*Cyperus esculentus*)	tubers
Water plantain (*Alisma geyeri*)	stems
Seepweed (*Suaeda depressa*)	seeds
Red sage (*Kochia americana*)	seeds
Pickleweed (*Allenrolfea occidentalis*)	seeds

at similar distances. Likewise, at Stillwater, when people were camped in the Stillwater Range taking pine nuts, the men went back to the marshes periodically for fresh supplies of waterfowl. Wuzzie George recalled that when she was a girl the trees around their pine nut camp were always decorated with drying ducks. When supplies ran out, her father went back for more.

Much less is said in the Pyramid Lake and Walker River ethnographies about the importance of waterfowl and the exploitation of water plants. Men in both areas made duck decoys, as they did at Stillwater and Lovelock. They held coot drives with tule balsa boats and made special duck arrows. But some of the specific techniques for taking ducks, such as with long nets strung above the water, are better described for Stillwater and Lovelock, both marshy areas where the poles of such nets could be implanted in shallow water. Drying Winnemucca Lake may also have served at various times, but apparently there were few suitable areas around Walker Lake to use this technique.[6] By far the most extensive lists of waterfowl species named in Northern Paiute also come from the marshes as opposed to the lake basins. As one of Park's consultants, interviewed at Pyramid Lake but raised in Lovelock, remarked, "you have to have lots of ducks" before netting is worthwhile. Pyramid Lake was apparently not well supplied, except for coots.[7]

Tule shoots, alkali bulrush seeds and cattail pollen, seed and inflorescences were eaten in all areas; but they were less important to the people at Walker River and Pyramid lake, at least within the memories of those interviewed by various ethnographers. The seeds common to the alkali flats at Stillwater were likely also present at Lovelock, but seem to have been rare in the Pyramid Lake and Walker River basins. Dominant economic seeds in these areas are Indian ricegrass, Great Basin wild rye, white–stem blazing star, and several others more typical of less alkali soils. As at Stillwater, women from both of these areas also went to the uplands in the spring to take roots, and they gathered valley seeds, thus suggesting that fishing alone was not considered sufficient. Nonetheless, Park was told by several people in both areas: "when all else fails, there are always fish."

But again, we are faced with the problem that the mere presence of resources does not necessarily assure success in their taking. There are certainly stories, most often told by those at the fisheries, of people from Lovelock and the lower Carson Basin reaching them at the time of spring fish runs in a starving condition. They gorged themselves on fish and some even died by overeating. But how often did this happen? And what do the stories really mean? Are the stories stereotypical of groups with seeming food abundances told about those in their eyes in less favorable areas, or what? Unfortunately these questions will remain, and certainly the ethnographies will not resolve them.

Table 3. Edible Plants of Carson Desert Lowlands

Name	Part Eaten
Carved seed (*Glyptopleura marginata*)	leaves
Prince's plume (*Stanleya pinnata*)	leaves
Onion (*Allium anceps*)	corms, leaves
Nevada onion (*Allium nevadense*)	corms, leaves
Cympoterus (*Cymopterus globosus*)	roots
Smoky mariposa lily (*Calochortus leichtlinii*)	bulbs
Sego lily (*Calochortus nuttallii*)	bulbs
Broomrape (*Orobanche fasciculata*)	stalk
Broomrape (*Orobanche corymbosa*)	stalk
Thistle (*Cirsium* spp.)	stalk
Prickly pear (*Opuntia polyacantha*)	buds
Sunflower (*Helianthus annuus*)	seeds
Tansy mustard (*Descurainia pinnata*)	seeds
Saltbush (*Atriplex argentea*)	seeds
White-stem blazing star (*Mentzelia albicaulis*)	seeds
Indian ricegrass (*Oryzopsis hymenoides*)	seeds
Curly dock (*Rumex crispus*)	seeds
Foxtail barley (*Horideum jubatum*)	seeds
Big sagebrush (*Artemesia tridentata*)	seeds
Fourwing Saltbush (*Atriplex canescens*)	seeds
Shadscale (*Atriplex confertifolia*)	seeds
Witchgrass (*Panicum capillare*)	seeds
Wheatgrass (*Agrophyron* spp.)	seeds
Bluegrass (*Poa* spp.)	seeds
Muhly (*Muhlenbergia* spp.)	seeds
Gooseleaf globemallow (*Sphaeralcea grossalariafolia*)	seeds
Silver buffalo berry (*Shepherdia argentea*)	berries
Wolf berry (*Lycium andersonii*)	berries
Cooper wolfberry (*Lycium cooperi*)	berries
Wild rose (*Rosa woodsii*)	hips

Nor will the ethnographies decide the issue as to whether these cultures were, to use current terminology, "limno–sedentary" or "limno–mobile" (see Thomas 1985: 18–20 for discussion). By first–hand accounts from Stillwater in the 1890s—a time of some changes in subsistence and technology—marsh, valley and mountain resources were available within an hour to at maximum a day's walk from the camp. Some camps had 20 or so cattail houses—the same house type as in the so–called sedentary villages of Owens Valley (Steward 1933).

Table 4. Edible Plants of the Stillwater Uplands

Name	Part Eaten
Nevada desert parsley (*Lomatium nevadense*)	roots
Yampa (*Perideridia bolanderi*)	roots
Spring beauty (*Claytonia umbellata*)	roots
Bitterroot (*Lewisia rediviva*)	roots
Sego lily (*Calochortus leichtlinii*)	bulbs
Arrowleaf balsamroot (*Balsamorhiza sagittata*)	seeds, roots
Hairy balsamroot (*Balsamorhiza hirsuta*)	seeds, roots
Onion (*Allium parvum*)	leaves
Onion (*Allium bisceptrum*)	leaves, bulbs
Onion (*Allium platycaule*)	leaves, bulbs
Wolly wyethia (*Wyethia mollis*)	seeds
Pinyon (*Pinus monophylla*)	seeds
Great Basin wild rye (*Elymus cinereus*)	seeds
Prairie sunflower (*Helianthus petiolaris*)	seeds
Blue elderberry (*Sambucus caerulea*)	berries
Service berry (*Amelanchier alnifolia*)	berries
Chockecherry (*Prunus virginiana*)	berries
Wild rose (*Rosa woodsii*)	hips
Current (*Ribes aureum*)	berries
Sagebrush gooseberry (*Ribes velutinum*)	berries
Silver buffalo berry (*Shepherdia argentea*)	berries

Other camps were smaller. People might leave for a month or even the winter in good pine nut years. But the men came back regularly to the marshes for waterfowl and fish. And not everyone left. The elderly, some small children and a few families often stayed behind. Houses were rebuilt every two to three years, sometimes in the same place, sometimes a short distance away. Everyone moved when there was a death. These camps appear to embody aspects of both sedentism and mobility. Similar patterns are present in the lake basins, and perhaps in the Humboldt basin as well [see for example, the site map for 26Ch 15 (Livingston, 1986:103–4)].

Material Culture Comparisons

Comparisons of the lake and marsh systems of material culture for the Northern Paiute and the archaeological Lovelock Culture lead to the conclusion that each had a varied technology for dealing with extant resources. And there is no real way of evaluating their comparative efficiency. The Northern Paiute and the Lovelock people certainly share a number of subsistence–related items of material culture, even though we might quibble about whether these are truly antecedent and descendant items in the historical sense. Part of the difficulty in answering the question of cultural relationships is the poor chronological control we have on the Lovelock sequence, especially in the Humboldt Sink where the richest deposits occur (Grosscup 1960).

Take, for example, fishing gear—hooks and lines, leisters, harpoons, etc. The uppermost level of Humboldt Cave yielded, in association with historic artifacts, a set line with tiny bone hooks (Figure 1a). The same type of line was recovered from Lovelock Cave (Loud and Harrington 1929: Plate 51). Stephen Powers collected the same type of line from the Pyramid Lake Paiute in 1876 (Figure 1b), called *winain.nu*, "throwing line." I suspect that all three are northern Paiute, and have nothing to do with the Lovelock Culture. Powers (1876) reports that they are used on "minnows," likely tui chub, which are known for schooling habits.

Cache 22, a fisherman's cache in Humboldt Cave, yielded several composite hooks with greasewood shanks and bone points with reverse barbs (Figure 2a). The greasewood shanks are reported to be beveled so that the bone fits snugly in place. There is lashing around the joint. Cache 22 was 45–60 cm below the surface (Heizer and Krieger 1956: 98). There is a suggestion by Grosscup (1960: 28) that two pieces of "wood," one of which was beveled, found loosely wrapped with tule and at a depth of 12 inches in Lovelock Cave might be a fishhook; but at 12 cm it is about one–third larger than the hooks from Humboldt Cave. Two other Lovelock Cave fishhooks are seemingly unprovenienced.

In 1916, Samuel Barrett collected a composite greasewood hook used for trout at Pyramid Lake (Figure 2b). The greasewood shank is also beveled so that both pieces fit snugly. But the forepart is not barbed. We do not know if Barrett's hook is a model or a functional piece. But in description it matches quite closely the construction of the Humboldt Cave and suggested Lovelock Cave fishhooks. Fishhooks from Pyramid Lake dated to Lovelock times do not appear to be of this type (Don Tuohy, personal communication 1988; see Tuohy, this volume). Again, we might suggest that this Humboldt Basin fishing gear is Northern Paiute and not from the Lovelock Culture. Gilbert Natches, interviewed by Loud (1929) in 1923, stated that each spring people from Lovelock went to the bend of the Truckee River to fish for trout. The size of these hooks is more suggestive of this quarry than any in the Humboldt. Caching of fish gear would also seem to follow under these circumstances.

The Northern Paiute of Pyramid Lake and Walker River made and used both fish spears and harpoons on trout, whitefish and suckers. The harpoon is well documented ethnographically to consist of a greasewood foreshaft or shafts with small toggled coyote or deer bone socketted points (Wheat 1967). The spear or leister was apparently the same, lacking the socketted points. There seems to be nothing illustrated in the Lovelock Culture materials that resembles these implements. Lacking large fish, the Humboldt Sink populations may not have had these implements in their inventories. The archaeological record at Pyramid Lake yields true bone leister parts (Tuohy, this volume).

At the major fisheries, the Northern Paiute used large lifting nets set on poles to fish from platforms in the river and perhaps in other locations. These nets have been collected ethnographically at Walker River and Pyramid Lake (Fowler and Bath 1981). They have a rather complex construction that resembles most closely nets used among California and Oregon (Klamath) fishermen (Kroeber and Barrett 1960). Two nets with the same construction details were supposedly removed from Hidden Cave in the Carson Basin (Ambro 1966). They contained historic cotton repairs and feature identical edge treatments to the ethnographically collected nets. Richard Ambro, who reported on them, cites unpublished notes by Heizer to the effect that nets of this sort were used in the Humboldt Sink as well, probably for chub. The mesh size in ethnographically collected nets matches these two nets, and thus they probably are indeed chub nets. Nothing like these has been excavated from Lovelock Culture sites, although what may be a linear gill net comes from Pyramid Lake (Don Tuohy, personal communication 1988). Gill nets are also attributable to the Northern Paiute (Fowler and Bath 1981).

Archaeological evidence for netting ducks is somewhat enigmatic. Loud (Loud and Harrington 1929: 88) identified some of the netting fragments from Lovelock Cave as possible duck nets and notes as well that a net with "birds" entangled was recovered from near Ocala. A careful comparison of mesh sizes might help in differentiating duck nets from rabbit nets. Loud's mesh dimensions were 16 cm between knots. Most ethnographic rabbit nets are less than that, 6–10 cm, so that the rabbits will not get through.

The use of tule duck decoys is well established for the archaeological culture in the Humboldt Sink (Figure 3a) and for all four ethnographic groups. Ethnographic decoys were collected as early as 1858 at Carson Lake (Simpson 1876) and there is an unbroken line of collections for that region to the present. The ethnographic and archaeological decoys differ in the number of details, most obviously in body construction and in feathering. Twined floats, hollow on the inside, characterize ethnographic decoys, whereas the Lovelock Cave decoys

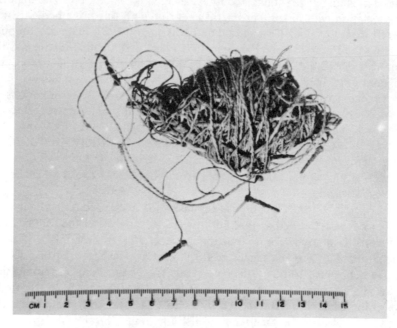

Figure 1a. Set line of native cordage, 36.6 m in length, with 183 tiny (1.2 cm) hooks suspended. Recovered from Humboldt Cave, Nevada. Courtesy of the Lowie Museum of Anthropology, University of California at Berkeley (Catalog number 1–42079).

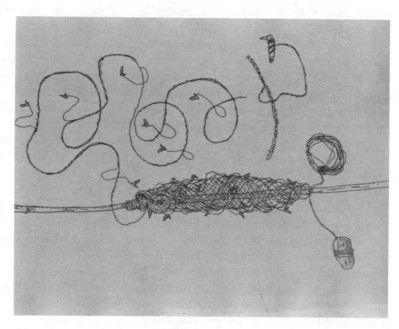

Figure 1b. Set line of native cordage, approximately 15 m in length, with 73 tiny hooks suspended. Collected by Stephen Powers at Pyramid Lake, Nevada in 1876. Note rod and rock sinker. Drawing by Susan Lohse of specimen in National Museum of Natural History, Smithsonian Institution (Catalog number 19047).

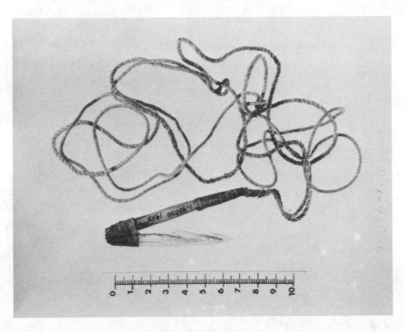

Figure 2a. Composite fishhook of bone and wood recovered from Humboldt Cave, Nevada. Courtesy of the Lowie Museum of Anthropology, University of California at Berkeley (Catalog number 1–43036).

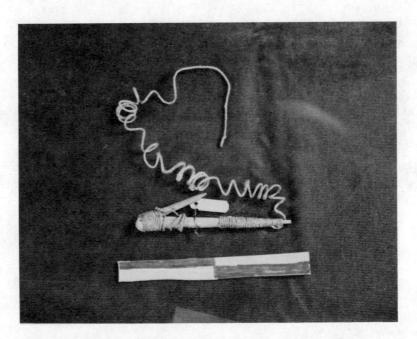

Figure 2b. Composite fishhook of greasewood with native cordage, designed to be suspended from a set line and used for trout. Collected in 1916 by Samuel Barrett in western Nevada. Milwaukee Public Museum (Catalog number 21970; 8.3 cm).

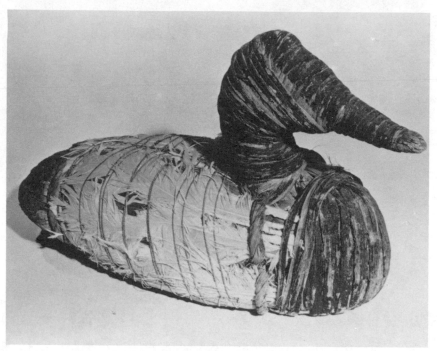

Figure 3a. Canvasback tule duck decoy recovered from Lovelock Cave, Nevada. Photograph by Carmelo Guadagno, courtesy of the Museum of the American Indian, Heye Foundation, New York (Catalog number 13/4512).

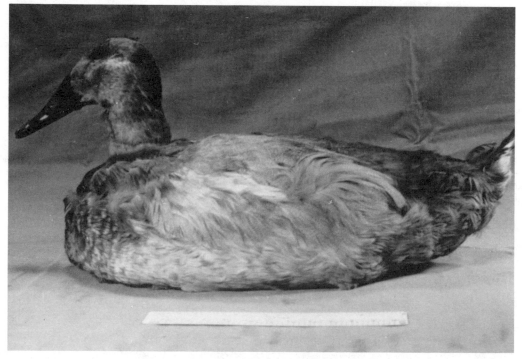

Figure 3b. Tule duck decoy covered with female canvasback skin. Collected by M. R. Harrington, Walker River Reservation, Nevada, 1924. Museum of the American Indian, Heye Foundation (Catalog number 13/4415).

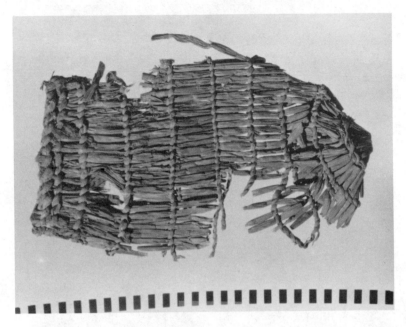

Figure 4a. Tule bag recovered from Humboldt Cave, Nevada. Note down–to–the–right work direction. Courtesy of the Lowie Museum of Anthropology, University of California at Berkeley (Catalog number 1–42285).

(probably all by one maker), have solid floats and less twining. Ethnographic decoy markers normally use whole duck skins to cover the tule float, whereas the archaeological specimens from Lovelock Cave feature individually attached feathers.[8] There are also some differences in treatment and attachment of heads, use of materials, etc. But then the ethnographic decoys also differ among themselves in a few details (Figure 3b). In spite of this, it is obvious that both the archaeological and the ethnographic groups practiced decoy hunting. The most famous archeological decoys are the canvasbacks from Lovelock Cave, although parts of Canada geese, white–fronted geese, coots, mergansers and others have been collected. The ethnographic decoys are canvasbacks, one redhead, one bufflehead and a pintail.

Evidence for the taking of waterfowl eggs is present indirectly in the archaeological record and is well documented ethnographically. Material culture correlates of the practice are small, twined tule and rush bags. Construction details differ, however, with the archaeological bags being conical, and made with the down–to–the–right twist in twining (Figure 4a). The ethnographically collected bags have a different start and an up–to–the–right twining direction (Figure 4b). Twining direction also differs in archaeological versus ethnographic matting, sandals, and the bulk of the basketry. Down–to–the–right work direction in tule technology is found at least among the Klamath (Barrett 1910) and possibly other California tribes. Tule sandals collected ethnographically are similar in construction plan (heel, warp turned up for a toe flap) to archaeological examples except in twining direction and overall fineness. The ethnographic specimens are probably models, and thus lack some refinements, but the work directional shift suggests discontinuity and a separate twining complex.

There is perhaps a material culture correlate for the processing of bulrush and other hard–shelled seeds particularly common in marsh areas. Ethnographically these are known by the term *wik^wan.u*, or hullers. They are commonly circular to elliptical in shape, flat and thin (Figure 5). They are common in both the Humboldt and Carson basins, but whether their distribution includes the Pyramid and Walker basins is not known. Three, and possibly six, were recovered from Lovelock Cave, but the bulk of those pictured in the report are from

Figure 4b. Mrs. Wuzzie George working on a tule duck egg bag.   Note up–to–the–right work direction. Photograph by C. S. Fowler, 1979.

surface sites in the Humboldt Basin (Loud and Harrington 1929).   Their distribution should be further documented.   Again, they may be Northern Paiute and not characteristic of the Lovelock culture.

Conclusions

As can be seen from the foregoing brief report, there remains much to do in bringing together the ethnographic and archaeological evidence for marsh and lake adaptations in western Nevada.   At the least, the archaeological material culture should be restudied from the perspective of the ethnographic materials, and additional efforts made to differentiate or unite the two. Preliminary assessments suggest that at least some of the artifacts types from the Humboldt Sink are protohistoric Northern Paiute and not necessarily Lovelock Culture. Others show more in the way of general technological continuities (as befitting similar adaptive strategies) than they do in specific details. The lake versus marsh–oriented adaptations should probably be re–examined as well, with more attention paid to the role of fishing, waterfowl hunting, and collecting specific plant types as opposed to the more generalized subsistence patterns obtaining elsewhere. Perhaps then we might make some better judgments as to the similarities and differences through time in this most interesting region of the Great Basin.

Figure 5. Selection of hullers for hard–shelled seeds, recovered from surface sites in the Humboldt Sink, Nevada. Plate 61, Loud and Harrington (1929).

Notes

[1]See, for example, Janetski (n.d.) on Utah Lake; Steward (1938, 1941) on Ruby Valley; Stewart (1941) on Harney Valley, Pyramid Lake, Walker River and Stillwater; and although outside the Great Basin, Barrett (1910) on the Klamath Basin.

[2]This journal is considered by many to be somewhat unreliable as to specific places where events were witnessed.

[3]On the taking of duck eggs and ducklings, see Henshaw (1879).

[4]Lists of mammals, land birds, insects and reptiles are not included here. Readers can get a good idea of the species involved by reviewing the pertinent tables in Fowler (1986) for designations "Nevada Northern Paiute."

[5]It is, of course, possible that the high figures represent the use of the area as a refuge from regions to the north and west that were by this time harder hit by emigration and settlement.

[6]Walker River residents do speak of shallow water areas near the southeast end of the lake that may have been suitable for netting ducks. Decoys were seen in a camp at the mouth of Walker River in 1845 by Edward Kern (1876: 480).

[7]Pyramid Lake also has the large American White Pelican rookery on Anaho Island. Several other species also nest there. Duck Lake, a small marsh (now dry) southwest of the lake, was favored in former times for coot drives.

References

Ambro, R. D.
  1966   Two Fish Nets from Hidden Cave, Churchill County, Nevada. *University of California Archaeological Survey Reports* 66:101–135. Berkeley.

Barrett, S. A.
  1910   The Material Culture of the Klamath and Modoc Indians of Northeastern California and Southern Oregon. *University of California Publications in American Archaeology and Ethnology* 5(4):239–93. Berkeley.
Curtis, E.
  1926   *The North American Indian: Being a Series of Volumes Picturing and Describing the Indians of the United States, and Alaska,* vol. 15. Plimpton Press, Norwood, Massachusetts.
DeOuille, D. (William Wright)
  1963   *Washoe Rambles.* Los Angeles, Westernlore Press.
Dodge, F.
  1860   Report of, Office of Indian Agent, Carson Valley, Utah Territory, January 4, 1859. In *Papers Accompanying the Annual Report of the Commissioner of Indian Affairs 1859,* No. 175. Exec. Docs., (Senate), 36th. Cong., 1st. Sess., Doc. No. 2, pp. 741–5. Washington, D.C.
Fowler, C. S. (editor)
  1989   *Willard Z. Park's Ethnographic Notes on the Northern Paiute of Western Nevada, 1933–1940.* University of Utah Anthropological Papers No. 114. Salt Lake City.
Fowler, C. S., and J. E. Bath
  1981   Pyramid Lake Northern Paiute Fishing: The Ethnographic Record. *Journal of California and Great Basin Anthropology* 3(2):176–186.
Fowler, C. S., and S. Liljeblad
  1986   Northern Paiute. In *Great Basin,* edited by W. L. d'Azevedo, pp. 435–465. Handbook of North American Indians, vol. 11, William G. Sturtevant, general editor. Smithsonian Institution, Washington, D.C.
Fremont, J. C.
  1845   *Report on the Exploring Expedition to the Rocky Mountains in the Year 1842 and to Oregon and Northern California in the Years 1843–1844.* Gales and Seaton, Washington.
Grosscup, G. L.
  1960   The Culture History of Lovelock Cave, Nevada. *University of California Archaeological Survey Reports* 52:1–71. Berkeley.
Heizer, R. F.
  1970   Ethnographic Notes on the Northern Paiute of Humboldt Sinks, Western Nevada. In *Languages and Cultures of Western North America: Essays in Honor of Sven S. Liljeblad,* edited by E. H. Swanson, Jr., pp. 232–245. Idaho State University Press, Pocatello.
Heizer, R. F., and A. D. Krieger
  1956   The Archaeology of Humboldt Cave, Churchill County, Nevada. *University of California Publications in American Archaeology and Ethnology* 47(1):1–90. Berkeley.
Henshaw, H. W.
  1879   Ornithological Report from Observations and Collections Made in Portions of California, Nevada, and Oregon, Appendix L. In *Annual Report upon Geographical Surveys of the Territory West of the 100th Meridian,* by G. M. Wheeler. Appendix OO of the Annual Report of the Chief of Engineers for 1879. Government Printing Office, Washington, D.C.
Janetski, J. C.
  n.d.   *The Ute of Utah Lake.* University of Utah Anthropological Papers No. 116. Salt Lake City, in press.
Kelly, I. T.
  1932   Ethnography of the Surprise Valley Paiute. *University of California Publications in American Archaeology and Ethnology* 31(3):67–210. Berkeley.
Kern, E. C.
  1876   Journal of Mr. Edward M. Kern of the Exploration of the Mary's River or Humboldt River, Carson Lake, and Owens River and Lake in 1876. Appendix Q in *Report of Explorations Across the Great Basin of the Territory of Utah for a Direct Wagon-Route from Camp Floyd to Genoa, in Carson Valley in 1859,* by Captain J. H. Simpson. Government Printing Office, Washington, D.C. (Reprinted by University of Nevada Press, Reno, 1983.)
Kroeber, A. L., and S. A. Barrett
  1960   Fishing Among the Indians of Northwestern California. *University of California Anthropological Records* 21(1):1–210. Berkeley.
Loud, L. L.
  1929   Notes on the Northern Paiute. In Lovelock Cave, by L. L. Loud and M. R. Harrington, pp. 152–164. *University of California Publications in American Archaeology and Ethnology* 25(1):152–164. Berkeley.
Loud, L. L., and M. R. Harrington
  1929   Lovelock Cave. *University of California Publications in American Archaeology and Ethnology* 25(1):1–183. Berkeley.
Powers, S.
  1876   Catalog of Artifacts, Accession 4856. Archives of the Office of the Secretary, Smithsonian Institution, Washington, D.C.
Reid, J. T.
  n.d.   The Papers of John T. Reid, Lovelock, Nevada. Ms. on file, Nevada Historical Society, Reno.

Shimkin, D. and R. M. Reid
    1970   Socio–cultural Persistence Among Shoshoneans of the Carson River Basin (Nevada). In *Languages and Cultures of Western North America: Essays in Honor of Sven S. Liljeblad*, edited by E. H. Swanson, Jr., pp. 172–200. Idaho State University Press, Pocatello.

Simpson, J. H.
    1876   *Report of Explorations Across the Great Basin of the Territory of Utah for a Direct Wagon–Route from Camp Floyd to Genoa, in Carson Valley, in 1859.* Government Printing Office, Washington, D.C. (Reprinted by University of Nevada Press, Reno, 1983.)

Steward, J. H.
    1933   Ethnography of the Owens Valley Paiute. *University of California Publications in American Archaeology and Ethnology* 33(3):233–350. Berkeley.
    1938   Basin–Plateau Aboriginal Sociopolitical Groups. *Bureau of American Ethnology Bulletin* No. 120. Washington, D.C.
    1941   Culture Element Distributions: XVIII. Nevada Shoshone. *University of California Anthropological Records* 4(2):209–359. Berkeley.

Stewart, O. C.
    1939   Northern Paiute Bands. *University of California Anthropological Records* 2(3):127–149. Berkeley.
    1941   Culture Element Distributions, XIV: Northern Paiute. *University of California Anthropological Records* 4 (3):361–446. Berkeley.

Thomas, D. H.
    1985   The Archaeology of Hidden Cave, Nevada. *Anthropological Papers of the American Museum of Natural History* 61(1):1–430. New York.

Wagner, W. F. (editor)
    1904   *Leonard's Narrative: Adventures of Zenas Leonard, Furtrader and Trapper.* Burrows Brothers, Cleveland.

Wheat, M. M.
    1950–1981   Manuscript, Photographic and Film Collection. Special Collections, Getchell Library, University of Nevada, Reno.
    1967   *Survival Arts of the Primitive Paiutes.* University of Nevada Press, Reno.

4

ARCHAEOLOGICAL SITES EXPOSED BY RECENT FLOODING OF STILLWATER MARSH CARSON DESERT, CHURCHILL COUNTY, NEVADA

Anan W. Raymond and Virginia M. Parks

Abstract

In the summer of 1985 the first of 51 large archaeological sites emerged from receding floodwaters at Stillwater Marsh, in the Carson Desert, Churchill County, Nevada. The sites contain cultural debris, features and human remains that mark a continuity of residential occupation in Stillwater Marsh from about 3000 B.P. to at least 700 B.P., if not 300 B.P.

Introduction

In the early 1980s, before the Stillwater Marsh flooded, Robert Kelly (1985) collected flake stone artifacts from the surface of over 100 sites in and around Stillwater Marsh. Kelly (1985, 1988, this volume) focused on how the artifacts informed on the settlement system that produced the sites. Kelly recognized the challenges posed by relic collectors, site erosion, sedimentation, toolstone availability and gemorphological change of the marsh. Time and scope forced him to limit analysis to surface flaked stone, leaving surface fire–cracked rock, groundstone and test excavation out of the equation. The data compelled Kelly to conclude that "there is no evidence of sedentism, semi–sedentism or focal use of the Carson Desert" (Kelly 1985:293). Although the wetlands in the Carson Sink produce abundant food resources, it did not support long term residential sites or sedentism because other areas were more productive (Kelly 1985:294).

More specifically, Kelly perceives a settlement shift about 1500 B.P. The pre–1500 B.P. period sites are identified by Elko series projectile points. Kelly proposes that during the Elko period the Carson Desert/Stillwater Marsh sites were produced by foragers with high residential mobility (1985:245, 1988, this volume). During the post–1500 B.P. period marked by Rose Spring, Eastgate, and Desert series points, Kelly notes a shift in the technological organization of flaked stone and attendant mobility strategy. Increased sedentism and logistic mobility is evident in the Carson Desert. Some sites indicate small logistical parties

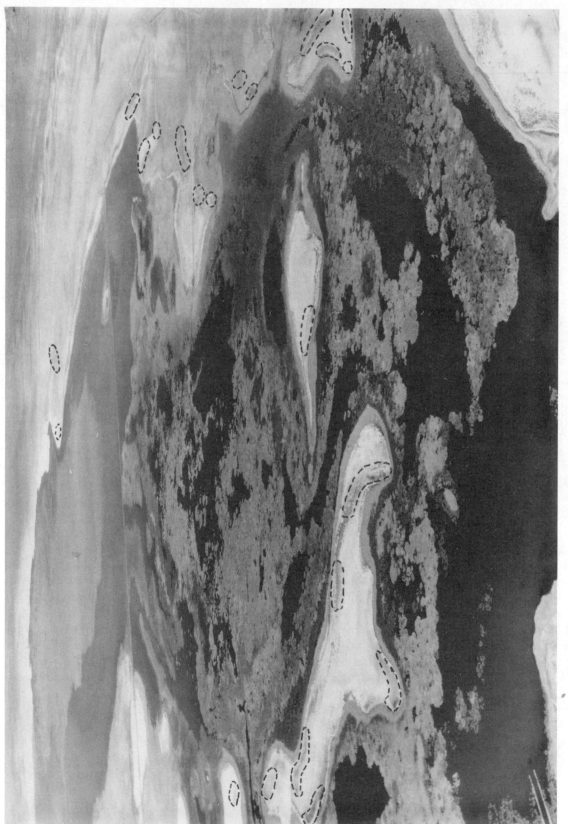

Figure 1. Oblique aerial photograph of the Nutgrass (foreground) and Big Water ponds in lower Stillwater Marsh. View is to the northeast with the Stillwater Range and Carson Sink in the background. Scale: bottom margin of the photograph covers 1.5 miles. Archaeological sites are marked. Base of photo to mountains along right margin covers 8 miles. (Copeland Photography, 1952, Oakland, California)

operating from residential camps outside the Carson Desert (1985:251, 293–294). Kelly also detects flaked stone evidence for increased residential mobility (1985:303), as well as short term residential use (1988:717). But he also encounters residential sites occupied for a long periods of time (this volume). Although the flaked stone data presents a confusing picture of the post–1500 B.P. mobility strategy, Kelly (this volume) argues that there is a shift from the pre–1500 B.P. strategy of high residential mobility.

A surface inventory of 51 flood–damaged sites in Stillwater Marsh (Raymond and Parks 1989) has returned data that contradicts Kelly's conclusions. The 51 sites are not the same sites examined by Kelly before the flood, although they occur in the same area—Stillwater Marsh. Nor was the flaked stone from these sites analyzed in the manner outlined by Kelly (1985). But, the flood exposed large sites containing cultural features, human burials, and middens with a marked residential aspect. The archaeological material has a density and abundance that, with the exception of the Humboldt Lakebed site, has no precedent in the western Great Basin. Of the 1024 circular cultural features mapped, many appear to be the remains of storage and residential structures. Projectile points and a few radiocarbon dates indicate that the sites date between 3250 B.P. and 700 B.P. The settlement shift perceived by Kelly (1985, 1988, this volume) at the cusp (about 1500 B.P) between the Elko and Rose Spring/Eastgate periods is not demonstrated. The size of cultural features and the frequency of sites, cultural features, ground stone tools, flaked stone tools, fire–cracked rock, and faunal remains is essentially the same in the pre–1500 B.P. period as the post–1500 B.P. period.

Before we examine the surface archaeology exposed by the flood let us outline the environmental context in which the sites are found.

Setting

Thirteen thousand years ago the Carson, Humboldt, Walker and Truckee Rivers all converged on giant Lake Lahontan. That lake stood 500 feet above the modern floor of the Carson Sink and Stillwater Marsh (Davis 1982). As the lake receded, dunes of sand, silt, and clay formed along the southern margin of Carson Sink (Katzer 1988). These dunes block the Carson River from spilling directly into the Sink, creating the maze of ponds and sloughs called Stillwater Marsh (Figure 1).

Melting snows feed the Carson River high in the Sierra Nevada. The Carson is well entrenched until it leaves its canyon upstream of Fallon, Nevada. There, the Carson splits into three streams which meander across a 240 square mile deltoid while dropping only 230 feet in elevation. One branch called the "Old" Carson River flows north to Carson Sink through the Fallon National Wildlife Refuge at Pelican Island Marsh. Another branch of the river cuts south and empties into Carson Lake Marsh. Carson Lake then spills north into Stillwater Slough which ultimately pours into Stillwater Marsh at the Stillwater Wildlife Management Area. The third branch, called the "New" River, was created by floods in 1867 and flows directly into Stillwater Slough and eventually into Stillwater Marsh (Figure 2).

As the lowest place in the western Great Basin (3,871 feet or 1,180 m) the Carson Sink also serves as the final pool for the Humboldt River. But the Humboldt River only reaches Carson Sink and Stillwater Marsh after it has filled Humboldt Sink. Floods in the 1880s (Russel 1885) and the 1980s sent water through the Humboldt Slough into Carson Sink. During the Holocene period the Walker River occasionally abandoned its usual course feeding Walker Lake and spilled north into the Carson River (Davis 1982). Floods, shifting sand dunes and rivers have influenced the size and location of Stillwater Marsh throughout the Holocene.

Marsh Habitats

In the late 1800s and 1900s Stillwater Marsh covered 35,000 acres (Sperry 1929). But recent agricultural diversions (Townley 1977) have eliminated the 17,000 acre marsh at Pelican Island and have shrunk Stillwater Marsh to 7,000 acres creating a bleak, unnatural landscape (Thompson and Merritt 1988). Under natural conditions Stillwater Marsh is a complex and fluctuating ecosystem. Silt lunette dunes, punctuating the flat expanse of water, create over 200 islands and a mainland shoreline of 225 miles (Giles et al. 1953). In the spring

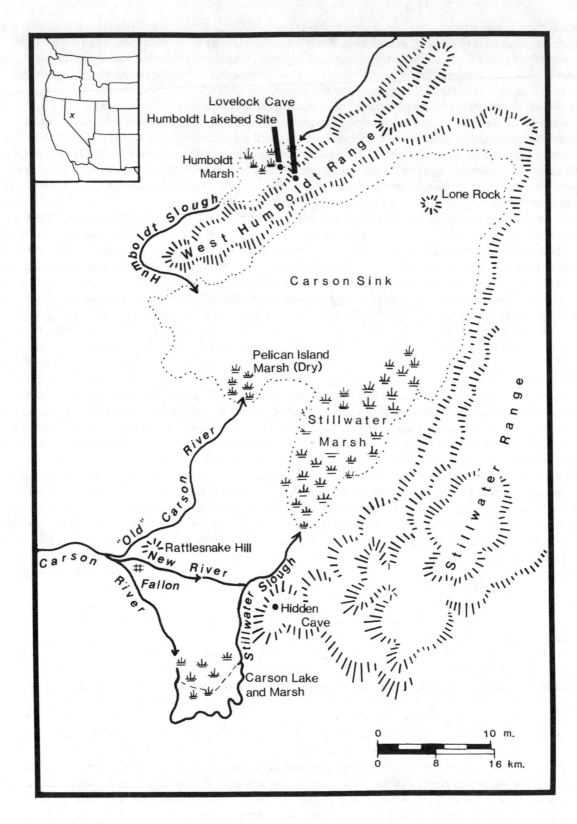

Figure 2. Map of Stillwater Marsh and the Carson Sink, Churchill County, Nevada.

the Carson delivers freshets from melting mountain snow. Water spreads over playas and shallow ponds. Emergents including cattail (*Typha* spp.), hardstem bulrush (*Scripus acutus*), and alkali bulrush (*Scripus maritimus*) rejuvenate. The nesting season begins in early March for geese, and continues through June for some ducks and ibis. In summer, 100° F temperatures partially evaporate downstream ponds and increase water salinity. Tui chub spawn and thousands of ducks and coots molt. Autumn slows the 4 to 5 foot annual evaporation rate. Submergent vegetation like sago pondweed (*Potomageton pectinatus*), widgeon grass (*Ruppia maritima*) and *Chara* sp. matures in the deeper ponds while the seeds of bulrush ripen in the drying ponds. These and other plants provide fuel to over a quarter of a million waterfowl which stop at the marsh in the fall on their way south along the Pacific flyway. By December most birds have left for points further south but some remain longer, including as many as 5,000 tundra swans. The swans will break up ice as it forms on ponds in early winter, thereby maintaining open water for themselves and the geese, ducks and coots which remain behind (Thompson 1987).

Water depth and water salinity influence the assemblage of flora and fauna in Stillwater Marsh (Thompson and Raymond 1988). Upstream ponds support vastly different vegetation than downstream ponds (Figure 3). The upstream ponds contain fresher water and do not evaporate completely. The downstream ponds hold saltier water, the result of evaporation, leaching, and flushing of upstream playas. Water depth crosscuts water salinity (Figure 4), producing a complex mosaic of habitats. Two feet of water in a downstream salty pond supports different plants and animals that two inches in the same pond, and different plants and animals than two feet of water in a fresh upstream pond. Stillwater Marsh, in a few miles, contains more environmental diversity than scores of miles in the pinyon/juniper zone on the adjacent Stillwater Range.

Marsh productivity and diversity is maintained by fluctuating water conditions. Fluctuating water budgets cause any one plant or animal species in any one location to undergo boom and bust cycles. Partial drying of shallow ponds produces dense micro–vegetation. This becomes food for aquatic invertebrates, which in turn become food for waterbirds and fish. Drying of deeper ponds allows decomposition of bottom organic deposits and aeration of the ground. A release of nutrients feeds a new surge of vegetation and invertebrates when water returns seasonally, or in dozens of years when seeds germinate after dormancy. An increase in water, like the recent flood, will wipe out emergent vegetation and the seeds and nesting they offer. But tui chub, annual plants and invertebrates explode, which attracts record numbers of pelicans and waterfowl. If a new water level is maintained for even a few years plants and animals will adjust, so that habitats initially lost are replaced elsewhere in the basin. As the water budget increases and decreases, the marsh will expand and contract, while retaining the same habitat structure illustrated in Figures 3 and 4 (Thompson and Raymond 1988).

The 1983–1986 Flood

In water years (October–September) 1982, 1983, 1984, and 1986 (USGS 1982–1986) the Carson and Humboldt Rivers delivered above average flows into the Carson Desert and Humboldt Sink. The Carson Sink, which has been mostly dry for the last 100 years, began to receive water from the Old Carson River, Stillwater Marsh and Humboldt Slough by mid 1983. By 1984 the ponds in the northeastern (or downstream) third of Stillwater Marsh stood 2.75 feet above normal level. Water began to lap against (then unknown) archaeological deposits by late winter. By summer 1984, Carson Sink posted a maximum elevation of 3,876.2 feet covering some 220,000 acres (Figure 5). Yet the water did not exceed 12 feet in depth (U. S. Fish and Wildlife Service 1988).

Like the Sink, Stillwater Marsh was transformed into a vast lake. But the exposed sites are confined to the downstream third of the marsh, where landforms were inundated with a meter and a half of water. Although the upstream portion of the marsh was also flooded, sites were not exposed. The upstream marsh lies about a half meter higher in absolute elevation than the downstream marsh. And, the upstream marsh did not experience severe wave and ice erosion. Large expanses of water and mudflat in the downstream third of the marsh allowed wind driven waves and ice to strip vegetation and topsoil from submerged islands and shorelines.

In July 1985 the first of 51 archaeological sites appeared in the downstream third of the marsh as floodwater began to retreat. The archaeological sites rest on silt lunette dunes which are normally vegetated with

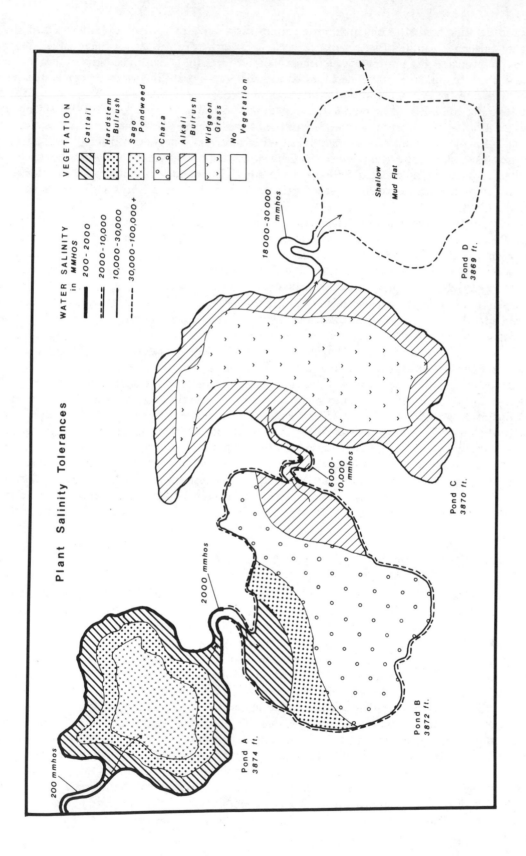

Figure 3. Stillwater Marsh habitats and water salinity.

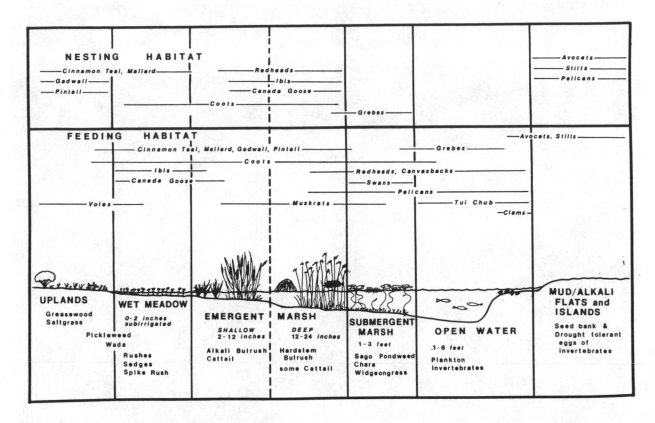

Figure 4. Stillwater Marsh habitats and water depth.

greasewood and saltgrass. Barren mudflats, open water, and dense stands of cattail and bulrush once surrounded the sites (Figure 1). Under historic conditions the sites occur in habitats like that described as Pond C in Figure 3, with smaller areas like Pond B and Pond D. Locally water is not potable. Water depth ranges between 1 and 3 feet, with large areas drying completely by autumn. The sites occur in a place known for its 3,000 acre nutgrass (alkali bulrush, *Scripus maritimus*) stand (Giles et al. 1953).

Since the flood, however, the landscape bears little resemblance to the historic condition. Floodwater killed the plants. Waves stripped up to 30 cm of topsoil, exposing the entire horizontal extent of many sites to the surface. Dead bulrush and cattail ringed landforms in windrows. Archaeological material became flotsam as the water eroded cultural deposits. Hundreds of human bones lay scattered across the surface. The bones and cultural debris were eroded from black midden deposits and scores of cultural features that dot each site. The sites also exhibit a veneer of redeposited cultural debris and sediments that blankets the dune slope leeward to the principal direction of wave action. Apparently, as the debris laden waves crested the dunes, water slowed enough to drop its load on the lee side of the landforms. As the water receded from the dunes it etched strandlines in the redeposited sediments, while wave fetch formed windrows of archaeological flotsam on the erosional slopes. The water receded to its "normal" level in spring 1987, making maps useful for navigation once again. Carson Sink held water until mid–summer 1987. By 1988, weeds and wind–deposited sand began to cover the sites.

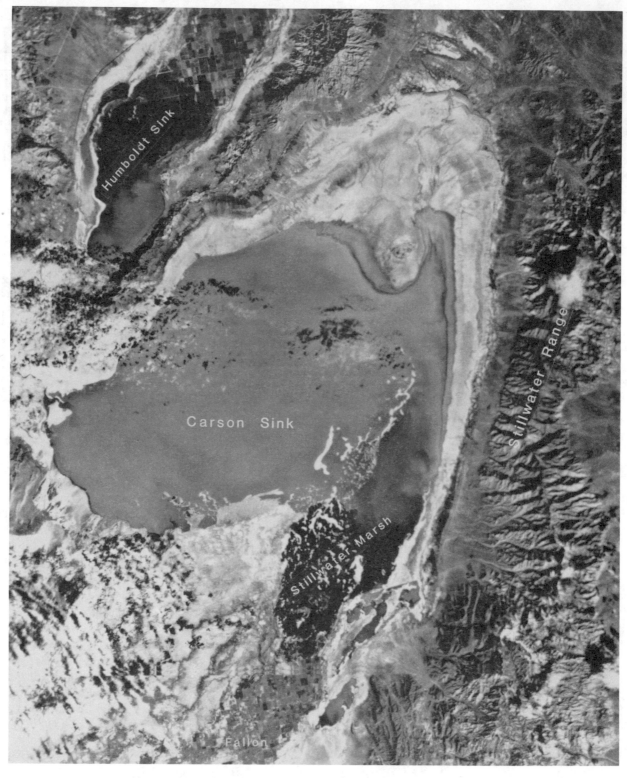

Figure 5. LANDSAT photograph of Stillwater Marsh and Carson Sink at the height of the 1983–1986 flood. (U.S. Geological Survey, October 27, 1984)

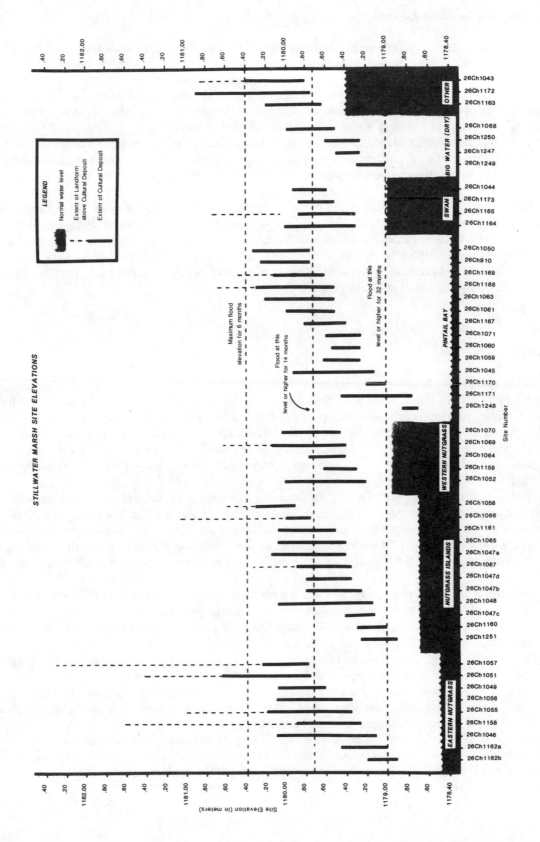

Figure 6. Elevation range of cultural deposits at sites in Stillwater Marsh.

Elevation and Depth of Deposits

The boundary of each site matches the boundary of the dune eminence upon which it is found. Because the flood stripped all vegetation and topsoil we could easily record the maximum and minimum elevations of archaeological deposits exposed across the profile of a dune. Aerial photogrammetry documented the depth and position of all cultural deposits relative to one another and to the rise and fall of the floodwater (Figure 6). Test excavations (Raven and Elston 1988) and soil probing confirm that the sites have depth at a value approximating the relief presented by the archaeological deposits exposed across the dune profile. At 39 sites the maximum elevation of archaeological deposits corresponds to the highest point on the landform today. Previous erosion, including the recent flood, has removed the upper deposits of these 39 sites. Small portions in the center of 12 sites remained above the maximum height (1,180.4 m) of the flood. These sites retain a protective cap over intact cultural deposits.

Some 43 sites have at least a portion of their cultural deposits lying at or below 1,179.73 m. These sites lay under water for at least 14 months and as much as 32 months. The flood stood at its highest elevation of 1,180.4 m for 6 months. Sites with deep (or high relief) deposits have escaped prolonged inundation. Shallow sites, or sites with little relief, often occur at low elevations and were thus completely submerged for over two years. Perhaps these sites have suffered several floods and years of deflation in the past. Another flood could wipe away shallow, low elevation sites altogether.

The Sites

Inventory

The Nevada State Museum (Tuohy et al. 1987) mapped and collected human bones and diagnostic artifacts from 30 sites in 1985 and 1986. The U.S. Fish and Wildlife Service (Raymond and Parks 1989) found 21 more sites and initiated a comprehensive mapping and inventory of all 51 sites in 1987 (Figure 7). The survey was designed to find sites significantly exposed by the flood. Sites were found opportunistically as archaeologists and biologists boated across Stillwater Marsh. Eventually all the shoreline and islands in Pintail Bay and the three Nutgrass ponds were surveyed. In adjacent ponds only shorelines and islands severely eroded by the flood were investigated.

We mapped each site to obtain basic information on topography, cultural debris and features. The project combined aerial photogrammetry with ground inventory and mapping. The low elevation (1:1800) color aerial photos (Figure 8) nicely resolved cultural features at some sites. Other sites showed no features on the photos despite their documentation by us on the ground. Ground mapping served to check the observations made on the aerial photographs. Both phases of the mapping project were meshed to draft base maps for each site (Figure 9).

Each site was inventoried across 23 data categories (Raymond and Parks 1989 Tables 1 and 2). Here we use a portion of the data to address Kelly's notion of a change in settlement of the Carson Desert around 1500 B.P. We have collapsed the data into 11 categories with sites grouped by the time period that associated projectile points indicate (Table 1 and Table 2).

The inventory of cultural debris and features was limited to data readily observable at the surface of the sites. Cultural features were counted, mapped and measured. The abundance of groundstone artifacts, fire-cracked rock and non-diagnostic culturally transported rock forced us to set an 8 cm (baseball-size) threshold below which searching and counting was abandoned. Flaked stone tools, including projectile points, hammerstones, and flaked stone cores were sought out and counted regardless of size. Only projectile points were collected. We estimated the abundance of flaked stone debitage, large faunal remains (greater than a duck humerus—7 cm), small faunal remains, and mussel shell. Table 2 shows how our field estimates translate to numerical values that permit comparison of sites. Let us first examine the temporal placement of the sites.

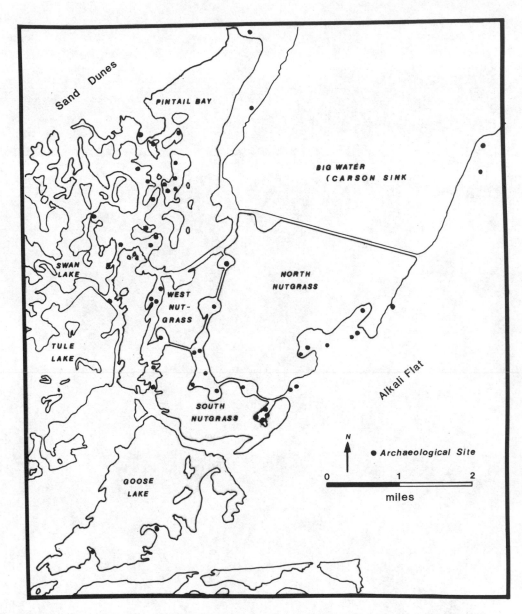

Figure 7. Map of lower Stillwater Marsh showing the location of archaeological sites.

Chronology

Elsewhere one of us (Raymond) has argued against using projectile points to mark time (Flenniken and Raymond 1986). Here, we retreat somewhat recognizing that projectile points offer an estimate of the age of the deposit from which they were recovered. Until more radiocarbon dates are obtained, projectile points must suffice. Indeed, projectile points are the only method that Kelly employs to document the timing of the purported change in settlement of the Carson Desert.

Kelly (1985, 1988, this volume) imports Thomas' (1981) Monitor Valley phases and projectile point typology. In Kelly's scheme Elko series points represent the pre–1500 B.P. period. Rose Spring/Eastgate points and Desert series points mark the post–1500 B.P. period. But for Thomas, Elko series points signal the Reville

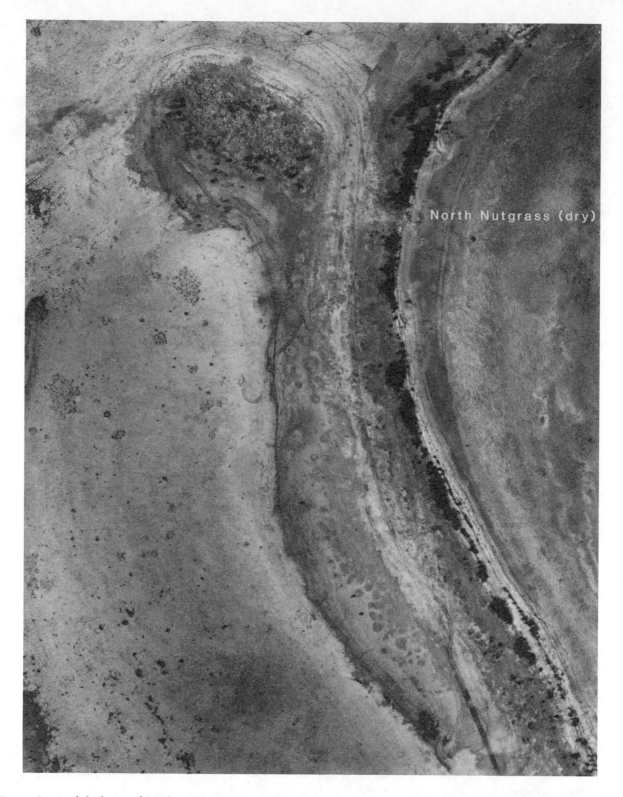

Figure 8. Aerial photo of 26Ch 1065, summer 1987, shows dark circular cultural features at southern end and numerous overlapping features in a complex midden deposit at the north end of the letter "q" shaped landform. Scale: length of photo = 250 meters. (Hammon, Jensen, Whallon, Oakland, California)

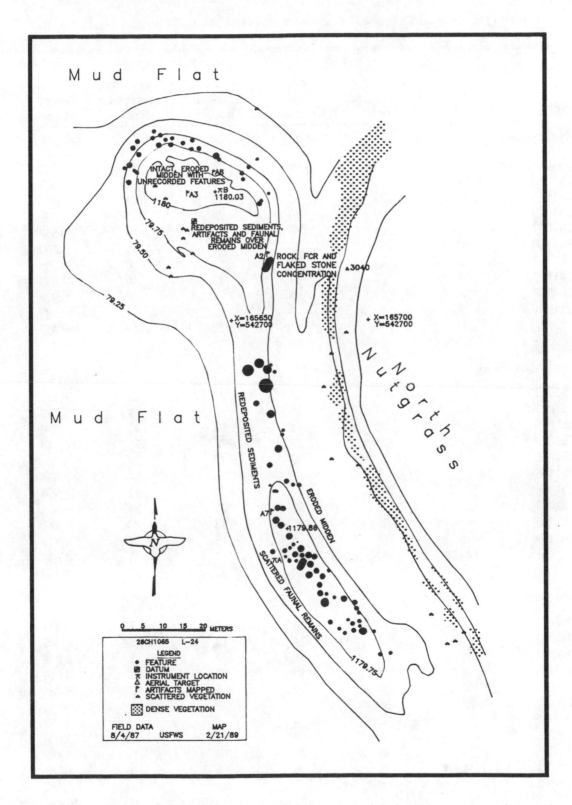

Figure 9. Site 26Ch 1065, one of 51 site maps combining data from aerial photogrammetry and ground survey. (U.S. Fish and Wildlife Service)

Table 1. Inventory of Cultural Debris and Features at Stillwater Marsh Sites

Site	Features	Groundstone Tools	Flaked Stone Tools	Fire-Cracked Rock	Culturally Transported Rock	Area in Square Meters	Burial
Period Arrow							
Ch1043	19	24	29	33	17	10,191	7
Ch1045	23	11	9	8	2	2,378	1
Ch1046	40	28	19	16	24	10,356	3
Ch1050	11	9	16	24	5	3,476	2
Ch1067	17	4	10	4	3	6,530	0
Ch1160	50	73	23	50	51	2,607	1
Ch1167	11	33	3	13	0	30,380	0
Ch1169	38	53	37	27	10	7,843	0
Ch1250	28	18	5	5	8	2,979	1
Ch1044	3	11	3	24	2	12,177	2
N	240	264	154	222	140	89,417	17
X	24	26	15	22	14	8,941	
Period Arrow/Dart							
Ch1047a	34	14	15	27	25	8,244	2
Ch1047d	14	7	15	8	9	3,285	1
Ch1048	109	60	44	83	42	7,780	2
Ch1049	7	15	23	22	22	4,346	Present
Ch1063	12	17	10	17	20	4,739	1
Ch1158	11	7	9	6	14	5,546	1
Ch1068	41	70	24	75	21	15,496	Present
Ch1051	23	18	28	29	26	9,951	1
Ch1065	88	97	117	95	27	7,242	1
Ch1159	5	4	5	5	17	4,374	4
N	344	309	290	367	223	70,603	13+
X	34	31	29	37	22	7,060	
Period Dart							
Ch910	11	12	12	7	7	3,884	5
Ch1047c	12	31	14	18	3	1,009	0
Ch1052	34	29	16	39	21	2,044	1
Ch1056	8	4	19	0	8	4,614	Present
Ch1161	12	4	7	5	2	8,121	Present
Ch1162a	25	30	36	32	24	10,943	0
Ch1162b	22	32	4	7	2	3,457	0
Ch1163	9	1	4	0	1	2,900	1
Ch1251	58	48	24	37	0	4,888	0
Ch1173	11	3	9	6	0	1,748	1
Ch1010	38	8	7	25	11	3,382	4
N	240	202	152	176	79	46,990	12+
X	22	18	14	16	7	4,272	

Table 1. (Continued)

Site	Features	Groundstone Tools	Flaked Stone Tools	Fire-Cracked Rock	Culturally Transported Rock	Area in Square Meters	Burial
Period Unknown							
Ch1047b	14	5	2	5	15	3,764	0
Ch1055	17	4	6	4	20	6,117	1
Ch1057	0	6	0	5	0	19,314	Present
Ch1058	25	4	4	16	9	4,600	3
Ch1059	1	13	3	1	0	7,821	0
Ch1060	71	18	4	12	18	8,202	1
Ch1061	9	5	2	4	1	2,718	0
Ch1064	8	9	7	4	0	2,146	3
Ch1066	0	2	2	3	0	1,995	0
Ch1069	33	18	8	19	7	4,828	1
Ch1071	13	6	2	3	10	6,017	0
Ch1164	5	4	1	8	0	5,357	0
Ch1165	14	8	1	10	0	3,153	0
Ch1168	34	28	8	15	9	13,631	0
Ch1170	0	42	2	15	0	7,814	0
Ch1171	36	6	4	6	7	7,814	0
Ch1172	9	11	19	18	9	6,768	0
Ch1247	5	6	5	5	0	2,336	0
Ch1248	1	12	1	1	1	17,622	0
Ch1249	10	96	21	50	0	10,159	1
N	305	303	102	204	106	35,731	10+
X	15	15	5	10	5	6,786	
Total	1,129	1,078	698	969	548		52

phase which lasts from 3250 B.P. to 1250 B.P. The Underdown phase, marked by Rose Spring and Eastgate Points, lasts from 1250 B.P. to 550 B.P. (Thomas 1981). Kelly does not cite a reason for this discrepancy. The cusp between the Elko period and the Rose Spring/Eastgate period lies around 1500 B.P. to 1250 B.P. The exact date is less important than Kelly's notion of a shift in the settlement strategy between Elko (dart) period sites and Eastgate/Rose Spring (arrow) period sites.

Some 170 projectile points were recovered from the 51 flood exposed sites (Tuohy et al. 1987, Raymond and Parks 1989). The points, like those recovered by Kelly in his earlier work in the Carson Desert and Stillwater Marsh, were typed using the Monitor Valley key (Thomas 1981). Table 3 permits comparison of the frequency of point types from Stillwater Marsh with other sites in the Carson and Humboldt Sinks. However, points from the Humboldt Sink sites were not submitted to Monitor Valley criteria.

Projectile points of the Elko and Rosegate series dominate 75% of the collection from Stillwater Marsh. In the Carson Desert surrounding Stillwater Marsh projectile points are more evenly distributed among the Gatecliff, Elko, Rosegate and Desert series (Kelly 1985:245). Rosegate series points comprise the majority at Stillwater Marsh, Lovelock Cave and the Humboldt Lakebed site. But these latter two sites do not obtain near

Table 2. Estimated Abundance of Cultural Debris at Sites in Stillwater Marsh

Site	Large Faunal Remains	Small Faunal Remains	Flaked Stone	Mussel Shell
Period Arrow				
Ch1043	2	3	3	2
Ch1045	0	1	1	1
Ch1046	1	3	3	2
Ch1050	1	2	1	0
Ch1067	1	1	2	1
Ch1160	1	1	2	0
Ch1167	0	1	1	2
Ch1169	1	1	2	2
Ch1250	1	2	1	1
Ch1044	0	1	1	1
Subtotal	8	16	17	12
Period Arrow/Dart				
Ch1047a	1	1	1	1
Ch1047d	1	1	2	0
Ch1048	3	3	2	1
Ch1049	2	3	2	1
Ch1063	1	3	2	1
Ch1158	1	1	1	1
Ch1068	1	2	2	1
Ch1051	1	2	3	1
Ch1065	2	3	3	2
Ch1159	1	0	1	0
Subtotal	14	19	19	9
Period Dart				
Ch910	2	2	2	1
Ch1047c	1	1	1	1
Ch1052	0	1	2	3
Ch1056	1	1	2	0
Ch1161	1	1	1	0
Ch1162a	1	1	2	3
Ch1162b	1	1	2	3
Ch1163	1	1	1	1
Ch1251	0	1	1	1
Ch1173	0	1	1	1
Ch1070	0	1	2	1
Subtotal	8	12	17	15

Table 2. (Continued)

Site	Large Faunal Remains	Small Faunal Remains	Flaked Stone	Mussel Shell
Period Unknown				
Ch1047b	1	1	1	1
Ch1055	0	1	1	0
Ch1057	0	1	1	0
Ch1058	0	1	1	1
Ch1059	1	1	1	2
Ch1060	1	1	1	1
Ch1061	0	1	1	0
Ch1064	1	1	1	1
Ch1066	0	0	1	0
Ch1069	1	1	2	2
Ch1071	0	0	1	1
Ch1164	0	1	1	0
Ch1165	0	0	1	0
Ch1168	1	1	1	2
Ch1170	0	1	1	1
Ch1171	1	0	0	1
Ch1172	1	1	3	1
Ch1247	1	1	1	0
Ch1248	1	1	1	0
Ch1249	0	2	1	0
Subtotal	10	17	22	14

0 = Absent.
1 = Rare — 1–50 items (mussel shell <100 items).
2 = Common — 50–200 items (mussel shell 100–1000 items).
3 = Abundant — more than 200 items (mussel shell >1,000).

the proportional frequency of Elko series points as that returned from Stillwater Marsh. Hidden Cave stands out from all sites with its abundance of Gatecliff series points.

To examine the chronological ordering of the Stillwater Marsh sites projectile points were allocated among four categories, two of which inform on site age (Table 4). The post–1500 B.P. types are arrow points, (Eastgate, Rose Spring, and Desert series). Dart points (Elko series, large side notch, and Gatecliff series) characterize the pre–1500 B.P. period. Humboldt series points and untypeable points are not time sensitive. Available radiocarbon dates are also used to sort site into a pre–or post–1500 B.P. period. Table 4 shows that 20% (n = 10) of the sites occur in the arrow point period. Twenty two percent (n = 11) of the sites occur in the dart points period. Forty percent (n = 20) contain no points, untypeable points, or Humboldt points only. Ten sites (20%) have both arrow and dart points and probably hold at least two prehistoric occupations. These data demonstrate that in the eroded marsh the number of places occupied was unchanged from Elko times through Eastgate/Rose Spring times. The scarcity of Desert series points suggests that the culture marked by Desert points did not use the downstream third of the marsh, or has eroded away, or arrived very recently.

Table 3. Frequency of Projectile Points from Sites in the Carson and Humboldt Sinks

Site	Gatecliff Series		Elko Series		Rosegate Series		Desert Series		Humboldt Series			Untypeable Out of Key
	N	%	N	%	N	%	N	%	N	%	Total	N
Hidden Cave[1]	153	76.1	13	6.5	8	4.0	0	0.0	27	13.4	201	64
Carson Desert[2]	15	8.1	36	19.5	42	22.7	57	30.8	35	18.9	185	132
Lovelock Cave[3]	5	4.1	22	18.2	53	43.8	11	9.1	30	24.7	121	10
Humboldt Lakebed Site[4]	62	4.3	113	7.8	695	47.7	427	29.3	159	10.9	1,456	345
Stillwater Marsh[5]	5	4.3	34	29.8	52	45.6	9	7.8	14	12.2	114	56

[1]Pendleton 1985:184.
[2]Kelly, Robert, 1990 personal communication.
[3]Clewlow and Napton 1970:68.
[4]Livingston 1988b:70.
[5]Tuohy 1987, Raymond and Parks 1989.

Table 4. Frequency of Projectile Point Styles Recovered from Stillwater Marsh (data from Tuohy et al. 1987, Raymond and Parks 1989; radiocarbon data Raven and Elston 1988; Robert L. Kelly, personal communication 1990; and Sheilagh Brooks, personal communication 1989)

Site Number	Arrow	Dart	Humboldt	Untypeable	Total Points	Carbon 14 Date
Period Arrow						
Ch1043	5	0	0	2	7	
Ch1045	1	0	0	0	1	
Ch1050	5	0	0	4	9	290±80
Ch1067	2	0	0	3	5	
Ch1160	3	0	0	2	5	
Ch1167	1	0	0	0	1	
Ch1169	1	0	0	0	1	
Ch1250	2	0	0	0	2	
Ch1044	0	0	1	0	1	1140±80
Subtotal	20	0	1	11	32	
Period Arrow/Dart						
Ch1046	7	1	1	3	12	
Ch1047a	2	1	1	0	4	
Ch1047d	3	2	1	1	7	
Ch1048	5	5	3	4	17	870±70
Ch1049	1	1	0	1	3	
Ch1051	5	1	1	3	10	
Ch1063	1	1	0	2	4	
Ch1065	6	1	0	1	8	
Ch1068	7	1	0	6	14	1320±100
Ch1158	2	3	1	0	6	
Ch1159	2	0	1	1	4	2265±70
Subtotal	41	17	9	22	89	
Period Dart						
Ch910	0	1	0	1	2	
Ch1047c	0	1	0	0	1	
Ch1052	1	2	1	0	4	3290±90
Ch1056	0	2	1	1	4	
Ch1070	0	2	0	0	2	
Ch1161	0	1	1	2	4	
Ch1162a	0	8	2	6	16	
Ch1162b	0	2	1	0	3	
Ch1163	0	2	0	1	3	
Ch1173	0	0	0	1	1	1350±70
Ch1251	0	2	0	0	2	
Subtotal	1	23	6	12	42	

Table 4.   (Continued)

Site Number	Arrow	Dart	Humboldt	Untypeable	Total Points	Carbon 14 Date
Period Unknown						
Ch1047b	0	0	0	0	0	
Ch1055	0	0	0	0	0	
Ch1057	0	0	0	0	0	
Ch1058	0	0	0	0	0	
Ch1059	0	0	0	1	1	
Ch1060	0	0	0	0	0	
Ch1061	0	0	0	0	0	
Ch1064	0	0	0	2	2	
Ch1066	0	0	0	2	2	
Ch1069	0	0	0	1	1	
Ch1071	0	0	0	0	0	
Ch1164	0	0	0	0	0	
Ch1165	0	0	0	0	0	
Ch1168	0	0	0	1	1	
Ch1170	0	0	0	0	0	
Ch1171	0	0	0	0	0	
Ch1172	0	0	0	0	0	
Ch1248	0	0	0	0	0	
Ch1249	0	0	0	0	0	
Ch1247	0	0	0	0	0	
Subtotal	0	0	0	7	7	
Total	62	40	16	52	170	

Site Area

As discussed above, the flood exposed the entire horizontal extent of the cultural deposits at most sites, making the measurement of each site's area straightforward. Table 1 shows that the mean size of arrow period sites is considerably larger than dart period sites. However one arrow period site with an area of over 30,000 square m has skewed the data. The size of a site does not directly reflect the intensity of site occupation. Some small sites (e.g. 26Ch 1160) are packed with features and archaeological debris while some very large sites (e.g. 26Ch 1248) have few cultural indications (Figure 10).

Cultural Debris

Table 1 and 2 summarize counts of groundstone tools, flaked stone tools, fire-cracked rock and non-diagnostic rock manuports as well as the estimated abundances of large faunal remains, small faunal remains, flaked stone debitage, and mussel shell. The most important conclusion from this data is that the basic activities represented by this cultural material were well established in Elko times and continued through Rose Spring/Eastgate time. The abundance and mix of cultural material is not significantly different between Elko times and Rose Spring/Eastgate times. Indeed, projectile points seem insignificant given the abundance of other

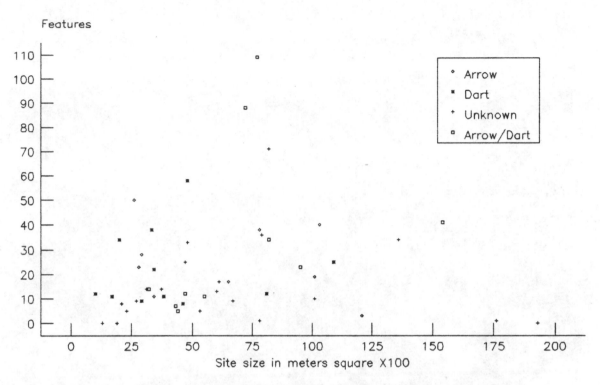

Figure 10. Total number of features by area (in square meters) at 51 Stillwater Marsh sites.

cultural material. Test excavations (Raven and Elston 1988) have shown how detailed analyses can sort out differences in site function within and across chronological boundaries. But the basic residential aspect with a focus on marsh resources will underlie most detailed interpretations. Sites with both dart and arrow points have the highest frequency of cultural material probably because of longer and more numerous occupations. The arrow period sites contain slightly more artifacts and cultural debris than the dart period sites. This may reflect a population increase during Eastgate/Rose Spring times, a phenomenon documented throughout the western Great Basin (Elston 1982). But more stone artifacts at later sites may also reflect scavenging of rock from earlier sites, a behavior not unexpected in rock poor Stillwater Marsh.

Most milling stones and burned rocks from the marsh are manufactured in basalt, a material that dominates the southern end of the Stillwater Range and comprises both Rattlesnake Hill on the Carson River in Fallon and Lone Rock in the center of Carson Sink. These landforms respectively lie 30, 27, and 11 km from the center of Stillwater Marsh. The abundance and size of basalt artifacts at marsh sites indicates a considerable effort dedicated to transporting stone. The mean weight of 9 nearly complete pestles from the marsh is 4.2 kg. The pestles imply the presence of mortars 4 to 7 times as heavy. Such artifacts probably had long use lives, perhaps used over a generation or two (cf. Horsfall 1987:342–343). Faunal remains occur in abundance on the surface of many sites. Analyses (Livingston 1988a, Dansie 1987) indicate that marsh animals compose, almost exclusively, the prehistoric diet. Sites from the arrow period contain more faunal remains and debitage on the surface than sites from the dart period. This may mark a population increase after 1500 B.P. but not a significant change in settlement. That 50 or more faunal elements occur on the surface of many sites, regardless of chronological placement, is significant. A plethora of faunal remains must lie below the surface [a fact confirmed by test excavations (Raven and Elston 1988)]. Activities implied by faunal remains (food acquisition, processing, consumption) are well represented across 3,000 years of prehistory at Stillwater Marsh. Detailed analysis will eventually sort out differences in the length and season of marshland subsistence pusuits. But the data demonstrates that the marsh served as a focus of subsistence in both Elko and Rose Spring/Eastgate times.

Figure 11. Circular cultural feature containing dark organic fill prehistorically excavated into a sterile matrix (26Ch 1047a, F34, 200 cm diameter). (U.S. Fish and Wildlife Service)

Debitage is rare (less than 50 items) at 30 sites (Table 2). Eight of these sites have more than the mean number (x = 22) of total features. And 7 sites with less than 50 items of debitage have more than the mean (x = 22) number of groundstone artifacts. Although the low frequency of debitage at the marsh sites reflects its low visibility and scarcity of siliceous stone around Stillwater Marsh (Elston 1988), it also demonstrates that the quantity of flaked stone debitage does not mirror the degree of prehistoric activity in Stillwater Marsh.

Burials

Over 4,000 human bones were recovered from 33 sites in Stillwater Marsh (Brooks et al. 1985). Of these, approximately 80 percent were displaced from their original depositional context by the flood. Twenty–seven sites contained 52 relatively intact *in situ* burials. The number of burials increases in arrow period sites over the sites occupied in earlier periods. Though this may reflect a population increase, the pattern of burying people at sites in the marsh was well established during the earlier period.

Figure 12. Noncircular cultural feature, F1, concentration of fire-cracked rock, at 26Ch 1050. (U.S. Fish and Wildlife Service)

Cultural Features

The most pervasive archaeological indicator of prehistoric occupation in Stillwater Marsh are cultural features. We recognized two types of features: circular and non-circular. Circular features appeared at the surface as round stains of dark organic soil filled with cultural debris including flakes, ground stone fragments, fire-cracked rock, mussel shell and faunal remains (Figure 11). Most non-circular features are concentrations of cultural debris unassociated with deliberate modifications of the soil, including piles of fire-cracked rock (Figure 12) and concentrations of ground stone artifacts. We mapped 1,024 circular features and 105 non-circular features at the 51 flood-exposed sites. Table 1 shows there is no significant difference in the total number and average number of features between sites of the arrow period and sites of the dart period. Perhaps because of longer or more numerous occupations, sites with both arrow and dart points contain more features than other sites.

The function of many circular features is unknown. Similar facilities at other sites in the western Great Basin have been cited as evidence for sedentary or semi-sedentary residential sites (Humboldt Lakebed site [Livingston 1986]; Lake Abert sites [Oetting, this volume]). Test excavations at Stillwater indicate that some circular features served as storage facilities, house foundations, and post holes (Tuohy et al. 1987, Raven and Elston 1988, Kelly this volume). Most features contain cultural debris, but feature content appears no different from the surrounding midden deposit (Raven 1988). Perhaps the contents of circular features have deteriorated

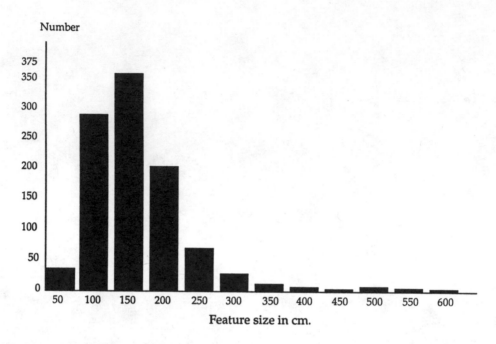

Figure 13. Frequency of circular features by 50 cm size class at flood exposed sites in Stillwater Marsh.

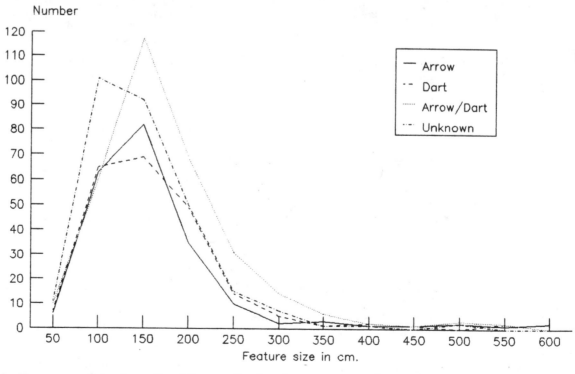

Figure 14. Frequency of circular cultural features by size class at arrow period, dart period, arrow/dart period, and unknown period sites.

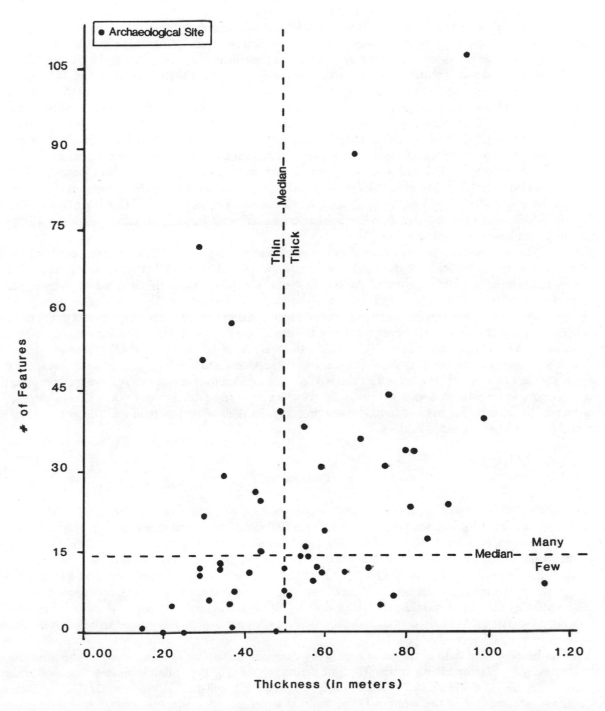

Figure 15. Scattergram of archaeological sites showing the total number of features by the thickness of the cultural deposit.

beyond recognition. And perhaps many features were emptied prehistorically and left open to accumulate midden dumped by later site occupants or washed in by rains and floods.

If we accept that the features represent some level of residential use and storage then their presence and abundance signals substantial settlement and use of the marsh over 3,000 years. The presence of 240 cultural features at eleven dart period sites (Table 1) does not square with Kelly's notion that the Carson Desert was used by foragers with high residential mobility. The 240 cultural features at ten arrow period sites, and the 344 features at the ten arrow/dart period sites marks a continuation of a pattern first seen in Elko times.

As we mapped the 1,024 circular features we measured their diameters (of 1,016) at the surface (Raymond and Parks 1989). Circular features ranged in size from 10 cm to 580 cm with a mean size of 142 cm. When grouped into 50 cm categories a histogram (Figure 13) of all circular features reveals that 84% (N = 854) of the circular features fall within 51 cm and 200 cm in diameter. In the western Great Basin circular cultural features in excess of 200 cm may represent habitation/residential facilities (e.g. Livingston 1986, Raven 1988). At Stillwater, 16% (N = 162) of the circular features have dimensions suggesting residential facilities. Figure 14 displays frequency curves of circular cultural features by size class at arrow period, dart period, arrow/dart period and unknown period sites. Dart and arrow/dart period sites contain slightly more features larger than 200 cm than arrow period sites. This may only reflect differential exposure and erosion by the recent flood. Sites lacking time-sensitive projectile points have many small features compared to other sites. This is partly explained by some sites which are so eroded that only the bottom cross section of features remain. Midden, artifacts and projectile points have been washed away.

Cultural features deserve the attention of future researchers at Stillwater Marsh. At the site level cultural features offer clues on intensity and stucture of occupation (Raven 1988). But depositional and erosional processes will temper the investigation of cultural features. Consider that prehistoric use of circular cultural features was accompanied by other activities at a site that would result in deposition of artifacts, midden, anddebris. Accordingly, the number of circular cultural features should be directly proportional to the thickness (relief) of the cultural deposit. However this is not the case. Several sites have total feature counts well above the median of 14 but have a thickness lying below the median of 50 cm (Figure 15). Perhaps these sites represent locations where many shallow features were excavated and used (e.g. as a field storage site or cemetery) to the exclusion of other activities that would cause midden to accumulate. A more likely explanation, however, offers water erosion and deflation as agents which have removed a once thicker cultural deposit. In other words, the circular features at thin sites are probably the shallow remnants of once deeper features that extended below the now eroded midden.

Conclusions

The 1983–1986 flood in the Carson Desert has taught us three important lessons about archaeology of Stillwater Marsh. First, residential groups were living in Stillwater Marsh and focusing on its resources since at least 3,200 years ago, to at least 550 B.P. if not 300 B.P. The cultures marked by Elko, Rose Spring and Eastgate projectile points are well represented at residential sites in the Marsh. The material matches that of the Lovelock culture described by Loud and Harrington (1929), Napton (1969), Grosscup (1960) and Hester (1973). Stillwater Marsh provides an excellent opportunity to employ and refine the Lovelock culture concept: sedentary or semi-sedentary marshside hamlets exploiting wetland plants and animals. It will require future excavations to determine the details of the residential occupation. Were sites permanent year-round settlements or seasonal habitations reoccupied year after year?

Second, based on the data obtained in the survey, there appears to be no significant change in settlement at the cusp between Elko and Rose Spring/Eastgate period around 1500 B.P. Slightly more archaeological debris is evident after the 1500 B.P. date. This probably represents a population increase in the Carson Desert, a phenomenon documented in the western Great Basin at that time. A settlement change may have occurred relatively recently, however. The flood exposed no sites with good associations of Desert series points. If Numic speakers and culture are marked by these points, radiocarbon evidence suggests their arrival in Stillwater Marsh was very recent. And, if the sites exposed by the flood are representative, the bearers of Desert series points did not settle in or subsist on Stillwater Marsh to the same manner as their predecessors.

Third, a single flood has dramatically changed our view of Carson Desert archaeology. Before the deluge the surface archaeology told a story of limited occupation and use of Stillwater Marsh. Erosion of 20 cm of topsoil has revealed resdidential sites with abundant cultural debris. Yet only one-third of the present day marsh was effected. Perhaps older or more recent occupations lie just under the surface of islands and shorelines elsewhere in Stillwater Marsh.

Acknowledgments

Many people helped us, especially Don Tuohy and Amy Dansie. They got the ball rolling. Amateur Charlie Gomes and U. S. Fish and Wildlife Service employees Eugene Duffney, Delvan Lee and Ernest Lantto helped find and refind sites in the flooded marsh. Norm Bergren, Bill Drummond, Dave DeVries and Bob Ducret assisted with land survey, aerial photogrammetry, and map drafting. Robin Benson, Liz Sobel, Jonathan Till, Elisabeth Raymond, Jo Reese, Campbell McNair, Carol Cote, Calista Early and Art Andrae aided various aspects of the fieldwork. The support of the Fallon Paiute-Shoshone Tribes concerning human remains contributed to the success of the fieldwork. Sharon Taylor and the Fallon Chapter of the CCCNAA helped in the field and in the lab. Steve Thompson taught us about the ecology of Stillwater Marsh. He conceived Figures 3 and 4. Many thanks to Carolyn Harriman and Mary Croston who typed the manuscript. We are grateful to Ron Anglin, Stillwater Wildlife Refuge Manager, who provided the time to implement and report on the project summarized here.

References

Brooks, S. T., M. B. Haldeman, and R. H. Brooks
   1988   *Osteological Analysis of the Stillwater Skeletal Series, Stillwater Marsh, Churchill County, Nevada.* Report submitted to U.S. Fish and Wildlife Service, Portland, Oregon.

Clewlow, C. W., and L. K. Napton
   1970   Additional Projectile Points and Lithic Artifacts from Lovelock Cave. *University of California Archaeological Research Facility* 7:64–72.

Dansie, A. J.
   1987   The Animal Bones. In *Final Report on Excavations in the Stillwater Marsh Archaeological District, Nevada,* by D. R. Tuohy, A. J. Dansie, and M. B. Haldeman, pp. 256–311. Nevada State Museum Archaeological Service Report to the U.S. Fish and Wildlife Service, Portland, Oregon.

Davis, J. O.
   1982   Bits and Pieces: The Last 35,000 Years in the Lake Lahontan Area. In *Man and Environment in the Great Basin,* edited by D. B. Madsen and J. F. O'Connell, pp. 53–75. SAA Papers No.2, Society for American Archaeology, Washington, D.C.

Drews, M. P.
   1988b Projectile Points. In *Preliminary Investigations in Stillwater Marsh: Human Prehistory and Geoarchaeology,* vol. 4, edited by C. Raven and R .G. Elston. Intermountain Research, Silver City, Nevada. Submitted to U.S. Fish and Wildlife Service, Portland, Oregon.

Elston, R. G.
   1982   Good Times, Hard Times: Prehistoric Culture Change in the Western Great Basin. In *Man and Environment in the Great Basin,* edited by D. B. Madsen and J. F. O'Connell, pp. 53–75. SAA Papers No.2, Society for American Archaeology, Washington, D.C.

   1988   Flaked Stone Tools. In *Preliminary Investigations in Stillwater Marsh: Human Prehistory and Geoarchaeology,* vol. 1, edited by C. Raven and R. G. Elston. Intermountain Research, Silver City, Nevada. Submitted to U.S. Fish and Wildlife Service, Portland, Oregon.

Flenniken, J. J., and A. W. Raymond
   1986   Morphological Projectile Point Typology: Replication, Experimentation and Technological Analysis. *American Antiquity* 51:603–614.

Giles, L. W., D. W. Marshall, and W. Barker
   1953   *Stillwater Wildlife Management Area.* Conservation in Action No. 9. Washington D.C.

Hester, T. R.
   1973   *Chronological Ordering of Great Basin Prehistory.* Contributions of the University of California Archaeological Research Facility, No. 17. Berkeley.

Horsfall, G.
    1987   A Design Theory Perspective on Variability in Grinding Stones. In *Lithic Studies Among the Contemporary Highland Maya*, edited by B. Hayden, pp. 332–377. University of Arizona Press, Tucson.
Katzer, K. L.
    1988   Age and Paleoenvironmental Significance of a Clay Dune Field in Stillwater Marsh, Carson Desert, Western Nevada (abstract). In *84th Annual Cordilleran Meeting Abstracts with Program*. Geological Society of America, p. 72.
Kelly, R. L.
    1985   *Hunter–Gather Mobility and Sedentism: A Great Basin Study*. Ph.D dissertation, Department of Anthropology, University of Michigan. University Microfilms, Ann Arbor.
    1988   The Three Sides of a Biface. *American Antiquity* 53(4):717–734.
Livingston, S. D.
    1986   Archaeology of the Humboldt Lakebed Site. *Journal of California and Great Basin Anthropology* (8)1:99–115.
    1988a   Avian Fauna. In *Preliminary Investigations in Stillwater Marsh: Human Prehistory and Geoarchaeology*, vol. 1, edited by C. Raven and R. G. Elston, pp. 287–306. Intermountain Research, Silver City, Nevada. Submitted to U.S. Fish and Wildlife Service, Portland, Oregon.
    1988b   The Avian and Mammalian Faunas from Lovelock Cave and the Humboldt Lakebed Site. Ph.D dissertation, Department of Anthropology, University of Washington. University Microfilms, Ann Arbor.
Loud, L. L., and M. R. Harrington
    1929   Lovelock Cave. *University of California Publications in American Archaeology and Ethnology* 25(1):1–183. Berkeley.
Napton, L. K.
    1969   *Archaeological and Paleobiological Investigations in Lovelock Cave, Nevada*. Kroeber Anthropological Society Papers, Special Publication No.2. Berkeley.
Pendleton, L. S. A.
    1985   Material Culture: Artifacts of Stone. In *The Archaeology of Hidden Cave*. Anthropological Papers of the American Museum of Natural History 61(1):183–218. New York.
Raven, C.
    1988   Cultural Features and Site Structure. In *Preliminary Investigations in Stillwater Marsh: Human Prehistory and Geoarchaeology* vol. 1 and 2. Intermountain Research, Silver City, Nevada. Submitted to U.S. Fish and Wildlife Service. Copies available from U.S. Fish and Wildlife Service, Portland, Oregon.
Raven, C., and R. G. Elston, (editors)
    1988   *Preliminary Investigations in Stillwater Marsh: Human Prehistory and Geoarchaeology* vol. 1 and 2. Intermountain Research, Silver City, Nevada. Submitted to U.S. Fish and Wildlife Service. Copies available from U.S. Fish and Wildlife Service, Portland, Oregon.
Raymond, A. W., and V. M. Parks
    1989   Surface Archaeology of Stillwater Marsh, Churchill County, Nevada. Ms. on file at Nevada State Museum, Carson City.
Russell, I. C.
    1885   *Geological History of Lake Lahontan, A Quarternary Lake of Northwestern Nevada*. United States Geological Survey Monograph 11.
Schmitt, D. N.
    1988   Mammalian Fauna. In *Preliminary Investigations in Stillwater Marsh: Human Prehistory and Geoarchaeology*, vol. 1, edited by C. Raven and R. G. Elston, pp. 257–286. Intermountain Research, Silver City, Nevada. Submitted to U.S. Fish and Wildlife Service, Portland, Oregon.
Sperry, C. C.
    1929   Report on Carson Sink. National Archives Records Group 22, Fallon–General 1931–32. Box 68. Washington D.C.
Stillwater Wildlife Management Area (SWMA)
    1979–1985 Annual Narrative Reports. Ms. on file at Stillwater Wildlife Management Area, Fallon, Nevada.
Thomas, D. H.
    1981   How to Classify the Projectile Points from Monitor Valley, Nevada. *Journal of California and Great Basin Anthropology* 3:7–43.
    1985   *The Archaeology of Hidden Cave*. Anthropological Papers of the American Museum of Natural History 61(1). New York.
Thompson, S.
    1987   Waterbirds. In *Annual Narrative, 1987: Stillwater Wildlife Management Area*. Ms. on file at Stillwater Wilflife Management Area, Fallon. Nevada.
Thompson, S., and K. Merritt
    1988   Western Nevada Wetlands: History and Current Status. *Nevada Public Affairs Review* (1):40–45.
Thompson, S., and A. Raymond
    1988   The Ecology of Stillwater Marsh: Implications for Prehistoric Hunter-gatherers. Paper presented at the 21st Great Basin Anthroplogical Conference, Park City, Utah.

Townley, J.
  1977   *Turn This Water into Gold: The Story of the Newlands Project.* Nevada Historical Society, Reno.
Tuohy, D. R., A. J. Dansie, and M. B. Haldeman
  1987   *Final Report on Excavations in the Stillwater Marsh Archaeological District, Nevada.* Nevada State Museum Archaeological Service
          Report to the U.S. Fish and Wildlife Service, Portland Regional Office.
U.S. Geological Survey
  1982–1986 *Water Resources Data, Nevada.* U.S. Geological Survey Water Resources Division, Carson City, Nevada. Davis.

5

THE DIETARY ROLE OF FRESHWATER SHELLFISH FROM STILLWATER MARSH

Michael P. Drews

Abstract

The sporadic occurrence of freshwater molluscs from archaeological sites within the Great Basin has prompted researchers to identify shellfish as a marginal dietary resource. Archaeological studies relating to freshwater molluscs have been most successful in the coastal and central portions of the United States, where the majority of ecological studies on living populations of shellfish remains has been conducted. Baseline data form these studies and archaeological evidence from Stillwater Marsh suggest that a re-evaluation of the role of freshwater molluscs in prehistoric diets is in order.

Introduction

S everal species of freshwater mollusc, including freshwater snails (Gastropods) and clams (Pelecypods), were recovered during testing at several sites within the Stillwater Marsh (Figure 1). Archaeologists frequently have used shell remains for purposes of site dating and environmental reconstruction, and as indices of seasonality and subsistence patterns. Archaeological studies relating to freshwater molluscs have been most successful in the coastal and central portions of the United States, where the majority of ecological studies on living mollusc populations has been conducted (see Cook 1946; Parmalee 1956; Petersen 1976; Parmalee and Klippel 1974; Clark 1979; Glassow and Wilcoxon 1988)). In the Great Basin, studies of molluscs have been oriented primarily towards the paleontology of Pleistocene lakes (Baily and Baily 1951; Roscoe 1963). The paucity of baseline studies of living mollusc populations within this region limits archaeological researchers to only the most generalized discussion of subsistence or seasonality.

Ethnographic references to the gathering and consumption of freshwater molluscs in the Great Basin are rare. Farnham (1843, cited in Steward 1938:9) states that the Paiute ". . . eat roots, lizards and snails . . ," while d'Azevedo's Washoe informants identify a place near McTarnahan Bridge on the Carson River as a good place

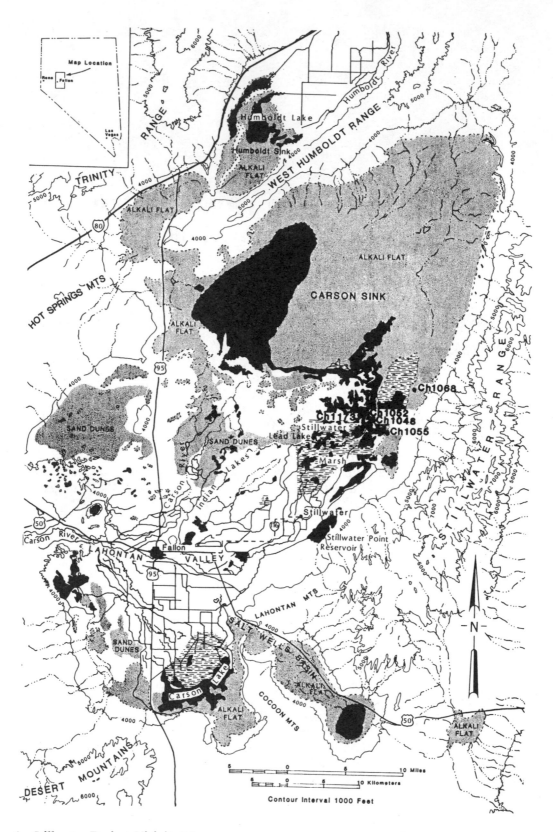

Figure 1. Stillwater Project Vicinity Map.

to procure "clams" (d'Azevedo 1978:72). In his account of Carson Lake, Simpson (1876:86) reports that ". . . the shores are covered with mussel shells . . ."

Recent archaeological investigations in the western Great Basin have revealed that few sites contain shell remains. Freshwater clams were identified in the earliest deposits of Last Supper Cave, dating between 9000 and 8000 B.P. (Layton 1979). While at the Old Humboldt Site (26Pe 670), clam shells associated with large fish and bison date as early as 11,000 B.P. (Davis 1984). A broad temporal distribution of clam shell is indicated at the Rye Patch Dam sites where they are present at all sites, but with decreasing frequency through time (Dansie 1987). Similar fluctuations are evident at South Fork Shelter (Heizer, et al. 1968). Shell remains also have been identified in Washoe Territory, at the Stewart Dump Site (Hattori 1978), the Vista Site (Drews 1986), and the Clear Creek Site (Kuffner 1987). In all cases, sites containing shellfish remains are located adjacent to hydrologic regimes capable of supporting populations of the species encountered at the site.

Research Orientation and Methods

Shell analysis from the Stillwater sites addresses subsistence strategies and the role of shellfish in the prehistoric diet, a topic of considerable debate. Several studies suggest that, based upon recovery cost and caloric yield, shellfish are a marginal resource used mainly as a starvation resource or low ranked dietary supplement (Bailey 1975; Parmalee and Klippel 1974). More recent researchers (Glassow and Wilcoxon 1988; Erlandson 1988) conclude that, while caloric yield may be low when compared to other food resources, the protein content of shellfish remains relatively high. As a result, shellfish may have played a more important role in the prehistoric diet than previously thought. We suggest that significant amounts of shellfish remains may indicate a dietary staple, while lower frequencies may reflect a dietary supplement.

Shell from the Stillwater sites was segregated by unit and level, then sorted by class. Bivalves from all sites appeared to be of a single species; *Anadonta* sp. This shell is of an extremely fragmentary nature with only a few salient hinge features identified. As a result, minimum number of individuals (MNI) using shell hinge data could not be calculated; instead, unit/level lots were weighed. Gastropods were also weighed and species within the sample were identified but not sorted.

Large quantities of shell were recovered from three sites (26Ch 1048, 26Ch 1052, and 26Ch 1068), providing somewhat redundant information. As a result, the shell remains from selected units were analyzed. These samples correspond with those selected by the faunal analysts so that the resulting data could later be compared with other faunal observations.

Nearly 100,000 grams of shell are represented by the samples (Table 1). The highest frequencies were observed at 26Ch 1052, the lowest at 26Ch 1055. The only species of Pelecypod recovered at the sites is *Anadonta* sp. (either *californiensis* or *nuttalliana*). Several species of Gastropods were identified, including two species of *Helisoma* (*Lymnaea stagnalis* and *Physa utahensis*). No clams were found at 26Ch 1055; snails, while present in small quantities at 26Ch 1052, are absent from the sample from that site.

Species Characteristics and Ecology

Anadonta (Figure 2) is a freshwater clam commonly found burrowed in the muddy waters of slow moving streams or lakes. Individuals may reach a maximum length of 90 mm and, unlike the free–swimming larvae of marine bivalves, temporarily become parasites during their larval stage, attaching themselves to the fins of small minnows (Pennak 1953:700–1, Lyman 1980).

While there are some exceptions, freshwater clams generally are found in substrates free of rooted vegetation; their distribution generally is limited to waters with a Ph below 7.0 (acid) or a bound carbon content less than 15.0 mg per liter (Pennak 1953:704–5). In favorable environments, as many as 5,000 individuals may inhabit a square meter of area (Pennak 1953:704). During temperatures below 10°C, freshwater clams will burrow deeper into their summer habitat, making collection more difficult (Pennak 1953:705).

MICHAEL P. DREWS

Table 1. Distribution of Freshwater Molluscs

Site Number	Total Weight Recovered	Analytic *Anadonta*	Sample Weight Gastropod	Soil Sample Size
26Ch 1048	450.50 g	42.20 g	14.40 g	.55m³
26Ch 1052	98,972.00 g	15,324.00 g	0.00	.25m³
26Ch 1055	9.70 g	0.00	9.70 g	1.65m³
26Ch 1068	430.10 g	78.50 g	96.60 g*	.50m³
26Ch 1173	8.40 g	8.40 g	0.00	1.35m³
Total	99,870.70 g	15,453.10 g	120.70 g	4.30m³

*81.4 grams from Unit 13.

Two living populations of *Anadonta* have been located in the present Stillwater Marsh (Steve Thompson, personal communication): one at the south end of Stillwater Point Reservoir and the other at Lead Lake (Figure 1). During late fall, literally thousands of shells were exposed in these areas by receding waters and population densities approached 2/m². Thompson and an associate easily gathered a bucketful by hand in approximately 15 minutes.

The three genera of Gastropods identified are all pulmonate (air breathing) snails that must rise to the surface for respiration. *Helisoma* sp. (Figure 3a) are disk-shaped snails that prefer rooted vegetation in slow moving or stagnant water. They commonly are found in ditches, mud flats, lakes, and intermittent ponds (Pennak 1953:704).

Lymnaea stagnalis (Figure 3b) are found in environments similar to that of *Helisoma*, but can tolerate a more intermittent water supply, surviving, for a time, in only slightly moist mud (Chamberlain and Jones 1929:5). They commonly are found on aquatic plants and tolerate increasingly alkaline environments.

Physa utahensis (Figure 3c) also prefers areas of rooted vegetation. It can be found in a variety of conditions including ponds, sloughs, and springs (Chamberlain and Jones 1929:158).

Figure 4 shows the vertical distribution of freshwater molluscs sampled from the Stillwater sites. Distributions reflect the surficial nature of three sites (26Ch 1055, 26Ch 1068, and 26Ch 1173), while at the deeper sites (26Ch 1048 and 26Ch 1052) highest frequencies occur in the lower deposits.

Nutritional Analyses

Several researchers (Cook 1946, Munson et al. 1971, Koloseike 1969) have discussed the nutritional significance of marine and freshwater clam shells in archaeological contexts. Parmalee and Klippel (1974) collected 39 species of freshwater mussel from several large river drainages in the midwestern United States, and provide baseline data for shell/meat/calorie ratios. Two species of *Anadonta* are identified in the study. While shell weight to meat ratios can vary greatly between species, shell weight/meat weight data for *Anadonta grandis* may approach that of the *Anadonta* species identified at the Stillwater sites. The meat weight of *Anadonta grandis* is approximately 25% greater than its shell weight (Parmalee and Klippel 1974: 424).

Table 2 shows the shell weight and relative meat weights for *Anadonta* shell recovered at each of the Stillwater sites. By factoring sample size and estimated site volume (area x average depth), total meat weights present at each site are estimated.

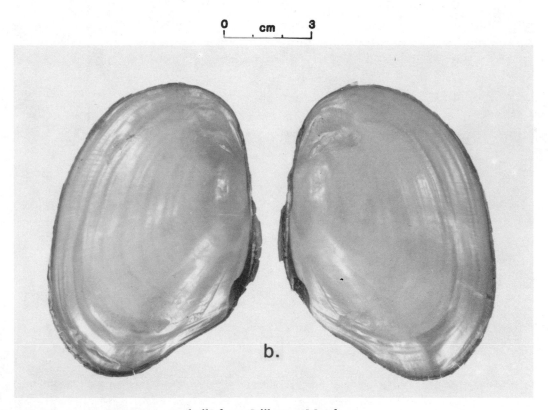

Figure 2. Contemporary *Anadonta* sp. shells from Stillwater Marsh.

(a) exterior aspect
(b) interior aspect

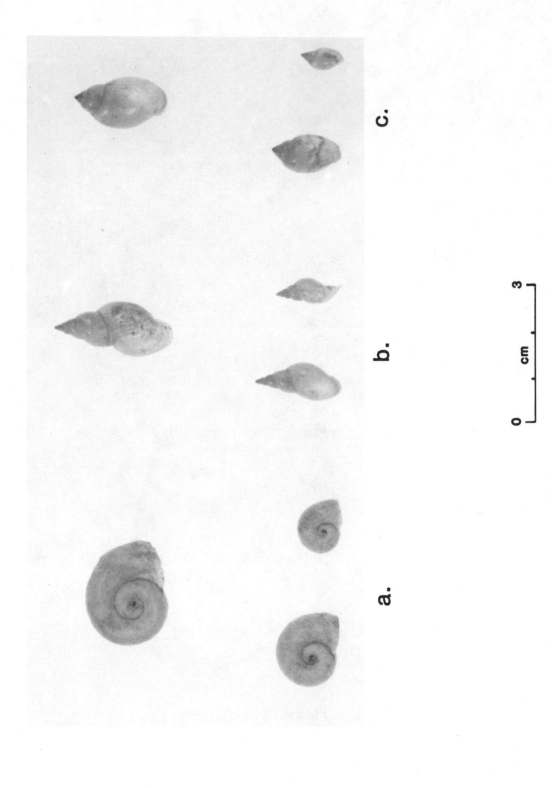

Figure 3. Contemporary gastropod shells from Stillwater Marsh.

(a) *Helisoma sp.*
(b) *Lymnaea stagnalis*
(c) *Physa utahensis*

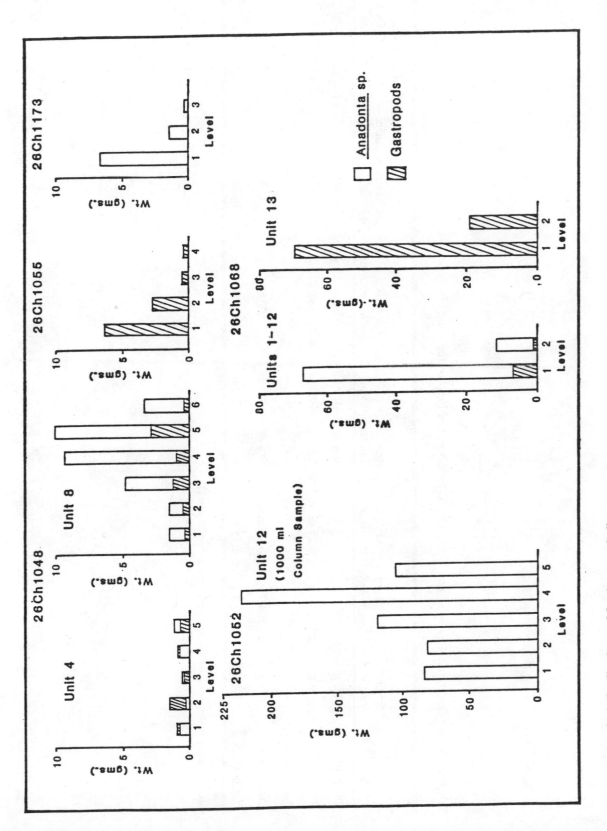

Figure 4. Vertical distributions of freshwater shell.

Table 2. Shell Weight, Meat Weight, and Estimated Caloric Yield of Freshwater Clams from Stillwater Marsh*

Site	Shell Weight	Estimated Meat Weight	Sample Size	Meat Weight/m	Site Volume	Estimated Meat Weight/Site	Estimated Calories (70 C/100 g/Site)	Calculated Person Days of Nutrition
26Ch 1048	42.2 g	56.3 g	0.55 m	102.4 g	4200 m	430,000.0 g	30,156 C	12.5 - 15.0 days
26Ch 1052	15,324.0 g	20,432.0 g	0.25 m	81,728.0 g	882 m	72,084,096.0 g	50,458,867 C	57.6 - 69.0 years
26Ch 1055	—	—	—	—	—	—	—	—
26Ch 1068	8.5 g	104.7 g	0.50 m	209.4 g	576 m	120,614.4 g	84,430 C	35.0 - 42.0 days
26Ch 1173	8.4 g	11.2 g	1.35 m	8.3 g	280 m	2,324.0 g	16,268 C	7.0 - 8.0 days

*Meat weight and caloric yield estimated from Parmalee and Klippel (1974).

Nutritional analyses of two smaller species of clam suggest that the caloric equivalent per 100 grams of meat is approximately 25% less than the meat weight (Parmalee and Klippel 1974:431). By factoring these data, caloric equivalents for shellfish remains at each site can be estimated, and, based upon a caloric requirement of 2,000 to 2,400 calories/day to maintain homeostasis (Parmalee and Klippel 1974:433), the food supply represented by shellfish remains calculated (Table 2). These data provide an index of potential nutritional importance of the resource.

Table 2 shows that only at 26Ch 1052 do shellfish remains occur in quantities significant to approach a staple nutritional resource. The relative dietary importance of shellfish will vary, however, depending upon the duration and intensity of occupation of the site. In contrast, the lower frequencies at the remaining sites strongly suggest that shellfish were utilized only as dietary supplements.

By considering the protein content of shellfish, their nutritional and economic importance increase. Erlandson (1988:105) shows that, by using the nutritional analysis in Parmalee and Klippel (1974), the actual number of shellfish needed to supply necessary protein is reduced by a factor of ten when compared to the number of shellfish needed to supply necessary calories. Thus, shellfish remains from 26Ch 1048 and 26Ch 1068 may represent a staple nutritional resource.

Gastropods As A Resource

Bobrowsky (1984) notes that the role of gastropods in archaeology poses a significant problem for the archaeomalacologist. Gastropods may enter the archaeological deposit as a source of food and/or ornamentation, as a non-cultural biological occurrence, or through accidental introduction.

It seems likely that snail shells from the Stillwater sites were deposited either accidentally or by non-cultural means. They occur in most sites (although none were encountered at 26Ch 1173), and their frequencies, while significantly lower, fluctuate in a manner similar to those of freshwater clam. Such frequencies might suggest that the snails were accidentally harvested with the clams. They also might have been transported to the site on aquatic plants. Introduction related to natural occurrence may be evident at 26Ch 1068 where some of the dark circular features on the lower portion of the site may be residual root masses of aquatic plants.

Although accidental or natural introduction seems evident, use as a food resource should not be discounted. The ethnographic record suggests that snails were eaten by the Paiute and the resource certainly would have been easily obtained within the Stillwater Marsh.

The use of snail shells for ornamentation is not evident at any of the sites; snail shell beads were not observed and none of the snail shell recovered appears to be refuse from such manufacture.

Future Directions

While beyond the scope of this analysis, shell remains potentially contribute to assessments of seasonality. Additional shell layers (annuli) are added, during the yearly cycle, growing most rapidly during summer months and gradually slowing through the winter. Researchers have successfully measured these growth increments (Weymouth 1923; Weide 1969; Chatters 1986), and used the results to infer season of death.

In order to assess seasonality, baseline data from living populations must be gathered and compared to growth rings on the fossil shell. Such baseline data could be applied Basin-wide. In order to determine seasonality, however, the fossil shell must retain some minimal attributes. Most successful determinations are made with complete shells. Measurements can, however, be made along external margins or along the resilial tuberosity of the shells' external ligament (see Chatters 1986).

While the *Anadonta* shell from the Stillwater sites is fragmentary, samples from 26Ch 1048, 26Ch 1052, and 26Ch 1068 suggest that identifiable hinges and lateral margins are present on some of the specimens. As a result, future seasonality studies might be pursued.

Isolated shell fragments occur sporadically in non–cultural contexts throughout the Carson Sink and Stillwater Marsh. Frequencies and geomorphology suggest natural deposition. Presently, off–site shell densities are unknown, and quantification of apparently non–cultural remains could be an important part of future research. Those frequencies could be contrasted against prehistoric sites containing low shell densities and natural or cultural deposition could be determined with more certainty.

The role of freshwater shell in the prehistoric diet remains somewhat clouded since real nutritional data has yet to be realized. The occurrence of living populations of *Anadonata* in the Stillwater marsh will, however, allow for further assessment.

Baseline nutritional data has not been compiled for species indigenous to the Great Basin but live capture and analysis would provide this. In an archaeological context, shell weights could then become a reliable means to determine meat weight, and time accounting during capture used to estimate caloric return.

References

Bailey, G. N.
   1975   The Role of Molluscs in Coastal Economies: The Results of Midden analysis in Australia. *Journal of Archaeological Science* 2:45-62.

Baily, J. L., and R. I. Baily
   1951   Further Observations on the Mollusca of the Relict Lakes in the Great Basin. *Nautilus* 65:46-53, 85-93.

Bobrowsky, P. T.
   1984   The History and Science of Gastropods in Archaeology. *American Antiquity* 49:77-93.

Chamberlain, R. V., and D. T. Jones
   1929   A Descriptive Catalog of the Mollusca of Utah. *Bulletin of the University of Utah Biological Series* 11(1). Salt Lake City.

Chatters, James C.
   1986   Shell of Margaritifera Margaritifera as a Source of Paleoenvironmental and Cultural Data. Pit 3, 4, 5 Project Shasta County, California. *Central Washington Archaeological Survey Archaeological Report* 86-5, pp. 1-31. Central Washington University, Ellensburg, Washington.

Clark, G. R.
   1979   Seasonal Growth Variation in the Shells of Recent and Prehistoric Specimens of *Mercenaria mercenaria* from St. Catherines Island, Georgia. In *The Anthropology of St. Catherines Island. 2. The Refuge-Deptford Mortuary Complex*, by D. H. Thomas and C. S. Larsen, Appendix, pp. 161-179. Anthropological Papers of the American Museum of Natural History 56(1). New York.

Cook, S. F.
   1946   A Reconsideration of Shell Mounds with Respect to Population and Nutrition. *American Antiquity* 12:50-53.

d'Azevedo, W. L.
   1978   Ethnohistorical Notes on Eagle Valley, Carson City, Nevada. In *The Archaeology of the Stewart Dump Site (26Or121)*, by E. M. Hattori, Appendix 2, pp. 69-75. Nevada State Museum Archaeological Services Report No. 13(2). Carson City.

Dansie, A. J.
   1987   The Stillwater Animal Bones and Burial Patterns. In *Final Report on Excavations in the Stillwater Marsh Archaeological District, Nevada*, by D. R. Tuohy, A. J. Dansie, and M. B. Haldeman, pp. 256–311. Nevada State Museum Archaeological Services Report. Carson City.

Davis, J. O.
   1984   *1983 Excavations at Archaeological Site 26Pe670, Rye Patch Reservoir, Nevada*. Social Sciences Center Technical Report No. 38, Desert Research Institute, Reno.

Drews, M. P.
   1986   Shell. In *The Archaeology of the Vista Site 26Wa3017*, by C. D. Zeier and R. G. Elston, pp. 275-282. Intermountain Research. Submitted to Nevada Department of Transportation, Carson City, Contract No. P51-84-013.

Erlandson, J. M.
   1988   The Role of Shellfish in Prehistoric Economics: A Protein Perspective. *American Antiquity* 53:102-109.

Glassow, M. A., and L. R. Wilcoxon
   1988   Coastal Adaptations Near Point Conception, California, with Particular Regard to Shellfish Exploitation. *American Antiquity* 53:36-51.

Hattori, E. M.
   1978   *The Archaeology of the Stewart Dump Site (26Or121)*. Nevada State Museum Archaeological Services Report 13(2):69-75. Carson City.

Heizer, R. F., M. Baumhoff, and C. W. Clewlow, Jr.
   1968   Archaeology of South Fork Shelter (NV-El-11), Elko County, Nevada. *University of California Archaeological Survey Reports* 71:1-58. Berkeley.

Koloseike, A.
1969   On Calculating the Prehistoric Food Resource Value of Molluscs. *Archaeological Survey Annual Report* No. 11. University of California, Los Angeles.

Kuffner, C. S.
1987   *Carson City Comprehensive Water Plan: Further Archaeological Investigation of the Nevada Medium Security Prison Farm, Carson City, Nevada.* Archaeological Research Services Report, Virginia City.

Layton, T. N.
1979   Archeology and Paleo-Ecology of Pluvial Lake Parman, Northwestern Great Basin. *Journal of New World Archeology* 3(3):41-56.

Lyman, R. L.
1980   Freshwater Bivalve Molluscs and Southern Plateau Prehistory: A Discussion and Description of Three Genera. *Northwest Science* 54(2):121-136.

Munson, P. J., P. W. Parmalee, and R. A. Yarnell
1971   Subsistence Ecology of Scovill, A Terminal Middle Woodland Village. *American Antiquity* 36:410-431.

Parmalee, P. W.
1956   A Comparison of Past and Present Populations of Fresh-Water Mussels in Southern Illinois. *Illinois State Academy of Science Transactions* 49:184-192.

Parmalee, P. W., and W. E. Klippel
1974   Freshwater Mussels as a Prehistoric Food Resource. *American Antiquity* 3:421-434.

Pennak, R. W.
1953   *Freshwater Invertebrates of the United States.* The Ronald Press Company, New York.

Peterson, C. H.
1976   Relative Abundances of Living and Dead Molluscs in Two California Lagoons. *Lethaia* 9:134-148.

Roscoe, E. J.
1963   Snails and Archaeology in the Great Basin. *American Antiquity* 65:134-136.

Simpson, J. H.
1876   *Report of Explorations Across the Great Basin of the Territory of Utah for a Direct Wagon-route from Camp Floyd to Genoa, in Carson Valley.* Corps of Topological Engineers, U.S. Army. Washington, D.C. (Reprinted by University of Nevada Press, 1983.)

Steward, J. H.
1938   Basin-Plateau Aboriginal Sociopolitical Groups. *Bureau of American Ethnology Bulletin* 120. Washington, D.C. (Reprinted by University of Utah Press, 1970.)

Weide, M. L.
1969   Seasonality of Pismo Clam Collecting at Ora-82. *UCLA Archaeological Survey Annual Report* No. 11. University of California Press, Los Angeles.

Weymouth, F. W.
1923   The Life History and Growth of the Pismo Clam. *Fish Bulletin* 7:1-120. California Fish and Game Commission. No. P51-84-013.

6

MAMMALS IN THE MARSH: ZOOARCHAEOLOGICAL ANALYSIS OF SIX SITES IN THE STILLWATER WILDLIFE REFUGE, WESTERN NEVADA

Dave N. Schmitt and Nancy D. Sharp

Abstract

Limited archaeological excavations and surface collections in Stillwater Marsh have returned thousands of animal bones. This paper presents mammalian faunal data retrieved from six sites in the marsh, including taxonomic presences and abundances, and inferences on large and small mammal use as human subsistence resources. Further, we present some regional research concerns to which future large scale archaeofaunal recovery and analysis can contribute significantly.

Introduction

T he Stillwater Wildlife Management Area, located approximately 18 miles northeast of Fallon, Nevada, is an open marshland containing numerous ponds and turgid sloughs (see Raven and Elston 1988). Severe flooding and subsequent erosion between 1982 and 1986 exposed hundreds of prehistoric human burials, cache pits, and houses (Kelly 1988). In response to site weathering and vandalism, The U.S. Fish and Wildlife Service scheduled several archaeological sites for test investigation in order to explore variation in site contents, contexts, and antiquity, both in the heart of the marsh and along its periphery. Here, we present mammalian faunal data retrieved from six of these sites: 26Ch 1048, 26Ch 1052, 26Ch 1055, 26Ch 1062, 26Ch 1068, and 26Ch 1173 (Figure 1).

Archaeological test excavations at these Stillwater sites returned abundant faunal remains consisting of tens–of–thousands of specimens. Excluding the enormous volume of fragmented shell recovered from site 26Ch 1052 (see Drews, this volume), animal bone, particularly of fish and bird (e.g., Livingston 1988), is the most abundant material type represented in each site assemblage. Here we focus on mammalian skeletal remains,

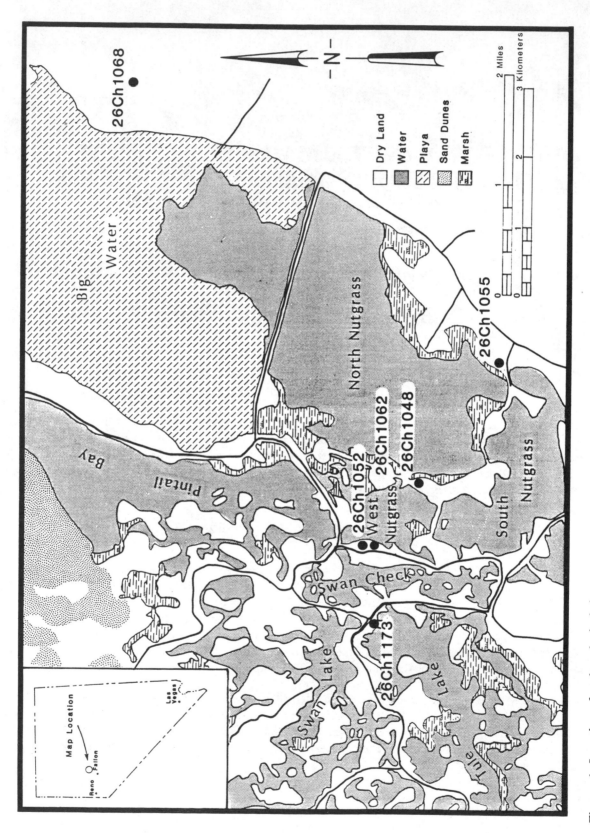

Figure 1. Location of archaeological sites.

Table 1. Unit/levels and Features Selected for Mammalian Faunal Analysis

Site	Unit (Features)	Levels	Percent of Total Assemblage
26Ch 1048	Surface Collections	—	19
	4	1 – 5	
	8	1 – 6	
26Ch 1052	12	1 – 5	12
26Ch 1062	(1, 3, 4, 5, 7, 9, 10, 14, 23) and non-feature midden	—	50
26Ch 1068	2, 6, 7, 12, 13	1 – 2	34

discussing the taxa represented and their abundances, evidence of human subsistence, and inter–site comparisons. Further, we present some zooarchaeological research concerns and analytic suggestions for future inquiries into prehistoric human wetland adaptations.

Methods

The faunal assemblages display considerable variation in both raw frequency and taxonomic diversity. At sites 26Ch 1055 and 26Ch 1173, skeletal remains are so few that all mammalian fauna could be analyzed. Conversely, the wealth of faunal material recovered from 26Ch 1048, 26Ch 1052, 26Ch 1062, and 26Ch 1068 precluded total assemblage analysis at these sites (Schmitt 1988a; Sharp 1990). Instead, representative samples were extracted for taxonomic identification and detailed analysis (Table 1); bone lots outside the sample units were scanned for "rare" taxa (i.e., those not represented in selected units or surface manifestations) and/or elements displaying evidence of butchery.

Table 2. Bone/Animal Size Classes (after Thomas 1969)

Class I – Mice, Shrews
Class II – Squirrels, Woodrats
Class III – Hares, Muskrat
Class IV – Coyote, Bobcat
Class V – Deer, Mountain Sheep

Mammal remains were identified by comparison with the Nevada State Museum (NSM) osteological collection and faunal collections at the Thomas Burke Memorial Museum, University of Washington. Fragmented remains lacking diagnostic attributes were sorted into animal size classes (Table 2) on the basis of bone size and thickness. Only the more reliable cranial and mandibular elements of small mammals (Classes I and II) were identified to the genus or species level; rodent post–cranial elements were tallied according to animal size class. All identified specimens were quantified by the number of identified specimens per taxon (NISP) (Grayson 1979, 1984).

Descriptive Summary

At least 14 species of mammals were recovered from the test excavations. Water screening through one–eighth inch mesh enhanced the recovery of both rodent remains and fragmented large mammal bones. The following is a summary of identified taxa and anatomical parts in each site assemblage. Discussions include methods employed in species identification and published records of various taxa in the Stillwater Marsh area.

Order Insectivora – Insectivores
Family Soricidae – Shrews
Sorex cf. *vagrans* – Vagrant Shrew

26Ch 1048: One complete mandible (1 specimen).
26Ch 1062: One skull fragment (1 specimen).
REMARKS: The vagrant (or wandering) shrew and water shrew (*Sorex palustris*) both occur in the Stillwater area (Hall 1946). The recovered specimens were identified on the basis of size; although morphologically similar, *S. vagrans* is smaller than *S. palustris*.

Order Lagomorpha – Rabbits, Hares, and Pikas
Family Leporidae – Rabbits and Hares

26Ch 1062: One skull fragment, 1 mandible, 1 vertebra, 2 humeri, 1 femur, 1 metatarsal, 1 phalanx (8 specimens).

cf. *Sylvilagus* sp. – Rabbit

26Ch 1068: One tibia shaft fragment, 1 calcaneum fragment (2 specimens).
REMARKS: Nuttall's cottontail (*Sylvilagus nuttallii*) is the only large rabbit currently found in the project area (Hall 1946), but the Audubon (or desert) cottontail (*S. audubonii*), currently extant in the southern portion of Nevada, may have occupied the Carson Desert during the Holocene (Grayson 1985).

cf. *Lepus* sp. – Hares

26Ch 1048: One proximal ulna fragment, 2 proximal tibiae, 1 tibia shaft fragment, 4 distal metapodials, 2 phalanx fragments (10 specimens).
26Ch 1068: One patella, 1 calcaneum fragment, 1 distal metapodial (3 specimens).

Lepus sp. – Hares

26Ch 1048: Two skull fragments, 4 mandible fragments, 10 isolated teeth, 2 proximal ulnae, 1 distal femur, 1 proximal tibia, 2 patellae, 1 metapodial, 1 astragalus (24 specimens).
26Ch 1062: Two skull fragments, 2 mandibles, 4 isolated teeth, 2 humeri, 2 carpals, 2 innominates, 3 tibiae, 3 femora, 2 astragali, 1 tarsal, 5 metapodials, 2 phalanges (30 specimens).
26Ch 1068: Two skull fragments, 2 mandible fragments, 3 isolated teeth, 1 axis fragment, 1 distal radius, 1 innominate fragment, 1 proximal tibia, 1 proximal metapodial (12 specimens).

26Ch 1173: One mandible fragment, 2 isolated teeth, 1 distal scapula, 1 vertebra fragment, 1 proximal femur, 1 distal femur (7 specimens).

REMARKS: The black-tailed jackrabbit (*Lepus californicus*) is the only species of hare currently found in the Stillwater Marsh area, including a published record near Fallon, elevation 1,220 m (4,000 feet) (Hall 1946:606). Since the snowshoe hare (*L. americanus*) and white-tailed jackrabbit (*L. townsendii*) once may have been present in the Stillwater vicinity (cf. Grayson 1982, 1985), identification of these fragmented specimens cannot be carried beneath the genus level.

Order Rodentia – Rodents
Family Heteromyidae – Pocket Mice, Kangaroo Mice and Rats
Perognathus sp. – Pocket Mice

26Ch 1048: One mandible fragment (1 specimen).

REMARKS: Both the little pocket mouse (*Perognathus longimembris*) and Great Basin pocket mouse (*P. parvus*) occur in the Carson Desert area. Although Hall (1946) does not report the long–tailed pocket mouse in the Stillwater area, *P. formosus* remains were abundant in Hidden Cave and the Fallen–in–Cave owl pellet collection (Grayson 1985:144–145).

Dipodomys sp. – Kangaroo Rats

26Ch 1048: Three mandible fragments (3 specimens).
26Ch 1062: One tibia (1 specimen).
26Ch 1173: One mandible fragment (1 specimen).

REMARKS: Three species of kangaroo rat occur in the project area: *Dipodomys ordii* (Ord kangaroo rat), *D. microps*, (chisel- toothed kangaroo rat), and *D. merriami* (Merriam kangaroo rat) (Hall 1946). The desert kangaroo rat (*D. deserti*) also is found in the Carson Sink, but it is larger than other members of the genus and the skeletal remains reported here.

Family Muridae – Rats and Mice
Peromyscus sp. – White–footed Mice

26Ch 1048: Eleven skull fragments, 4 edentulate mandible fragments (15 specimens).
26Ch 1055: One mandible fragment (1 specimen).
26Ch 1062: Five edentulate mandibles (5 specimens).
26Ch 1068: One skull fragment, 2 edentulate mandible fragments (3 specimens).

Peromyscus cf. *crinitus* – Canyon Mouse

26Ch 1062: One maxilla with M2, 1 mandible with M1-2 (2 specimens).

Peromyscus maniculatus – Deer Mouse

26Ch 1048: One mandible with M1, 1 mandible with M3 (2 specimens).

REMARKS: Three members of the genus *Peromyscus* are found in the Stillwater area: deer mouse, canyon mouse, and, although not found in the Fallon area today, piñon mouse (*P. truei*) (see Grayson 1985:146-147). Published records for *P. crinitus* in Churchill County include a single specimen approximately five km east of the Stillwater Marsh at Mountain Well, elevation 1,710 m (5,600 feet) (Hall 1946), and 28 specimens on Eetza Mountain in elevations ranging from 1,250 m (4,100 feet) to 1,320 m (4,330 feet) (Grayson 1985).

Table 3. Measurements (mm) of 26Ch 1048 and *26Ch 1062 *Peromyscus* Mandibles with Teeth (after Grayson 1985)

| Specimen Number | Alveolar Length | Occlusal Length | | | Identification |
		M1	M2	M3	
5061-5-17	3.57	—	—	.99	*P. maniculatus*
5063-3-6	3.52	1.41	—	—	*P. maniculatus*
*	—	1.35	—	—	*P. cf. crinitus*

Records of *P. maniculatus* include specimens examined in Fallon and from three miles north of the town of Stillwater (elevation 1,220 m [4,000 feet.]) (Hall 1946).

Due to the morphological similarity displayed by many species of *Peromyscus*, the high variability of dental elements that characterize them (see Grayson 1985:147 and references therein), and the lack of sufficient comparative specimens, most of the assemblage was not identified beneath the genus level. Identifications of *P. crinitus* and *P. maniculatus* were based on mandibular measurements (Table 3) compared with modern *P. crinitus* and *P. maniculatus* molar and/or alveolar (occlusal) lengths (cf. Grayson 1985:147-149) and tooth morphology.

Subfamily Microtinae – Voles

26Ch 1062: Two hundred eight skull fragments, 175 mandibles, 2 isolated teeth (385 specimens).

Microtus sp. – Meadow Voles

26Ch 1048: Two hundred forty–one skull fragments, 270 mandible fragments, 306 isolated teeth (817 specimens).
26Ch 1052: Eighty–seven skull fragments, 116 mandible fragments, 238 isolated teeth (441 specimens).
26Ch 1055: Six skull fragments, 22 mandible fragments, 9 isolated teeth (37 specimens).
26Ch 1062: Six skull fragments, 60 mandible fragments, 183 isolated teeth (249 specimens).
26Ch 1068: Fifty–two skull fragments, 55 mandible fragments, 64 isolated teeth (171 specimens).
26Ch 1173: Twenty–one skull fragments, 22 mandible fragments, 18 isolated teeth (61 specimens).

Microtus cf. *montanus* – Montane Vole

26Ch 1048: Six skull fragments (6 specimens).
26Ch 1055: One skull fragment (1 specimen).
26Ch 1068: Five skull fragments (5 specimens).

Microtus montanus – Montane Vole

26Ch 1048: Seven skull fragments, 2 mandibles (9 specimens).
26Ch 1062: Thirty-four skull fragments (34 specimens).
26Ch 1068: Two Skull fragments (2 specimens).

Microtus cf. *longicaudus* – Long–tailed Vole

26Ch 1068: One skull fragment (1 specimen).

REMARKS: Three species of Microtine rodents are present in the Stillwater Marsh area: *Microtus montanus*, *M. longicaudus*, and *Lagurus curtatus* (the sage vole) (Hall 1946). As presented above, *Microtus* remains are abundant in each site investigated here. During faunal sorting and cataloging of both selected analytic unit/levels and those not included for detailed analysis, we examined literally hundreds of Microtine skulls, mandibles and posterior (aboral) mandible fragments. Because every specimen that possessed a mandibular foramen and/or M3 exhibited characteristics diagnostic of *Microtus* (cf. Chomko 1980; Grayson 1983), Schmitt liberally identified some fragmented cranial and mandibular elements as *Microtus*; conversely, Sharp left the nondiagnostic specimens as Microtinae.

Specimens identified as *M. montanus* possessed ridged interorbital regions (when present) and constrictive incisive foramina (cf. Grayson 1985; Lyman 1985a and references therein).

cf. *Ondatra zibethicus* – Muskrat

26Ch 1048: One skull fragment, 1 proximal radius, 1 distal metapodial (3 specimens).
26Ch 1052: One isolated tooth fragment, 1 metapodial fragment (2 fragments).
26Ch 1068: One isolated tooth fragment, 1 vertebra fragment, 1 caudal vertebra fragment (3 specimens).

Ondatra zibethicus – Muskrat

26Ch 1048: One skull fragment, 1 complete skull, 2 mandible fragments, 1 isolated tooth, 1 proximal humerus (epiphysis), 1 distal humerus, 1 thoracic vertebra, 1 sacrum fragment, 5 caudal vertebrae, 1 proximal femur, 1 distal femur (epiphysis), 1 astragalus (17 specimens).
26Ch 1052: One skull fragment, 1 isolated tooth, 1 proximal radii, 2 caudal vertebrae, 2 metapodials (7 specimens).
26Ch 1062: Twenty-nine skull fragments, 9 mandibles, 35 isolated teeth, 2 clavicles, 3 vertebrae, 9 scapulae, 12 humeri, 4 radii, 4 ulnae, 2 metacarpals, 5 innominates, 13 femora, 15 tibiae, 9 astragali, 11 calcanea, 15 carpal/tarsals, 18 metatarsals, 25 phalanges, 3 metapodials (223 specimens).
26Ch 1068: One complete mandible, 3 mandible fragments, 2 isolated teeth, 2 distal scapulae, 2 proximal humeri (epiphyses), 1 lumbar vertebra, 6 caudal vertebrae, 4 caudal vertebrae epiphyses, 1 femur, 3 distal femora (epiphyses), 1 calcaneum, 1 astragalus, 1 metapodial, 1 distal metapodial (29 specimens).
REMARKS: Muskrats occupy wetland areas throughout northern Nevada (Hall 1946).

Order Carnivora – Carnivores
Family Canidae – Coyote, Wolves, Foxes, and Dogs
Canis sp. – Coyote, Wolves, and Dogs

26Ch 1048: Two isolated teeth, 1 atlas, 2 astragali, 1 carpal, 1 proximal metapodial, 1 distal metapodial, 3 phalanges (11 specimens).
26Ch 1062: One mandible fragment, 1 isolated tooth, 1 vertebra, 1 carpal, 2 innominate fragments, 1 tibiae, 2 tarsals, 7 phalanges (16 specimens).

Canis sp. – Wolf–dog Hybrid

26Ch 1048: One mandible, 1 distal humerus shaft (2 specimens).
REMARKS: Canid bones were present in large numbers on the surface of 26Ch 1048, including previously identified remains of coyote (*Canis latrans*), large and small domestic dogs (*Canis familiaris*), gray wolf (*C. lupus*), and massive canids which appear to be wolf–dog hybrids (*Canis* sp.) (Dansie 1987a:262–264; see also

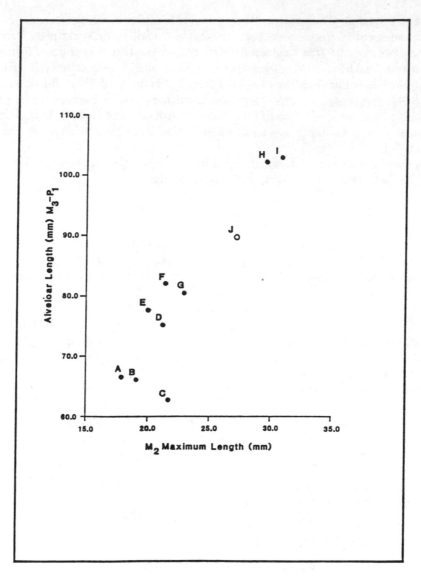

Figure 2. Relationship between mandibular alveolar length and maximum length of M2 in selected Nevada Canis.

    (a) *Canis familiaris*; 26Ch 1049*
    (b) *Canis familiaris*; 26Ch 1048*
    (c) *Canis familiaris*; 26Wa 275
    (d) Coyote-dog hybrid; Nevada State Museum (NSM) OCC "Eetza"
    (e) *Canis latrans*; NSM OCC Number 1064
    (f) *Canis latrans*; NSM OCC Number 55
    (g) *Canis latrans*; NSM OCC Number 1040
    (h) *Canis lupus*; NSM OCC display
    (i) *Canis lupus*; L-16, 16-1*
    (j) Specimen 6058; 26Ch 1048

* See Dansie 1987a

Dansie, this volume). The excavated and surface–collected assemblages reported here contain an equally diverse collection of *Canis* remains, including what appears to be a wolf–dog hybrid mandible. Figure 2 presents mandibular measurements of prehistoric domestic dogs from the Stillwater Marsh and Pyramid Lake (see Dansie 1984b, 1987a), modern coyotes and wolf, a known coyote–dog hybrid, and the 26Ch 1048 specimen (Catalog Number. Admittedly a small sample, this comparison does, however, illustrate the robustness of the individual, probably representative of a small wolf or wolf–dog hybrid.

Canis cf. *latrans* – Coyote

26Ch 1048: One isolated tooth, 1 innominate (2 specimens).
26Ch 1052: One skull fragment (1 specimen).
26Ch 1068: One proximal tibia (1 specimen).

Canis latrans – Coyote

26Ch 1048: One mandible fragment (1 specimen).
REMARKS: Coyotes are ubiquitous in Nevada and most of western North America (e.g., Hall 1946). Schmitt observed coyote tracks, scatological remains (see Schmitt 1988b), and numerous wary individuals during field operations in the Stillwater Marsh.

Vulpes (fulva) – Red Fox

26Ch 1048: One mandible (1 specimen).
REMARKS: A single record of *Vulpes* is reported east of the Stillwater Marsh in Fairview Valley (Hall 1946:232-233); red fox skeletal remains were recovered at Hidden Cave (Grayson 1985:152).

Family Mustelidae – Weasels, Skunks, and Allies

26Ch 1062: One skull fragment (1 specimen).

cf. *Mustela vison* – Mink

26Ch 1048: One distal scapula, 1 distal humerus, 1 calcaneum (3 specimens).
26Ch 1052: One isolated tooth fragment (1 specimen).
26Ch 1173: One isolated tooth fragment (1 specimen).

Mustela vison – Mink

26Ch 1048: Two mandible fragments (2 specimens).
26Ch 1052: Four skull fragments, 4 isolated teeth (8 specimens).
26Ch 1062: One skull fragment, 1 mandible fragment, 2 radii, 1 ulna, 1 calcaneus (6 specimens).
26Ch 1068: One mandible fragment (1 specimen).

Lutra canadensis – River Otter

26Ch 1048: One mandible fragment (1 specimen).
REMARKS: Although Hall (1946) does not report mink or river otter in the Fallon area, their skeletal remains were found in several archaeological sites in Stillwater Marsh (Dansie 1987a). Mink remains are reported at Hidden Cave as well (Grayson 1985:154).

cf. *Taxidea taxus* – Badger

26Ch 1048: One proximal humerus (1 specimen).

Taxidea taxus – Badger

26Ch 1048: Two skull fragments (2 specimens).
26Ch 1062: Three femur fragments (3 specimens).
REMARKS: The badger is found throughout the Great Basin and in most of the western United States. The three femur fragments recovered at 26Ch 1062 may have come from the same individual; all were recovered from midden deposits in the same analytic unit (Sharp 1990).

Family Felidae – Cats and Allies
Lynx rufus – Bobcat

26Ch 1068: One calcaneum (1 specimen).
REMARKS: Bobcats are widely distributed throughout the Great Basin, including all of Nevada. Hall (1946:282) reports specimens examined in Fallon and at Carson Lake.

Order Artiodactyl – Even–toed Ungulates

26Ch 1062: One scapula, 1 tibia, 1 sesamoid, 1 metatarsal, 1 metapodial (5 specimens).

Family Bovidae – Bovids
cf. *Ovis canadensis* – Mountain Sheep

26Ch 1048: One isolated tooth fragment, 1 proximal ulna fragment (2 fragments).

Ovis canadensis – Mountain Sheep

26Ch 1048: One calcaneum (1 specimen).
26Ch 1062: One phalanx (1 specimen).
REMARKS: Mountain sheep occur throughout Nevada (Hall 1946), and were particularly abundant during prehistoric times (see Pippin 1979). Dansie (1987a) collected mountain sheep remains from numerous sites in the Stillwater Marsh, including five specimens from 26Ch 1068 displaying evidence of butchery.

26Ch 1048

One thousand five hundred sixty mammal bones from 26Ch 1048 were segregated for analysis. Of the six sites investigated, mammalian fauna at 26Ch 1048 represent the largest and most taxonomically diverse assemblage. Nine hundred thirty specimens (60%) were identified (some tentatively), to the genus and/or species level (Table 4).   Voles (*Microtus*) are most abundant, followed distantly by mice (*Peromyscus* sp.), muskrat, jackrabbits, and canids.

Twenty-four percent of the specimens examined at 26Ch 1048 are burned. Similar to taxonomic abundances, most are burnt *Microtus* (and other rodent) remains. The ample occurrence of burnt rodent remains in Stillwater Marsh archaeological sites is discussed below.

Table 4. Number of Identified Specimens per Taxon/Animal Size Class by Site at Stillwater Marsh

Taxon	26Ch1048	26Ch1052	26Ch1055	26Ch1062	26Ch1068	26Ch1173	Total
Sorex cf. *vagrans*	1	—	—	1	—	—	2
Leporidae	—	—	—	8	—	—	8
cf. *Sylvilagus* sp.	—	—	—	—	2	—	2
cf. *Lepus* sp.	10	—	—	—	3	—	13
Lepus sp.	24	—	—	30	12	7	73
Perognathus sp.	1	—	—	—	—	—	1
Dipodomys sp.	3	—	—	1	—	1	5
Peromyscus sp.	15	—	1	5	3	—	24
P. cf. *crinitus*	—	—	—	2	—	—	2
P. maniculatus	2	—	—	—	—	—	2
Microtinae	—	—	—	385	—	—	385
Microtus sp.	817	441	37	249	171	61	1,776
M. cf. *montanus*	6	—	1	—	5	—	12
M. montanus	9	—	—	34	2	—	45
M. cf. *longicaudus*	—	—	—	—	1	—	1
cf. *Ondatra zibethicus*	3	2	—	—	3	—	8
O. zibethicus	17	7	—	223	29	—	276
Canis sp.	13	—	—	16	—	—	29
C. cf. *latrans*	2	1	—	—	1	—	4
C. latrans	1	—	—	—	—	—	1
Vulpes vulpes	1	—	—	—	—	—	1
Mustelidae	—	—	—	1	—	—	1
cf. *Mustela vison*	3	1	—	—	—	1	5
M. vison	2	8	—	6	1	—	17
Lutra canadensis	1	—	—	—	—	—	1
cf. *Taxidea taxus*	1	—	—	—	—	—	1
T. taxus	2	—	—	3	—	—	5
Lynx rufus	—	—	—	—	1	—	1
cf. *Ovis canadensis*	2	—	—	—	—	—	2
O. canadensis	1	—	—	1	—	—	2
I - II	491	257	61	240	139	46	1,234
III	59	6	4	163	20	4	256
IV	44	1	—	23	10	2	80
V	29	1	—	6	7	—	43
Total	1,560	725	104	1,397	410	122	4,318

26Ch 1052

Seven hundred twenty-five mammal bones from 26Ch 1052 were analyzed (see Table 4). Voles *(Microtus* sp.) are most abundant (constituting 96% of the identified specimens), while mink and muskrat are rare. In collapsing small mammals into a single faunal aggregate, rodents constitute 97% of the assemblage, the highest percentage of small mammal remains found in the six sites investigated. Mammalian fauna are present throughout the deposits, with over one-half (55%) occurring between 30–50 cm below surface.

Burned bone constitutes 20% of the mammalian specimens examined from 26Ch 1052, and is most abundant in the lower 30 cm of excavated deposits in Unit 12 where 26% are burned (see Raven and Elston 1988 for unit locational data and feature descriptions here and throughout).

26Ch 1055

Mammal remains recovered at 26Ch 1055 are represented by 104 specimens. Excluding four unidentifiable class III fragments, the entire assemblage consists of rodent remains. *Microtus* dominates the identified assemblage (see Table 4), with a single *Peromyscus* mandible fragment found in Feature 4. Based on uniform staining, the variety of anatomical portions in unit/level aggregates, and the recovery of complete, undamaged bones, most of the rodents appear to have accumulated via natural circumstances.

26Ch 1062

One thousand three hundred ninety-seven mammal bones from 26Ch 1062 were identified to taxon or size class. Voles, muskrats, and hare are most abundant (combined constituting 94% of the taxonomically identified specimens) with sparse occurrences of bighorn sheep, kangaroo rat, white–footed mouse, and unidentified canid.

Overall, the wealth of muskrat and Leporid remains at 26Ch 1062 (cf. Table 4) suggests intensive prehistoric utilization of these species for subsistence resources. Combining all size class III specimens, the proportion of burned (also commonly fragmented) bone reaches 24.4%, significantly more than the proportion of burned bone in the non-class III mammal assemblage (i.e., 7.4%).

26Ch 1068

Four hundred ten mammal bones from 26Ch 1068 were examined. Two hundred thirty-four specimens (57%) were identified (some tentatively) to the genus level, representing at least eight taxa (see Table 4). Voles *(Microtus* sp.) are most abundant, followed by muskrat and jackrabbit. Mink, bobcat, and a possible coyote *(Canis* cf. *latrans)* are each represented by a single specimen.

Most specimens (N=233, 57% of the total) were recovered above Feature 4 in level 1 of Unit 12. This level also contained the most taxonomically diverse mammalian assemblage including most (83%) of the identified jackrabbit remains and numerous muskrat and unidentified large mammal (classes IV-V) bone fragments.

26Ch 1173

A total of 122 mammal bones was recovered from test excavations at 26Ch 1173. Of the four taxa present, *Microtus* are most abundant, followed by rare occurrences of jackrabbit, kangaroo rat *(Dipodomys* sp.), and a possible mink (see Table 4). As at 26Ch 1055, clusters of rodent remains in excavation unit/levels and relative skeletal completeness indicate that most accumulated by non-cultural processes. Only two bones recovered from the site are burned.

Human Subsistence

Zooarchaeological literature focusing on processes of fossil accumulations and modifications is abundant (see for example Gifford 1981 and references therein). As actualistic and taphonomic studies increase, faunal analysts discover (often to their dismay) more and more natural processes that leave marks on bone similar to those produced by humans during subsistence activities. The following section empirically addresses bone damage indicative of human subsistence activities in the large mammal and small mammal bone assemblages.

Large Mammals

Prehistoric large mammal use in Stillwater Marsh is evident in nine skeletal elements displaying butchering marks. The following discussion of animal butchery follows recent recommendations outlined by Lyman (1987) and includes data from surface–collected materials recovered by the Nevada State Museum (Dansie 1987a) as well as from the present collections.

At 26Ch 1048, a large *Canis* (wolf-dog?) femur displays evidence of butchering in faint striations and an impact fracture on the posterior surface above the distal condyles (Table 5; Figure 3b). The striae are "bent" within the impact zone, indicating that percussion occurred subsequent to cutting. Specimen 7102–1–1 is a mink (*Mustela vison*) cranium from 26Ch 1052 possessing striae on its dorsal surface indicative of skinning (Figure 3d). Dansie (1987a:301) illustrates a mink skull from site 26Ch 910 in the marsh exhibiting similar cut marks.

A mountain sheep (*Ovis canadensis*) first phalanx from 26Ch 1055 exhibits numerous striae (i.e., skinning marks) on the latero–distal condyle (Figure 3a). Because the specimen is artifactual (see Tuohy 1987), modifications may represent both hide removal and bone extraction for tool manufacture.

Six mountain sheep elements from 26Ch 1068 displaying various stages of butchery were recovered. Two are first phalanges representing a single hoof; the entire foot was present in the excavation unit/level (including second and third phalanges and sesamoids), and the anatomical location of the cut marks correspond (see Figure 3c). These striae are characteristic of hide removal. Other butchered bones at 26Ch 1068 exhibit evidence of dismemberment (2 atlases and 2 distal humeri) and filleting (vertical striae on a distal tibia). All dismemberment striae are located in joints of medium tightness in terms of the natural skeletal disarticulation sequence described by Hill (1979) (see also Lyman 1987:283).

Mountain sheep remains are recovered frequently from Great Basin archaeological sites (e.g., Dansie and Ringkob 1979; Grayson 1988; see especially Thomas and Mayer 1983), but the number of modified elements recovered from limited surface reconnaissance and test excavation at 26Ch 1068, an open, low–elevation site, is intriguing (cf. Table 5). Recently, Lyman (1987:253) has discussed the numerous cultural and natural variables that may affect a butchering episode. One such variable which may be of particular significance at 26Ch 1068 is geographic location in terms of accessibility. Because valley bottoms are not favorable habitat for mountain sheep (see Pippin 1979 and references therein), their occurrence at 26Ch 1068 suggests the transport of whole carcasses and/or manageable butcher units to the site, probably the result of logistical hunting trips to higher elevations during site occupation.

Atlases and phalanges are low utility items while humeri and tibiae are of much higher utility (see Binford 1978 for artiodactyl utility values; see also Lyman 1985b). If, as presented above, butcher units were brought to the site for the final stages of processing and subsequent consumption, these low utility items may have been part of a high utility unit. In particular, atlases may have been transported to the site in articulated vertebral columns with ribs. Similarly, phalanges may have been introduced to the site via a high utility articulated appendage, or the mixture of both high and low utility elements at 26Ch 1068 represent the transport of whole carcasses to the site for processing and consumption. Clearly, larger samples are required to address the issue of whole–carcass versus butcher unit transport and processing at these sites.

Table 5. Butchering Marks on Mammal Bones by Site

Site	Specimen Number	Species	Element	Mark Type, Location	Figure	Type *	Function
26Ch 1048	5202–1–1	*Canis* sp.	Distal Femur	Two-three parallel (acute) striae and impact fracture on posterior shaft.	3b	Fd–1 or Fd–4	Dismemberment or filleting
26Ch 1052	7102–1–1	*Mustela vison*	Cranium	Multiple, parallel striae transversing dorsal surface of maxillary and frontal bones.	3d	—	Skinning
26Ch 1055	2–14	*Ovis canadensis*	1st Phalanx	Multiple, horizontal and acute striae on latero–distal condyle.	3a	—	Skinning
26Ch 1068	1181–14–1	*Ovis canadensis*	1st Phalanges	Multiple, horizontal striae on postero–distal shafts.	3c	—	Skinning
26Ch 1068	33–1	*Ovis canadensis*	Atlas	Multiple horizontal striae transversing dorsal and ventral surfaces.	76**	CV–1	Dismemberment
26Ch 1068	47–1	*Ovis canadensis*	Atlas	Multiple horizontal striae across the dorsal arch.	77**	—	Dismemberment
26Ch 1068	48–1	*Ovis canadensis*	Distal Humerus	Multiple horizontal and acute striae acorss medial surface.	78**	Hd–2	Dismemberment
26Ch 1068	57–1	*Ovis canadensis*	Distal Humerus	Chopping marks on antero-lateral surface.	78**	Hd–2 or Hd–6	Dismemberment or filleting
26Ch 1068	32–2	*Ovis canadensis*	Distal Tibia	Vertical, parallel striae on anterior surface at the medial malleolus.	79**	Td–4	Filleting

* Most similar to Binford's 1981 type.
** See Dansie (1987:296-299)

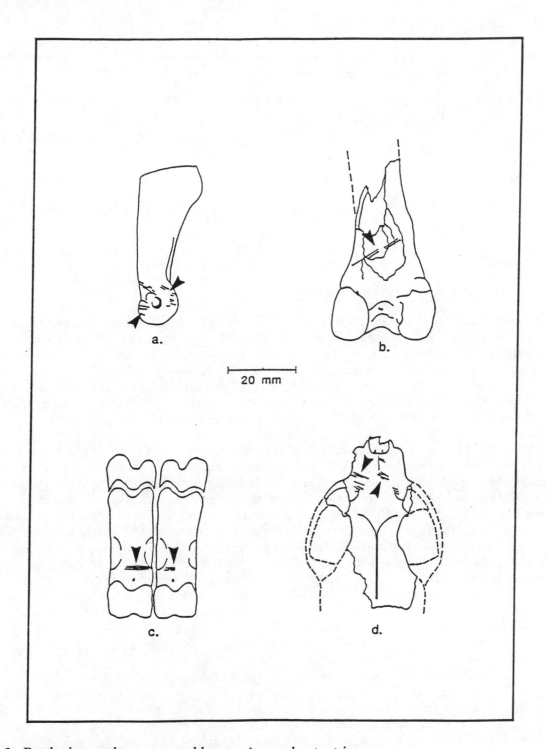

Figure 3. Butchering marks on mammal bones. Arrows locate striae.

(a) 26Ch 1055: Specimen 2–14.
(b) 26Ch 1048: Specimen 5202–1–1.
(c) 26Ch 1068: Specimen 1181–14–1.
(d) 26Ch 1052: Specimen 7102–1–1.

Table 6. Burned Small Mammal Bone Frequencies by Site

	26Ch 1048	26Ch 1052	26Ch 1055	26Ch 1062	26Ch 1068	26Ch 1173
Number of Rodent Bones	1,378	698	100	91	321	108
Number Burned	284	139	0	69	19	2
Percentage Burned	21	20	0	8	6	2

Small Mammals

> On reaching our camping-place, which I call the Middle Gate, I saw a naked Indian stretched out on the rocks at an angle of about 20 degrees. He was so much of the color of the rocks as to escape our notice for some time. . . . He seemed particularly pleased when he saw the long string of wagons coming in and laughed outright for joy. I counted twenty-seven rats and one lizard lying about him, which he had killed for food (Simpson 1876, entry for June 3, 1859).

Small mammal remains are common in western Great Basin archaeological sites (e.g., Dansie 1987b; Grayson 1985; Schmitt 1986a), often constituting the majority of faunal items recovered. Because rodents can be incorporated into archaeological deposits through numerous taphonomic processes (cf. Schmitt 1988b), and commonly lack the evidence of cultural utilization found on larger mammal bones (e.g., butchering marks), the agencies responsible for their accumulation are difficult to identify; analyses commonly focus on paleoenvironmental issues through taxonomic presences and abundances of small mammals (e.g., Grayson 1983). While such analyses are important, they tell us little about the role of small mammals in prehistoric human subsistence.

Stahl (1982) has pointed out the potential importance of small mammals in prehistoric diets due to their high ratio of edible meat to total weight. Although population densities and methods of procurement would affect caloric return rates to some extent, small mammals rank higher than most Great Basin plant resources (see Simms 1987). Ethnographic records of most Great Basin cultures discuss small mammals as major elements of the aboriginal diet (cf., Steward 1941; Stewart 1941). Because rodents were roasted and consumed whole or pounded up for soup, the best evidence for their utilization as human food resources is found in human coprolites (e.g., Bryant 1974, Dansie 1984a; Roust 1967). Archaeological evidence for the roasting of small mammals also might be discerned in the recovery of charred bone, the result of elements falling off the carcass during cooking or the discard of elements too large and/or dense for human consumption (cf. Dansie 1984a).

Numerous elements displaying corrosion, polishing, and other attrition diagnostic of partially digested bone have been identified in the Stillwater assemblage. Some specimens may be items from disaggregated human coprolites, but most appear to be bone digested by terrestrial carnivores and avian predators; these taphonomic implications have been addressed elsewhere (see Schmitt 1988b). The following discussion focuses on the rather copious occurrence of burned small mammal bone.

Bones can be become burned by many cultural and non–cultural processes including brush fires (cf. Grayson 1988), house fires (Schmitt 1986b), cooking, and refuse disposal into a hearth. At archaeological sites in the Stillwater Marsh, burned small mammal bone was observed in five site assemblages (Table 6), with color variations (i.e., black to "chalky" white) indicating differential stages of heating (cf. Shipman et al. 1984). Some specimens probably burned inadvertently (e.g., a hearth constructed in association with natural skeletal accumulations), but many probably represent cultural subsistence refuse.

Burned rodent bone was observed throughout the cultural deposits at 26Ch 1048. In Unit 4, charred rodent remains are most abundant (25%) in Levels 2 and 3 (34%, combined). Most (92%) are burned *Microtus* cranial and mandibular fragments, which strongly suggests roasting (i.e., very little muscle and tissue is available to insulate bones from burning), but cranial abundances may reflect recovery techniques; it is likely that many long bones passed through our one–eighth inch mesh during water screening. While the frequency of burned bone at 26Ch 1052 is similar to that of 26Ch 1048 (see Table 6), charred small animal remains are rare at the remaining four sites.

Only a few (often isolated) burned rodent bones are present in the 26Ch 1062 and 26Ch 1068 assemblages. Small mammals may have been roasted and consumed there, but to a much lesser degree than at 26Ch 1048 and 26Ch 1052. Burned bone was virtually absent at 26Ch 1055, and only two specimens were observed at 26Ch 1173. The paucity of bone damage and recognition of relatively complete individuals (e.g., burrow deaths) at these sites suggests that most small mammal accumulations are the result of non-cultural processes.

In sum, the occurrence of charred small mammal remains suggests that, in some instances, rodents were roasted and consumed at 26Ch 1048, 26Ch 1052, and 26Ch 1068. Based on these data, it is suspected that small mammals were also processed by other techniques (e.g., pounded and stewed) and used as food items. The wealth of identified *Microtus* remains (both burned and unburned) indicates that this species was abundant in the marsh and, at least in some instances, was taken as a food resource. Compared to other small mammals in the area, *Microtus* is relatively slow, does not hibernate or estivate (Pearson 1985:561), and is active day and night, thus exposing itself to risk from both nocturnal and diurnal predators, including humans.

Summary

Mammalian faunas at the six sites investigated display a great deal of variation. The mammal remains from 26Ch 1048 represent the largest and most taxonomically diverse assemblage. Carnivore remains indicate that numerous species were exploited, probably both for their pelts and as food resources. Similarly, jackrabbit and muskrat were acquired for various resources. Small mammal bone appears to be representative of both non-cultural and cultural accumulations. The numerous charred rodent remains suggest that some carcasses were roasted and consumed.

The assemblage from 26Ch 1052 also reflects the utilization of small mammals for food, as evident by the recovery of numerous fragmented and charred rodent remains. A mink cranium with butchering marks indicates the removal of a pelt and probable (subsequent) use as food. Likewise, fragmented *Canis* and muskrat remains suggest exploitation of these species for usable and consumable resources.

Although rodents and large mammals may have been exploited for subsistence resources at 26Ch 1062, more convincing evidence exists for exploitation of class III mammals, including muskrat and jackrabbit. The high proportion of fragmented and burned bone in this size range and the uneven distribution of both burned and unburned bone across excavated features suggest processing, consumption, and disposal of size class III mammals at the site. Size class III specimens identified to taxon indicate that jackrabbit and, especially, the locally abundant muskrat, were frequently exploited by the 26Ch 1062 inhabitants.

26Ch 1068 contains numerous mountain sheep remains exhibiting cultural modification. Although large mammal remains are present at other sites, the data suggest that mountain sheep were exploited as a food resource more intensively at 26Ch 1068. Conversely, small mammal utilization at the site was rare.

Assemblages recovered from 26Ch 1055 and 26Ch 1173 are small mammal accumulations displaying no evidence of cultural utilization. Burned bone is virtually absent, and unit/level aggregates indicate that most specimens are compilations of skeletal elements from natural deaths on or near the sites.

Future Research

The following discussion addresses some regional research concerns to which the Stillwater mammalian archaeofauna can contribute significantly. General methods as to how these data might be acquired are also presented.

Canids

The abundance and variety of *Canis* in Stillwater Marsh is quite remarkable. Of particular importance are the domesticated dogs (*C. familiaris*) and species showing evidence of hybridization. Similar to prehistoric dogs found throughout the New World, aboriginal Indian dogs in Nevada are represented by a variety of shapes and sizes (cf. Dansie 1984b, 1987a). Because dog breeds can be altered to suit the needs of human populations, the types of dogs present may be consistent with, though not necessarily indicative of, the human economies with which they are associated (Dansie and Schmitt 1986:252). Further, data relevant to the origins, historical distributions, and fates of New World dog varieties should result from each find. The recovery and subsequent metric and qualitative analyses of additional dogs in Stillwater Marsh can contribute significantly to such studies.

Surface Reconnaissance

Mammalian and other faunal remains are present on the surface of numerous archaeological sites in the Carson Desert (Dansie 1987a; Schmitt 1988a, 1990). For example, at site 26Ch 1048 hundreds of faunal specimens possessing valuable zoogeographic and human subsistence data lie exposed as a result of recent flooding and subsequent exfoliation.

During field operations, Schmitt recorded the various species present in surface manifestations at five sites. With the exception of numerous muskrat (*Ondatra zibethicus*) remains deposited by flooding, most of the bones appear to be from the subsurface deposits on which they now lie; too, faunal remains are scarce where no cultural material was present. Table 7 presents a generic presence-absence tally of various mammalian taxa observed in surface manifestations and those recovered from excavated deposits at the five sites. Clearly, taxonomic richness, diversity, and abundance are dictated by sample size (Grayson 1984), but, with the exception of 26Ch 1052 where *Anadonta* shell obscured ground visibility, taxonomic diversity on the surface seems to parallel that of the buried deposits, particularly with respect to the larger mammals.

Although lacking the provenience necessary for many types of analyses and interpretations, identification of bones in conjunction with other artifact classes in surface assemblages may serve as a valuable tool in addressing the range of site variability in the marsh, particularly in assessing intensity of occupation. Further, a taxonomic inventory (i.e., species list) of surface materials also may provide insights into historic zoogeography and paleoenvironmental conditions, both factors to which prehistoric peoples adapted (e.g., Lyman 1986).

Excavation

Faunal remains at most archaeological sites in the Stillwater Marsh are numerous, and exhibit remarkable preservation. Within these assemblages lies the potential to address the question of seasonality of site occupation(s) through, for example, analyses of age and sex compositions. Extracting seasonal data from vertebrate remains is a common analytic endeavor, but is plagued with many difficulties, compounded by the uniformitarian assumption that modern and prehistoric animal populations are ontogenetically similar. The storage and transport of dried foods, and natural inclusions in introduced assemblages also complicate analysis (e.g., Grayson and Thomas 1983; Lyman 1982; Monks 1981). Because large samples and multiple indicators generally produce more valid estimates of seasonality (cf. Monks 1981), the wealth and variety of mammals and avifauna in Stillwater Marsh archaeological sites offer a relatively high degree of analytical accuracy.

Clearly, through large scale and refined excavation of archaeological deposits, the research concerns presented above can be addressed with much greater resolution and reliability. Additional recovery and analysis of Stillwater mammalian remains in association with detailed stratigraphic and chronological controls offer the potential to construe changes in environmental conditions, faunal distributions and abundances, and human subsistence and settlement in Great Basin wetlands.

Table 7. Identified Small (top) and Large (bottom) Mammalian Taxa by Site: Surface Versus Excavated Assemblages

	26Ch 1048		26Ch 1052		26Ch 1055		26Ch 1068		26Ch 1173	
	Sur.	Exc.	Sur.	Exc.	Sur.	Exc.	Sur.	Exc.	Sur.	Exc.
Sorex	−	+	−	−	−	−	−	−	−	−
Perognathus	−	+	−	−	−	−	−	−	−	−
Peromyscus	−	+	−	−	−	+	−	+	−	−
Microtus	+	+	−	+	+	+	+	+	−	+
Dipodomys	−	+	−	−	−	−	−	−	−	+
Sylvilagus	−	−	−	−	−	−	−	+	−	−
Lepus	+	+	−	−	−	−	+	+	+	+
Ondatra	+	+	−	+	−	−	+	+	−	−
Mustela	+	+	−	+	−	−	−	+	−	+
Lutra	−	+	−	−	−	−	(+)	−	−	−
Taxidea	+	+	−	−	−	−	(+)	−	−	−
Lynx	−	−	−	−	−	−	−	+	−	−
Vulpes	+	−	−	−	−	−	−	−	−	−
Canis	+	+	−	+	−	−	+	+	−	−
Artiodactyl	+	+	−	+	(+)	−	+	+	−	−
Total	8	12	0	5	2	2	7	9	1	4
Total Large Mammal	7	7	0	4	1	0	6	7	1	2

( ) Nevada State Museum surface collections (Dansie 1987a).

References

Binford, L. R.
  1978 *Nunamiut Ethnoarchaeology.* Academic Press, New York.
  1981 *Bones: Ancient Men and Modern Myths.* Academic Press, New York.
Bryant, V. M., Jr.
  1974 Prehistoric Subsistence in Southwest Texas: The Coprolite Evidence. *American Antiquity* 39:407–420.
Chomko, S.
  1980 Identification of North American Rodent Teeth. In *Mammalian Osteology*, by B. M. Gilbert, pp. 72–99. Modern Printing Co., Laramie, Wyoming.
Dansie, A. J.
  1984a Human and Carnivore Modification of Small Mammals in the Great Basin. Paper presented at the 1st International Bone Modification Conference, Carson City, Nevada.

1984b Prehistoric Dogs in Nevada. Paper presented at the 19th Great Basin Anthropological Conference, Boise, Idaho.
1987a Stillwater Animal Bones. In *Final Report on Excavations in the Stillwater Marsh Archaeological District*, by D. R. Tuohy, A. J. Dansie, and M. B. Haldeman, pp. 257–311. Nevada State Museum Archaeological Services Reports, Carson City.
1987b Archaeofaunas: 26Pe450 and 26Pe366. In *Studies in Archaeology, Geology and Paleontology at Rye Patch Reservoir, Pershing County, Nevada*, edited by M. K. Rusco and J. O. Davis, pp. 156–181. Nevada State Museum Anthropological Papers No. 20. Carson City.

Dansie, A. J., and T. Ringkob
1979 Faunal Analysis of the Glendale Site Assemblage. In *The Archaeology of the Glendale Site (26Wa2065)*, by M. M. Miller, and Robert G. Elston, pp. 184–220. Nevada Archaeological Survey. Submitted to the Nevada Department of Transporation. Carson City.

Dansie, A. J., and D. N. Schmitt
1986 Aboriginal Dogs from the Vista Site. In *The Archaeology of the Vista Site 26Wa3017*, by C. D. Zeier and R. G. Elston, pp. 241-252. Intermountain Research, Silver City, Nevada. Submitted to Cultural Resources Section, Nevada Department of Transportation, Carson City.

Gifford, D. P.
1981 Taphonomy and Paleoecology: A Critical Review of Archaeology's Sister Disciplines. In *Advances in Archaeological Method and Theory*, vol. 4, edited by M. B. Schiffer, pp. 365-438. Academic Press, New York.

Grayson, D. K.
1979 On the Quantification of Vertebrate Archaeofaunas. In *Advances in Archaeological Method and Theory*, vol. 2, edited by M. B. Schiffer, pp. 199–237. Academic Press, New York.
1982 Toward a History of Great Basin Mammals During the Past 15,000 Years. In *Man and Environment in the Great Basin*, edited by D. B. Madsen and J. F. O'Connell, pp. 82-101. SAA Papers No. 2. Society for American Archaeology, Washington, D.C.
1983 The Paleontology of Gatecliff Shelter: Small Mammals. In *The Archaeology of Monitor Valley 2. Gatecliff Shelter*, by D. H. Thomas, pp. 99-126. Anthropological Papers of the American Museum of Natural History 59(1). New York.
1984 *Quantitative Zooarchaeology*. Academic Press, Orlando.
1985 The Paleontology of Hidden Cave: Birds and Mammals. In *The Archaeology of Hidden Cave*, edited by D. H. Thomas, pp. 125-161. Anthropological Papers of the American Museum of Natural History 61(1). New York.
1988 *Danger Cave, Last Supper Cave, and Hanging Rock Shelter: The Faunas*. Anthropological Papers of the American Museum of Natural History 66(1). New York.

Grayson, D. K., and D. H. Thomas
1983 Seasonality at Gatecliff Shelter. In *The Archaeology of Monitor Valley 2. Gatecliff Shelter*, by D. H. Thomas, pp. 434-438. Anthropological Papers of the American Museum of Natural History 59(1). New York.

Hall, E. R.
1946 *Mammals of Nevada*. University of California Press, Berkeley.

Hill, A. P.
1979 Disarticulation and Scattering of Mammal Skeletons. *Paleobiology* 5:261-274.

Kelly, R. L.
1988 Archaeological Context. In *Preliminary Investigations in Stillwater Marsh: Human Prehistory and Geoarchaeology*, edited by C. Raven and R. G. Elston, pp. 5-20. Intermountain Research, Silver City, Nevada. Submitted to the U.S. Fish and Wildlife Service, Portland, Oregon.

Livingston, S. D.
1988 Avian Fauna. In *Preliminary Investigations in Stillwater Marsh: Human Prehistory and Geoarchaeology*, edited by C. Raven and R. G. Elston, pp. 287-306. Intermountain Research, Silver City, Nevada. Submitted to the U.S. Fish and Wildlife Service, Portland, Oregon.

Lyman, R. L.
1982 Archaeofaunas and Subsistence Studies. In *Advances in Archaeological Method and Theory*, vol. 5, edited by M. B. Schiffer, pp. 357-403. Academic Press, New York.
1985a The Paleozoology of the Avey's Orchard Site. In *Avey's Orchard: Archaeological Investigations of a Late Prehistoric Columbia River Community*, edited by J. R. Galm and R. A. Masten, pp. 243-319. Eastern Washington University Reports in Archaeology and History 100-42.
1985b Bone Frequencies: Differential Transport, *In Situ* Destruction, and the MGUI. *Journal of Archaeological Science* 12:221-236.
1986 On the Analysis and Interpretation of Species List Data in Zooarchaeology. *Journal of Ethnobiology* 6(1):67-81.
1987 Archaeofaunas and Butchery Studies: A Taphonomic Perspective. In *Advances in Archaeological Method and Theory*, vol. 10, edited by M. B. Schiffer, pp. 249–337. Academic Press, New York.

Monks, G.
1981 Seasonality Studies. In *Advances in Archaeological Method and Theory*, vol. 4, edited by M. B. Schiffer, pp. 177-240. Academic Press, New York.

Pearson, O. P.
1985 Predation. In *Biology of New World Microtus*, edited by R. H. Tamarin, pp. 535-566. American Society of Mammalogists Special Publication No. 8. Shippensburg University, Shippensburg, Pennsylvania.

Pippin, L. C.
1979   Bighorn Sheep and Great Basin Prehistory. In *The Archaeology of Smith Creek Canyon, Eastern Nevada*, edited by D. R. Tuohy and D. L. Rendell, pp. 332-361. Nevada State Museum Anthropological Papers No. 17. Carson City.

Raven, C., and R. G. Elston (eds.)
1988   *Preliminary Investigations in Stillwater Marsh: Human Prehistory and Geoarchaeology.* Intermountain Research, Silver City, Nevada. Submitted to the U.S. Fish and Wildlife Service, Portland, Oregon.

Roust, N. L.
1967   Preliminary Excavations of Prehistoric Coprolites from Four Western Nevada Caves. *University of California Archaeological Survey Reports* 70:49-88. Berkeley.

Schmitt, D. N.
1986a   Faunal Analysis. In *The Archaeology of the Vista Site (26Wa3017)*, by C. D. Zeier and R. G. Elston, pp. 209-239. Intermountain Research, Silver City, Nevada. Submitted to Cultural Resources Section, Nevada Department of Transportation, Carson City.

1986b   *Zooarchaeological and Taphonomic Investigations at Site 36JA42, Upper Applegate River, Southwestern Oregon.* Unpublished Master's thesis. Department of Anthropology, Oregon State University, Corvallis.

1988a   Mammalian Fauna. In *Preliminary Investigations in Stillwater Marsh: Human Prehistory and Geo-archaeology*, edited by C. Raven and R. G. Elston, pp. 257-286. Intermountain Research, Silver City, Nevada. Submitted to the U.S. Fish and Wildlife Service, Portland, Oregon.

1988b   Some Observations on Vertebrate Taphonomy and Site Formational Processes in Stillwater Marsh. In *Preliminary Investigations in Stillwater Marsh: Human Prehistory and Geoarchaeology*, edited by C. Raven and R. G. Elston, pp. 353-365. Intermountain Research, Silver City, Nevada. Submitted to the U.S. Fish and Wildlife Service, Portland, Oregon.

1990   Appendix A; Human and Non-human Skeletal Remains. In *Islands in the Sink: Archaeological Patterns at the Margin of the Carson Sink*, by C. Raven. Intermountain Research, Silver City, Nevada. Submitted to the Bureau of Reclamation, Sacramento, California.

Sharp, N. D.
1990   The Mammalian Fauna at 26Ch1062. In *The Archaeology of 26Ch1062*, by R. L. Kelly, in preparation.

Shipman, P., G. Foster, and M. Schoeninger
1984   Burnt Bones and Teeth: An Experimental Study of Color, Morphology, Crystal Structure and Shrinkage. *Journal of Archaeological Science* 11:307-325.

Simms, S. R.
1987   *Behavioral Ecology and Hunter-Gatherer Foraging: An Example from the Great Basin.* BAR International Series 381. Oxford.

Simpson, J. H.
1876   Report of Explorations Across the Great Basin of the Territory of Utah for a Direct Wagon-route from Camp Floyd to Genoa, in Carson Valley. (Re-issued by University of Nevada Press, 1983.)

Stahl, P. W.
1982   On Small Mammal Remains in Archaeological Context. *American Antiquity* 47:822-829.

Steward, J. H.
1941   *Culture Element Distributions XIII: Nevada Shoshone.* University of California Anthropological Records 4(2). Berkeley.

Stewart, O. C.
1941   *Culture Element Distributions XIV: Northern Paiute.* University of California Anthropological Records 4(3). Berkeley.

Thomas, D. H.
1969   Great Basin Hunting Patterns: A Quantitative Method for Treating Faunal Remains. *American Antiquity* 12:29-60.

Thomas, D. H., and D. Mayer
1983   Behavioral Faunal Analysis of Selected Horizons. In *The Archaeology of Monitor Valley 2. Gatecliff Shelter*, by D. H. Thomas, pp. 353-391. Anthropological Papers of the American Museum of Natural History 59(1). New York.

Tuohy, D. R.
1987   The Artifacts from the Refuge. In *Final Report on Ecavations in the Stillwater Marsh Archaeological District*, by D. R. Tuohy, A. J. Dansie, and M. B. Haldeman, pp. 215-255. Nevada State Museum Archaeological Series Report. Carson City.

UNUSUAL EBURNATION FREQUENCIES IN A SKELETAL SERIES FROM THE STILLWATER MARSH AREA, NEVADA

Sheilagh Brooks, Michele B. Haldeman, and Richard H. Brooks

Abstract

Unusual eburnation frequencies on adult epiphyses were observed during the analysis of a skeletal series from the Stillwater Marsh region in west central Nevada. This series consisted of 144 relatively complete skeletons and 272 single bones or incomplete skeletons, making a total of 416 possible individuals. Eburnation is sometimes described as the end result of degenerative arthropathies. Eburnation occurred on vertebrae, a tempero–mandibular joint, humeri, ulnae, radii, femora, tibiae, patellae, podials, metapodials and phalanges. Skeletons of eight males, three females, and two unknown sex adults were observed with eburnation in individuals with age ranges from 17 or 18 to 55+. The left side was effected more often than the right and in seven cases both sides were eburnated. Ingestion of mycotoxins produced by spores growing on stoned seeds may be a possible causative factor.

Introduction

A number of archaeological site areas on marshy hillocks were exposed, after the subsidence of flood water destroyed the covering vegetation in the Stillwater Reservoir portion of the Carson Sink, west central Nevada. Human skeletal remains were recovered from sites located in about a four mile square section of the Stillwater Wildlife Refuge Management area through archaeological field salvage research. Approximately 416 possible individuals were identified from the comingled bones; 144 were relatively complete skeletons from which age and/or sex could be determined (Brooks et al. 1988). The identification of the remaining 272 individuals was derived from single bones or several skeletal elements from which neither age nor sex could be estimated. Based on the 144 relatively complete skeletons, 31.3% were male, 19.4% were female and 49.3% of unknown sex. The latter were mostly juveniles under 18 years of age at death. Radiocarbon dates from four

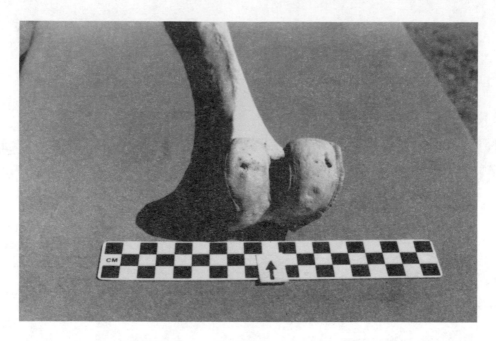

Figure 1. L1–60–4a, female, 45±, left femur with pitting and osteophytes, but no eburnation.

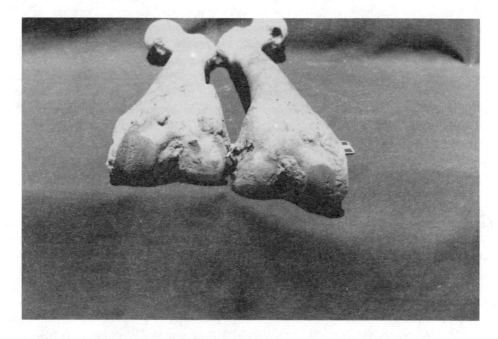

Figure 2. L21–1, male, 50± years, showing the appearance of the distal facets of the right and left femora with osteophytes and eburnation. The eburnated areas made direct contact with the proximal facets of the right and left tibiae in Figure 4.

already broken long bones ranged from about 848 A.D. ± 50 years to 1698 A.D. ± years, although artifacts found during the salvage research may indicate an earlier initial time of 2,000 to 3,000 years ago.

Description of Pathology

During the anthropometric and anthroposcopic analyses (quantitative and qualitative skeletal research), marked arthropathies (disease effecting joints) were observed in the adults. Certain arthropathies are evidenced skeletally through the presence of osteophytes, which are extra bony growths around a joint surface. These are frequently recorded for Great Basin Indian skeletal series (Stark 1983; Brooks et al. 1988). Osteophytes occur most often in the vertebrae and are observed in prehistoric skeletal series in the late twenties or early thirties. They also are recorded around the joint surfaces of hand bones, elbow and knee joints, as well as the sacro–iliac joint. This type of arthropathy in mature individuals relates to biological aging, and a reduction of the ability of the cartilage to repair itself. In younger individuals osteophytes are attributed to trauma or inflammation in an effected joint. Repeated minor trauma or "wear and tear" on the joints gradually produces degenerative changes in the articular or hyaline cartilage—soft tissue padding that occurs at all contact points between bones. At the same time osteophytes develop around the joint facets of the bones involved.

Merbs (1983) divided one arthropathy, osteoarthritis, into a sequential set of three changes, based on this observations of Inuit Eskimo skeletons. The first minor indications visible are the porous or pitted appearance of the joint surfaces and the second when new bone or osteophytic growth begins along the edges of the joint facets (Figure 1). The last phase of his sequence is called eburnation, where the cartilage padding has become completely eroded, exposing the underlying bone. Friction caused by continued rubbing of bone on bone through ongoing usage can polish, or eburnate, the joint facet surfaces. Although the eburnated compact bone is dense and hard, it is thin and the trabecular, or spongy, and bone underneath shows through as porosities on the joint facets. The effected joint surfaces display a smooth or polished appearance and shallow grooves may appear in the eburnated areas (Figures 2 and 3).

Distribution of Pathology

Osteophytes were recorded in the Stillwater series for almost every bone in the body, including the tempero–mandibular joint. Among the pathologies recorded for Stillwater adults, osteophytes effected the greatest number of individuals in the skeletal series, 67 or 16.1% of the 416 total count. Osteophytes were most frequently observed surrounding the vertebral bodies or centra (Figure 4). The development of osteophytes on the centra of vertebrae is usually the first indication of age and/or problems of physical strain. Osteophytic growth rimming the contact facets was also recorded for many other joints. Osteophytes can and do occur independently or eburnation, but all cases of eburnation observed in the Stillwater series had marked osteophytic growth around that joint.

Eburnation is one of the more acute changes of an arthropathy and a total of 38 joint surfaces in the Stillwater series demonstrated evidence of eburnation (Brooks et al. 1988). These ranged from slight to well–polished joint facets, usually with "mushroom–shaped" osteophytes (Figure 5 and 6). The term "mushroom–shaped" is used to describe a large osteophyte around an articular facet, curving over a section of the adjacent long bone shaft. In 13 Stillwater individuals at least one bone contained an eburnated facet. Nine of these are from relatively complete burials and four from single bones or a few bones catalogued together as a probable individual. The percent of eburnation for the 144 relatively complete burials is 6.3%, for the total Stillwater series, or 416 burials, 3.1% (Brooks et al. 1988:102). This is an unusual frequency for Nevada Great Basin prehistoric human remains, since in a study of 250 skeletons from various regions of Nevada, there were only a few recorded cases of eburnation (Stark 1983).

Figure 7 shows that distribution of the eburnation by bone and the incidence of the pathology for each bone. The 38 bones observed with eburnation include vertebral superior or inferior facets on the atlas, axis, cervicals C3 through C7, a thoracic T6 and a sacrum. Other effected joints are the tempero–mandibular joint, one proximal humerus, four distal humeri, one distal ulna, three proximal radii, five distal femora, two proximal

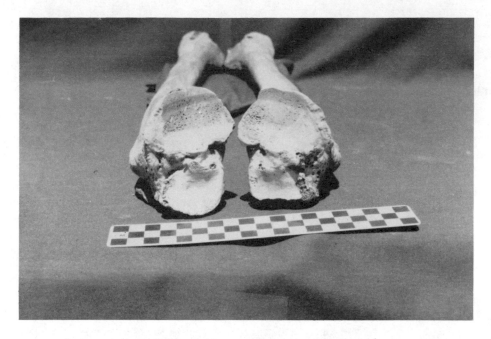

Figure 3. L21–1, male, 50± years, matching right and left tibiae proximal facets to Figure 2, with eburnation and osteophytes. Note the porosities and the wear or grooving on the eburnated areas.

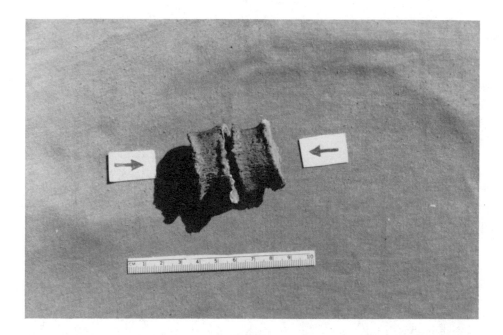

Figure 4. L2–2, male 55± years, showing osteophytic growths around the margins of the lumbar vertebrae.

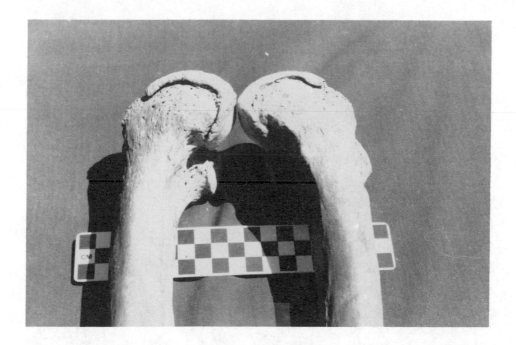

Figure 5. L21–1, male, 50± years, showing "mushroom–shaped" osteophytes around the distal facets of the right and left femora.

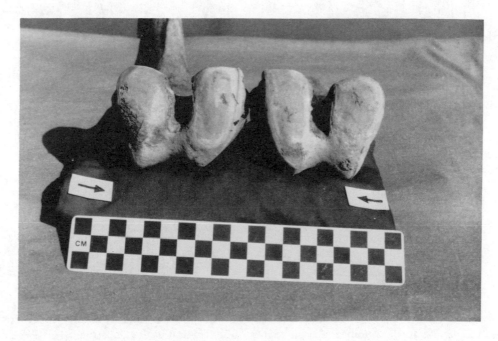

Figure 6. L2–2, male, 55± years, with eburnation and osteophytes on the distal facets of right and left femora. Note the porous appearance of the eburnated bone.

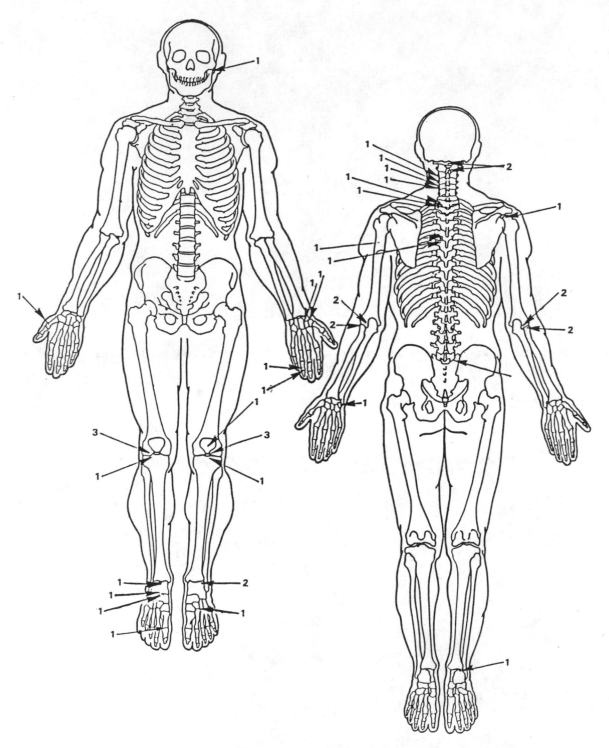

Figure 7. Incidence and distribution of eburnation in the Stillwater skeletal series, Nevada. Numbers between (1) and (3) indicate the number of occurrences of eburnation at that location.

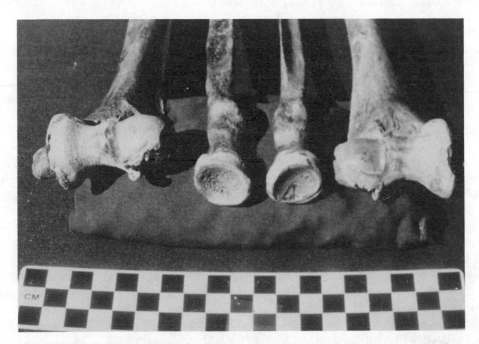

Figure 8. L2–2, male, 55± years, with eburnated facets of both humeral distal capituli, which made contact with both radial proximal head facets. Note the osteophytes, porosities and irregular bony growths. Both proximal ulnae, not shown, had osteophytic growths, but no eburnation.

tibiae, two distal tibiae, one patella, four podials, two metapodials, and one phalange. Seven cases of eburnation involved right and left sides of a joint from the same individual (Figure 8); overall right sides totaled 15 and left sides 19. Two instances included the central facet of the atlas and the dens of the axis. The dens is the superior extension of the axis that fits on a facet of the atlas, allowing the head to turn.

Thirteen individuals had eburnation in a least one joint, of these eight were males, 61.5%, three were females, 23.1%, and two were of unknown sex, 15.4% (Brooks et al. 1988). Among the 144 relatively complete burials 4.2% have two or more joints effected. These included shoulders, elbows (Figure 7), knees, cervicals, and podials. The age range for those individuals with eburnation is one 17–18 year–old and a 23–26 year–old, the degree of eburnation was examined and the polishing had just started, as only a small area was eburnated and there were no osteophytes (Brooks et al. 1988).

Causative Factors

Initially two possible causes were suggested for the unusual eburnation frequency, both related to the wetlands environment of the Stillwater Marsh. Today there are high arsenic levels in the marsh waters, and this as well as selenium, were thought to have effected the bones of the joints. Studies made on living populations with higher than usual amounts of either arsenic (Savory and Sedor, 1977 and Dinman, 1960) or selenium (Cooper 1967) show these two substances only effect soft tissues in areas other than joints when present in the environment above minimal levels, not apparently bone or associated cartilage.

In Merbs' study (1983) of osteoarthritis in the Inuit Eskimo skeletal remains, he suggested these manifestations, from pitting and porosities to osteophytes and eburnation, were derived from continued, repetitive daily activities. The key factor in his conclusions is that constant strain or stress created by the repetitive activity would first lead to destructive effects on the cartilagineous tissue and, eventually, the bony element as well.

There are a series of daily tasks that would have been performed by the Stillwater men and women in their normal cultural patterns. These included every aspect of their lives from making fire, carrying burdens, cutting and scraping skins, weaving baskets or sewing, chopping wood, to bringing in killed game, and so on endlessly. Some of these activities were conducted daily, others in certain weekly or monthly cycles. The problem in assuming these tasks alone would lead to the development of eburnation is that almost the same cultural activities apply to many of the prehistoric peoples in the Nevada Great Basin, not just those living in and around the Stillwater Marsh. Yet skeletons from other Nevada sites do not demonstrate any frequency of eburnation and the few recorded cases from widely scattered locales (Stark 1983) do not manifest the extreme eburnation observed in some of the Stillwater skeletal series. Another possible cause might be the effects of the damp, cold winter climate, but again human skeletal remains from sites around other lacustrine areas in the Great Basin have not demonstrated the severe eburnation, nor the frequency recorded (Stark 1983), as at Stillwater.

No other causative factors were proposed during discussions with paleopathologists until the European Anthropological Association meetings in Budapest. There Drs. Comis and Flinn (1988) described the effects of mycotoxins effecting stored wheat as a possible nutritional cause. Research with people in an area of Siberia, where eburnation was almost endemic, discovered a mycotoxin, produced by spores of the parasitic fungus *Fusarium*, effected the wheat stored in this damp cold region. When the wheat was eaten by people (or dogs in an experiment) the mycotoxin destroyed the hyaline cartilage (cartilage found between joint surfaces), leading to eburnation (Nesterov, 1964). Comis and Flinn (1988) had observed severe eburnation in a medieval English monastery, which they believe resulted from wheat stored in the damp climate being effected by *Fusarium* mycotoxins. As the monks ate the wheat, the mycotoxins eventually caused destruction of their hyaline cartilage. In combination with their daily activity patterns, eburnation was the eventual result.

Wheat is not indigenous to the New World, but was introduced after European contact. The prehistoric Great Basin Indians in the Stillwater Marsh area were not agriculturalists, but hunters and gatherers. The question then is, does the *Fusarium* parasitic fungus, or some related type of fungus, effect those plants that were domesticated in the New World, such as corn, beans, and squash? More importantly, would this fungus effect the harvested wild plants or seeds that the west central Great Basin Nevada Indians collected and stored? The key factor for the development of the mycotoxins appears to be the storage of grains or seeds especially in a damp, cold environment.

Based on ethnographic information from C. Fowler (personal communication 1988), the local Indian groups in the Stillwater region collected various wild seeds, including tule seeds in the marshes, and stored them. Tuohy et al. (1987) encountered evidence of storage pits in the earth hillocks within the Stillwater Marsh, where the archaeological excavations were conducted. After a series of attempts to discover whether *Fusarium* or another parasitic fungus would effect stored wild seeds of Great Basin varieties, contact was made with Dr. Hesseltine, U.S. Department of Agriculture, a mycological specialist. Published date (Hesseltine, 1979) indicate that *Fusarium* does effect New World plants, including corn and other wild grass seeds, when they are stored in a cold, damp environment. The Stillwater Marsh region appears to have been an excellent situation for the development of *Fusarium* mycotoxins effecting the wilde seeds, stored in the pits located in the marshy hillocks. It should be emphasized that more research is needed to substantiate this assumption.

Conclusions

The unusual frequencies of eburnation among the skeletal remains from the Stillwater Marsh appear to be related, at least in part, to the wetlands environment of the Marsh. Probably also the disintegration of the hyaline cartilage resultant from the presumed effects of ingesting the mycotoxins was further aggravated by the daily, repetitive activities necessary for survival. These prehistoric cultural patterns are interpreted by the archaeologists from the artifacts recovered from the Stillwater area and the information provided by Great Basin Indian ethnologists. Following Merbs' reasoning (1983) the daily stress and strain on joints could lead to arthropathy problems. These difficulties would be amplified with the loss of hyaline cartilage between the joints and this combination could easily be the causative factor involved in the unusual frequencies of eburnation in the Stillwater skeletal series. The effects obviously varied between individuals, dependent on reactions to mycotoxins, amounts of contaminated seeds eaten, metabolism and other physiological factors, since only a percentage of the Stillwater human remains were effected.

The research on the Stillwater skeletal material is ongoing, even though the human remains were reburied in the fall of 1988. Fortunately they were radiographed previously, although x-rays do not show the actual eburnation only the so-called "mushroom-shaped" osteophytes (Rogers 1989). Numerous photographs and slides were taken, particularly of the eburnation itself, with closeups of the polished areas of the facets. The problem now is to determine whether *Fusarium* mycotoxins will be found in the Stillwater Marsh prehistoric storage pits or archaeologically recovered remains of seeds. Although, as Dr. Hesseltine said in a letter: "The fact that eburnation occurred in this marsh area fits the picture of mold toxins" (1988). His statement provides a basis for the tentative assumption of a causative factor for the eburnation frequencies observed in the human skeletal remains from the Stillwater Marsh area.

References

Brooks, S. T., M. B. Haldeman, and R. H. Brooks
   1988 *Osteological Analyses of the Stillwater Skeletal Series, Stillwater Marsh, Churchill County, Nevada.* Prepared for U.S. Fish and Wildlife Service, Stillwater National Wildlife Refuge.

Comis, S. D., and R. M. Flinn
   1988 Severe Joint Disease—A Nutritional Cause? Paper presented at the 6th Congress of the European Anthropological Association, Budapest, Hungary.

Cooper, W. E.
   1967 Selenium Toxicity in Man. In *Symposium: Selenium in Biomedicine*, edited by O. H. Muth, J. E. Oldfield, and P. H. Weswig, pp. 185–199. Avi Publishing Company, Inc., Westport, Connecticut.

Dinman, B. D.
   1960 Arsenic: Chronic Human Intoxication. *Journal of Occupation Medicine* 2:137–141.

Hesseltine, C. W.
   1979 *Interactions of Mycotoxins in Animal Production.* Symposium, National Academy of Sciences, Washington, D.C.

Merbs, C. F.
   1983 *Patterns of Activity-Induced Pathology in a Canadian Inuit Population.* Archaeology Survey of Canada Paper No. 119. National Museum of Man Mercury Series, Ottawa.

Nesterov, A. I.
   1964 The Clinical Course of Kashin-Beck Disease. *Arthritis and Rheumatism* 7:29–40.

Rogers, J.
   1989 Osteoarthritis of the Knee Joint in Skeletal Material—Visual Observation and Radiographic Findings. Paper presented at the Paleopathological Association Meetings, San Diego, California.

Savory, J., and F. A. Sedor
   1977 Arsenic Poisoning. In *Clinical Chemistry and Chemical Toxicology of Metals*, edited by S. S. Brown, pp. 271–286. Elsevier North-Holland Biomedical Press.

Stark, C. R.
   1983 *The Determination of Variation in Skeletal Remains in Nevada Through the Use of Discrete Morphological Traits and Anthropometry.* Unpublished Master's thesis, Anthropology Department, University of Nevada, Las Vegas.

Tuohy, D. R., A. J. Dansie, and M. B. Haldeman
   1987 *Final Report on Excavations in the Stillwater Marsh Archaeological District, Nevada.* Nevada State Museum Archaeological Services Reports. Carson City.

8

SETTLEMENT PATTERNING AND RESIDENTIAL STABILITY AT WALKER LAKE, NEVADA: THE VIEW FROM ABOVE

David Rhode

Abstract

Use of wetland environments by prehistoric hunter-gatherers in the Great Basin was integrated into regional land use patterns incorporating surrounding upland and desert habitats, in which land use in different Great Basin wetlands influenced land use in these surrounding habitats, and vice versa. The density and distribution of archaeological remains in upland areas of the Walker River drainage suggest that the wetland environment at Walker Lake exerted a significant effect on prehistoric settlement patterns of the uplands: uplands near the lake were primarily occupied for relatively short-term, logistic foraging from presumed residential bases located near the lake, while uplands further from the lake were occupied on a more long-term, residential basis. The evidence, indirect though it is, suggests that Walker Lake was a long-term residential focus in the region. While the nature of this wetlands residential pattern remains uncertain, it is likely to have differed significantly from lakeshore adaptations known from the Carson and Humboldt Sinks.

Introduction

In this paper I discuss prehistoric settlement variability in the uplands of the Walker River drainage, western Nevada (Figure 1). Such a topic might appear out of place in a volume devoted to wetland adaptations, but as our understanding of prehistoric settlement of lakeshore areas of the western Great Basin has expanded, the fact that such settlement must be considered in the context of the larger region has become increasingly clear. Understanding prehistoric occupation of uplands surrounding lake basins is critically important for understanding how prehistoric settlement patterns in the wetland areas of the Great Basin were articulated into regional land use systems. The particular role of upland occupation in the settlement systems found in different lake basins remains a problem of considerable interest, and it is this role in the Walker River drainage that I consider here.

Figure 1. Major wetland habitats in the Lahontan Basin, western Great Basin (after Russell, in Snyder 1917).

The Regional Perspective

Over the decades, archaeologists have shown increasing interest in settlement patterning and the relationships of land use in different environments around the lakes of the western Great Basin. And, over the decades, the size of the "region" thought to be important in the lacustrine settlement system has correspondingly increased. Loud and Harrington (1929), working from the relatively restricted perspective of Lovelock Cave, tentatively began a regional outlook by connecting the occupation of sites on the Humboldt lakebed to the occupation of the cave. Later, Heizer and his colleagues (Heizer 1967; Heizer and Napton 1970; Napton 1969) greatly expanded the regional scope by postulating a "limno-sedentary" settlement pattern in the Carson and Humboldt Sinks, that featured long-term residential stability around the wetland environment and a strong subsistence emphasis on wetland plants and animals. They set this lacustrine subsistence pattern apart from the much more generalized subsistence pattern of Shoshonean groups in the central Great Basin described by Steward. More recently, the work of Thomas and his colleagues in the Carson Sink (Thomas 1985; Kelly 1985, 1988) has

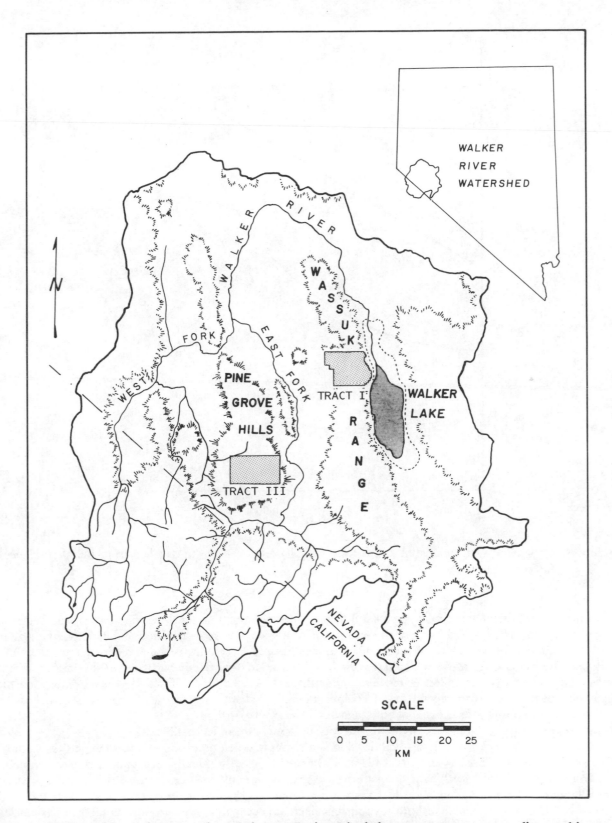

Figure 2. Walker River drainage, southern Lahontan Basin. Stippled areas are survey tracts discussed in text.

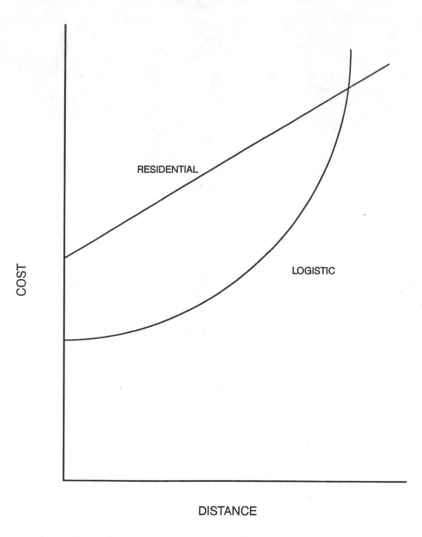

Figure 3. Comparison of residential and logistic mobility costs relative to distance from initial residence to farthest destination.

expanded the pertinent settlement region still further, in suggesting that the lacustrine biome was but one of many environments exploited by western Great Basin groups in a more generalized and wide-ranging pattern.

At issue here are the types of units and relationships used in creating regional settlement models in the valleys of the western Great Basin. First, the kinds of occupation occurring in particular environments form the units of such models. Included in the units of settlement are the kinds of activities carried out and their frequency over time. The second major component is the relationships between those units; that is, how occupation of one unit affects occupation of another. These relationships serve to integrate the model, place it in the context of the actual space involved, and provide a measure of its spatial scale.

In the case at hand, these issues boil down to some simply stated problems: First, what was the nature of occupation in lakeshore environments? Was it a principal focus of residential occupation, or was it a habitat used on a more limited basis? Was the pattern of use stable through time, or intermittent? Second, what was the relationship between occupation in lakeshore environments, and of other environments surrounding the lakeshore? Did proximity to lakeshore environments increase occupation of environments surrounding the lake, lessen that occupation, change the kinds of activities involved, or have no effect?

The Walker Watershed Project

These were some of the problems guiding my research in the Walker River drainage (Rhode 1987). In particular, I wanted to know what kind of effect lakeshore occupation might have had on the settlement of the uplands around the lake, if any, and if this pattern could be detected archaeologically.

In order to examine the effects of the Walker Lake environment on upland settlement in the region, I looked at two upland areas that differed mainly in their distance to the lake (Figure 2). These areas were located in the northern Wassuk Range and in the central Pine Grove Hills. If lakeshore occupation did have an effect on upland occupation and use, that effect should be responsive to distance from the lake, particularly travel time considerations among other factors.

The effect of travel time on occupation can be shown using some simple cost-benefit models. If we divide activities involving residential mobility from those involving logistical mobility (Binford 1980; Kelly 1983), the following relationship between those activities at different distances may generally apply (Figure 3). The costs of initially outfitting a logistical trip should generally be lower than the cost of outfitting a residential move. Costs of actual movement may also be initially higher for the residential group than the (by definition) smaller logistical group. But at some critical distance, logistical movement costs will rise at a steeper rate than residential movement costs -- for one reason because the logistical group, which by definition moves goods to consumers, must effectively make a round trip, while the residential group, by definition moving consumers to the goods, need only go one way. In the case of bulky goods such as pinyon nuts, these round-trip costs may be multiplied by the number of trips necessary to move enough to provision the consumers. At some critical distance, it will be cheaper to move residentially than to move logistically. Thus we can anticipate that distance between resource areas will be an important factor in how occupation of those areas is related (cf. Jones and Madsen 1989).

Distance-mediated relationships between occupation of resource areas can be identified archaeologically only if the spatial relationship is stable through time. If residential locations shift frequently, then positioning between resource areas will be highly unstable, and distance factors will be effectively canceled out over the long term. Only if there is a stable residential patterning will the effects of distance on settlement of otherwise similar resource areas be recognized in the archaeological record. In this manner, if such patterns can be recognized with respect to distance from a lakeshore environment, then a temporally-stable residential pattern with respect to the lake and its surroundings can be inferred.

Methods

In each upland area investigated, a simple random sample of 24 quadrats measuring 200 m on a side were surveyed (Figures 4 and 5). Each quad was traversed by 12 transects, each 2 m wide and spaced 18 m apart, and all surface artifacts within these transects were collected in 2 m intervals. Thus, both upland areas had equivalent levels of coverage. This collection procedure resulted in detailed spatial control of artifact density along the transects, suitable for the creation of maps to be used to identify artifact clusters (sites) of different sizes and densities, and to discriminate between those clusters and the background distribution of artifacts in the region.

Results

The two upland samples differ in both artifact density and content. Most striking is the difference in total artifact abundance (Table 1). A total of 36 artifacts were found in the Wassuk Range sample, located nearer the lake, while the Pine Grove Hills sample contained 5810 artifacts, a difference of some 1600 per cent. The artifacts in the Wassuk Range sample are also relatively dispersed, and not as strongly clustered into "sites" as those of the Pine Grove Hills sample. The variance/mean ratio (Grieg-Smith 1964:63; Hodder and Orton

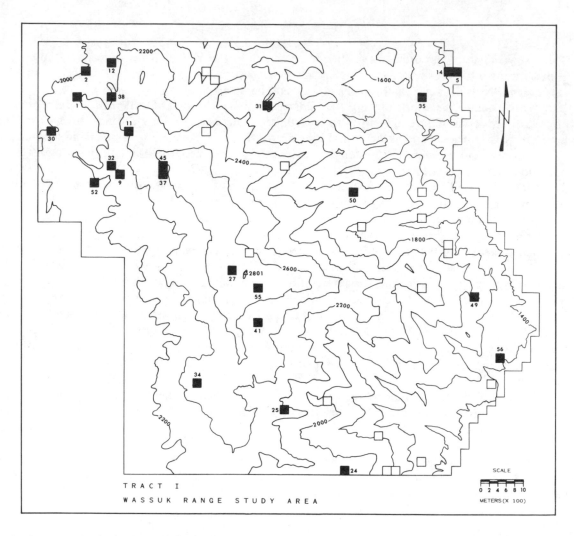

Figure 4. Survey sample in Tract I, located near Walker Lake in the Wassuk Range. Surveyed quadrats are filled and numbered squares, unsurveyed quadrats (for reasons of steepness) are open and unnumbered.

1976:34) of artifact density for the Wassuk Range sample is 6.37. The variance/mean ratio for the Pine Grove Hills sample is 1692.13, indicating a sample significantly more clustered in space that the Wassuk sample.

The low number of artifacts in the Wassuk Range, and the great disparity in the numbers of artifacts found between the two areas, made statistical comparison of formal and functional characteristics a problem. Therefore, we returned to sites that had been found in the Wassuk Range during our systematic sampling and made complete point-provenienced surface collections. These site collections (Table 1) were then compared to samples of similar artifact density in the Pine Grove Hills.

Detailed formal and functional comparisons between the artifacts of the two upland areas show that the Pine Grove Hills assemblage are strongly dominated by waste materials from lithic tool manufacture, whereas the Wassuk Range samples have a greater proportion of shaped artifacts (Table 1). The raw materials used in chipped stone technology in the Pine Grove Hills were almost exclusively obsidian, primarily from sources over 30 km away. Exotic obsidian also dominates the Wassuk technology, though chert materials are better represented in the Wassuks. The Pine Grove Hills debitage is comprised mainly of small flakes with little or

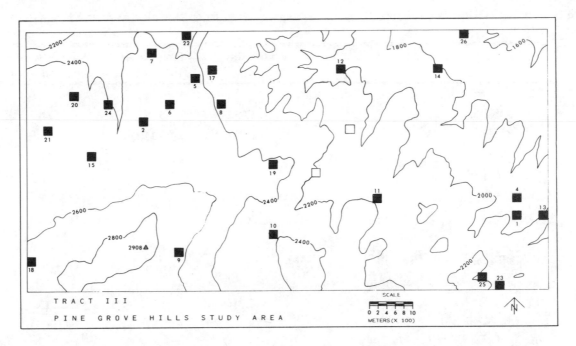

Figure 5. Survey sample in Tract III, located farther from Walker Lake in the Pine Grove Hills. Surveyed quadrats are filled and numbered squares, unsurveyed quadrats (for reasons of steepness) are open and unnumbered.

Table 1. Number of Artifacts Recovered in Random Sample Tracts and in Site Collections

Artifact Class	Wassuk Range Sample	Pine Grove Hills Sample	Wassuk Range Site Collection
Debitage	18	5,163	672
Worn Flakes	4	406	115
Cores	0	31	20
Retouched Flakes	3	82	37
Bifaces	4	67	42
Projectile Points	7	36	27
Groundstone	0	4	23
Historic Materials	0	5	17
Faunal	0	7	26
Total	36	5,801	979

Table 2. Characteristics of Chipped Stone Artifacts Recovered from Wassuk Range and Pine Grove Hills

	Wassuk Range Sample	Pine Grove Hills Sample	Wassuk Range Site Collection
Raw Material:			
Obsidian	17	5,591	574
Chert	11	160	251
Quartzite	0	15	45
Basalt	5	20	21
Other	3	7	14
Total	36	5,794	912
Flake Type:			
Number (mean weight in grams)			
Cortical	9 (7.7)	430 (1.7)	112 (13.2)
Non-cortical	9 (2.7)	4,733 (0.4)	560 (1.2)
Total	18	5,163	672
Platform Type on Flakes:			
Cortical	1	55	18
1–2 Facets	3	938	165
3+ Facets	2	553	62
Crushed	1	227	24
Unknown	11	3,390	403
Total	18	5,163	672
Platform Angle on Flakes, in Degrees:			
20–40	1	249	30
50–70	2	790	102
80–100	3	651	130
110+	0	47	5
Unknown	1	78	9
None present	11	3,348	396
Total	18	5,163	672

no cortex and with acutely angled, facetted platforms (Table 2); the debitage assemblage appears to best represent reduction of bifacially worked cores. This technology is also present in the Wassuks, but the Wassuk technology also contains a significantly larger component of cortical flakes, larger flakes, and flakes with simple or cortical platforms (Table 2), that probably represent reduction of more irregular cores.

Table 3. Characteristics of Edge Wear on Chipped Stone Tools.

Wear Class	Wassuk Range Sample	Pine Grove Hills Sample	Wassuk Range Site Collection
Wear Type:			
Chipped	13	643	172
Stepped	4	115	32
Crushed	0	46	23
Abraded	0	4	15
Total	17	808	242
Location:			
Edge Only	6	100	33
Unifacial	6	552	177
Bifacial	5	158	34
Total	17	810	244
Shape of Edge:			
Straight	6	424	154
Convex	8	209	52
Concave	3	120	28
Complex	0	55	10
Total	17	808	244
Edge Angle, in degrees:			
45 or less	10	511	132
over 45	7	295	112
Total	17	806	244

Tools represented in the Pine Grove Hills are most often found on unmodified flakes, whereas such "expedient" tools are less common in the Wassuk sample (Table 1). The kinds of wear representing those tools are quite similar between the two upland sample areas, though the Pine Grove Hills assemblage tends to have more chipped stone tools, made on variously curved, acutely angled edges, and exhibiting mainly unifacial wear, than their counterparts in the Wassuk Range, the edge tools of which are steeper-edged and straighter (Table 3). These characteristics are consistent with greater use of "expedient" flakes as tools in the Pine Grove Hills. The general overall similarity of tool types represented in the two upland areas suggests that the same kinds of activities were represented in each area, at this scale of measurement.

Wassuk sites are functionally similar to certain classes of sites found in the Pine Grove Hills, in terms of artifact abundance (usually a low to moderate debitage scatter), tool content, the presence of groundstone and architectural features. Most sites in the Wassuks are lithic scatters of moderate density and quantity, associated with stone circles probably representing foundations of habitation structures. The Pine Grove Hills have a more

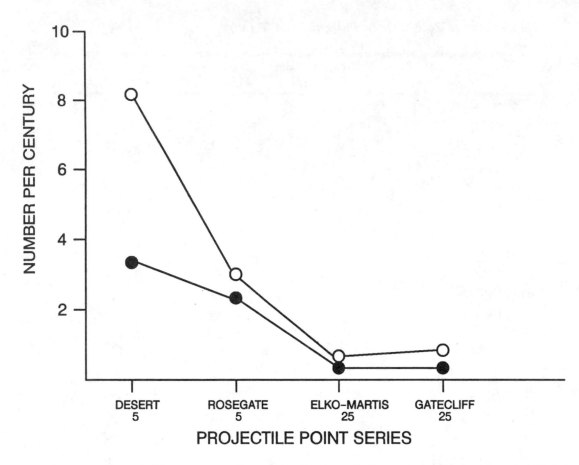

Figure 6. Relative number of different projectile point series deposited per century in the Wassuk (filled circles) and Pine Grove Hills (open circles) samples. Numbers below the projectile point series marks the number of centuries the series were assumed to be extant.

diversified array of site types represented, including several classes of sites which are not found in the Wassuks: very small lithic scatters of debitage, stone circles associated with few or no artifacts, dense lithic scatters lacking groundstone or architecture, and extremely dense lithic scatters that contain groundstone and architecture (see Rhode 1987:Chapter 8 for details).

The chronology of occupation of the two areas appears to have been quite similar, using time-sensitive projectile point styles as a guide. Both areas have been occupied since at least the middle Archaic period (points dating to earlier periods have been found near both sample areas, including a fluted point in the Pine Grove Hills). Both areas were most heavily occupied during the late prehistoric and historic periods, with an abundance of components containing Desert Side-notched points and/or historic materials (Figure 6). This increase in upland occupation during the late prehistoric/historic period agrees with results found elsewhere in the western Great Basin (Bettinger 1976, 1977; Pippin 1980). The archaeological records of the two upland samples are therefore products of contemporaneous occupations, within the limits of current archaeological measurement.

Interpretations

Differences in the settlement of the two uplands suggest greater intensity of occupation in the Pine Grove Hills than in the Wassuk Range. While many of the same activities were carried out in the Wassuk Range and the Pine Grove Hills, the Pine Grove Hills supported a greater variety and frequency of those activities, especially residential activities (domestic dwellings and facilities, tool manufacture and repair).

The reason for these settlement differences toward which I most incline is that they represent the effect of a stable residential pattern that was focussed at the mouth of the Walker River, on the north shore of Walker Lake. People residing at this location could make use of the adjacent Wassuk upland resources more inexpensively using logistical mobility (bringing the upland resources back to the lakeshore residential bases) than by using residential mobility. This was not the case for groups occupying the Pine Grove Hills. This pattern of occupation would result in less evidence of residential occupation (and more evidence of logistical occupation) in the Wassuk Range than the Pine Grove Hills. I interpret the sites in the Wassuk Range as principally short-term pinyon-gathering sites located near residential bases at Walker Lake, while the Pine Grove Hills archaeological record consists of a more diversified suite of occupations associated primarily with residential occupation in the pinyon zone. This hypothesized settlement pattern existed through the period represented by Rosegate and Desert series points, and into historic times.

My interpretation is obviously only one of several possible explanations for the observed differences (see Rhode 1987 for a discussion of other scenarios). But it should be emphasized that these settlement differences would not occur if lacustrine and upland settlement were unrelated in a regional settlement system, nor would they occur if the regional geography of residential settlement was temporally unstable. In these cases, upland settlement would be expected to differ only to the extent that one upland area was inherently better for occupation than the other. While the two uplands do exhibit some environmental differences, they are not different enough to account for the great differences in settlement observed. The inference I draw is that long-term residential patterning in the region was stable, and that it affected the uplands in a manner consistent with a residential focus located at Walker Lake.

It should also be apparent that all the evidence I have concerning occupation at Walker Lake is indirect, and my proposed relationships between lacustrine and upland settlement literally begs the question of what prehistoric occupation near Walker Lake was actually like. I have been unable to investigate the archaeological record near the mouth of Walker River, so cannot answer this question using direct archaeological evidence, but the nature of occupation at the mouth of Walker River is clearly a question of critical importance at this point, one which I hope can be answered in the near future.

The Walker Lake environment has several characteristics that set it apart from wetland environments in the Humboldt and Carson Sinks, and prehistoric residential patterning may be expected to have differed accordingly. Walker Lake is large and deep, with a relatively steep shoreline over most of its extent. The shoreline is more gradual on the northern and southern ends, but the position of that shoreline fluctuates widely in space when lake level varies, as it does almost every year. These conditions do not promote stable wetland habitat, especially marshes. The principal biota suitable for subsistence are mainly anadromous fish: large populations of Lahontan cutthroat trout and tui chub existed in the lake and spawned each year in great runs up Walker River. Indeed, ethnographic work among the residents of the Walker Lake region show fishing in the lake and river to have been a major source of subsistence (Stewart 1943; Bath 1978; cf. also Fowler and Bath 1981).

In contrast, the wide variety of subsistence evidence we have from Lovelock Cave, Hidden Cave, Humboldt Cave, and the open sites in the Humboldt Basin and Carson Sinks (Ambro 1967; Budy 1988; Cowan 1967; Follett 1967, 1970; Heizer 1967; Heizer and Krieger 1956; Heizer and Napton 1970; Livingston 1986, 1988; Loud and Harrington 1929; Napton 1969; Napton and Heizer 1970; Roust 1970; Smith 1985; Thomas 1985; Wheat 1967; Wigand and Mehringer 1985) all suggest the importance of marsh biota in the subsistence of groups inhabiting those more shallow and marshy lake basins. It is for this reason that I doubt the marsh-oriented subsistence and settlement patterning found in the Humboldt and Carson Sinks occurred around Walker Lake. This is not to say that an important residential focus at or near the mouth of Walker River should not be expected; I would be quite surprised if it did not exist. But I anticipate occupation of this locality would be rather different from those occupations found at Stillwater or Humboldt.

Patterns of prehistoric occupation in the lower Walker River valley may have resembled those found along the lower Truckee River and near Pyramid Lake, which had a similar type of lake environment. However, a major difference between the Walker Lake and Pyramid Lake regions is that the mountains around the latter contain no pinyon, a fact that should make detectable differences in both upland, and I would argue lowland,

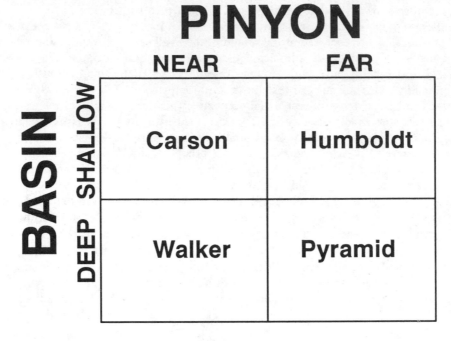

Figure 7. Dimensional classification of environmental characteristics of major lake basins in the Lahontan Basin.

settlement patterns in the two regions. Indeed, one can divide the four major lake basins in the western Great Basin into separate categories based on the abundance of marshlands, on the one hand, and the proximity to upland pinyon resources, on the other (Figure 7). I think that detailed regional-scale comparisons of both upland and lowland archaeological records in these contrastive environments will bring us much closer to identification of the regional environmental factors that resulted in the variety of settlement patterns we see around the lakes of the western Great Basin.

References

Ambro, R. D.
   1967   Dietary-Technological-Ecological Aspects of Lovelock Cave Coprolites. In *Papers on Great Basin Archaeology*. University of California Archaeological Survey Reports No. 70 pp. 37-47. Berkeley.

Bath, J.
   1978   *Lake Margin Adaptations in Great Basin Prehistory*. M.A. thesis, Department of Anthropology, University of Nevada, Reno.

Bettinger, R. L.
   1976   The Development of Pinyon Exploitation in Central Eastern California. *Journal of California Anthropology* 3(1):80-95.
   1977   Aboriginal Human Ecology in Owens Valley: Prehistoric Change in the Great Basin. *American Antiquity* 42:3-17.

Binford, L. R.
   1980   Willow Smoke and Dogs' Tails: Hunter-gatherer Settlement Systems and Archaeological Site Formation. *American Antiquity* 45:4-20.

Budy, E. R.
   1988   Plant Macrofossils. In *Preliminary Investigations in Stillwater Marsh: Human Prehistory and Geoarchaeology*, 2 vols., edited by C. Raven and R. G. Elston, pp. 339-352 . Intermountain Research Reports, Silver City, Nevada.

Cowan, R. A.
   1967   Lake Margin Ecologic Exploitation in the Great Basin as Demonstrated by an Analysis of Coprolites from Lovelock Cave, Nevada. In *Papers on Great Basin Archaeology*, pp. 21-35. University of California Archaeological Survey Reports No. 70. Berkeley.

Follett, W. I.
1967   Fish Remains from Coprolites and Midden Deposits at Lovelock Cave, Churchill County, Nevada. In *Papers on Great Basin Archaeology*, pp. 93-116. University of California Archaeological Survey Reports No. 70. Berkeley.
1970   Fish Remains from Human Coprolites and Midden Deposits Obtained During 1968 and 1969 at Lovelock Cave, Churchill County, Nevada. In *Archaeology and the Prehistoric Great Basin Lacustrine Subsistence Regime as Seen from Lovelock Cave, Nevada*, by R. F. Heizer and L. K. Napton, pp. 163-175. Contributions of the University of California Archaeological Research Facility No. 10. Berkeley.

Fowler, C. S., and J. Bath
1981   Pyramid Lake Northern Paiute Fishing: the Ethnographic Record. *Journal of California and Great Basin Anthropology* 3(2):176-186.

Grieg-Smith, P.
1964   *Quantitative Plant Ecology*. Methuen, London.

Heizer, R. F.
1967   Analysis of Human Coprolites from a Dry Nevada Cave. In *Papers on Great Basin Archaeology*, pp. 1–20. University of California Archaeological Survey Reports No. 70(1). Berkeley.

Heizer, R. F., and A. D. Krieger
1956   The Archaeology of Humboldt Cave, Churchill County, Nevada. *University of California Publications in American Archaeology and Ethnology* 47(1):1-190. Berkeley.

Heizer, R. F., and L. K. Napton
1970   *Archaeology and the Prehistoric Great Basin Lacustrine Subsistence Regime as Seen from Lovelock Cave, Nevada*. Contributions of the University of California Archaeological Research Facility No. 10. Berkeley.

Hodder, I., and C. Orton
1976   *Spatial Analysis in Archaeology*. Cambridge University Press, Cambridge.

Jones, K. T., and D. B. Madsen
1989   Calculating the Cost of Resource Transportation: A Great Basin Example. *Current Anthropology* 30(4):529-534.

Kelly, R. L.
1983   Hunter-gatherer Mobility Strategies. *Journal of Anthropological Research* 39:277-306.
1985   *Hunter-gatherer Mobility and Sedentism: A Great Basin Study*. Ph.D. dissertation, Department of Anthropology, University of Michigan. University Microfilms, Ann Arbor.
1988   The Three Sides of a Biface. *American Antiquity* 53:717-734.

Livingston, S. D.
1986   The Archaeology of the Humboldt Lakebed Site. *Journal of California and Great Basin Anthropology* 8(1):99-115.
1988   *The Avian and Mammalian Faunas from Lovelock Cave and the Humboldt Lakebed Site*. Unpublished Ph.D. dissertation, Department of Anthropology, University of Washington, Seattle.

Loud, L. L., and M. R. Harrington
1929   Lovelock Cave. *University of California Publications in American Archaeology and Ethnology* 25(1). Berkeley.

Napton, L. K.
1969   The Lacustrine Subsistence Pattern in the Desert West. In *Archaeological and Paleobiological Investigations in Lovelock Cave, Nevada*, by L. K. Napton, pp. 28–97. Kroeber Anthropological Society Special Papers No. 2. Berkeley.

Napton, L. K., and R. F. Heizer
1970   Analysis of Human Coprolites from Archaeological Contexts, with Primary Reference to Lovelock Cave, Nevada. In *Archaeology and the Prehistoric Great Basin Lacustrine Subsistence Regime as Seen from Lovelock Cave, Nevada*, by R. F. Heizer and L. K. Napton, pp. 87-109. Contributions of the University of California Archaeological Research Facility No. 10. Berkeley.

Pippin, L. C.
1980   *Prehistoric and Historic Patterns of Lower Pinyon-Juniper Woodland Ecotone Exploitation at Borealis, Mineral County, Nevada*. Desert Research Institute Technical Report No. 17. Reno.

Rhode, D.
1987   *The Mountains and the Lake: Prehistoric Lacustrine-Upland Settlement Relationships in the Walker Watershed, Western Nevada*. Unpublished Ph.D. dissertation, Department of Anthropology, University of Washington, Seattle.

Roust, N. L.
1967   Preliminary Examination of Prehistoric Human Coprolites from Four Western Nevada Caves. In *Papers on Great Basin Archaeology*, pp. 49-88. University of California Archaeological Survey Reports No. 70 Berkeley.

Smith, G. R.
1985   Paleontology of Hidden Cave: Fish. In *The Archaeology of Hidden Cave, Nevada*, edited by D. H. Thomas, pp. 171-178. Anthropological Papers of the American Museum of Natural History 61(1). New York.

Snyder, J.
1917   The Fishes of the Lahontan System of Nevada and Northeastern California. *U.S. Bureau of Fisheries Bulletin* 35:33-86. Washington, D.C.

Stewart, O. C.
1941   Culture Element Distributions: XIV. Northern Paiute. *University of California Anthropological Records* 4(3). Berkeley.

Thomas, D. H.
  1985   *The Archaeology of Hidden Cave, Nevada*. Anthropological Papers of the American Museum of Natural History 61(1). New
          York.
Wheat, M. M.
  1967   *Survival Arts of the Primitive Paiutes*. University of Nevada Press, Reno.
Wigand, P. E., and P. J. Mehringer, Jr.
  1985   Pollen and Seed Analyses. In *The Archaeology of Hidden Cave, Nevada*, edited by D. H. Thomas, pp. 108-124. Anthropological
          Papers of the American Museum of Natural History 61(1). New York.

9

PYRAMID LAKE FISHING: THE ARCHAEOLOGICAL RECORD

Donald R. Tuohy

Abstract

The Lower Truckee Basin in western Nevada is comprised of two adjacent and connected basins; one holding the living Pyramid Lake, the other a playa, holding the former Lake Winnemucca. They were both fed largely by runoff from the Sierra Nevada via the Truckee River. An extensive freshwater fishery, the Lower Truckee Basin formerly supplied one of the most important staple foods of the region, fish. The principal prehistoric (and historic) food fishes were the tui chub, the kuyui, the Lahontan cutthroat trout, and the Tahoe sucker. The surviving Northern Paiute took these fishes and some others by using a number of ethnographic traits both in the use of lake fishing and river fishing. In this paper these ethnographic traits used in the taking of fish are compared with the archaeological record. The archaeological record, with dates going back nearly 10,000 years, seems to be unrelated to the ethnographic record.

The "kin–ordered mode" of fish production (Wolf 1982:88–96) was used for 9,000 years, and when the "capitalist mode" took over about A.D. 1850, it spelled a death knell to the cutthroat trout by A.D. 1940. The U.S. government now subsidizes a sports fishery operation run by the Pyramid Lake Paiutes.

Introduction

Fowler and Bath (1981:176–186) and Fowler (1989) have illuminated the ethnographic record for Northern Paiute fishing, particularly at Pyramid Lake, a large freshwater fishery located in west–central Nevada. Their studies were based on original field research of museum collections of fishing gear, data drawn from the unpublished field notes on the Pyramid Lake Paiutes made by the ethnographer Willard Z. Park, and a comparative ethnological study of lake margin cultural adaptations made by Bath (1978). Thus, a succinct and accurate portrayal of the material culture and behavioral patterns utilized in river and lake fishing by the Northern Paiutes exists, particularly when supplemented by data drawn from the reports of Lowie (1924), Curtis (1926), Stewart (1941), Fowler and Matley (1978), Powers (Fowler and Fowler 1970), and Knack and Stewart (1984).

The ethnographic pattern for the Lower Truckee River Basin, comprised of Lake Winnemucca and Pyramid Lake, is that of the *Kuyuitikadi Paiutes*, or black sucker eaters, (after *Chasmistes cujus*, or kuyui, a distinctive black sucker that thrives in the Lahontan Basin). The *Kuyuitikadi* not only relied upon kuyui, but other endemic fish species of the Basin, including the Lahontan cutthroat trout (*Salmo clarki henshawii*), the Tahoe sucker (*Catostomus tahoensis*), the Lahontan tui chub (*Gila bicolor*), the Lahontan redside (*Richardsonius egregious*), and the Lahontan speckled dace (*Rhinichthys osculus*) (LaRivers 1962:193–592).

On the basis of their studies, Fowler and Bath (1981) concluded that some of the features of western Nevada ethnographic fishing show a continuum from the Klamath area to the Pacific Coast, as noted previously by Kroeber and Barrett (1960), and that these features ". . . seem to have been well established in the western Great Basin in the prehistoric past" (Fowler and Bath 1981:186).

The Problem

Fishing has long been recognized as enhancing the economic intensification of hunters and gatherers the world over. The bountiful, but usually seasonal, nature of fishery resources often has led to increased social complexity among hunters and gatherers. A review of the archaeological record of fishery exploitation in the Lower Truckee Basin, when compared to the known ethnographic record of *Kuyuitikadi* fishing, ought to provide further insights into lakeside cultural adaptations through time in a desert environment. It is toward this goal that the majority of this paper is structured.

The Lower Truckee Basin Fishery

Geographically, the lower Truckee Basin lies to the northeast of Reno in Washoe County, Nevada (Figure 1). Pyramid Lake itself is 300 feet deep and 35 miles long, about the size of Lake Tahoe, but unlike the latter, its width varies from 4 to 12 miles, and it is much shallower, with a maximum depth of 330 feet. Lake Winnemucca, its sister basin, is much narrower and also shallower although it too, is about 35 miles long. The Winnemucca Basin is presently a playa, and both basins form the evaporative pan for the Truckee River. Both lakes contain a high percentage of dissolved solids, and their waters are highly saline and alkaline, but potable.

An original reference work on fishes on the Lahontan system, of which Pyramid Lake is the deepest part, was published by Snyder (1917). At the time, Snyder named some new species, later corrected by LaRivers (1962:24), and those endemic species mentioned above comprised the principal aboriginal food fishes in the Lower Truckee Basin. Two of the six species, the "black sucker," or kuyui, and the cutthroat trout, were the principal focus of Northern Paiute subsistence activities, particularly during annual spawning runs up the Truckee River (Wheat 1967:60–61 and Brink 1969:42).

Since the spawning runs were determined by natural processes, not cultural, it is fair to speculate that the timing of the runs was essentially the same in the prehistoric past as in the ethnographic present. Fowler and Bath (1981:177) note that fishing was potentially a year–round activity for the Pyramid Lake Paiute. This was due in part to the winter and spring timing of the two cutthroat runs, the late spring *kuyui* run, and the spring runs of the lesser food fishes, such as the Tahoe suckers, redsides, speckled dace and the tui chub (Zeier and Elston 1986:361, Figure 100).

The Ethnographic Baseline

A variety of techniques and fishing technology was used by Northern Paiutes of the Desert West. Of the nine Northern Paiute "fishing" tribes represented, the Pyramid Lake Paiutes, had the highest number of "fishing traits"—twelve. Among them were: weir fishing from a platform, white rock paving of the stream channel, sack dip net, gill net, trot line, pole with a line and hook, river bank platform, boat or raft, V–frame dip net, weir

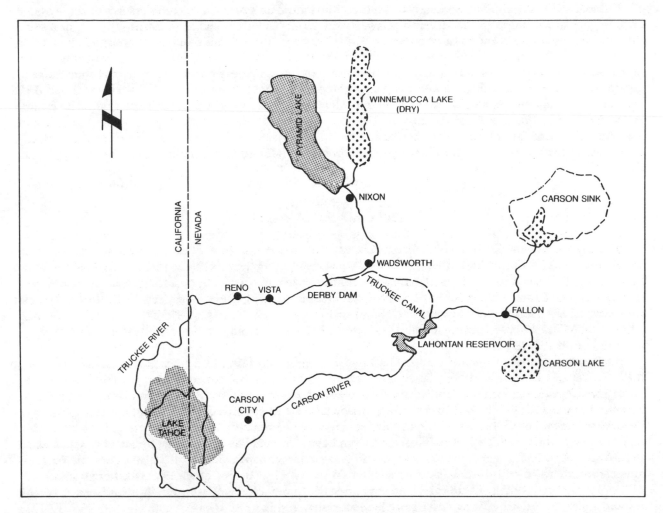

Figure 1. Sketch map of the Lower Truckee Basin, Pyramid Lake and Winnemucca Lake, in western Nevada. Map after Born (1972:41, Figure 31). It is 35 miles from Reno to Wadsworth.

plus a basket trap, basket trap and a harpoon or a spear used to catch fish (Bath 1978:96). These techniques were used for fishing in both the lake and the river.

Weirs and platforms were used in river fishing in conjunction with both dip nets and basket traps. The weir would span the river completely enough to obstruct fish. On the downstream side a basket trap would be secured to the weir. Also used in river fishing was a trap secured by two sticks which were fixed in the river bottom. Weirs, platforms, harpoons and spears were used in several ways in river fishing. Very often in conjunction with platforms, the river would be paved with white rocks to increase visibility. Harpoons of the unilaterally barbed bone type were used from platforms from the river bank but also on the lake shore.

Along with fishing platforms and weirs used by the ethnographic Northern Paiute of western Nevada, Fowler and Bath (1981:177–184) indicate that lifting nets, fish baskets, dip nets made with a carved wooden shuttle and wooden gage, two types of basket traps, and a weir–and–basket trap, single and double pointed harpoons and a bipointed leister were used in river fishing. Some very interesting insights into fishing at Winnemucca Lake as well as Pyramid Lake and Truckee River are found in Follett (1982) who interviewed Harry Winnemucca, a Pyramid Lake Paiute.

Ethnographic lake fishing apparently was more of an individual enterprise accomplished with set lines, gill nets, single–barbed harpoons, and trident spears (Bath 1978:42–52; Fowler and Bath 1981:183). Elliptical stone sinkers were used on set lines and on sticks used in gill netting. Rock weights were also attached to each end of the gill net. Fishhooks for minnows were gorge hooks of sharpened rabbit bone, or composite hooks made of split–willow folded in half with a tiny bone pin in the bite. Trout hooks were composite, and were made of greasewood with the shank of the hook having a concave socket to receive the cylindrical barb (Fowler and Bath 1981:184). Fowler and Bath (1981:185) also describe a triangular–shaped obsidian knife used for filleting *kuyui* by the Northern Paiutes of Pyramid Lake.

Thus, the material culture traits used in fishing by inhabitants of the Lower Truckee Basin are clearly demarcated. Prehistoric fishing techniques presumably may be inferred by comparing similar artifact types with the known ethnohistoric ones.

The Archaeological Record

The archaeological recovery of fish remains of species endemic to the Lahontan Basin is not at all uncommon. W. I. Follett (1963, 1969, 1970, 1974, 1977, 1980, 1982, and 1985) has reported the bulk of these finds. Other fish remains have been identified as constituents in coprolites or as ecofacts at other archaeological sites (Zeier and Elston 1986; Schmitt et al. 1986:359; Dansie 1987b:33; Tuohy and Clark 1979:328,465; Napton and Heizer 1970; Heizer and Napton 1970; Heizer and Krieger 1956:33; Riddell 1956:17; Orr 1956:6, 1952:12; Hubbs and Miller 1948:41; and Loud and Harrington 1929:36). A summary of most of these finds by species is listed in Follett (1982:183).

Archaeological evidence demonstrates that Lahontan Basin food fishes have been utilized since about 9000 B.P. (Rusco and Davis 1987:193). There are a number of radiocarbon dates that support this contention. Stratigraphic evidence includes fish bones themselves, recovered from a "Pre–Mazama" site in the lower Humboldt River Valley, 26Pe 670, one of which was identified as a specimen of a large trout (Dansie 1987a:145). The oldest known Lower Truckee Basin fishing line, made of sagebrush bark, yielded a date of 9660 ± 170 B.P. (GX–13744) (Tuohy 1988:225), while the oldest known Lower Truckee Basin fishing net fragment has been dated at 7,830 ± 350 B.P. (L–289KK) (Orr 1974:50). In a fairly recent paper, Follett (1982:188) gives the range or radiocarbon dates of 49 fish remains from about 9600 to 600 B.P. (Berger et al. 1965:340; Berger and Libby 1966:472; Shutler 1968:25). There can be no doubt that the Lower Truckee Basin with its abundance of protein resources was an extensive fishery ever since humans discovered it.

Yet the archaeological record of those technological adjustments and changes will always be deficient to some extent. Some of the more fragile items, such as vegetable fiber fishing lines, nets and baskets disintegrate rapidly after having been submerged, and usually buried, and then, again, having been exposed to sunlight. The northwest shore of Pyramid Lake, deflating rapidly, seems to have been an area where much of that kind of perishable artifact deposition and reappearance has taken place (Tuohy 1988).

Two recent perishable finds of fishes in the Lower Truckee Basin are important as examples of prehistoric storage of fish. Hidden away in the collections area of the Nevada State Museum, we found 971 Tui chubs, from Stick Cave at the northeastern end of Winnemucca Lake (Figure 2). They came from several caches and the largest fish was 12 cm in length and the shortest, 7.5 cm. According to Anan Raymond (personal communication 1989), Fish and Wildlife archaeologist, these tui chubs were of comparable size and conformation compared to the ones recently found in the flooding of the Stillwater Wildlife Refuge near Fallon, Nevada.

A second find was sent to the Nevada State Museum by a Californian who had excavated a cave on the northeast end of Winnemucca Lake. In the cave he found a cache, consisting of some bunch grass, a filleted kuyui, and an open–work, twined–style, conical–shaped basket. The fish had been split along the back bone and the entrails removed, but the head was still attached to the dorsal half. The two halves of the fish were still attached to one another, as shown in Figure 3. Baskets had been found at sites in the northwest section of Pyramid Lake, but they were of the close twining type, and not the open–work, conically–shaped type of carrying basket (Figure 4) (Tuohy 1988:212). The whole cache was of some interest to us, as it showed just how food

Figure 2. Tui chub (*Gila bicolor*) from Stick Cave (25Pe 1a) on the northeast corner of **Winnemucca Lake**. The photo shows 31 of the 917 chubs that were found there. The collection is in the **Nevada State Museum**, photograph by Anan Raymond.

fishes were preserved by drying them whole for a later meal. As in the case of the 971 tui chubs, this cache of the whole *kuyui* was placed in a cave, we think, as a grave offering (a later visit to the site found human bone on the back dirt pile). The Paiutes continued the tradition of drying fish for subsistence use until the 1920s and 1930s, when this activity declined. Some fish, without heads, are shown in Knack and Stewart (1984:Plate 10) air-drying for future use.

In addition to lengths of fishing line or net line, the Pyramid Lake Basin, in particular, has yielded literally thousands of historic and prehistoric artifacts, mostly net sinkers, associated with fishing. Only a fraction of this total has been professionally recorded or sampled. Nevertheless, the range of artifact classes recovered is believed sufficient to portray the equipment types utilized throughout human use of the fishery. The following sections review the material remains that refelct fishing practices. To make comparisons with the ethnographic record easier, the artifact classes will be divided into those presumably associated with either river or lake fishing.

Archaeological Evidence of the Ethnographic Period Fishing (Post A.D. 1840)

No structural remains of fishing platforms, weirs, or white-rock river bottom pavement areas have been recorded archaeologically for the Lower Truckee River Basin. Dam construction, siltation and erosion of the Truckee River bed, and archaeological sampling errors may account for this dearth of recorded sites with historic structural features. The most common structural feature noted in the Pyramid Lake Basin is a low circular stone wall, one or more rock courses high, and ranging in size from one to four meters in diameter. When found on

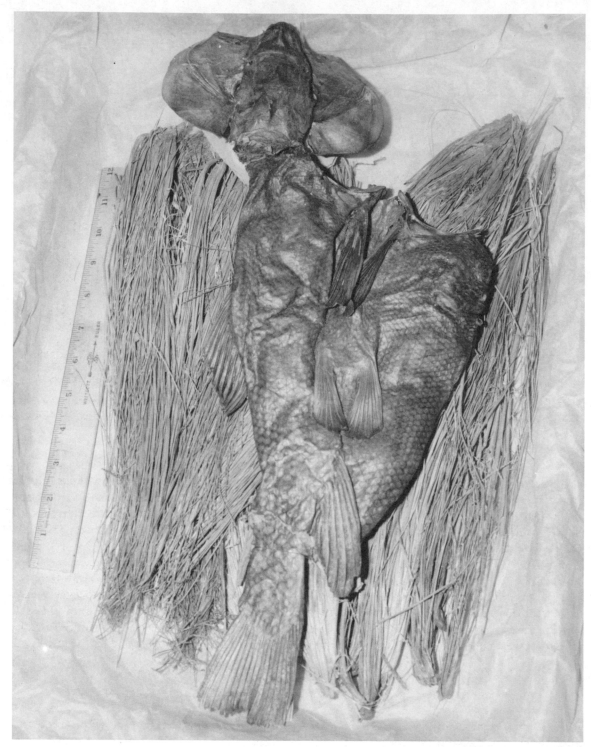

Figure 3. Mummified fish, *kuyui* (*Chasmistes cujus Cope*), found in a disturbed cave with two clumps of bunch grass and a carrying basket in association. Each *kuyui* was split along the backbone with the head still on and left to dry. R. G. Allen collection at the Nevada State Museum. Photograph by Phil Hutchinson.

Figure 4. One of two baskets of twined construction used in fishing and found on the flats on the northwestern corner of Pyramid Lake by Steve Wallmann. He donated it to the Nevada State Museum where it was preserved by Amy Dansie.

historic lake shorelines, these features have been interpreted as historic–period, small boat anchorages, or mooring areas, or temporary open–air camps.

In addition to these structural features, there were historic period fishery artifacts made by Europeans that were manufactured and distributed over the Pyramid Lake Basin. This artifact inventory includes all the metallic hooks, sinkers, spinners and weights that comprise modern fishing gear. The time frame for these artifacts is extended backwards to around A.D. 1800 as trade goods preceded the arrival of the first European. A sampling of these goods is shown in Figures 5 and 6.

As an example of the latter, an historic European's fishing kit was discovered in a cave on the western shore of Winnemucca Lake in 1956. This cache was unearthed by Leroy Giles and it is presently on display in the Nevada State Museum's historical gallery. The artifacts include camp gear, armament, and fishing gear. They were found with an 1889 newspaper and are attributed to a date of 1893.

By 1869, Anglo trespass upon the Pyramid Lake fishing grounds was well established (Knack and Stewart 1984:154-178). The Anglo fishermen were pretty well equipped. The camp gear in the fishing cache included seven items, including a coffee grinder and a box full of matches. Armament included 49 items including a can of Prussian blue paint and 18 cartridges in a box labelled: "centre-rimmed metallic cartridges adapted to U.S. Springfield muskets." But the fishing gear was most impressive, and it included the following:

1. One metal oar lock
2. One five–inch spinner, painted red
3. One two–inch spinner, painted red
4. One five–inch spinner, metallic
5. One box of metal fishhooks
6. One fishing line, wrapped on wooden holders
7. Fourteen, round lead sinkers
8. Two, wooden net shuttles
9. Three fish net floats of wood
10. One wooden template for making fish spinners
11. Two pairs of shears
12. One brass spring balance; up to 40 lbs.

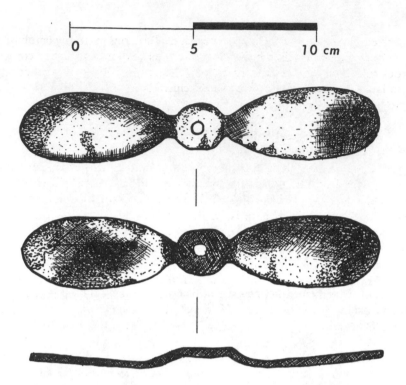

Figure 5. A modern metallic propeller retrieved from site 26Wa 233A/423, a site on the northwest corner of Pyramid Lake. Harry Norcross, Jr., collection. Drawing by June Eustice.

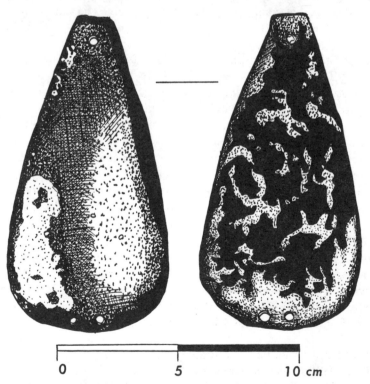

Figure 6. A metallic spinner retrieved from the northwest shore of Pyramid Lake from site 26Wa 233A/312. The Harry Norcross, Jr., collection. Drawing by June Eustice.

These artifacts emphasize the Anglos new techniques of fish capture, but primarily emphasize wooden boats for use on the open lake. Other techniques used by Anglos were the use of nets stretched completely across the Truckee River during trout runs, and the use of a "grab hook". The "grab hook" was a hooked metal gaff for raking fish ashore. These latter two techniques were used exclusively for river fishing.

Archaeological Evidence of Prehistoric Fishing

As noted, the collection of prehistoric fishing apparatus from Pyramid Lake is extensive, numbering over 500 specimens (including net sinkers), from the northwest quadrant of the lake alone. The excavations that were carried out at seventy-plus sites at Pyramid Lake yielded their share of fishing equipment, too, and part of it is illustrated in this paper. But the emphasis here is on the private collections made at Pyramid Lake, and subsequently donated to the Nevada State Museum. As an example, part of the fishing gear was studied by Peter Ting, Sr., (1966, 1967 and 1983) and part of it was studied by Harry A. Norcross and Frances Riddell (1974). I also published a paper on a group of Ting's fishing sinkers (Tuohy 1968), but all previous studies were incomplete or ignored one aspect or another of the fishing gear entirely. With the donation of the Peter Ting, Sr., collection and the Harry Norcross collection to the Nevada State Museum, steps may be taken to establish a typology for all types of fishing gear.

Typology of Fishhooks and Spears

The initial classification of Pyramid Lake fishhooks was made by Peter C. Ting, Sr., who was president of the Am-Arcs of Nevada, a Reno, Nevada archaeological society, in 1968. The article he wrote included a total of 32 fishhooks he and his son, Peter Ting, Jr., had gathered from the shores of Pyramid Lake. His classification included seven types of hooks including the following (Ting 1968:5-10):

1. Unilaterally barbed; tang with one surface beveled (9)
2. Leister type; unilaterally barbed; tang knobbed (2)
3. Multipointed type; barbless (8)
4. Simple cylindrical; tang beveled, same width as base of point (3)
5. Simple willow-leaf shaped; tang carved on all sides, narrower than base of point (1)
6. Bi-pointed (8)
7. Composite harpoon

The first classification of fishhooks in the western Great Basin occurred when Lovelock Cave was published in 1929 (Loud and Harrington 1929). That publication showed two types of hooks: (1) a set line, 22 feet long, with twelve hooks with bone barbs set at a right angle on the fiber shanks, a so-called "trot line" and (2) two fishhook barbs with unbarbed tips about an inch long, and attached to a wooden shaft. When Heizer and Krieger (1956) published on the archaeology of Humboldt Cave they named the two hooks they found, Types 1 and 2. Hook type 1 showed barbed bone hooks attached to wooden shanks, and Hook Type 2 was the familiar "trot line," with the right-angle hooks. But there was another hook type shown in their illustration (Heizer and Krieger 1956:Plate 143a) which was not given a number. It is a fishhook with a bone point (that is unbarbed) attached to a wooden shaft. So, all in all, there were three types of fishhooks represented in the archaeological literature until the 1960's. Only the "trot line" was said to be used both in prehistoric and historic times (Heizer and Krieger 1956:77).

These three types of fishhooks should be incorporated into a typology which includes all of their features. In a reassessment of the Peter Ting, Sr., classification of Pyramid Lake fishhooks, I have eliminated two of his categories: his "category 5," simple willow-leaf shaped carved bone fishhook, with the tang curved on all sides, and narrower than the base of the point, and "category 7," the composite harpoon. The reason for eliminating "category 5" was that it was a bipointed hook represented by a total of three examples. I thought that these stout hooks would fit in with the bipointed hook having rounded cross–sections. His "category 7" composite harpoon, is a single instance of a toggle type harpoon which he put together from three parts. Two parts, believed to be spurs, were found by his son, and ten feet away was the center piercing point. However, a third spur was found several yards away from the find spots of the former. They were not tied together, and I believe Ting made a mistake when he typed the parts. As he says himself: "As the Pyramid Lake "harpoon" is not identical to any known type of composite harpoon, the author will be the first to admit that his interpretation may be wrong" (Ting 1968:10). Both double and single pointed harpoons were made by the Pyramid Lake Paiute (Fowler and Bath 1981:Figures 7 and 8, 182–183), and these were made from a socketed bone head fitted to a greasewood foreshaft.

Peter Ting, Sr., only had 32 fishhooks to type, and he wound up with 7 types of fishhooks. Including the Peter Ting, Sr., collection, the Harry Norcross collection and the Louis Sabini collection, there are now over 100 fishhooks to type. These came from sites situated in the Quaternary alluvial deposits surrounding Pyramid Lake. My typology of Pyramid Lake fishhooks follows:

I. Barbed
   A. Fixed barb spear points
   B. Leister type, unilaterally barbed
II. Unbarbed
   A. Bipointed hooks
      1. Round to oval cross–sections
         a) Hafted at the end
         b) Hafted in the center
      2. Half–round to flat cross–sections
         a) Hafted at the end
         b) Hafted in the center
   B. Single–pointed hooks
      1. Large (more than 5 cm in length)
      2. Small (less than 5 cm in length)
   C. Other types of hooks
      1. V–shaped, made of bone
      2. Lozenge–shaped hooks
III. Fishhook blanks

Barbed–Fixed Spear Points

The unilaterally barbed bone harpoons are shown in Figure 7. They were first described for Pyramid Lake by Rendall (1966) and by Ting (1967). At first, some credence was given to the bone harpoons being transported into Pyramid Lake from elsewhere. But when more of them became known, it was decided that they were of local manufacture, after all.

They vary in length from 122 mm to 266.6 mm, and in width to a maximum of 18.5 mm, and in thickness from about 6 mm to about 9 mm. The number of barbs on the known harpoons vary from three to a maximum of twenty. The barbs are carved at about a 30 to a 45 degree angle to the longitudinal axis. Ting (1967:5) noted the similarity in the Pyramid Lake barbed bone spear point to certain Fuegian fixed barbed spear points (Mason 1902:212, Plate 2) and to certain Magdalenian barbed bone or antler points (Oakley 1950:85, Figure 39c). Two of the fixed barb spear points are in the Peter Ting, Sr., collection and all the rest are in private hands.

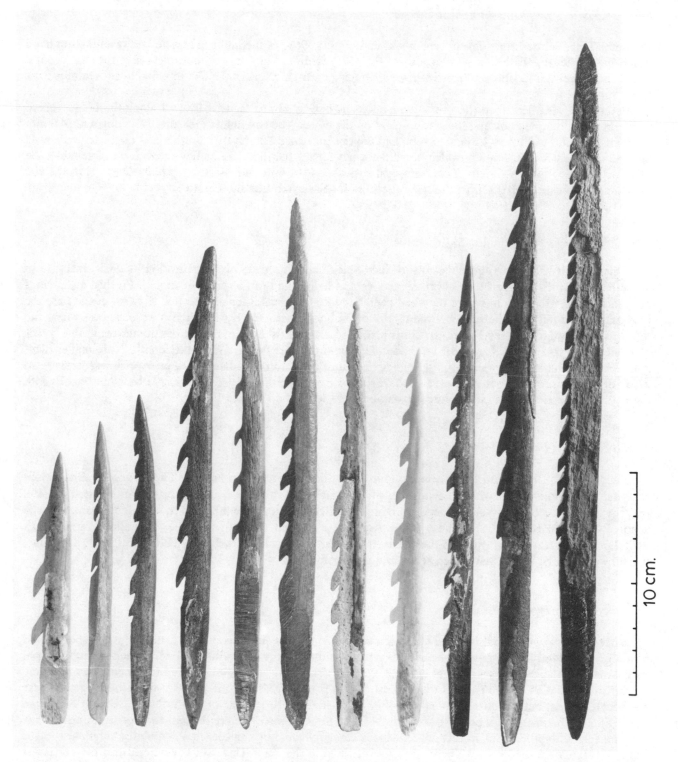

Figure 7. Fixed unilaterally barbed spear points from the northwest end of Pyramid Lake, used in lake fishing. They were borrowed by Peter Ting, Sr., from several private collectors, and five of them belong in the Peter Ting, Sr., collection or the Peter Ting, Jr., collection. One of them, 2392-G-1124, the third from the left, is still in the Peter Ting Sr., collection at the Nevada State Museum.

Barbed–Leister Type Hooks (not illustrated)

Peter Ting, Sr., described leister type hooks in 1967 and 1968. In the latter paper, he had two hooks in hand which he considered as leister. As Rostlund (1952:105) said, ". . . in a leister the function of the side prongs, which are somewhat flexible and provided with in–facing barbs, is to grasp the fish in a manner resembling that of ice tongs."

Peter Ting, Sr., described the leister type hooks as having inward facing barbs all along the hook. There were ten barbs on one hook and there were eight on the other. The two points measured 43.5 mm and 54.0 mm in length, and the width was 4 mm to 5 mm, and the thickness was 2.0 mm to 2.3 mm. Leister spears were used on the Northwest Coast, some of which had a detachable head, but there are so few recovered at Pyramid Lake that perhaps they were a variety of two–pronged spear heads (Driver and Massey 1957:201–208). Nonetheless, Fowler and Fowler (1981:192) list the use of leisters for the Pyramid Lake Paiutes.

Unbarbed–Bipointed Hooks

This category has been entirely changed since Peter Ting, Sr., made his classification in 1968. Included in it are bipoints with rounded to oval cross–sections and half–round to flat cross–sections. Further distinctions are made among them as to where they had been hafted, in the center, or on one point. Most of the time the typologist could tell the difference between styles of fishhooks, particularly where there were grooves where the line was to be attached (see Figure 8). This bipointed class of fishhooks is the most numerous in the Lower Truckee Basin collection. Sizes varied considerably, but most were two to four cm in length. The smaller ones, hafted in the middle and with a hook on either end, are believed to have been used in river fishing because so many of them were found at sites next to the Truckee River (see Figure 9). The larger bipointed hooks with the rounded cross–sections (see Figure 10) are believed to be used in lake fishing.

Unbarbed–Single–Pointed Hooks

Single–pointed hooks are hard to separate from the double pointed examples. The former have one blunt end that is not pointed but which may be shaped for attachment to the point, but most often, it is not. In size, they vary from less than two cm in length to more than 10 cm. They were attached to a wooden shank to make a hook ("type 2") (Figure 11). These hooks were set at a right angle to take fish in shallow water. Such "trot–line" hooks turn cross–ways in the fishes' throat. In line fishing, a weight is tied to one end of the line, but no weights tied to line have been recovered archaeologically.

Unbarbed–Other Types of Fishhooks

There are two additional types of fishhooks that were not previously considered, although they both could have been included in the "bipointed class." We recovered two pairs of bipointed bone fishhooks from a burial cave on the east shore of Pyramid Lake, site 26Wa 315. The bone points were lashed together with a very fine mesh fishing cord. The two pairs of them are shown in Figure 12. The bone points were lashed together near the beveled ends, but we do not know how they were attached to a spear or to the line. Because they were found next to the lake, these bone hooks were believed to be involved in lake fishing, and not in stream fishing.

The second type of hook in this miscellaneous category could be considered a "bipointed" hook also. It is called a lozenge–shaped hook. There were five of them in the Peter Ting, Sr., collection from the northwest shore of Pyramid Lake, and they are not illustrated in this paper. They look like more robust versions of the bipointed hooks shown in Figure 8, but they did not have the central grooved area for hafting. These lozenge–shaped hooks were also hafted in the central area with the two sharpened points sticking out on each side.

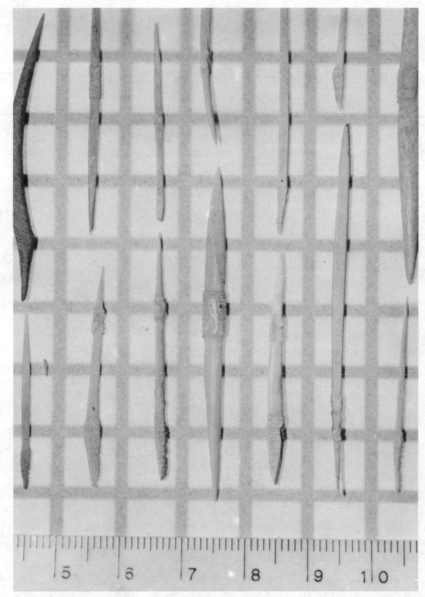

Figure 8. Fourteen bone bipointed hooks showing the place where they were hafted to the line in a medial position, or at one end of the hook. All of them came from sites at the northwest end of Pyramid Lake. Peter C. Ting collection 2392-G-1100 through 2392-G-1200. Photograph by Phil Hutchinson.

Fishhook Blanks

These are shown in the extreme right of the bottom row of the Sabini collection (Figure 9), and in the last row of the Harry Norcross collection (Figure 13p). There are a total of four hooks which can be considered "blanks." They all need more work to shape them off into one type of hook or another.

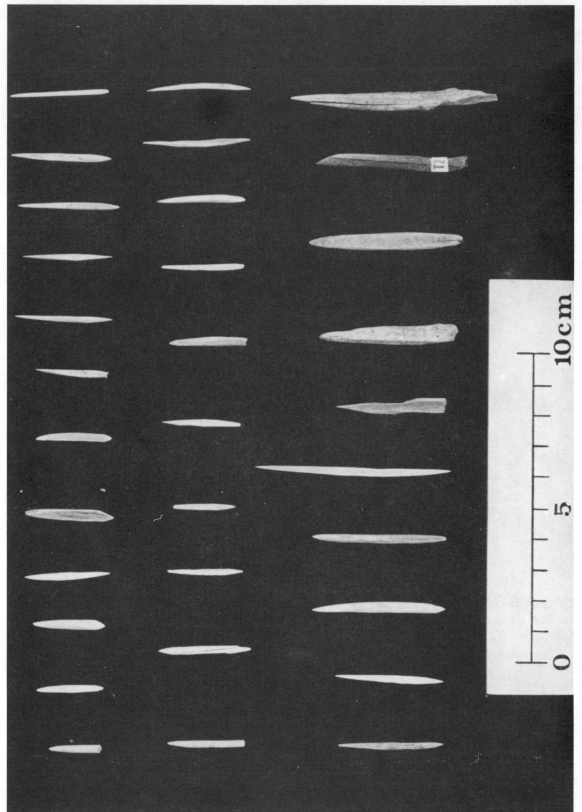

Figure 9. Fishhooks used in river fishing. They all came from sites in the vicinity of Marble Bluff, next to the Truckee River. Shown are 23 bipointed hooks, 5 single pointed hooks, one large single pointed hook (third from left in the last row), and awls and fishhook blanks (the last four pieces in the third row). Sabini collection, uncataloged; still in private hands.

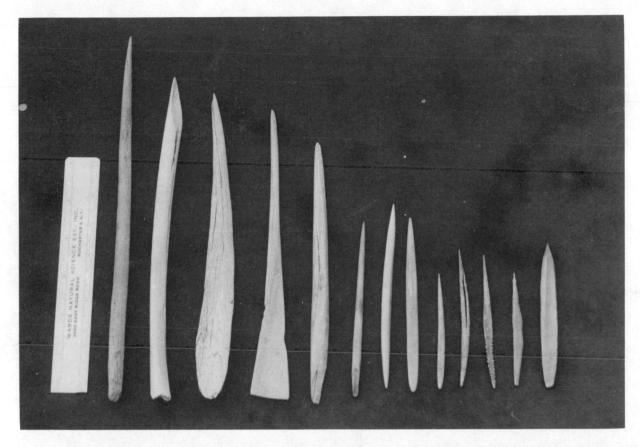

Figure 10. Awls and fishhooks from the Peter Ting, Sr., collection. The five awls are on the left, and the eight fishhooks are on the right. There are two bipoints on the right and the rest of the fishhooks are single-pointed. Peter Ting, Sr., Collection 2392-G, Plaque 6.

The Oldest Surface Collection of Fishhooks from Pyramid Lake

What is purported to be the oldest collection of fishhooks from Pyramid Lake is shown in Figure 13. The collection came from site 26Wa 221 at the northwest corner of Pyramid Lake. The Harry Norcross, Jr., collection was made in 1965 when the lake was at its lowest point, about 3,789 feet. The fishhooks were collected from the lower level, that is, the newly exposed beach, at this site. Other types of artifacts provide clues as to the age of the site. Harry Norcross, Jr., and Fritz Riddell (1974:4) recorded some large Northern Side–notched, Elko, Pinto, and Martis points and a couple of crescents from this site. The upper level of this site, that is, the higher beach, extending from 3,790 to 3,800 feet, yielded Northern Side–notched, Elko, Pinto, and Humboldt points, and also a rather remarkable collection of atlatl weights. In addition to these artifacts, there were a variety of knobbed and grooved sinkers, and several centrally perforated stone discoidals (see Net Sinkers section below). The list of artifacts from the lower portion of the site, according to Norcross and Riddell (1974:4) included:

> . . . a scapula saw, numerous gorge hooks, flaking tools, bone pins, parts of composite fishhooks, and a unilaterally barbed point. . . . Spatulate bone (hair?) pins and an L–shaped scapula awl (pin?) enrich the inventory. Sinkers and atlatl weights also occur.

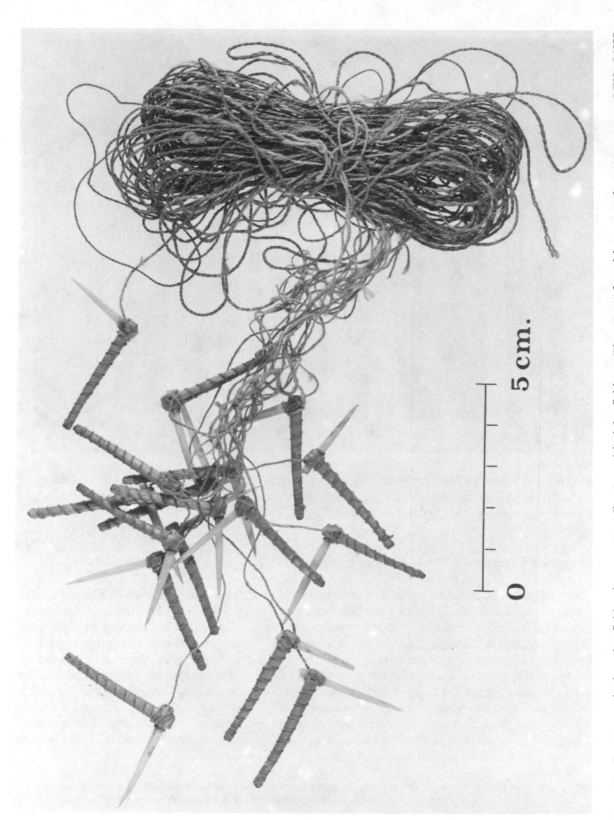

Figure 11. Seventeen single point fishhooks on a "trot line," used in lake fishing. They were found in a potted-out cave, near 26Wa 348H, on the east side of Pyramid Lake. Wheat collection, 101 in the Nevada State Museum.

5 cm.

0

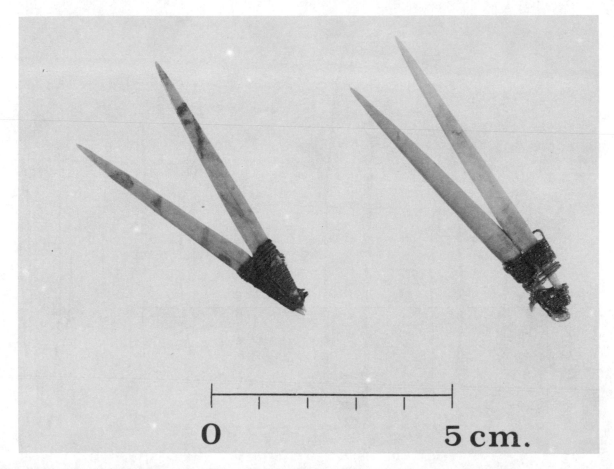

0   5 cm.

Figure 12. Composite hooks made of bone for lake fishing. They were found at 26Wa 315, a site on the east shore of Pyramid Lake. Nevada State Museum collection, 268 and 497.

The Harry Norcross, Jr., collection spent several years in the State Indian Museum in Sacramento, California, before it was turned over to the Nevada State Museum in Carson City. Including the fishhooks presented here, there are more than 765 specimens in that collection. These came from all around the lake, and they will be described in a future paper. The one pertinent radiocarbon date on a three ply fishing line, 9960 ± 170 B.P. (Gx-13744, Tuohy 1988) came from one of eight sites (26Wa 217) that were located with precision to the northwest section of Pyramid Lake. That site was on the same lake level, 3,780 to 3,800 feet, as the site yielding the collection of fishhooks (26Wa 221), and our estimate is that these two sites were coeval. When all of the artifacts have been described, we may come to a different conclusion, but right now, the inference is made that this collection of fishhooks in the oldest known from Pyramid Lake.

Originally there were 27 fishhooks in the Norcross collection, but only sixteen of them were illustrated in Figure 13. It is to be noted that six types of fishhooks are represented in the collection, and they are: the fixed unilaterally barbed bone spear point (Figure 13c); the bipointed hook having a round to oval cross-section (Figure 13d, e, h, i, j, k, m, n, and o); the bipointed hook with the round to oval cross-section hafted in the center (Figure 13f); the single-pointed hooks, large (Figure 13a, b, and p); the single pointed hooks, small (Figure 13g and l); and the fishhook blank (Figure 13g).

This variety of fishhook types indicates the inference that the native people of Pyramid Lake knew (at a very early time period) the kinds of fish they wished to catch, and they adapted their bone technology to this purpose. The husbanding of animal bones and antlers to make fishhooks could be considered a step toward making hunters and gatherers become more reliant upon their lacustrine environment.

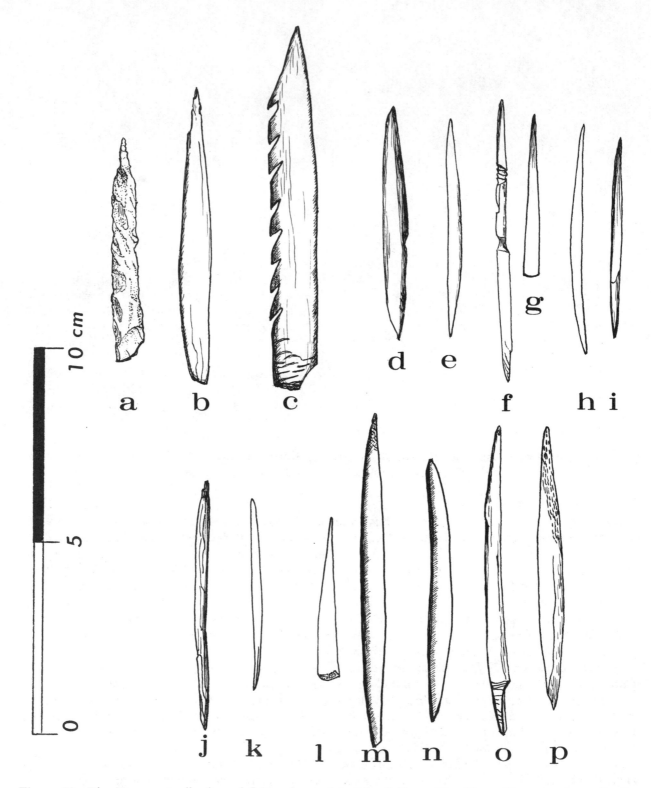

Figure 13. The Norcross collection of fishhooks used in lake fishing. The Harry Norcross, Jr., collection, 26Wa 221B/14 through 26Wa 221B/41, all from the northwest portion of Pyramid Lake.

Figure 14. Three wooden artifacts from the northeastern end of Winnemucca Lake which were identified as "fishhooks" by Phil Orr (1952:13, Figure 5) but were later identified as parts to a trap utilizing a scissors snare (Janetski 1979:Figure 8b).

Before bringing this discussion of Pyramid Lake fishhooks to a close, there is one error about fishhooks in the literature that the Nevada State Museum perpetrated. In the Nevada State Museum *Bulletin Number 1* "Preliminary Excavations of Pershing County Caves," Orr (1952:12-13) describes two small "fishhooks." Orr (1952:12) identifies them as ". . . made of the natural branch of a twig, and the "point" is very dull." Further research of these hooks, and three others shown in our Figure 14, showing the attached lines, demonstrated that they were not fishhooks, but triggers to a scissors snare (Janetski 1979:Figure 8b). Thus, parts of a rodent or small animal trap were confused in the literature of the western Great Basin as fishhooks.

Other Types of Archaeological Fishing Equipment

Besides the various types of fishhooks that have shown up in the surface archaeology, there are also some other types of fishing equipment that have appeared in the Lower Truckee Basin. I have already mentioned the sagebrush bark fishing line collected at 26Wa 217. It was Z-twisted, and it came in two-ply and three-ply gauges. There are also a home-made wooden float, canoe anchor stones, and various types of net weights. The latter occur in clusters at Pyramid and Winnemucca Lakes and are often picked up and taken home by the collectors.

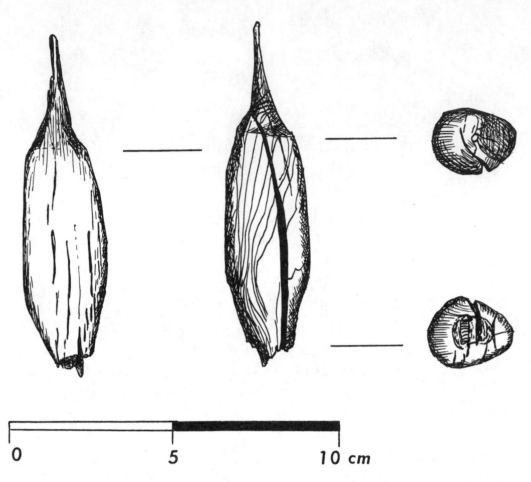

0   5   10 cm

Figure 15. Homemade wooden float used in line fishing. It came from a cave site near the Pyramid at Pyramid
Lake. Pyramid Lake surface collection PL505-802. Drawing by June Eustice.

In a systematic survey which the Nevada State Museum carried out in the middle sixties, we made an attempt
to rescue as many anchor stones and net weights as possible, but the largest number are in the Peter Ting, Sr.,
and the Harry Norcross, Jr., collections. Those collections were made independently, mostly at the northwest
corner of Pyramid Lake. We do have about 30 or so canoe anchor stones in the Nevada State Museum
collection. The smaller grooved canoe anchor stones may grade into net weights, and we have more than 3,000
of the latter. I have prepared a revised classification of the net weights for this paper. Peter Ting, Sr., came
up with the first classification of net weights from Pyramid Lake in 1966 (Ting 1966:8–9), and I revised his
terminology in a later paper (Tuohy 1968:211–215). Just recently, another whole class of net weights was
discovered in the Harry Norcross, Jr., collection. It is comprised of oval shaped stones, beach pebbles, without
any modification whatsoever. Where they were wrapped with cordage, the cordage preserved the original hue
of the pebble, and the rest of the pebble is coated with calcium carbonate, which tends to lighten the pebble's
hue. All in all, we came up with eight classes of net weights from Pyramid Lake. I will first describe the wooden
float used in line fishing, the canoe anchor stones, and finally the net weights.

Wooden Float Used in Line Fishing

The wooden float used in line fishing came from a cave site near the Pyramid on the east side of Pyramid Lake. It was made of a non–native species of wood and it could be historic. The piece was hand–carved with a dull knife, and was meant to be spindle–shaped, but one of the spindles was broken off. It is 10.6 cm in length and 2.57 cm in diameter (Figure 15).

Anchor Stones

This category was conceived by Peter Ting, Sr., and he and Harry Norcross, Jr., noted some sagebrush rope near the vicinity of a heavy grooved stone, and Ting decided to call these stones "canoe anchors or fish net stones." He said they were used as end weights for longer fish nets (Ting 1968:8). These grooved stones weigh from two to thirty-five pounds, and they very often included large, shaped milling stones with grooves for rope attachment. The surface survey conducted by the Nevada State Museum revealed a variety of types, most with one groove, but many with two or more grooves for line attachment. The anchor stones from the Harry Norcross, Jr., collection are shown in Figure 16. We do not know whether tule rafts were used in conjunction with lake fishing at the northwest sector of Pyramid Lake. The anchor stones remain somewhat enigmatic.

Net Sinkers

These net sinkers were described first by Peter Ting, Sr., (1966) and then they were reclassified by Tuohy (1968:211–215). It is time to reclassify them, taking into consideration the previous classification of Elsasser (1958:32–33) and the Norcross collection. Accordingly, I have divided the more than 300 net sinkers in the Ting and Norcross collections into eight classes and twenty–one types. They are listed as follows:

Revised Typology of Lower Truckee Basin Net Sinkers

   I. Unmodified
      A. Ovate pebble type (Figure 17)
  II. Perforated (Figure 18)
      A. Perforated net sinker (Loud and Harrington 1929:147)
  III. Knobbed (Figure 19)
      A. Hook–shaped (Tuohy 1968:213)
      B. Foot–shaped (Tuohy 1969:214)
      C. Ovate (Tuohy 1968:214)
      D. Globular (Tuohy 1968:214)
  IV. Grooved (Figure 16)
      A. Centrally encircling groove, tapered ends (Loud and Harrington 1929:127)
      B. Centrally encircling groove, rounded ends (Loud and Harrington 1929:127)
      C. Edge grooved, or partially grooved
      D. Single girdled (Cressman 1960:54)
      E. Double girdled (Cressman 1960:54)
   V. Chipped (not illustrated)
      A. Chipped and battered, roughly rectangular shaped (Osborne 1957:48)
  VI. Notched (Figure 20)
      A. Asymmetrical with strait sides (Elsasser 1958:32–34)
      B. Symmetrical, smooth, rectangular (Elsasser 1958:32–34)
      C. Smooth, ovoid or leaf–shaped (Elsasser 1958:32–34)
      D. General, irregular shaped (Elsasser 1958:32–34)

E. Two–notched (Cressman 1960:54)
F. Three–notched (new type)
G. Four or more notches (Cressman 1960:54)
VII. Bipointed (not illustrated)
A. Spindle shaped or bipointed (Tuohy 1968:214–215)
VIII. Effigy sinkers (not illustrated)
A. Made in the shape of an effigy (Ting 1966:8)

This classification should serve the Western Great Basin for all fish net sinkers found in the future. This classification includes Elsasser's (1958) typology of the net sinkers from the Humboldt Sink and Ting (1966) and Tuohy's (1968) typology combined. For purposes of this paper, there simply was not enough time to count the totals for each class of net sinker, and figure the percentages. But we can say, subjectively, that there were fewer "effigy" and "chipped" net sinkers than any other kind, and there were more "bipointed", "grooved", and "knobbed" sinkers among the collections from Pyramid Lake.

I have outlined the ethnographic baseline following Fowler and Bath (1981), and I have described the prehistoric fishing apparatus, which was in use since about 7000 B.C. The next section of this paper discusses several archaeological sites that contain evidence, both artifactual and faunal, of the use of the Pyramid Lake–Truckee River fishery.

Comparative Discussion of Archaeological Sites

This discussion begins in the Lower Truckee Basin with sites already excavated there. Not too much is known about fishing apparatus or about fish remains themselves elsewhere in the western Great Basin. The bulk of the archaeological information on fishing gear comes from Truckee River and Pyramid Lake. We shall begin with some surface collections that were made at Pyramid Lake and Lake Winnemucca.

Pyramid Lake

In a recent collection of papers dealing with the Clovis–Archaic interface in the Far Western North America, Dansie, et al. (1988:153–200), report on three Late Pleistocene mammals, two camels (*Camelops hesternus*), and one horse (*Equus cf. pacificus*) from Pyramid Lake dated at 25,500 years B.P. These fossils were found in the vicinity of several archaeological sites at the northwest end of the lake. In explaining the nearby surface archaeology, I had to know whether these fossils were coeval with the artifacts (Tuohy 1988:201–216). Apparently the fossils and the cultural material were not the same age, because the three ply sagebrush fishing line found at one of the sites yielded a date of 9660 ± 170 B.P. The paper by Dansie, et al. (1988:153–200) shows why the fossils are older than the artifacts.

The type of artifacts recovered here were mostly large stone knives and other chipped stone tools, but six of the sixty artifacts, represent fishing gear. There were fragmentary materials of two woven, twined bags (one of which is shown in Figure 4), one bone fishhook (Tuohy 1988:213, Figure 5, lower), and three stone net sinkers (Tuohy 1988:205, Figure 3, lower). The bone fishhook was of the single pointed, unbarbed, large type of hook made out of a flat, long–bone splinter. It was 130 mm long, 7 mm wide and 3.6 mm thick. The stone net sinkers were of three different types. There was one "hook shaped" sinker made of marble, one "bipointed" net sinker made of tufa, and one "knobbed" marble net sinker that may have been used as an atlatl weight (Tuohy 1988:205, Figure 3). All of these artifacts are characteristic of prehistoric patterns of lake fishing at Pyramid Lake.

At the lower end of Pyramid Lake where the Truckee River empties into Pyramid Lake, David T. Clark and I excavated three sites between 1973 and 1978. These three sites, 26Wa 1014I, 26Wa 1016, and 26Wa 1020

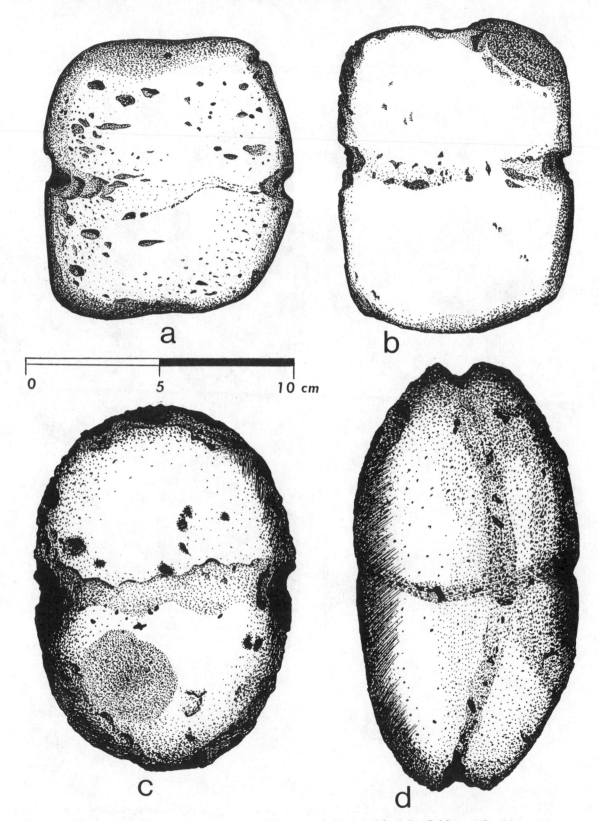

Figure 16. Canoe anchor stones, or large, grooved net weights used in lake fishing. The Harry Norcross, Jr., collection from site 26Wa 233A. Drawing by June Eustice.

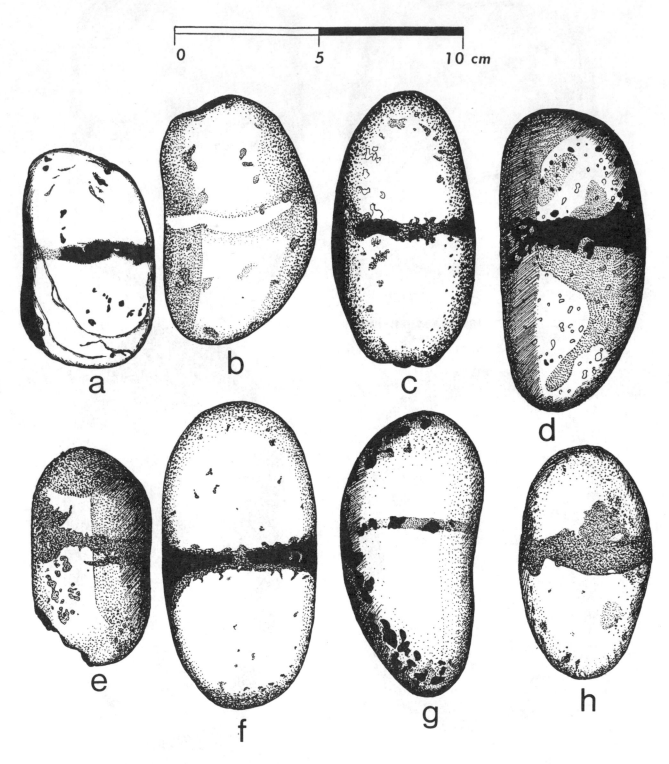

Figure 17. Class I, unmodified ovate pebble type of net sinker. This type of sinker was unmodified except for where the lines were tied to them. The Harry Norcross, Jr., collection from sites 26Wa 217B and 26Wa 233, lake fishing sites. Drawing by June Eustice.

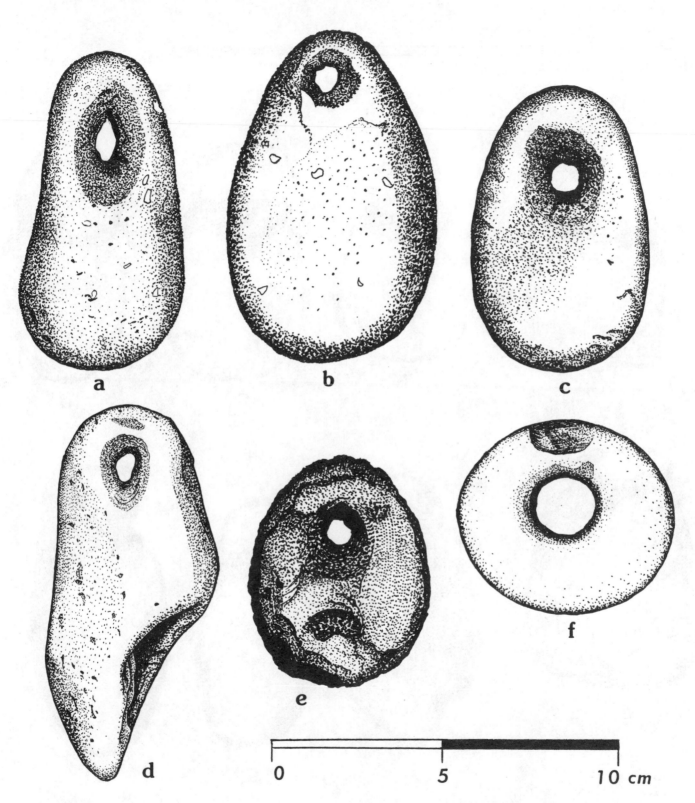

Figure 18. Class II, net sinkers from Pyramid Lake. These are perforated net sinkers used in lake fishing. The Harry Norcross, Jr., collection, 26Wa 217A and 26Wa 221B. Drawing by June Eustice.

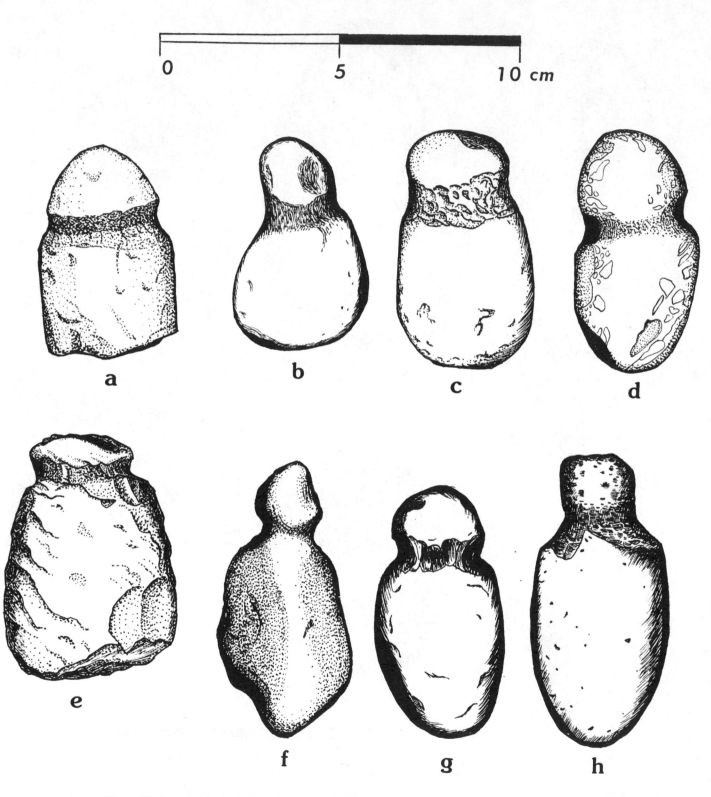

Figure 19. Class III, knobbed net sinkers from Pyramid Lake, used in lake fishing. The Harry Norcross, Jr., collection from sites 26Wa 221B and 26Wa 218. Drawing by June Eustice.

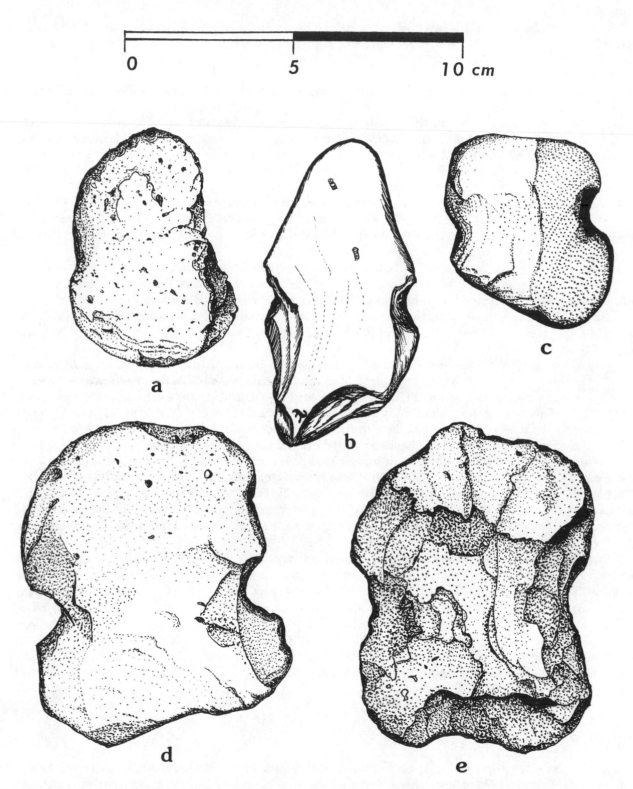

Figure 20. Class IV notched stone net sinkers from Pyramid Lake. These exhibit two notches to four notches, and were used in lake fishing. The Harry Norcross, Sr., collection from sites 26Wa 233A and 26Wa 180. Drawing by June Eustice.

The first site (26Wa 1014I), is hypothesized to be a Northern Paiute winter village house site. It yielded an uncorrected date of 290 ± 90 (WSU–2385) on some charcoal from the floor. This date correlates with two others from Pyramid Lake; Water Bottle Cave (26Wa 372) dated to 380 ± 100 (Gak–2385), and Paul Bunyan's Cave, 240 ± 100 years (Gak–2389). These three sites or components of these three sites are considered to be "*kuyui* Phase" or protohistoric sites, characterized by Desert side–notched points and/or twill–twined perishables (Tuohy and Clark 1979:131).

A single, three–notched pebble fishing sinker was recovered from the house floor at 26Wa 1014I. Manufactured of a light gray granite, the sinker was 4.9 cm in length, 3.9 cm wide, and 0.9 cm thick, and weighed 26.2 grams. Unlike fishing–related artifact types, which were rare, fish bones were abundant with 81% of the total 1,631 bone specimens identified as fish. These specimens were not indentified to species, so we do not know how many lake trout versus *kuyui* suckers or other species of fish were taken (Tuohy and Clark 1979:109).

At 26Wa 1016, 61 complete and nine fragmentary bipoint fish hooks were found (Tuohy and Clark 1979:287). These were largely associated with Burial III which was dated to about 1820 ± 180 B.P. (I–2846), or the Middle Pyramid Phase. Also found with Burial III was a fish–shaped effigy which resembled those discovered previously at the same site (Tuohy 1969:104, Figure 5b).

In addition to these artifacts a total of 21,280 fish bones, or 80.3% of the total animal bones were recovered at 26Wa 1016. Most of them, 75.6%, were too deteriorated, or too fragmentary for analysis. The Lahontan cutthroat trout was represented by 782 bones with a minimum of 21 individuals cutthroats present. The rest of the fish remains were split among the three species that occur at Pyramid Lake, including the kuyui, the Tahoe sucker, and the tui chub. Fifty–two percent of the analyzed fish elements were indentified as *kuyui* (Tuohy and Clark 1979:340).

At the third site, 26Wa 1020, also located at the mouth of the Truckee River, there were no stone or bone artifacts, but there were 9,642 fish bones recovered. This figure represents 74.6% of the total faunal assemblage. The *kuyui* was the most numerous fish (1,780 bones). Second most abundant was the tui chub (840 specimens identified); the Tahoe sucker was third (445 bones); fourth was the Lahontan cutthroat trout (186 bones). Thus, we can see that the most popular sites at the mouth of the Truckee River yielded the most complete inventory of fish remains, with the *kuyui* and the Lahontan cutthroat trout the most popular fishes at those three sites.

At other sites in the Pyramid Lake Basin, we retrieved eleven coprolites from three caves located along the east side of Pyramid Lake, 26Wa 275, 26Wa 385 (Thea Heye Cave), and 26Wa 525. Although the constituents were not broken down to species, Napton and Heizer (1970:120, Table 10) did report "fish bones" from five of their samples from Pyramid Lake, and "fish scales" were present at four of them. Also, Harrington recovered the desiccated remains of 19 fish, including at least nine kuyui, and one Tahoe sucker, from Thea Heye Cave in 1927 (Follett 1977:59–70).

Other Pyramid Lake sites in which fish remains were encountered are shown in Tuohy and Clark (1979:400, Figures VI–I). Their map of Pyramid Lake shows the percentage (by weight) of fish bones recovered from excavated sites on the Pyramid Lake Reservation. These figures come from a study by Walter Stein, a paleozoologist. Of the 42 sites reported, eight sites had less than 1% fish bones; 11 sites had 1 to 10%; 7 sites had 11% to 20%; 7 sites had 21& to 30%; 3 sites had 31% to 40%; one each had 41% to 50% fish bones; and two had 61% to 70% fish bones (Tuohy and Clark 1979:400, Map VI–I). It will take more sorting to find out the percentages of each species, and this analysis will be done in the near future. Right now we can say that two cave sites yielded the highest proportions of fish remains: Thea Heye Cave 26Wa 385, a riverine site, and Warrior Point Cave, 26Wa 729T, a lake edge site.

Winnemucca Lake

Turning now to an adjacent basin, the Winnemucca Playa, Hester (1974:11) reports an attributed date of from A.D. 600 to A.D. 110, for some fishes from a site at the south end of the playa. This site was excavated by an amateur, although W. I. Follett examined the fish remains, most of which are scales embedded in pieces of skin or adhering to biface knives. He found four species of fish represented, a cutthroat trout, a tui chub, a by an amateur, although W. I. Follett examined the fish remains, most of which are scales embedded in pieces of skin or adhering to biface knives. He found four species of fish represented, a cutthroat trout, a tui chub, a kuyui, and a Tahoe sucker (Follett 1974:37–41). He said this site further corroborates the evidence from other sites on Winnemucca Lake that these four fishes were used as food by the aboriginal peoples of Pyramid and Winnemucca Lakes (Follett 1974:39).

Twelve sites at Falcon Hill at the northwest end of Winnemucca Lake were excavated by Richard Shutler, Jr., and Donald R. Tuohy between 1959 and 1961 and reported by Hattori (1982:181–203). Follett (1982:181–203) analyzed 1,089 fish bones from ten of the sites. Of the 622 remains identified to species, 357 were Lahontan cutthroat trout, 240 were tui chub, 20 were kuyui, and 5 were Tahoe sucker. These all were food fishes in the Lower Truckee Basin.

In his description, Follett (1982:191–194) also gives a firsthand account of the Northern Paiute fishing techniques as practiced by a tribal member, Mr. Harry Winnemucca. Winnemucca said his people speared the *kuyui* in the Truckee River using a gaff of greasewood with a bent handle of spliced willow. He also said the Pyramid Lake Paiute caught cutthroat trout with a net which would allow the tui chubs to pass through (Follett 1982:191). Hook and line fishing was also practiced. The "cork" line was buoyed by floats made out of cottonwood (see Figure 15), and the "lead" line was weighted by grooved rocks. Harry Winnemucca gave some other details about Pyramid Lake fishing, but most are presented by Fowler and Bath (1981). It is interesting to note that Follett (1982:194) says in footnotes that one Pyramid Lake Paiute fishhook was made from a bird's claw, as was recorded by Earll (1884:825–1030). That hook must be one of a kind.

The Truckee Meadows

About 35 miles upstream from Pyramid Lake the Truckee River leaves the Truckee Meadows, a flat plain about 20 miles wide, which contains the cities of Reno and Sparks. Robert Elston and associates have done most of the archaeological work in and around the Truckee Meadows. There are five sites to be considered here: 26Wa 3236 on the lower Truckee River (Drews and Juell 1986); the Vista site (James, et al. 1982; Zeier and Elston 1986); the Glendale site (Miller and Elston 1979); the Truckee River Canyon (Elston, et al. 1977); and sites 26Wa 1696 and 26Wa 1697 which were excavated by the State of Nevada Highway Department (Turner 1986). We will start with site 26Wa 3236, located on the lower Truckee Canyon.

The Lower Truckee Canyon Site

This site is situated about 17 miles downriver from the Truckee Meadows and about the same distance from Pyramid Lake. The site, 26Wa 3236, is located in a sand dune overlying low bluffs, 250 meters north of the Truckee River. The sand dune is about eight meters higher than a high terrace of the Truckee River, and it is crescentic in plan. The sand dune is composed of light–colored clays and silts (Drews and Juell 1986:5).

A program including surface collecting and test excavation was carried out at two sites in the region, and fish remains came from one of them, site 26Wa 3236. The eleven readily identifiable fish remains came from two test units, and included kuyui, Tahoe sucker, and the Lahontan tui chub. The fish remains were confined to the lower component of the test pits, and a radiocarbon date of 2580 ± 160 years B.P. is thought to apply to the fauna. That is, the most intensive use of the site occurred slightly before 630 B.C. (Drews and Juell 1986:56). The site chronology on the basis of limited testing runs from possibly the pre–Archaic of 8,000 years ago until the Late Archaic period which began about A.D. 500 and lasted until the historic contact period in the middle of the nineteenth century.

The Vista Site

The Vista site was reported by Zeier and Elston (1986). The site is located a short distance north of the Truckee River in the eastern Truckee Meadows where the river enters a narrow canyon on its way downstream to Pyramid Lake. The Vista site featured six housepit depressions, ranging between 3.0 and 5.5 meters, although on housepit measured 6 by 8 mctcrs, and a variety of other medium and small size pits. The site was determined to be a multicomponent site ranging from the Spooner Phase (4000 to 7000 B.P.) until the Historic Period (ca. 800 B.P.). The faunal analysis from the Vista site was done by Dansie and Schmitt (1986:209–239). Schmitt reports that there were 439 fish remains in the faunal collection. He reports them as follows (Schmitt 1986:295):

> Although some identifications are tentative the species represented include tui chub (*Gila bicolor*), the Lahontan cutthroat trout (*Salmo clarki henshawii*), and possible kui–ui (cf. *Chasmistes cujus*).

The soil flotation analysis added to this total. Out of the analysis of the 23 bulk samples, came the following notes on fish remains (Budy and Juell 1986:311–321):

> The best species candidates for representation by the larger bone are *kuyui* (*Chasmistes cujus*), Tahoe sucker (*Catostomus tahoensis*), tui chub (*Gila bicolor*) and Paiute cutthroat trout (*Salmo clarki*), but none were identified to species.

In addition to the fish remains themselves, there were six bone tool fragments that appeared to have been fishing implements, probably fishhooks (Drews and Schmitt 1986:303, Figure 90). Two are bipointed and are referred to as "gorges". Three others had blunt, rounded bases and a single point on the opposite end. The latter three would be placed in my single–pointed category. The sixth fishhook was a highly modified bone splinter with a basal tenon, apparently modified to fit into a hole in the shaft of a hook. The latter composite fishhook is apparently unique. It came from the deepest level of the site, 60 to 70 cm in a presumed house floor. Five of the six fishhooks from Vista resemble the Pyramid Lake specimens, and although the Vista site is considered an antecedent "Washoe" site, dating to the King's Beach times (ca. A.D. 500 to about A.D. 1100), it well may relate to the Pyramid Lake sequence of prehistoric cultures.

The Glendale Site (Sparks)

The Glendale site was an archaeological site located along a highway corridor within the city limits of Sparks, Nevada (Miller and Elston 1979). It was located in the Truckee Meadows along Glendale Avenue where that avenue crosses the Truckee River. The initial reconnaissance located a site on the grounds of the Nevada Mental Health Institute where prehistoric and historic artifacts were found. Subsequent tests revealed housepits and hearths believed to be parts of a known Washoe winter village (d'Azevedo 1956). Work at the site commenced in September, 1977 and concluded in December, 1977.

As the Glendale site was situated on terraces of the Truckee River, it was proposed that it was the remains of a winter fishing site. The excavations proved otherwise. The fish remains consisted of a few cutthroat trout or sucker bones. Leporids (rabbits) constituted the major taxonomic group at the site (Dansie and Ringkob 1979).

Among the artifact groups recovered were Martis style projectile points, typical of the Lake Tahoe area in California, mixed with typical Great Basin series points. This had been noted before in the Truckee Meadows (Elston 1971). There was only one prehistoric artifact that could have been used in fishing and that one was a possible net weight with two notches on either side (Miller and Elston 1979:Plate 36). Although the authors confirm the winter time use of the site, they state:

> There is no evidence that the site was used as a fishing base camp. Fish remains are present but very sparse and no item of fishing gear was recovered (Miller and Elston 1979:322).

Northwest Truckee Meadows (Reno)

Four prehistoric and one historic sites were discovered by Nevada Department of Transportation crews during a survey of McCarran Boulevard in northwest Reno. Two of the prehistoric sites (26Wa 1696 and 26Wa 1697), considered to be non–riverine base camps were excavated in late 1977 and early in 1978. At this writing the manuscript has been edited, and is due to be published in late 1990 (Turner 1986). One small "possible" fish skull bone came from site 26Wa 1696 and four fish vertebrae from the other site, 26Wa 1697 (Turner 1986:16–15).

After taking into account the 1,376 fish remains from the flotation sample, Amy Dansie, who did the analysis, (Turner 1986:16–16) concludes that there were ten species of native fish in the Lahontan Basin that could have contributed to the sample. Her best estimate of "likely candidates" are the Tahoe sucker and the tui chub. The Tahoe sucker could have been gathered in the Truckee Meadows, but the tui chub would have come from Pyramid Lake, the Lower Truckee River, Washoe Lake, or Lake Tahoe.

Fish remains from 26Wa 1697 are all small vertebrae, too fragmentary for identification, but Dansie (Turner 1986:16–23) notes that fish remains do constitute .06 percent of the fauna in a non–riverine open site, several miles from a fish habitat.

There was one artifact from 26Wa 1696 which may have functioned as a perforated net weight. It was manufactured from a relatively flat stream–worn cobble, and it measured 8.5 cm in length and was 7.5 cm wide and 2.0 cm thick. It was biconically drilled, and the opening was 10mm in diameter (Turner 1986:13–22). These two sites, 26Wa 1696 and 26Wa 1697, had twenty–three rock lined hearths or roasting pits associated with them. The two dated occurrences of fish from two of these features were 880 ± 70 B.P. and 940 ± 80 B.P. (WSU 1974), which would put these two sites in an Early King's Beach phase which extended from about A.D. 500 to about A.D. 1200.

Comparison of Ethnographic and Archeological Fishing Gear

As indicated previously, a goal of this paper is to compare ethnographic *Kuyuitikadi* fishing gear (Fowler 1989:29–41) with the archaeological record, partially portrayed in this report. At the beginning of these comparisons over the last 9,000 years or so, we have relied largely on the collections of private individuals to compile the archaeological baseline for fishing gear on the Lower Truckee Basin. Thanks to the collections of Peter C. Ting and Harry Norcross, Jr., both of whom collected artifacts at a rather propitious time (in the mid-1960s), we can now say more about the prehistoric fishing apparatus that was used at Pyramid Lake. We will have more to say about this topic when the analysis of the complete collection from 102 excavated sites at Pyramid Lake is analyzed and reported.

With respect to the fish resource and the seasonality of the fish runs, we have very little to add to Park's notes which were recently published by Fowler (1989:29–41). The timing of the fish species and their seasonal runs up the Truckee River in the winter and spring remained more or less constant throughout the year. The Pyramid Lake Paiute fisherman fished almost every day in the winter and spring and quite a bit during the summer and fall (Fowler 1989:30), and we think that was true prehistorically as well.

During the mid–1960s, the Nevada State Museum using Fleischmann Foundation funds conducted a surface survey of the Pyramid Lake Reservation, but we did not survey the Truckee River banks all the way from Wadsworth to Nixon, a distance of almost 20 miles. During a second period of field work, from 1973 to 1978, we covered both of the river banks from the Nixon bridge to the mouth of the Truckee River at Pyramid Lake. The Corps of Engineers wanted to line the curves of the river with heavy–duty rip–rap, and eventually did so, lining three miles from the Nixon bridge downstream to Pyramid Lake. We found that five large sites would be affected by this construction, and comparisons from three of them are reported in this report (see the "Pyramid Lake" section in the "Comparative Discussion of Archaeological Sites"). But the point to be stressed here is that a survey of both river banks from Wadsworth to the Nixon bridge needs to be accomplished before we can say much about the remnant fishing weirs and platforms for them which often were constructed together on the river banks during the historic period.

There are various net fragments from the 102 sites that were excavated during the 1960s, but they are completely unanalyzed at this time. But the date of 7830 ± 350 years B.P. on the fish net from Level 4 in Fishbone Cave in the Winnemucca Sink (Orr 1974:50) suggests very early use of such devices. Several styles of fish nets were used to take different species of fish in the Lower Truckee Basin during historic times (Fowler 1989:32), but the comparison of net sizes and types will have to wait until the archaeological nets from Pyramid Lake are analyzed. Needless to say, net–making existed in the Lower Truckee Basin for a very long time, as it did in the Humboldt Sink (Loud and Harrington 1929:258, Plate 42).

The harpoons and spears used by the Pyramid Lake Paiutes (Fowler 1989:34–35), seem very different in form and function from those used prehistorically. The historic, single–pronged, fish harpoon with a willow shaft, and the double–pronged harpoon with the bone points as described by Park (Fowler 1989:34, Figure 1b) do not seem to have counterparts in the prehistoric harpoons from Pyramid Lake. Compare, for example, the unilaterally–barbed spear points made of bone shown in Figure 7 with the bident spears said to be of Paiute manufacture by Park (Fowler 1989:34, Figure 12d). Although there are no dates on the long, unilaterally barbed bone spear points from Pyramid Lake, they are found at apparently old sites that were underwater throughout the length of the contact period (ca. 1850–1965). Among other archaeological bone points, Ting (1968:6, Figure 1b) also reports finding two leisters, as did Fowler and Fowler (1981:192) who reported leisters for the Pyramid Lake Paiutes. So it looks like there were some changes in the technology of the harpoon and in the bone spear points, but not in the leister, unless the archaeological–found leisters belong to the contact period. But this we do not know because the leisters were both recovered by amateurs.

The same correspondences obtain for fish hooks and lines; the ethnographic models are different from the archaeological ones. Park shows a model of a compound trout hook, made from greasewood that has a shaft 8.3 cm in length, and a point about half that length (Fowler 1989:34, Figure 12d). This fish hook was not duplicated in the archaeological materials, and as we have explained, the all–greasewood hook–shaped pieces from Winnemucca Lake were identified as parts to a trap utilizing a scissor's snare (Figure 14, this paper).

Fowler (1989:37) reports that hooks and lines of two sizes were used to take trout, suckers and smaller fishes, such as chub, redside, and dace. These smaller fishes were called collectively "minnows" by Paiute informants, and trot lines were used to take minnows, likely tui chub. Trot lines were recovered in the uppermost level of Humboldt Cave (Figure 1a), and Lovelock Cave (Loud and Harrington 1929:Plate 51). Fowler notes that these "trot lines" were called *winain.nu*, (throwing line) by the Pyramid Lake Paiutes and she suspects all three of the trot lines belonged to the Northern Paiute (C. Fowler, this volume). One other Paiute line was recovered archaeologically. Unfortunately, it came from a potted–out cave (26Wa 348H), on the eastern shore of Pyramid Lake, so we do not know the archaeological position of this trot line either. The bigger hooks shown in this report, I think, were used to take trout and suckers, while the smaller ones were used to take minnows, for use as bait.

As for the larger bone hooks recovered archaeologically at Pyramid Lake, we cannot correlate them to any of the known types of hooks used by the Pyramid Lake Paiutes. The smaller hooks hafted to the line in a medial position (Figure 8) were trot lines hooks and I think the ungrooved smaller hooks were trot line hooks, too. But there is no estimate of age for these smaller hooks, and some were found in a collection from the oldest known open sites at Pyramid Lake (Figure 13). We should date the sites and fish hooks from them in order to find out which hooks are antecedent and which of them are descendant, but that has not been done yet.

We can tell more about rock weights used as fish sinkers than we can about other fishing gear. We can compare types of net sinkers with the known archaeology and get a seriation of types across time. When we come to compare the net sinkers to the historic Paiute ones, there is not enough detail in Park's ethnographic account to make the comparison (Fowler 1989:29–39). We do not know the shape of the "rock weights," but in the archaeology we have two categories, anchor stones, which are heavy stones, and net sinkers, which are lighter in weight.

Discussion

A second goal of this paper is to attempt to understand the cultural processes that affected the Lower Truckee River Basin fishery and eventually led to its demise. To do this we need to take a broader view of the world's fisheries and the modes of production used to exploit them. We shall rely upon a collection of articles on the present day fishing communities of the world (Clay 1987:2–52), and the commercial expansion and the industrial capitalism that shaped them (Wolf 1982:73–180).

For example, Wiley (1987:2), considers how and why contemporary fishing communities exist. He notes that most fishing communities today choose men as fishermen, and further, how advanced processes, like refrigeration on ships, will affect the catch. He also considers how an aquatic animal, such as a fish, gets from the water into a human stomach:

> At first, a fish is part of the natural ecosystem. Then, someone catches it, making it part of a haul that is distributed among, for example, a crew of fishermen. The fish may be eaten right away, but more likely it is destined for later consumption, locally or perhaps many miles away. Fish, being highly perishable must be processed. . . . In passing through these stages, a fish moves from a natural state to a cultural one (Wiley 1987:2).

As an ethnologist Wiley (1987:2) wants to know more about the ecological and ethnological questions surrounding the fish catch, more about the fishing technology, and also more about the complex socioeconomic system that will handle the fish prior to local consumption, or further processing for foreign consumption. In other words, what were the modes of production and distribution in the several surviving fishing communities?

Likewise, Wolf (1982) considers modern day society and the forces that shaped it by examining the world in A.D. 1400 before the European mercantile expansion achieved world–wide dominance after the industrial revolution. Wolf (1982:73–100) presents, as an outgrowth of Marxist thinking, three "modes of production": (1) the capitalist mode, (2) the tributary mode, and (3) the kin–ordered mode. Only the capitalist mode and the kin–ordered mode apply to the Paiute people of Pyramid Lake. The "tributary mode" of production did not obtain at the Pyramid Lake fishery, because the Pyramid Lake Paiutes were not sufficiently socially organized to have had a "head chief" who would coerce "by political or military means" tribute from underlings (Wolf 1982:80).

What had happened in the Lower Truckee River Basin (Pyramid Lake and Lake Winnemucca) fishery was that for more than 9,000 years the Pre–Mazama people, the Early Archaic people, the Lovelock people, and the Northern Paiute people did not have the technology to completely exploit the fishery. A primary reason for this is technological; these people didn't have wooden boats for use on the open lake, metallic fishhooks and spinners, and the other trappings later introduced to them by the Anglo society with whom they were in contact. The native peoples had what would be called in Wolf's terms (1982:88) a "kin–ordered" mode of production. That is, the Paiutes were a group of people living together which includes the family and those with extended patterns of kinship. The Paiutes had "fishing cliques," a group of men (and women) who would go fishing together (Bath 1978:53,62), and there is also inferential evidence that fishing cliques were prevalent in earlier societies at Pyramid Lake. Despite the succession of Indian groups over the 9,000 plus years, it was not until the latter half of the 19th century that the "kin–ordered" mode of production changed to the "capitalist" mode.

So, while the Pyramid Lake Indian Agency was forming, fifteen years before the Executive Order was signed in 1874 (Knack and Stewart 1984:92), the Lower Truckee Basin was subjected to fishing by a cultural system operating with a "capitalist mode" of production to feed the markets in nearby towns. The Anglo fishermen were thick by 1869 and the Indian Agent Lee (Knack and Stewart 1984:161) reported:

> . . . white–owned fishing nets and lines stretching completely across the river in more than 20 different places on the lower two miles of river, well within the reservation boundaries.

Lee also states (Knack and Stewart 1984:160):

> Upon my arrival at the reservation I was soon convinced that it was nothing more nor less than a rendezvous for white fishermen, men engaged in prospecting for mines and self–constituted fishermen and traders and others.

As we have seen by the appearance of historic period fishing artifacts, described previously, and the fishing nets at the mouth of the Truckee River, the capitalist mode of production was in full vogue in 1869. The tools for fish production were provided by an alien culture, in part, by a desire to provide the higher–income Comstock miners with fresh meat for their table fare. Later on, when refrigeration of railroad cars came in, the Paiutes also participated in the "capitalistic" mode of fish production. Between the spring of 1888 and the spring of 1889, the Wells Fargo Express and the railroad freight lines hauled away 100 tons of fish (Trelease 1969:5–6). This is equal to 10,000 ten–pound trout!

Of course, the Lower Truckee River fishery could not sustain this yield, so by the early 1940s the cutthroat trout vanished from Pyramid Lake. The nets across the Truckee River and the Pyramid Lake Indian's deadly gaff–hook had taken their toll. Also, the roe from the female cutthroat trout were used as bait for catching more trout, probably because of the sexual excitement it aroused in the male (Trelease 1969:9). But an ardent fisheries expert, Trelease (1969:9), does not blame the loss of the fish on the capitalist mode of fishery exploitation practiced by the Indians and the Anglos. He blames the demise of the fishery on the construction of Derby Dam and its faulty fish ladder, 25 miles east of Reno. The faulty fish ladder on Derby Dam prevented ". . . the brood fish from reaching the upriver spawning grounds" (Trelease 1969).

The Lower Truckee River fishery eventually recovered with the help of brood stock cutthroats originally from Heenan Lake in California, and later on, from Summit Lake in Nevada. In 1967, brood stock supplies of cutthroats were being raised principally in Catnip Reservoir and Marlette Lake in Nevada (Trelease 1969:14). Eventually, breeding was taken over by the Pyramid Lake Tribe (Cerveri 1977) in a government sponsored fish hatchery established on the reservation. Today, fishing and recreation are available to the general public for a nominal fee.

Summary

In summary, we have traced the aboriginal use of fish in the Lower Truckee River Basin lakes, Pyramid Lake and Lake Winnemucca, and these lakes contributed, as did other parts of the known aboriginal environment, from about 7000 B.C. on to historic times, ca. 1850 A.D. Using the ethnographic baseline for fishing as one vector and the archaeological baseline for fishing as the other, we have defined the technological gear men have used to catch fish in the Lower Truckee Basin. We have also defined the socio–archaeological processes at work. The "kin–ordered" (Wolf 1982:88–96) mode of fish production was prevalent for 9,000 years. After about A.D. 1850, the anglo "capitalist mode" (Wolf 1982:77) of fishing took over, and this strategy combined with the effects of the construction of the Derby Dam, demolished the prime game fish in the Lower Truckee Basin (the cutthroat trout) within 90 years. Since about the 1960s the game fish of Pyramid Lake have recovered in a government–subsidized sports fishery operation run by the Pyramid Lake Tribe.

Note

Parts of the above paper were delivered at the 1978 Great Basin Anthropological Conference on October 20, 1978, and at the 1979 Southwestern Anthropological Association Meetings held at Santa Barbara, California, March 28–31 where I chaired the symposium "Fish and Man in the Far West."

References

Bath, J. E.
　　1978　*Lake–Margin Adaptations in Great Basin Prehistory.* Unpublished Master's thesis, Department of Anthropology, University of Nevada, Reno.
Berger, R. G., J. Fergusson, and W. F. Libby
　　1965　UCLA Radiocarbon Dates IV. *Radiocarbon* Vol. 7, pp. 336–371. Los Angeles.

Berger, R., and W. F. Libby
1967 UCLA Radiocarbon Dates VI. *Radiocarbon*, Vol. 9, pp. 479–480. Los Angeles.

Born, S. M.
1972 Late Quaternary History, Deltaic Sedimentation, and Mudlump Formation at Pyrmaid Lake, Nevada. *Center for Water Resources Research Desert Research Institute*, the University of Nevada System, pp. 1–97. Reno.

Brink, P. J.
1969 *The Pyramid Lake Paiute of Nevada*. Unpublished Ph.D. dissertation, Boston University, Boston.

Budy, E., and K. E. Juell
1986 Soil Flotation Analysis. In *The Archaeology of the Vista Site 26Wa3017* by C. D. Zeir and R. G. Elston, pp. 311–322. Intermountain Research, Silver City, Nevada. Contract No. P51–84–013. Submitted to the Cultural Resources Section, Nevada Department of Transportation. Carson City.

Cerveri, D.
1977 *Pyramid Lake Legends and Reality*. Western Printing and Publishing Co., Sparks.

Clay, J. (editor)
1987 Fishing Communities. In *Cultural Survival Quarterly* 11(2):1–80.

Cressman, L. S., D. L. Cole, W. A. Davis, T. M. Newman, and D. J. Scheans
1960 Cultural Sequences at the Dalles, Oregon. *Transactions of the American Philosophical Society*, New Series 50(10).

Curtis, E.
1926 *The North American Indian*, vol. 15. Cambridge University Press.

Dansie, A. J.
1987a Archaeofaunas: 26Pe450 and 26Pe366. In *Studies in Archaeology, Geology and Paleontology at Rye Patch Reservoir, Pershing County, Nevada*, edited by M. K. Rusco and J. O. Davis, pp. 137–147. Nevada State Museum Anthropological Papers No. 20. Carson City.
1987b Rye Patch Archaeofauna: 26Pe670. In *Studies in Archaeology, Geology and Paleontology at Rye Patch Reservoir, Pershing County, Nevada* by M. K. Rusco and J. O. Davis, pp. 69–72. Nevada State Museum Anthropological Papers No. 20. Carson City.

Dansie, A. J., J. O. Davis, and T. W. Stafford, Jr.
1988 The Wizards Beach Recession: Farmdalian (25,000 yr B.P.) Vertebrate Fossils Co–occur with Early Holocene Artifacts. In *Early Human Occupation in Far Western North America: The Clovis Archaic Interface* edited by J. A. Willig, C. M. Aikens, and J. L. Fagan, 156–200. Nevada State Museum Anthropological Papers No. 21. Carson City.

Dansie, A. J., and T. Ringkob
1979 Faunal Analysis of the Gendale Site Assemblage. In *The Archeology of the Glendale Site (26Wa2065)* by M. M. Miller and R. G. Elston, pp. 184-220. Nevada Archaeological Survey. Submitted to the Nevada Department of Transportation. Carson City.

Dansie, A. J., and D. N. Schmitt
1986 Aboriginal Dogs from the Vista Site. In *The Archaeology of the Vista Site (26Wa3017)*, edited by C. D. Zeier and R. G. Elston. Intermountain Research, Silver City, Nevada. Contract No. P51–84–013. Submitted to the Cutural Resources Section, Nevada Department of Transportation, Carson City.

d'Azevedo, W. L.
1956 *Washoe Placenames*. Ms. on file, Anthropology Department, Nevada State Museum. Carson City.

Drews, M., and K. Juell
1986 *An Intensive Evaluation of Archaeological Sites 26Wa3236 and 26Wa3308 in The Truckee River Canyon, Washoe County, Nevada*, Intermountain Research, Silver City, Nevada. Submitted to SEA Engineering and Planners, Sparks, Nevada.

Drews, M., and D. Schmitt
1986 Other Prehistoric Artifacts. In *The Archaeology of the Vista Site 26Wa3017*, by C. D. Zeier and R. G. Elston, pp. 283–310. Intermountain Research, Silver City, Nevada. Contract No. P51–84–013. Submitted to the Cultural Resources Division, Nevada Department of Transportation. Carson City.

Driver, H. E., and W. C. Massey
1957 Comparative Studies of North American Indians. *Transactions of the American Philosophical Society* N.S. 47(2):165–456. Philadelphia.

Earll, R. E.
1884 Catalogue of the Apparatus for the Capture of Fish Exhibited by the United States National Museum. *Bulletin of the United States National Museum*, vol. 27 pp. 825–1030. Washington, D.C.

Elsasser, A. B.
1958 The Surface Archaeology of Site 26–Pe–5, Pershing County, Nevada. In *Part 2. Some Archaeological Sites in Western Nevada* edited by R. F. Heizer, pp. 26–61. Reports of the University of California Archaeological Survey No. 44. Berkeley.

Elston, R. G.
1971 A Contribution to Washo Archaeology. *Nevada Archaeological Survey Research Paper* No. 2. Reno.

Elston, R., J. O. Davis, A. Leventhal, and C. Covington
1977 The Archaeology of the Tahoe Reach of the Truckee River. *Northern Division of the Nevada Archaeological Survey,* University of Nevada. Reno.

Follett, W. I.
1963   Preliminary Report on Fish Remains from the Falcon Hill Sites, Washoe County, Nevada. In *1962 Great Basin Anthropological Conference*, edited by R. Shutler, Jr., pp. 33–34. The Nevada State Museum Anthropological Papers No. 9. Carson City.
1969   Fish Remains from Coprolites and Midden Deposits at Lovelock Cave, Nevada. In *Papers on Great Basin Archaeology*, edited by R. F. Heizer, pp. 21–35. University of California Archaeological Survey Report No. 70. Berkeley.
1970   Fish Remains from Human Coprolites and Midden Deposits Obtained During 1968 and 1969 at Lovelock Cave, Churchill County, Nevada. In *Archaeology and the Prehistoric Great Basin Lacustrine Subsistence Regime as Seen from Lovelock Cave, Nevada*, by R. F. Heizer and L. K. Napton, pp. 163–175. Contributions of the University of California Archaeological Research Facility, No. 10. Berkeley.
1974   Fish Remains from Site NV-WA-197, Winnemucca Lake, Nevada. In *Four Papers on Great Basin Anthropology*. Contributions of the University of California Archaeological Research Facility, No. 21, pp. 37. Berkeley.
1977   Fish Remains from Thea Heye Cave, NV-Wa-305 Washoe County, Nevada. *Contributions of the University of California Archaeological Research Facility*, No. 35, pp. 59–80. Berkeley.
1980   Fish Remains from the Karlo Site (CA-Las-7), Lassen County, California. *Journal of California and Great Basin Anthropology* 2(1):114–122.
1982   An Analysis of Fish Remains from Ten Archaeological Sites at Falcon Hill, Washoe County Nevada, With Notes on Fishing Practises of the Ethnographic Kuyuidtkadt Northern Paiute. In *The Archaeology of Falcon Hill, Winnemucca Lake, Washoe County, Nevada* by E. M. Hattori, pp. 179–203. Nevada State Museum Anthropological Papers No. 18. Carson City.
1985   Analysis of Selected Fish Remains, Dryden Cave, Nevada Appendix VIII. In *Excavations at John Dryden Cave (26Wa3051), Smoke Creek Desert, Washoe County, Nevada*, by Basin Research Associates. VIII, pp. 1–5. Bakersfield.
Fowler, C. S.
1989   *Willard Z. Park's Ethnographic Notes on the Northern Nevada Paiute of Western Nevada, 1933–1934*, vol. 1. University of Utah Anthropological Papers, No. 114. Salt Lake City.
Fowler, C. S., and J. E. Bath
1981   Pyramid Lake Northern Paiute Fishing: The Ethnographic Record. *Journal of California and Great Basin Anthropology* 3(2):176–186.
Fowler, D. D., and C. S. Fowler (editors)
1970   Stephen Powers' The Life and Culture of the Washo and Paiutes. *Ethnohistory* 17(3–4):117–149.
Fowler, D. D., and J. F. Matley
1978   *The Palmer Collection from Southwestern Utah, 1875*. Miscellaneous Paper 20, University of Utah Anthropological Papers No. 99. Salt Lake City.
Hattori, E. M.
1982   The Archaeology of Falcon Hill. Winnemucca Lake, Washoe County, Nevada. *Nevada State Museum Anthropological Papers*, No. 18. Carson City.
Heizer, R. F., and A. D. Krieger
1956   The Archaeology of Humboldt Cave, Churchill County, Nevada. *The University of California Publications in American Archaeology and Ethnology* 47(1). Berkeley and Los Angeles.
Hester, T. R.
1984   Archaeological Materials from Site NV-WA-197, Western Nevada: Atlatl and Animal Skin Pouches. Paper 1, Four Papers on Great Basin Anthropology. *Contributions of the University of California Archaeological Research Facility* Number 2(1–36). Berkeley.
Hubbs, C. L., and R. R. Miller
1948   The Zoological Evidence. In *The Great Basin with Emphasis on Glacial and Postglacial Times*. Biological Series Vol. X, No. 7. Bulletin of The University of Utah Vol. 38, No. 20. Salt Lake City.
James, S. R., B. Brown, and R. G. Elston
1982   *Archaeological Investigations at the Vista Site (26Wa3017) Washoe County, Nevada: With an Appendix on Subsurface Tests Near 26Wa3018*. Intermountain Research, Silver City, Nevada. Submitted to the Nevada Department of Transportation. Carson City.
Janetski, J. C.
1979   Implication of Snare Bundles in the Great Basin and Southwest. *Journal of California and Great Basin Anthropology* 1:306–321.
Kroeber, A. L., and S. A. Barrett
1960   Fishing Among Indians of Northwest California. *University of California Anthropological Records* 21(1):1–120.
Knack, M. C., and O. C. Stewart
1984   *As Long as the River Shall Run, An Ethnohistory of Pyramid Lake Indian Reservation*. University of California Press, Berkeley.
LaRivers, I.
1962   *Fishes and Fisheries of Nevada*. State Printing Office, Carson City.
Loud, L. L., and M. R. Harrington
1929   Lovelock Cave. *University of California Publications in American Archaeology and Ethnology* 25(1). Berkeley.
Lowie, R. H.
1924   Notes on Shoshonean Ethnography. *American Museum of Natural History Anthropological Papers* 20(3):185–314. New York.
Mason, O. T.
1902   Aboriginal American Harpoons. *Annual Report, Smithsonian Institution for 1900*, Part 2. Washington D. C.

Miller, M. M., and R. G. Elston
  1979   *The Archaeology of The Glendale Site.* Archaeological Survey. Submitted to the Nevada Department of Transportation. Carson City.
Napton, Lewis K., and Robert F. Heizer
  1970   Analysis of Human Coprolites from Archaeological Contexts with Primary Reference to Lovelock Cave, Nevada. In *Archaeology and the Prehistoric Great Basin Lacustrine Subsistence Regime as Seen from Lovelock Cave, Nevada*, by R. F. Heizer and L. K. Napton, pp. 87–130. Contributions of the University of California Research Facility, No. 10. Berkeley.
Norcross, H., and F. A. Riddell
  1974   The Surface Archaeology of the Pyramid Lake Region, Nevada. Paper presented at the 20th Great Basin Anthropological Conference, Carson City.
Oakley, K. P.
  1950   *Man the Tool Maker.* 2nd ed. Bartholomew Press, Dorking, Great Britain.
Orr, P. C.
  1952   *Preliminary Excavations of Pershing County Caves.* Nevada State Museum Department of Anthropology Bulletin No. 1. Carson City.
  1956   *Pleistocene Man in Fishbone Cave, Pershing County, Nevada.* Nevada State Museum Department of Anthropology Bulletin No. 2, pp. 1–20. Carson City.
  1974   Notes on the Archaeology of the Winnemucca Caves, 1952–58. In *Collected Papers on Aboriginal Basketry*, edited by D. R. Tuohy, and D. L. Rendall, pp. 47–59. Nevada State Museum Anthropological Papers No. 16. Carson City.
Osborne, D.
  1957   *Interagency Salvage Program River Basin Surveys Papers Number 8: Excavating in the McNary Reservoir Basin Near Umatilla, Oregon.* Smithsonian Institution Bureau of American Ethnology Bulletin 166. Washington, D.C.
Rendall, D. L.
  1966   A Barbed Antler Point Found at Pyramid Lake, Nevada. *American Antiquity* 31(5):740–2.
Riddell, F. A.
  1956   Final Report on the Archaeology of Tommy Tucker Cave. *University of California Archaeological Survey Reports* 35(44):1–25. Berkeley.
Rostlund, E.
  1952   Freshwater Fish and Fishing in Native North America. *University of California Publications in Geography* vol. IX. Berkeley.
Rusco, M. K., and J. O. Davis
  1987   *Studies in Archaeology, Geology and Paleontology at Rye Patch Reservoir, Pershing County, Nevada.* Nevada State Museum Anthropological Papers No. 20. Carson City.
Schmitt, D., C. D. Zeier, and E. Budy
  1986   Subsistence Patterns. In *The Archaeology of the Vista Site (26Wa3017)*, by C. D. Zeier and R. G. Elston, pp. 357–362. Intermountain Research, Silver City, Nevada. Contract No. P51-84-013. Submitted to Cultural Resource Section, Nevada Department of Transportation. Carson City.
Shutler, R., Jr.
  1968   The Great Basin Archaic. In *Archaic Prehistory in the Western United States*, edited by C. Irwin-Williams, pp. 24–26. Eastern New Mexico University Contributions in Anthropology 1(3). Portales.
Stewart, O. C.
  1941   Culture Element Distribution XIV: Northern Paiute. *University of California Anthropological Records* 4(3). Berkeley.
Ting, P. C.
  1966   North American Indian Fishing Sinkers. *Western Collector* 4(10). San Francisco.
  1967   A Pyramid Lake Surface Artifact Assemblage Located at or Near the 3800 Foot Elevation. *Nevada Archaeological Survey Reporter* I(8):4–11.
  1968   Bone Points from Pyramid Lake. *Nevada Archaeological Survey Reporter* II(3):4–13.
  1983   Publications in Archaeology, by P. Ting, Sr. *Nevada Archaeologist* 4(1):2–25. Carson City.
Trelease, T. J.
  1969   The Death of a Lake. *Nevada Outdoors Wildlife Review* 3(4):4–9.
Tuohy, D. R.
  1968   Stone Sinkers from Western Nevada. *American Antiquity* 33(2):211–215.
  1969   The Test Excavations of Hanging Rock Cave, Churchill County, Nevada. In *Miscellaneous Papers on Nevada Archaeology 1–8*, pp. 26–67. The Nevada State Museum Anthropological Papers No. 14. Carson City.
  1988   Artifacts from the Northwestern Pyramid Lake Shoreline. In *Early Occupation in Far Western North America: The Clovis–Archaic Interface*, edited by J. A. Willig, C. M. Aikens, and J. L. Fagan, pp. 201–216. *Nevada State Museum Anthropological Papers* No. 21. Carson City.
Tuohy, D. R., and D. T. Clark
  1979   *Excavations at Marble Bluff Dam and Pyramid Lake Fishway, Nevada.* Parts I, II,I II, IV, V, and VI. Submitted to Bureau of Reclamation Mid–Pacific Regional Office. Sacramento.

Turner, T. H.
  1986   The Archaeology of Five Sites in the Northwest Truckee Meadows. Ms. on file, Nevada Department of Transportation. Carson City.
Wheat, M. M.
  1967   *Survival Arts of the Primitive Paiutes*. University of Nevada Press, Reno.
Wiley, J.
  1987   Introduction: Fisherfolk. *Cultural Survival Quarterly* 11(2):2–5.
Wolf, E.
  1982   *Europe and the People Without History*. University of California Press. Berkeley.
Zeier, C. D., and R. G. Elston (editors)
  1986   *The Archaeology of the Vista Site (26Wa3017)*. Intermountain Research, Silver City, Nevada. Contract No. P51–84–013. Submitted to the Nevada Department of Transportation. Carson City.

PREHISTORIC CARNIVORE USAGE IN THE WETLAND HABITATS OF WESTERN NEVADA

Amy J. Dansie

Abstract

Archaeofauna data demonstrate a high frequency of carnivores in the wetland habitats of western Nevada. Stillwater Marsh produced the most diverse cultural carnivore assemblage with Pyramid Lake, Winnemucca Lake and the lower Humboldt River showing significant occurrences of aboriginal dogs, wolves, coyotes, foxes, badgers, and bobcats. Otters and mink, aquatic mammals at the top of the food chain, provide evidence that Stillwater Marsh was a stable, fresh water ecosystem for long periods of time during which humans exploited the marsh intensively. Of particular note, the presence of wolves in the lower valleys of the western Great Basin are further evidence that the wetlands provided significant biomass to terrestrial carnivores (including humans). Meadow voles, archaeologically abundant, were perhaps the mainstay of the wolves and coyotes and were also exploited by humans. The factors of local abundance, competition for small game in intensively exploited habitats, defense against predators and scavengers, and use of fur pelts probably combined to stimulate intensified exploitation of carnivores in the wetlands more so than in the upland areas of the western Great Basin. The keeping of dogs is documented only from the Carson Sink, lower Humboldt River, Pyramid Lake and Winnemucca Lake (Northern Paiute Territory), and the Truckee Meadows (Washo Territory) in northern Nevada. The presence of large fisheries and bird rookeries is hypothesized to explain this geographic distribution. An ideological component of carnivore use is evidenced by numerous carnivore bone artifacts, indicating that carnivores were an integral part of the human culture during the Great Basin Archaic in the wetlands, lakes, and riverine areas.

Introduction

Human exploitation of wetlands in the Desert West has been one of the most intensely discussed archaeological issues of the region, matched only by the topic of early man and the Numic spread. Current research demonstrates that human adaptations to wetlands may be pivotal to both of these other topics (Willig et al. 1988, Aikens and Witherspoon 1986). The focus here is on a previously unnoticed pattern of prehistoric human behavior in the ecological context of the Lahontan Basin wetlands and lakes. Archaeofaunal data show a high frequency of carnivores in this area, unmatched elsewhere in the Great Basin. A series of ecological and cultural factors are evaluated to help explain why this might have happened. As will be shown, there can be no simple explanation for this particular archaeological pattern, except that the complex ecological web within which the humans exploited carnivores both allowed and stimulated diversification into the total available food chain.

As just one small part of the overall behavior system, the use of carnivores demonstrates that when the wetlands were at maximum productivity and stability, humans exploited them fully. Perhaps even more significant, the presence of so many carnivores, whether cultural or not, implies that the marshes offered a natural productivity to terrestrial predators which serves as independent evidence of the vast biomass ecologically available in desert marshes and lakes. This reconstruction applies to any time period when the marshes developed optimum ecological diversity, and no attempt to compare chronological changes will be offered at this time. Current research in both the western and eastern Great Basin wetlands following the El Nino flooding of the 1980s will soon provide such data, not yet fully available at the level of dated analyzed faunal assemblages.

Background

Loud and Harrington (1929) reported 30 coyote bone tubes and 2 coyote bone awls from Lovelock Cave, 32% of the modified bones. Additionally, of the 153 unmodified bones, 92 (65%), are coyote bones. Other carnivores totaled 2.7%. Notable among these other carnivores is a stuffed mink skin. Although Loud and Harrington (1929:35) concluded that most unmodified bones were deposited in the cave by natural agencies, rather than by man, Ambro (1967:40) and Livingston (1988) concluded that many of the carnivore and bird bones were culturally deposited. Many of the Lovelock Cave coyote bones stored at the Nevada State Museum show subtle cultural modification, including skinning scars on mandibles, and end–snapped, unfinished long bone tubes (Dansie 1988).

Faunal remains recovered from archaeological sites in the Great Basin since the excavation of Lovelock Cave have not duplicated this high frequency of cultural carnivore bone, with the outstanding exceptions of sites at Pyramid Lake, Winnemucca Lake and Stillwater Marsh (Dansie 1988). Nightfire Island, in the lower Klamath Basin, also produced numerous dogs, wolves, coyotes and otter bones along with lacustrine avifauna, fish, and mussels (Howe 1979). The Nevada sites producing abundant dog and coyote remains show a curious geographic correlation with the distribution of Lovelock Culture traits, prompting the analysis of the role of dogs, coyotes and other carnivores in the Lovelock Culture area (Dansie 1988).

Recent archaeological research in Great Basin wetlands has stimulated new interpretations and models of "lacustrine" adaptations in the Northern Great Basin (Tuohy et al. 1988; Janetski 1986, 1990; Madsen 1982; Raven and Elston 1988; Livingston 1988; Kelly 1990). Carnivores have not been included in these broader discussions, in part because the bulk of the carnivore data are incompletely analyzed and unpublished from the large collections at Pyramid Lake and Winnemucca Lake. This chapter summarizes the archaeological carnivore data for northern Nevada and attempts to place these data into an ecological framework relevant to questions of human adaptations to wetlands habitats.

The Carnivores

Most carnivores are hunters but some, like the coyote, are also scavengers and omnivores who will eat anything. Many carnivores also have thick fur coats which have been used world–wide by humans for warmth and beauty. Carnivores are not usually considered food in most cultures, but there are several exceptions (noted below). Western Great Basin carnivores are listed on Table 1.

The Great Basin carnivores are often rare in the local ecosystem due to their position high in the food chain. Many are nocturnal, and many mustelids live only near water, limiting their occurrence to stream or wetland habitats (Hall 1946). These factors of rarity and restricted habitat are probably the primary reasons carnivores are not often found in quantity in Great Basin archaeological sites, and why they are most common in wetlands

Table 1. Western Great Basin Carnivores

Taxa	Common Name	Genus, Species
Canids:	kit fox	*Vulpes macrotis*
	red fox	*Vulpes vulpes*
	gray fox	*Urocyon cinereoargenteus*
	coyote	*Canis latrans*
	wolf	*Canis lupus*
	Aboriginal Indian dog	*Canis familiaris*
	Wolf/Coyote/Dog hybrids	*Canis* sp.
Mustelids:	weasel	*Mustela freneta*
	mink	*Mustela vison*
	striped skunk	*Mephitis mephitis*
	spotted skunk	*Spilogale gracilis*
	river otter	*Lutra canadensis*
	badger	*Taxidea taxus*
	marten	*Martes nobilis*
	wolverine	*Gulo luscus*
Procyonids:	raccoon	*Procyon lotor*
	ringtail cat	*Basariscus astutus*
Felids:	bobcat	*Lynx rufus*
	mountain lion/cougar	*Felis concolor*
Ursids:	black bear	*Ursus americanus*
	grizzly bear	*Ursus horribilus*

or lacustrine sites. However, the increased human exploitation of desert carnivores in wetlands sites suggests there are some distinctive ecological factors involved in human adaptive behavior around wetlands which lead to an increase in carnivore predation by humans when the marshes were at optimum productivity.

The Geographic Scope

Most of the archaeofaunas discussed here occur in western Great Basin valleys that historically held lakes of some kind: Winnemucca Lake, Pyramid Lake, Humboldt Lake, The Carson Sink, including Stillwater Marsh, and Walker Lake. Major site collections outside this area are briefly reviewed for comparable patterns.

Ethnographic Baseline

A brief review of the ethnographic uses and cultural attitudes toward carnivores helps place the archaeological data into a local perspective. The two most common carnivores found archaeologically, coyotes and dogs, are emphasized in order to understand their potential cultural significance.

Coyote

The importance of coyote in the Northern Paiute and Washo cultures is well known within the realm of folklore and mythology, virtually all recorded stories include coyote as a main character. He was the trickster, the person who made all the mistakes humans are prone to make, and the stories serve as important guides to behavior training. His big brother, wolf, was wise and powerful, usually saving coyote from the consequences of his mistakes.

Coyote was also viewed as kin to human beings, even as Creator of humans among the Ute (Goss 1972; Fowler 1986). This attitude is reflected in a Paiute statement documented in Stewart (1941:426) "We don't eat coyote, because he is uncle to everyone." The aversion to eating coyote is universal in the Great Basin ethnographic literature, even starving people would rarely resort to eating coyote, and those who did reported being unable to "keep it down" (Stewart 1941:228), perhaps due to the carrion eating habits of coyotes. Coyotes were considered food by the Modocs (Ray 1963), and by some Numic groups (Fowler and Liljeblad 1986), along with several other carnivores, demonstrating the variability in carnivore food aversions among the ethnographic neighbors of the Lahontan Basin inhabitants. Northern Paiutes reported a means of trapping coyotes and bobcats (Loud and Harrington 1929), using a large deadfall, which indicates they used these carnivores, perhaps for their hides primarily.

Dogs

Ethnographic accounts of dogs in the Northern Paiute area are extremely limited (see Dansie 1984 for a literature review). Most references suggest that dogs were of minimal importance, used occasionally for hunting, but also regarded as camp companions. Dogs were also subject to food taboos, apparently due to their relationship to coyotes. In other Indian cultures, the Pawnee and Hidatsa, for example, dogs were sometimes considered fully acceptable food animals, often in ceremonial contexts (Wilson 1924; Bozell 1988). Paiute, Shoshone and Washo ethnographic data strongly indicate that dogs were not considered food, even in lean times (Stewart 1941; Steward 1938; Riddell 1978; Price 1962, 1980; Downs 1966). The Modoc and the Klamath valued dogs, claiming they would never eat them (Ray 1963, Spier 1930). The general impression is that only when cannibalism was considered an option in severe famines were dogs considered a source of survival food in the Intermountain West (Driver 1961; Driver and Massey 1957).

Riddell (1978:67) noted that dogs as pack animals, along with horses, were just beginning to arrive from the Bannocks to the north when the White Man arrived in the Great Basin. Dogs are usually not included in Great Basin folk stories, which might support the recent acquisition of dogs among the Northern Paiute. The Honey Lake Paiute word for dog is "walking horse" meaning you could pack it, but couldn't ride it, a recent Plains element (Riddell 1960). A Lovelock Paiute informant stated that dogs were acquired fairly recently from former inhabitants of the Humboldt Sink, and that they were used as watch dogs and to assist in digging out rodents and badgers. This use of dogs was augmented by covering the forefeet with badger skin to protect the dog's feet as they were used almost daily for this purpose (Reid n.d.).

The New World aboriginal Indian dog is well-documented from North and South America (Allen 1920). The American Indian dog is a true dog, that is, it is derived from domesticated Old World wolves, and probably arrived in America with the first immigrants over the Bering Land Bridge. A trait unique to these dogs is found in about 70% of the known populations, including the Nevada dogs; that is, many lack the first permanent premolar on one or more jaw and often all four are missing (Allen 1920).

Wherever several aboriginal dogs are found archaeologically, there are usually at least two sizes, larger than a coyote and smaller than a coyote, and wolf-dog hybrids are not uncommon (Bozell 1988, Allen 1920, Haag 1948, Walker and Frison 1982). Ethnographic records indicate that intentional cross breeding with wolves was common, in efforts to increase the strength and size of the larger dogs (Walker and Frison 1982). In the Great Basin, the descriptions of dogs, rare as they are, indicate that some of the Indian dogs were small and frequently cross-bred with coyotes (DeQuille 1963), probably unintentionally.

The photograph of an Indian encampment at Stillwater around 1912 shows a small dog in the foreground (Wheat 1967:18). This might represent an aboriginal dog, or a hybrid with European dogs. Comparisons with the famous black and white Basketmaker dog mummy (Wormington 1959:47) and the few descriptions lead me to conclude that this is what the small Indian dog most likely looked like. Larger dogs described from California and Nevada were said to have yellow hair (Reid n.d.; Dansie 1984), perhaps similar to the large Basketmaker dog mummy.

Other Carnivores

Little specific ethnographic data exists regarding the other carnivores, beyond casual and common reference to eating bobcats, badgers and foxes, using them all for skins. Wolf, as noted above, was regarded as Coyote's older and wiser brother in many folktales, and the "Boss" of the human realm in Ute cosmology (Goss 1972). Weasels are also common characters in folk tales. Other carnivores are variably, but rarely, listed as food animals in the Great Basin cultures. The Modoc, in contrast, apparently considered all carnivores except dogs as game food (Ray 1963:189), but the Klamath considered only the bear, mink, otter and racoon as food among the carnivores, listing all others as "not eaten" (Spier 1930:156), especially dogs.

Archaeological Data

Table 2 summarizes the distribution of archaeological carnivores in the northern Great Basin from a representative sample of sites (Dansie 1988). The combined abundance of coyote, dog, wolf and mustelid remains at Stillwater stands out as unique in the Nevada sites. Stillwater Marsh produced the most diverse assemblage of culturally modified carnivores including otter, mink, badger, weasel, dogs, wolves, wolf–dog hybrids, and 15 minimum individual coyotes, based on complete mandibles (Dansie 1987b), despite having the third smallest sample size. The abundance of coyote bones, the three coyote awls, and one coyote femur tube are reminiscent of Lovelock Cave.

The unmodified faunal remains from Hidden Cave have a similar coyote, wolf, and mustelid pattern and contains only a few carnivore tubes and no carnivore awls. Hidden Cave has the most diverse carnivore assemblage, including the now extinct Nobel marten (Grayson 1985).

As noted, Lovelock Cave contains many fine coyote bone tubes, but also abundant coyote mandibles, some bobcat bone tubes, a variety of mustelids, including stuffed weasel and mink, bear and raccoon hair, but no dog bones (but possibly dog hair), and no carnivore awls (Ambro 1967; Livingston 1988; Loud and Harrington 1929).

Pyramid Lake (personal observation of collections) sites yielded numerous dog and coyote remains, and a few wolf and wolf–dog hybrid bones in the mortuary caves, but few mustelids, and few carnivore bone artifacts. Sites on the east side of Winnemucca Lake had many well-preserved dog and coyote bones, a bobcat and coyote bone tube cache, a wolf bone tube, a coyote radius artifact, possibly a coyote rib loop (Roust 1958), but beyond a few badgers, virtually no mustelids. In contrast, the west side of Winnemucca Lake, narrowly dating to early Lovelock Culture times, has rare coyotes, no dogs, rare mustelids, no carnivore tubes or awls, but it did contain a mountain lion skull.

Carnivores as a dominant component of the archeofauna do not appear outside the Lovelock Culture area, nor in predominantly "natural" assemblages, such as Gatecliff, but are common within it; carnivore bone tubes and awls are rare outside the Lovelock Culture area, but common to abundant within it; and mustelids are rarely found outside this area in any quantity, but frequently found in relative abundance within it. Dogs are rare outside the Lovelock Culture area, but are also virtually absent in the core area around Lovelock Cave itself, being common only at Pyramid Lake, East Winnemucca Lake and Stillwater, present at Walker Lake and Washo Sites, absent at Falcon Hill, Hidden Cave, and Honey Lake.

Comparisons with more distant lacustrine site areas show that the carnivores of the Chewaucan Culture of the Northern Great Basin appear limited to coyote and bobcats associated with waterfowl, fish and mussels (Pettigrew 1980, 1985) but the large village sites have not been excavated extensively yet. Photographs in Howe

Table 2. Carnivores in Selected Great Basin Archaeological Sites

Site	Mammal Total	Carnivore Percent	Carnivore Total	Coyote	Dog	Wolf	Canid	Fox	Bobcat	Badger	Otter	Mink	Weasel	Skunk	Raccoon	Carnivore	Bear
Dangberg Site	18,726	.20	41	2	2	—	26	1	9	1	—	—	—	—	—	—	—
Gatecliff	13,041	.20	20	3	2	—	—	1	6	—	—	—	—	8	—	—	—
Pyramid Lake Caves	10,000	.51	51	38	9	2	—	1	1	—	—	—	—	—	—	—	—
Rye Patch	7,487	2.90	68	9	10	—	28	2	—	10	6	—	2	1	—	—	—
Hidden Cave	6,853	2.10	159	51	—	3	—	34	4	21	4	2	29	6	—	4	1
Hogup Cave	3,440	1.20	67	15	2	—	—	7	25	12	—	—	4	2	—	—	—
Ezra's Retreat	1,823	2.20	40	—	—	—	10	—	16	—	—	—	—	—	14	—	—
Vista	1,694	9.50	55	4	2	—	41	—	8	—	—	—	—	—	—	—	—
Winnemucca Lake East	1,214	9.30	134	32	6	1	38	2	7	2	—	—	—	—	—	46	—
Karlo	869	4.00	36	35	—	—	—	—	1	—	—	—	—	—	—	—	—
Stillwater	165	72.12	119	53	22	1	16	1	—	6	10	4	1	—	—	3	—
Lovelock Cave	156	67.00	106	92	1	2	—	1	1	5	—	1	1	—	1	—	1
Humboldt Cave	146	11.00	16	8	—	—	—	4	3	1	—	—	—	—	—	—	—
Total	65,614		912	342	56	9	159	54	81	58	20	7	37	17	15	53	2

(1979) document dogs, wolves, coyotes and otters associated with Nightfire Island middens from Modoc country, showing similarities between this lacustrine–oriented culture and the Lovelock culture. Few faunal data are reported from Utah Lake sites, but Janetski (1986:160) notes an older reference (Beeley 1946:25) to a "surprisingly large number of wolf bones" as well as bear and skunk at the Beeley Site. Hogup cave, located near a wetland habitat during some of its prehistory, contained only desert carnivores (coyotes, bobcat, badger, fox, weasel and skunk) in its vast faunal assemblage (Aikens 1970). None of these sites duplicate the high frequency and diversity of cultural carnivores found at Stillwater Marsh.

Although canids are repeatedly found around Pyramid Lake, this deep lake habitat yielded fewer other carnivores than the marshland sites. This suggests there may be significant contrasts in the carnivore availability between true lacustrine habitats (deep lakes) and marsh habitats (shallow water with emergent vegetation). Archaeological sites containing dogs in Washoe territory are associated with riverine fisheries, and show a distinctive subset of carnivores in winter village assemblages which includes dogs, coyotes, and bobcats. The use of canids (dog and coyotes) as food in Washo winter villages is strongly indicated and that use is interpreted as a subsistence stress adaptation (Dansie 1987; Dansie and Schmitt 1986; Schmitt 1986). These data suggest that fisheries may foster increased canid density, especially the ability to keep dogs, in the absence of marsh habitats, and that cultural exploitation of canids may well vary independently of the other carnivores.

The largest non–lacustrine faunal assemblage available for comparison, Gatecliff Shelter (Grayson 1983), produced only 20 carnivore bones out of 13,041 identified specimens (0.2%), but included a dog and a coyote femur artifact closely comparable to the Lovelock Cave coyote femur artifact. Many other non–lacustrine faunal assemblages were reviewed during my research, and none had a strong carnivore assemblage; most lacked carnivores remains of any kind.

Interestingly, the Rye Patch Reservoir archaeofauna produced a diverse assemblage of carnivores including dog, coyote, kit fox, otter, badger, skunk, and weasel within a large assemblage (7487 identified bones) dominated by jackrabbits and containing considerable waterfowl bone and egg, fish, and mussels (Dansie 1987a). These sites are along the lower Humboldt River and represent a linear pond–marsh habitat somewhat comparable to the marshland in the Humboldt and Carson sinks. Although the Southfork Shelter site near the upper Humboldt River has a faunal assemblage reflecting the presence of a stream (fish and mussel), it produced only 18 coyote bones out of 2,101 bones and no other carnivores (Heizer et al. 1968). Ezra's Retreat on the north fork of the Little Humboldt River (Bard et al. 1979) has a distinctive riparian stream assemblage with more raccoon bones than any other site, 14 elements, with 10 coyote and 16 bobcat bones rounding out the carnivore assemblage. Riverine habitats vary in the degree of marsh habitat, and the patterns of carnivore use by prehistoric peoples reflect the specific local variations.

Dogs and coyotes are by far the most common carnivore in this sample, but bobcats, wolves, otter and mink show repeated occurrences as well. Many sites have canids tabulated as a group because the small Indian dog and coyote are extremely difficult to distinguish, especially when comminuted as food bone, a common occurrence in the Washo territory samples.

In summary, although no one site area exemplifies the entire pattern, there does seem to be a pattern of carnivore usage within the geographic area of the Lovelock Culture which is distinctive and not a part of the regular Desert Archaic animal food exploitation realm of Basin hunter–gatherers.

The Ute cosmology discussed in Goss (1972), and the overwhelming preponderance of carnivores in the Washo and Numic folktales (d'Azevedo 1986), indicates that the perceptual kinship of humans with the carnivores might have fostered a special treatment of their physical remains within the culture as a whole. The archaeological evidence fully documents a variety of non–food cultural manipulation of carnivore remains within the Lovelock Culture area.

Chronology

Most of the carnivore assemblages reviewed here date to the period between 3500 and 650 years ago, during which time the Lovelock Culture flourished and Elko and Rosegate points were made in the Western Great Basin. The lacustrine carnivore usage pattern is not postulated as a continuous adaptive behavior any more than lacustrine subsistence systems were continuous in the Great Basin. Rather, during some extensive time periods the marshes were stable enough to foster distinctive exploitation systems focused on marsh resources. The dating of such mesic periods is beyond the scope of this paper, and subject to revisions based on current Stillwater research (cf. Raven and Elston 1988).

Discussion

This section will focus on the essential hypotheses and supporting data regarding aboriginal Indians dogs and prehistoric carnivore use in the Lahontan Basin.

Why are Dogs More Common in Wetland Sites?

Although humans keep dogs as pets and subsistence aids over most of the planet, dogs were kept within the ecological constraints of the overall subsistence system. The fundamental questions are: (1) how were they fed, (2) what did they contribute to the economy; (3) how were they perceived (how did they fit into the cultural system)?

1. The primary reason dogs are more common in the lacustrine habitat zones is that they could be kept alive on lake and marsh bulk–resource by–products during normal productivity, (for example, fish and bird entrails and bones, and tuber, insect and seed gruel).

2. (a) When times were lean, dogs were an immediately available source of famine food. If managed carefully, a few dogs for breeding might be saved, except for during the most severe famines. Butchered dogs are documented from Pyramid Lake (Dansie 1984).

   (b) Dogs as garbage disposers would provide an important function in an island marsh setting. The attraction of dangerous scavengers and disease–carrying insects are two obvious dangers of accumulating odoriferous garbage near habitations, and dogs are a functional answer to this survival problem worldwide.

   (c) As small game extractors (digging out rodents), and aids in bird, rabbit or rodent drives, small dogs might have added to the yield of various human predatory efforts significantly enough to justify investment of food to keep them alive.

   (d) Large dogs may have been kept as special hunting dogs, genetically upgraded intentionally with wolves, a common North American Indian tradition (Walker and Frison 1982). Evidence of wolves in Stillwater, Pyramid Lake and Hidden Cave and very large wolf–dog hybrids found at Stillwater and Pyramid Lake are factual evidence that this occurred locally (Dansie 1984, 1988, Schmitt 1988; Grayson 1985).

3. Carefully buried dogs display strong evidence of human perception of some dogs as important entities. In particular the mummy of a large, yellow–haired Indian dog in Crypt Cave, Winnemucca Lake, Nevada (Orr 1972, Dansie 1984), found wrapped in fine fish netting like human burials, and possessing a badly healed fracture of the left femur, represents years of lameness and care by his human associate. This is further evidence of the importance of large dogs to particular humans, perhaps due to mutual life support over much of a lifetime. Dogs are more common in mortuary caves around Pyramid Lake than in the food middens of the open sites. At least one dog burial at Stillwater and one at the Vista site near Reno (Elston and Zeier 1987) are further evidence of intentional burials suggesting that dogs held a special place within the perceptions of the people who fostered their survival.

Thus there are many human reasons why dogs would be kept if they could be supported economically, and as the only domestic animal available, offered all the benefits of the symbiosis between wolves and humans that dogs provide.

Why Are Other Carnivores Also More Common in Lacustrine Sites?

The high incidence of other carnivores in the lacustrine area sites of the Western Great Basin compared to other large faunal assemblages remote from marshes and lakes is part of a larger phenomenon in which increased local availability, competition within confined resource zones, and usefulness for fur clothing, bone tools, quivers, etc., combined to increase the incidence of human predation on local carnivores. Ideological values tied to the ceremonial use of carnivore parts also may have led to increased use of carnivores in lacustrine culture areas.

Livingston (1988) hypothesized that the Lovelock area people who used Lovelock Cave and 26–CH–15 relied on the marshes year round, adapting to natural fluctuations in marsh productivity by diversifying subsistence pursuits in the local area. The carnivore data support this view. Wolves are of particular interest in this context. They are extremely rare historically (noted only from northern and northeastern Nevada [Hall 1946]), and would not be predicted to occur in the Lahontan lowlands prehistorically, based on estimates of large game prey densities. However, now that we know they occurred in Hidden Cave, Lovelock Cave, Stillwater Marsh and at Pyramid and Winnemucca lakes, it is possible to account for their adaptation to the wetlands biomass abundance in much the same way that humans exploited the lacustrine ecology.

When human groups focused much of their seasonal round in the large open valleys of the Lahontan sinks, they also decreased their access to larger game in the mountains. The longer a lacustrine resource remained productive, the greater the hunting pressure on the local big game habitats between the large valleys, reducing the capture rate even more. Low frequencies of artiodactyl bone in the Humboldt and Carson sinks (Livingston 1988, Dansie 1988, Schmitt 1989) suggest that decreased use of big game actually occurred among valley bottom marsh dwellers. This would stimulate an increase in small game procurement for protein, fat and other essential nutrients. The greater the intensification of this subsistence focus, the greater the importance of small game in the diet of the group as a whole. Although small game can be abundant in the lacustrine habitat zones, attracting a higher population of desert carnivores, bulk capture by humans could reduce populations in a confined area enough to make competition with other predators a potentially significant subsistence threat. Human predation on carnivores in response to competition in lacustrine settings is in this sense predictable. Add to that the value of carnivore hides as warm clothing in damp lacustrine environments and the intensified exploitation of carnivores in these areas is not surprising.

The high incidence of dogs in lacustrine areas is essentially independent of the increased use of other carnivores. However, in confined settlements around and in marshes, where dry land is at a premium, accumulation of odoriferous drying bulk meat and associated garbage could be expected to attract predators and scavengers which would threaten either the safety or the food supplies of the human group. Even if not used for hunting, large dogs could be used for defense against wolves and coyotes, while many small dogs could be functional as watch dogs and defense against coyotes.

Although available data do not allow in–depth ecological analysis of the relationships between humans and carnivores in the Western Great Basin, the correlation of archaeological carnivores with lacustrine geographic areas suggests that humans utilizing wetlands resources also utilize carnivores more intensively than humans in desert or mountain regions. It has yet to be demonstrated why this is so.

The fact that all carnivores are also fur–bearers might account for their use for warm clothing wherever encountered, but does not explain their greater use in the marsh areas, as it gets seriously cold all over northern Nevada. Greater natural abundance of carnivores in lacustrine and marsh areas is probably the most critical factor in the higher usage rates by prehistoric humans. This is obviously so for the aquatic otters and minks.

Due to a greater overall biomass, in lacustrine areas with fish and waterfowl added to the desert ecosystem resource base, and with increased rabbit and rodent densities near wetlands carnivores are expected to have higher density in these areas. Voles (*Microtus* sp.) in particular were found in high frequencies in cultural contexts at Stillwater and natural contexts in Lovelock Cave (Schmitt 1988, Livingston 1988) and can reach densities of 12,000 per acre in peak population cycles (Hall 1946:542).

Aquatic fauna would have been accessible to terrestrial predators in maximum quantities when the water levels invaded the broken terrain of the Carson Sink. Seasonal water–level fluctuations would have stranded fish in shallow embayments, and nesting water fowl would have been easy prey in the shallow water areas. Greater competition between carnivores and humans for animal prey in restricted resource areas is hypothesized to explain some of the increased use of carnivores where humans practice *in situ* diversification as adaptations to lacustrine resource zones.

In my analysis of the Rye Patch archaeofauna (Dansie 1987) I proposed that carnivores were used as food under conditions of subsistence stress. In the same vein, diversification into the exploitation of carnivores as part of the overall intensification of lacustrine resources can be seen either as subsistence stress or effective adaptation. I will not belabor the subtle differences in these concepts, but will note that this analysis does not contradict my earlier views on the implications of carnivore usage.

Summary

The apparent restriction of carnivore bone tubes and other ceremonial paraphernalia to the time and geographic distribution of the archaeological Lovelock Culture could mean there is a strong "ideotechnic" component to the higher incidence of carnivore usage. Conversely, the carnivore data also suggest that the marshes were more stable and productive ecologically during the time the lacustrine cultures flourished, possibly leading to carnivore usage in proportion to natural availability alone. A combination of these factors (abundance, competition, usefulness, and cultural perceptions) is probably involved in the lacustrine carnivore usage pattern.

Fish and waterfowl taken in quantity produce copious amounts of discarded animal parts which probably significantly increased the feasibility and value of keeping dogs. The ability of dogs to survive on bulk vegetal foods allowed their survival during off–seasons of bulk animal processing. The factors of available dog food, usefulness in hunting large and small game, protection from predators and scavengers, garbage disposal and use as famine food combined to enhance the keeping of dogs in lacustrine areas more than in other areas of the Northern Great Basin. The cultural perception of dogs as valued components of society (worthy of burial) probably derives in part from the above functional factors making it possible to keep dogs, but may of course include such human values as companionship and affection. A Honey Lake Paiute informant told Riddell (1978:67), in time of famine they would "always try to eat someone's else's dog."

Conclusions

The carnivores were direct competitors with the humans who hunted and gathered all the same foods in the Lahontan Basin. Practitioners of a specialized lacustrine subsistence system, of necessity distant from the best big game hunting in the mountains, and maximizing all local resources (including small rodents and carnivores), could be predicted to intensify that adaptation through eliminating all controllable competition for the small and large game, fish and fowl of the immediate lacustrine ecological environment, even if they did not eat the carnivores. This might explain in functional terms the apparent emphasis on the carnivores in a specialized lacustrine geographic area, in contrast with other Desert West habitats.

References

Aikens, C. M.
 1970   *Hogup Cave.* University of Utah Anthropological Papers No. 93. Salt Lake City.
Aikens, C. M., and Y. T. Witherspoon
 1986   Great Basin Numic Prehistory: Linguistics, Archaeology, and Environment. In *Anthropology of the Desert West, Essays in Honor of Jesse D. Jennings,* edited by Carol J. Condie and Don D. Fowler, pp. 7–20. University of Utah Anthropological Papers No. 110. Salt Lake City.

Allen, G. M.
  1920   Dogs of the American Aborigines. *Bulletin Museum of Comparative Zoology* 63(9):431-517. Harvard University, Cambridge.
Ambro, R. D.
  1967   Dietary-Technological-Ecological Aspects of Lovelock Cave Coprolites. *University of California Archaeological Survey Report* 70:37-47. Berkeley.
Bard, J. C., C. I. Busby, and L. S. Kobori
  1979   *Ezra's Retreat: A Rockshelter/Cave Occupation Site in the North Central Great Basin.* Center for Archaeological Research at Davis Publication No. 6. Davis.
Beeley, S. J.,
  1946   *The Archeology of a Utah lake Site.* Unpublished Master's thesis, Department of Anthropology, University of Utah, Salt Lake City.
Bozell, J. R.
  1988   Changes in the Role of the Dog in Protohistoric-Historic Pawnee Culture. *Plains Anthropologist* 33(119):95-111.
d'Azevedo, W. L., editor
  1986   *Great Basin.* Handbook of North American Indians, vol. 11, W. G. Sturtevant, general editor. Smithsonian Institution, Washington, D.C.
Dansie, A. J.
  1979   Analysis of Faunal Material from Sites 4Las317 and 26Wa1676. In *The Archaeology of U.S. 395 Between Stead, Nevada and Hallelujah Junction, California* by R. G. Elston. Submitted to the California Department of Transportation and Nevada Department of Highways by the University of Nevada, Reno.
  1980   Great Basin Zooarchaeology. Paper presented at the 17th Great Basin Anthropological Conference, Salt Lake City, Utah.
  1984   Prehistoric Dogs in Nevada. Paper presented at the Great Basin Anthropological Conference, Boise, Idaho.
  1987a The Rye Patch Archaeofaunas: Change Through Time. In *Studies in Archaeology, Geology and Paleontology at Rye Patch Reservoir, Pershing County, Nevada,* by M. K. Rusco and J. O. Davis, pp. 156-181. Nevada State Museum Anthropological Papers No. 20. Carson City.
  1987b The Stillwater Animal Bones and Burial Patterns. In *Final Report on Excavations in the Stillwater Marsh Archaeological District, Nevada,* by D. R. Tuohy, A. J. Dansie, and M. B. Haldeman, pp. 256-311. Nevada State Museum Archaeological Services Reports. Carson City.
  1988   Prehistoric and Ethnographic Variation in Carnivore Usage in the Lovelock Culture Area of Western Nevada. Paper presented at the 21st Great Basin Anthropological Conference, Park City.
Dansie, A. J., and T. Ringkob
  1979   Faunal Analysis of the Glendale Site Assemblage. In *The Archeology of the Glendale Site (26Wa2065)* by M. M. Miller and R. G. Elston, pp. 184-220. Submitted to the Nevada Department of Highways by the Nevada Archaeological Survey, University of Nevada, Reno.
Dansie, A. J., and D. N. Schmitt
  1986   Aboriginal Dogs from the Vista Site. In *The Archaeology of the Vista Site (26Wa3017),* edited by C. D. Zeier and R. G. Elston, pp. 241-252. Intermountain Research Reports, submitted to the Cultural Resources Section, Environmental Services Division, Nevada Department of Transportation, Carson City.
Dansie, D. P.
  1975   John T. Reid's Case for the Redheaded Giants. *Nevada Historical Society Quarterly* 18(7):152-167.
DeQuille, D. (William Wright)
  1963   *Washoe Rambles.* Westernlore Press, Los Angeles.
Downs, J. F.
  1966   *The Two Worlds of the Washo.* Holt, Rinehart and Winston, New York.
Driver, H. E.
  1961   *Indians of North America.* University of Chicago Press. Chicago.
Driver H. E., and W. C. Massey
  1957   Comparative Studies of North American Indians. *Transactions of the American Philosophical Society* 47(2). Philadelphia.
Fowler, C. S.
  1986   Subsistence. In *Great Basin*, edited by W. L. d'Azevedo, pp. 64-97. Handbook of North American Indians, vol. 11, W. G. Sturtevant, general editor. Smithsonian Institution, Washington, D.C.
Fowler, C. S., and S. Liljeblad
  1986   Northern Paiute. In *Great Basin*, edited by W. L. d'Azevedo, pp. 435-465. Handbook of North American Indians, vol. 11, W. G. Sturtevant, general editor. Smithsonian Institution, Washington, D.C.
Goss, J. A.
  1972   A Basin-Plateau Shoshonean Ecological Model. In *Great Basin Cultural Ecology, a Symposium*, edited by Don D. Fowler, pp. 123-128. University of Nevada, Desert Research Institute Publications in the Social Sciences No. 8. Reno.
Grayson, D. K.
  1983   The Paleontology of Gatecliff Shelter: Small Mammals. In *The Archaeology of Monitor Valley. 2. Gatecliff Shelter* by D. H. Thomas, pp. 99-126. Anthropological Papers, American Museum of Natural History 59(2):1-552. New York.

1985   The Paleontology of Hidden Cave: Birds and Mammals. In *The Archaeology of Hidden Cave*, edited by D. H. Thomas, pp. 125–161 Anthropological Papers, American Museum of Natural History, 61(1)1–430. New York.

Haag, W. G.
1948   An Osteometric Analysis of some Aboriginal Dogs. *Reports in Anthropology, University of Kentucky, Lexington* VII(3):108-264.

Hall, E. R.
1946   *Mammals of Nevada*. University of California Press, Berkeley.

Heizer, R. F., M. A. Baumhoff, and C. W. Clewlow
1968   The Archaeology of South Fork Shelter (NV-EL-11), Elko County, Nevada. In *Papers on Great Basin Prehistory*, pp. 1-58. University of California Archaeological Survey Reports No. 71. Berkeley.

Howe, C. B.
1979   *Ancient Modocs of California and Oregon*. Binford and Mort, Portland.

Janestski, J. C.
1986   The Great Basin Lacustrine Subsistence Pattern: Insights from Utah Valley. In *Anthropology of the Desert West, Essays in Honor of Jesse D. Jennings*, edited by Carol J. Condie and Don D. Fowler, pp. 145–168. University of Utah Anthropological Papers No. 110. Salt Lake City.
1990   The Role of Lake Edge Resources in Hunter–Gatherer Subsistence: Faunal Evidence from the Eastern Great Basin. Paper presented at the 55th Annual meeting of the Society for American Archaeology, Las Vegas.

Kelly, R.
1990   The Archaeology of Great Basin Wetlands: Subsistence, Sedentism and Storage. Paper presented at the 55th annual meeting of the Society for American Archaeology, Las Vegas.

Livingston, S. D.
1988   *The Avian and Mammalian Faunas from Lovelock Cave and the Humboldt Lakebed Site*. Unpublished Ph.D. dissertation, University of Washington, Seattle.

Loud, L. L., and M. R. Harrington
1929   Lovelock Cave. University of California *Publications in American Archaeology and Ethnology* 25(1):1-183. Berkeley.

Madsen, D. B.
1982   Get it Where the Gettin's Good: A Variable Model of Great Basin Subsistence and Settlement Based on Data from the Eastern Great Basin. In *Man and Environment in the Great Basin*, edited by D. Madsen and J. O'Connell, pp. 206–226. SAA Papers No. 2. Society for American Archaeology, Washington, D.C.

Orr, Phil C.
1972   The Eighth Lake Lahontan (Nevada) Expedition, 1957. In *National Geographic Society Research Reports, 1955-1960*, pp. 123–126. National Geographic Society, Washington, D.C.

Pettigrew, R. M.
1980   The Ancient Chewaucanians: More on the Prehistoric Lake Dwellers of Lake Abert, Southwestern Oregon. *Association of Oregon Archaeologists, Occasional Papers* No. 1. pp. 49–67. Portland.
1985   *Archaeological Investigations on the East Shore of Lake Abert, Lake County, Oregon*. University of Oregon Anthropological Papers No. 32. Eugene.

Price, J. A.
1962   *Washo Economy*. Nevada State Museum Anthropological Papers No. 6. Carson City.
1980   *The Washo Indians: History, Life Cycle, Religion, Technology, Economy and Modern Life*. Nevada State Museum Occasional Papers No. 4. Carson City.

Raven, C., and R. G. Elston
1988   *Preliminary Investigations in Stillwater Marsh: Human Prehistory and Geoarchaeology*, 2 vols. Intermountain Research Reports, Silver City, Nevada.

Ray, V. F.
1963   *Primitive Pragmatists, The Modoc Indians of Northern California*. University of Washington Press, Seattle.

Reid, J.
n.d.   The Papers of John T. Reed, Lovelock, Nevada. Ms. on file, Nevada Historical Society. Reno.

Riddell, F. A.
1960   The Archaeology of the Karlo Site (Las-7). *University of California Archaeological Survey Report* 53:1-110.
1978   *Honey Lake Paiute Ethnography*. Nevada State Museum Occasional Papers No. 3. Carson City.

Roust, N. L.
1958   Archaeological Materials from Winnemucca Lake Caves. *University of California Archaeological Survey Report* 44(2):1-3.

Rusco, M. K., and J. O. Davis
1987   *Studies in Archaeology, Geology and Paleontology at Rye Patch Reservoir, Pershing County, Nevada*. Nevada State Museum Anthropological Papers No. 20. Carson City.

Schmitt, D. N.
1986   Faunal Analysis. In *The Archaeology of the Vista Site (26Wa3017)*, by C. D. Zeier and R. G. Elston, pp. 209-239. Intermountain Research, Silver City, Nevada. Submitted to Cultural Resource Section, Nevada Department of Transportation, Carson City. Contract No. P51-84-013.

1988   Mammalian Fauna. In *Preliminary Investigation in Stillwater Marsh: Human Prehistory and Geoarchaeology*, edited by C. Raven and R. Elston, pp. 262–290. Intermountain Research Reports, Silver City, Nevada.

Spier, L.
1930   *Klamath Ethnography*. University of California Publications in American Archaeology and Ethnography vol. 30. Berkeley.

Steward, J. H.
1938   *Basin-Plateau Aboriginal Sociopolitical Groups*. Smithsonian Institution Bureau of American Ethnology Bulletin 120. U.S. Government Printing Office, Washington, D.C.

Stewart, O. C.
1941   *Culture Element Distribution XIV: Northern Paiute*. University of California Anthropological Records 4(3). Berkeley.

Tuohy, D. R., A. J. Dansie, and M. B. Haldeman
1987   *Final Report on Excavations in the Stillwater Marsh Archaeological District, Nevada*. Nevada State Museum Archaeological Services Reports. Carson City.

Walker, D. N., and G. Frison
1982   Studies on Amerindian Dogs, 3: Prehistoric Wolf/Dog Hybrids from the Northwestern Plains. *Journal of Archaeological Science* 9:125–172.

Wheat, M.
1967   *Survival Arts of the Primitive Paiutes*. University of Nevada Press, Reno.

Wilson, G. L.
1924   *The Horse and the Dog in Hidatsa Culture*. Anthropological Papers of the American Museum of Natural History, 15(2). New York.

Willig, J. A., C. M. Aikens, and J. Fagan
1988   *Early Human Occupation in Far Western North America: The Clovis–Archaic Interface*. Nevada State Museum Anthropological Papers No. 21. Carson City.

Wormington, H. M.
1959   *Prehistoric Indians of the Southwest*. The Denver Museum of Natural History Popular Series No. 7. Denver.

Zeier, C. D., and R. G. Elston,
1986   *The Archaeology of the Vista Site (26Wa3017)*. Intermountain Research, Silver City, Nevada. Submitted to Cultural Resource Section, Nevada Department of Transportation, Carson City. Contract No. P51–84–013.

11

A WETLANDS AND UPLANDS SETTLEMENT–SUBSISTENCE MODEL FOR WARNER VALLEY, OREGON

William J. Cannon, C. Cliff Creger, Don D. Fowler, Eugene M. Hattori, and Mary F. Ricks

Abstract

Recent archaeological research in Warner Valley, Oregon is reported. Data indicate prehistoric occupations from Paleo-Indian to historic times. Previous research suggested a valley floor-centered settlement-subsistence system with upland utilization confined to hunting and toolstone acquisition. Data reported herein indicate that villages were occupied in the uplands as well as on the valley floor, and that the uplands were a major resource area for plant and animal foods, as well as toolstone.

Introduction

The northwestern section of the Great Basin is characterized by valley basins containing one or more lakes, or lake–systems. These include Summer Lake, Lake Abert, Surprise Valley, Warner Valley, Massacre Lake and the Harney–Malheur area. Unlike many other basins to the south and east, these basins generally have sufficient water to support marsh plants, fish, and water fowl. Hence, the basin floors can be characterized as wetlands areas.

Cressman (1936, 1937, 1942) conducted perfunctory surveys in some of these basins in the 1930s. However, systematic work was initiated by Margaret Weide (1968, 1974), who conducted a series of surveys in Warner Valley in the late 1960s–early 1970s. M. Weide proposed a lakeside settlement–subsistence model that is discussed below. M. Weide's work was followed by O'Connell's (1975) surveys and excavations in Surprise Valley, Fagan's (1974) work in the general region, Aikens and Greenspan's (1988) work at Malheur, and Pettigrew's and Oetting's (Pettigrew 1980, 1985; Oetting and Pettigrew 1987) work at Lake Abert. In addition, there have been numerous CRM surveys in many portions of the region (Bureau of Land Management 1975–1989), and an on–going rock art survey in Lake County, Oregon (e.g., Cannon and Ricks 1986). Since 1987, the University of Nevada, Reno has conducted an archaeological field school in Warner Valley (Fowler et al. 1989). The results of these projects, as well as others not cited, suggest that M. Weide's (1968, 1974) model of lake–side adaptation in the northern Great Basin should be extended. Her model postulated that settlements clustered around valley floor lakes close to the available marsh–plant, bird and fish resources, as well as the plant and small animal resources available on the adjacent flats and foothills. Use of the uplands was confined largely to hunting and toolstone acquisition. More recent data suggest that this model needs to be expanded, as will be discussed below. Warner Valley is used here as an example. However, the data from adjacent basins suggest that the expanded model has more general applicability in the northern Great Basin.

The Setting

Warner Valley (Figure 1) is located in Lake County, southern Oregon (the extreme northern end of the valley is in Harney County). The valley proper is a dog–legged basin extending some 130 km north–south, and 5 to 15 km east–west, with a drainage area of 3,600+ square km. The valley is dominated on the east by the fault scarp of Hart Mountain and its northward extension, Poker Jim Ridge, with elevations ranging from 2,280 to 2,640 m. On the west is Lynch's Rim, at 2,030 m, and the Coyote and Rabbit hills, at roughly 1,700 to 1,900 m elevation.

Warner Valley, together with Abert and Goose Lake valleys on the west, and Guano Valley on the east, form a transition area between the tabular basalt fields of the Columbia Plateau to the north and the fault–block mountains of the Basin and Range Province to the southeast. All three valleys have tilted blocks of Tertiary volcanics along their east sides with steep, west–facing scarps. Behind the scarps are gentle (5–10 degree) backslopes. The southwestern side of Warner Valley is similarly bounded by an east–facing fault scarp, Lynch's Rim, with a westward–inclined backslope, Drake's Flat.

In Pluvial times the valley floor was covered by Lake Warner. Its last high stand, about 11,000 B.P., was 98 m above the valley floor, with a surface area of ca. 1,310 square km, including a northwestward–extending bay that covered much of the Rabbit Basin. Following this high–stand, the lake receded in early Holocene times, leaving remnant playas that form the present valley–floor lake–marsh system. The valley floor lies at an elevation of about 1,360 m, On it is a series of shallow, interconnected lakes and sloughs. The lakes and sloughs form a wetlands system with over 480 km of shoreline. The system is fed primarily by runoff from the Warner Mountains to the west, **via** the Honey Creek, Deep Creek, and Twenty Mile Creek drainages. Other major sources of runoff are the Abert backslope–Rabbit Basin drainage, and some runoff from Hart Mountain.

The lake–slough system fills from south to north, with Crump and Hart lakes being its "reservoirs." D. Weide, (1975) estimates that when storage volume in the system exceeds 81.4 million cubic meters per water–year, the sloughs and lakes north of Hart Lake begin to fill. During the 1984–86 wet years, there was an estimated maximum of 490 million cubic meters of water in storage in the system. But, the water volume fluctuation is wide and rapid. In 1959 there was an estimated 72 million cubic meters in storage, and during the 1930s drought, very little water indeed. However, the system has never fully dried up: it contains four indigenous species of fish, and one fresh–water clam species.

Arcuate Dunes

Major features of the lake–slough system are arcuate, stabilized, clay–silt dunes, up to eight m high and five km long, on the leeward sides of lake beds. The dunes are of eolian origin. According to D. Weide (1975:198):

"Clay dunes are formed of sand–size aggregates of silt–clay particles stripped from dry crusts formed on desiccated lake floors, rolled into pellets, and deposited on the downwind side of the lake basin as a single, large foredune. Once such a clay dune begins to form, seasonal rains saturate the silt–clay particles wherein they become adhesive and plastic, preventing migration of the dune. Growth, in general, occurs when infrequent dry spells expose the surface of the adjoining lake basin to the action of a strong prevailing wind."

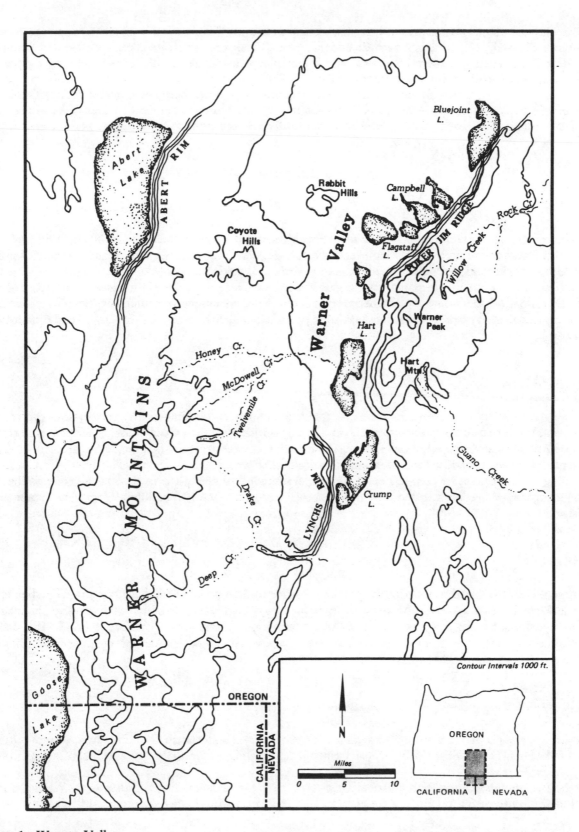

Figure 1. Warner Valley

The clay–silt dunes occur primarily in the northern end of Warner Valley around Anderson, Swamp, Mugwump, Flagstaff, Upper and Lower Campbell, Stone Corral, and Bluejoint lakes. West of the Campbell lakes there is an extensive system of sloughs bounded by playas, low dunes, stabilized arcuate dune ridges, and drainage terraces. The area is referred to locally as the Pot Holes, a term used herein. In southern Warner Valley, south of the Narrows, arcuate dunes are less common. However, there is a remnant dune in the middle of Crump Lake, and there are dune areas associated with both Greaser Lake and Coleman Lake in the south end of the valley. The arcuate dunes were occupied recurrently during prehistoric times, as discussed below.

Biological Resources

Wetlands Flora

According to D. Weide (1975:135), the lake–slough system reached its present form by about 8700 B.P., as Lake Warner waned during the early Holocene. From then, until twentieth century irrigation projects lowered the water table, there was about 4,200 ha of marsh–lands in the south end of the valley. There were several hundred hectares of additional marsh land around the Honey Creek delta, at the northwest end of Hart Lake. When the system overflows into the northern playas and sloughs, ephemeral strip marshes form, here and there, along the shorelines. The principal marsh plants are tule (*Scirpus* sp.), baltic rush (*Juncus* sp.), and some cattails (*Typha* sp.).

Valley Floor Flora

Vegetation on the non–marsh areas of the valley floor is dominated by greasewood (*Sarcobatus vermiculatus*), intermixed with various grasses and woody shrubs, including spiny hopsage (*Grayia spinosa*) and shadscale (*Atriplex confertifolia*). Lower bajada slopes with rocky substrate are dominated by big sage (*Artemisia tridentata*). Grasses found in the valley include saltgrass (*Distichlis* sp.), squirrel tail (*Sitanion* sp.), wild rye (*Elymus* sp.), and cheat grass (*Bromus* sp.). Although rare today, probably due to grazing and competition with cheat grass, Indian rice grass (*Oryzopsis hymenoides*) is present. It was possibly a major food resource in prehistoric times.

Uplands Flora

The uplands, the broad backslopes of the fault rims, generally above 1,630 m, have many small graben lakes, particularly the backslope of Hart Mountain. There are two upland biotic communities, a big–sage/bunchgrass community with scattered junipers, and a low–sage/bunchgrass community on shallow lithosols. The shallow lithosols support extensive stands of lomatiums, camas, yampa, bitterroot, and numerous other food, fiber and medicinal plants of known ethnographic use.

Fauna

Warner Valley is on the Pacific Flyway, and over 30 species of water and shore birds nest, or rest—often in great numbers—in the valley marshes. These include pelicans, grebes, herons, coots, geese, ducks, swans, cranes, snipe, and avocets.

The Warner lakes have four endemic species of fish: the redband trout (*Salmo* sp.), Warner sucker (*Catostomus warnerensis*), tui chub (*Gila bicolor*), and speckled dace (*Rhinichthys osculas*). In addition there are introduced modern game fish species (Greenspan 1989). Freshwater clams inhabit the lakes, and clam shell fragments are found in quantity in and on archaeological sites in the Pot Holes area and elsewhere.

The nearby uplands of Hart Mountain and Poker Jim Ridge support herds of antelope (*Antilocapra americana*) and bighorn sheep (*Ovis canadensis*). Although the bighorn sheep are twentieth century reintroductions into the area, they were a major element of the prehistoric fauna. Mule deer (*Odocoileus hemionus*), jack rabbit (*Lepus californicus*), and cottontail rabbit (*Sylvilagus* sp.) are also observed within the valley.

Archaeological Resources

Surveys by M. Weide, subsequent CRM surveys, and test excavations conducted in 1987–88 have demonstrated a range of archaeological site types in Warner Valley. Based on diagnostic projectile point types occupation is suggested from Paleo Indian times (>11,000 B.P.) to historic times. It should be noted that this chronology is based principally on cross–dating. Stratified sites have been badly vandalized over the past 50–75 years. Undisturbed stratigraphic sections in such sites are rare. Those cultural materials that have been excavated from undisturbed deposits date earlier than 4,000 B.P. (Fowler et al. 1989:8–31).

Diagnostic projectile points include possible Clovis forms: basal fragments exhibiting basal grinding and made on the same material as Clovis points from the Dietz site, located some 50 km to the northwest (Fagan 1988, Willig 1988). The full range of Archaic forms is present in the valley, from Great Basin Stemmed through Desert Side–notched (Fowler et al. 1989:33–44 and Figures 1–5).

Site Types

Types of archaeological sites found on the valley floor are as follows: marsh–edge processing sites, pit houses villages, dune camp sites, and rock art sites. In the uplands there are rock rings (probable hunting blinds as well as house rings), pit houses, plant gathering areas, hunting areas, small rockshelters, quarry areas, and rock art sites.

Marsh–edge processing sites are located on low benches adjacent to stands of marsh plants on lake shores or along slough areas. Three such sites are known in the Narrows area, a slough that connects Crump and Hart Lakes. Two of these were tested in 1987–88. A number of other similar sites are known in the valley, but are on private land and not accessible. All have been badly vandalized. The sites are characterized by one to two meters of black, greasy midden. There are literally hundreds of manos, and broken flat grinding slabs, and mortars (the whole specimens have been removed by collectors) on the sites and in the adjacent slough areas. The midden deposits contain quantities of clam shell fragments and fish bones, as well as bird bones, egg shells, and rabbit, antelope, and big horn sheep bones. Surprisingly, there are **very** few bones of aquatic mammals (Dansie 1989:A1–3). Diagnostic point types on both tested sites, again range from Great Basin Stemmed to Desert Side–notched forms.

Earlier reports spoke of these sites as "pit house villages." No evidence of floor or wall features, post–molds, etc. were found in the test excavations. Some of the vandal holes are old and overgrown with brush and grasses. Surficially, they look a great deal like the pit houses elsewhere in the general region: shallow plant–filled depressions. On the other hand, the vandalism is so extensive that clear evidence of houses has been destroyed and therefore missed by the test excavations.

What these sites appear to be are lake–side "grocery stores"—procurement areas for marsh plants (tules and cattails), birds, bird eggs, fish, and clams. Rabbits and ground squirrels could be taken on the adjacent benches and slopes, and antelope and big horn sheep were procured in the adjacent uplands. The marsh resources would have been available from early spring until late fall.

Valley floor pit house villages occur on gravel benches a few meters above the lake shores or sloughs. In the Narrows area, there is a (badly vandalized) series of eight to ten possible house depressions on a bench overlooking the slough connecting Hart and Crump lakes, and a second on the west shore of Crump Lake. Both remain to be tested. There are similar sites in the south end of the valley; these too remain to be tested. It is suggested that the pit house villages were, minimally, winter–village locales, although possibly having some occupants throughout the year, while others exploited resources elsewhere.

Rock art sites occur on large boulders at the bases of talus slopes along the edges of the valley floor. There is a concentration of such sites near the Narrows marsh and village sites.

As noted above, there are extensive arcuate dunes along the lee sides of the Warner lakes, particularly in the north half of the valley. The very high water of 1984–86 resulted in wave–action erosion of the dune faces. As the waters receded in 1987, hundreds of chipped and ground stone artifacts were eroded from the dunes and deposited on the beaches. In addition to the full range of Archaic point types, there were utilized flakes, and flat tabular, rectangular stone artifacts with edge chipping as well as chipped notches on the long sides. These are presumed to be sinkers for nets and set–lines. There were also manos, slab grinding stones, and broken mortars (Fowler et al. 1989:44–53).

Test excavations in arcuate dunes at Flagstaff and Campbell lakes demonstrated that here, as elsewhere, dune stratigraphy is extremely complex. Problems include relatively younger inset dunes at the bases of older dunes, secondary deposits and various other complexities. It was hoped that evidence of living floors or use areas would be found. A small cache pit lined with pond weed (cf. *Potamogeton* sp.) matting was found, together with two hearths, but no other clear evidence of occupation was seen. Given the plethora of artifacts on the beaches, it is clear that the dunes were occupied recurrently over a long time period. But, the artifacts were also winnowed from hundreds of cubic meters of dunes. Large scale machine–aided testing of dunes for both archaeological and geo–archaeological purposes will be required to gain a clearer understanding of the dynamics of dune building and deflation and the sequencing of prehistoric dune occupations.

In the Potholes area, there are dune fields rimming alkali flats. These dunes are lower and smaller than the lake–edge arcuate dunes. Here artifacts are found in deflated areas, and eroding from deflating leeward sides of the dunes. Both chipped stone and ground stone artifacts occur in these locales, together with animal bone and clam shell fragments.

The available evidence suggests that the arcuate dunes were locales for the taking of fish and clams when there was sufficient water in the adjacent lakes. Both arcuate and other dunes may have been locales for the collecting of native seed plants. However, the dunes have been badly over–grazed over the past century, so much so that the native plant situation cannot be determined at present. There is only one stand, of any size, of Indian rice grass (*Oryzopsis hymenoides*) known in the valley, near Plush. Currently, the valley soils are being mapped by the Soil Conservation Service, and a botanical survey is being undertaken by the Bureau of Land Management. Data from these studies will allow predictive modelling of past ethnobotanical resource areas.

Uplands site types include hunting areas, as noted. We refer here specifically to areas around shallow graben lakes and springs on the backslope of Hart Mountain, and in the Rabbit Basin area on the west side of the valley. The lakes/ponds and springs provide permanent, or semi–permanent, "water holes" and hence were focal points for hunting larger mammals, as well as rodents. The Rabbit Basin drains several thousand hectares of the backslope of the Abert Rim. Except during heavy rains, most of the drainage is sub–surface. However, at one point the water comes to the surface, forming a small one to three hectare pond, rimmed by marsh plants. There are surface concentrations of chipped and ground stone artifacts over a radius of 2+ km. around the pond. Diagnostic point types suggest intermittent use of the area over several thousand years. M. Weide (1968) reports a similar artifact concentration around Petroglyph Lake on Hart Mountain. A systematic survey of areas around the springs and lakes/ponds on Hart Mountain and Lynch's Rim remains to be done, for areas not previously covered, e.g., by Fagan (1974).

On the backslopes of Hart Mountain and Lynch's Rim there are extensive concentrations of root and seed plants of known ethnographic usage (Fowler 1986, Couture et al. 1986), including lomatiums, camas, yampa, bitterroot, wild onion etc. Assuming a similar, or even more extensive, pre–grazing distribution of these resources, there would have been numerous major plant–gathering areas available in prehistoric times.

The use of the plant gathering areas is suggested by the presence, in the upland areas, of pit houses, associated with large numbers of ground stone implements, both bedrock and portable, as well as concentrations of rock art (Ricks and Cannon 1989).

In addition to pit house village locales, there are rock ring sites situated in various "overlook" areas, e.g., on Lynch's Rim (Bureau of Land Management 1975–89). Some of these sites may have served primarily as hunting blinds; others may have served as uplands summer houses. Sites of this type are scheduled for test excavation to determine their functions.

In "rim" areas on both sides of the valley there are a number of small rockshelter locales. These are usually situated at the bases of cliffs. Most have been thoroughly vandalized. They may have served as equipment cache sites and temporary hunting camps.

Finally, there are toolstone procurement areas in the uplands; sources for nodular obsidian and aphanitic basalt (M. Weide 1968).

Given the data at hand, the settlement–subsistence model proposed by M. Weide (1968, 1974) was quite appropriate, and, indeed, innovative at a time when "site specific" archaeology was the norm in the Great Basin. However, data accumulated since M. Weide's work (Cannon and Ricks 1986, Bureau of Land Management 1975–89, Fowler et al. 1989) suggest that M. Weide's model can be extended. As indicated previously, M. Weide proposed that during Archaic times, the primary foci of both settlement and subsistence were the lake edges and valley floors. The uplands were visited principally for hunting and the acquisition of toolstone.

Much of the data not available to M. Weide derive from the uplands (well over 100 sites). Ethnobotanical observations indicate that the upland back–slopes are major areas for edible seeds, roots, and bulbs used in ethnographic times (Coutere et al. 1986; cf. Fowler 1986, Fowler and Liljeblad 1986), and presumably earlier. There are hundreds of hectares of such resources on the Hart Mountain and Lynch's Rim backslopes and in the Rabbit Basin, as noted previously. In addition to lithic scatters, there are apparent pit houses and above–ground rock house rings with numerous associated grinding implements, both bedrock and portable. Given these data, Ricks and Cannon (1989:7) propose:

" . . . that the populations which wintered in the lowland areas surrounding Warner Lake during the past 7,000 years were using a tethered subsistence strategy, with the lowland lake basin as the primary focus of subsistence activity. During the late spring and summer, the upland areas of the Warner Basin became a secondary focus of activity. . . . A substantial portion of the period between April and August [was spent] in the uplands, harvesting and processing plant materials such as Bitterroot (Lomatium spp.), Wild Onion (*Allium* spp.), Sego Lily (*Calochortus macrocarpus*), Camas (*Camassia quamash*), Wild carrot (*Perideridia* spp.), Ponderosa Pine (*Pinus ponderosa*), Chokecherry (*Prunus virginiana*), Wild Currant (*Ribes aureum* and *Ribes cerum*), and Huckleberry (*Vaccinium membranaceum*). While in the uplands they also hunted, procured lithic materials and gathered wood. Recent Harney Valley Paiute, according to informants [Coutere et al. 1986], met with members of neighboring groups in large upland gatherings, where activities included gambling, trading, arranging of marriages, and general socializing. We would suggest that this pattern may be of long standing, and that archaeological investigation of the sites identified as major upland occupation sites will show additional evidence of these activities."

The combined M. Weide and Ricks and Cannon models are schematically represented in Figure 2.

Much research remains to be done to verify and expand the model. Paleoenvironmental research currently being conducted by the Desert Research Institute in the northern Great Basin, including Warner Valley, will add substantially to the data base required. As indicated, soils and botanical surveys are presently underway. An extensive ethnobotanical survey of the Warner Valley is under development, focussing on the uplands areas. An overall research design for the "Tri–Corners" region—the area at which the states of California, Nevada, and Oregon converge—is in draft form and is currently being refined (Bunten et al. 1989). The research design calls for an extensive program of systematic survey, test excavations, and paleoenvironmental and taphonomic research in the region. Together with data being generated by researchers in adjacent valley basins, we expect that understanding of prehistoric cultural–environmental interactions in the northern Great Basin will improve substantially in the years ahead.

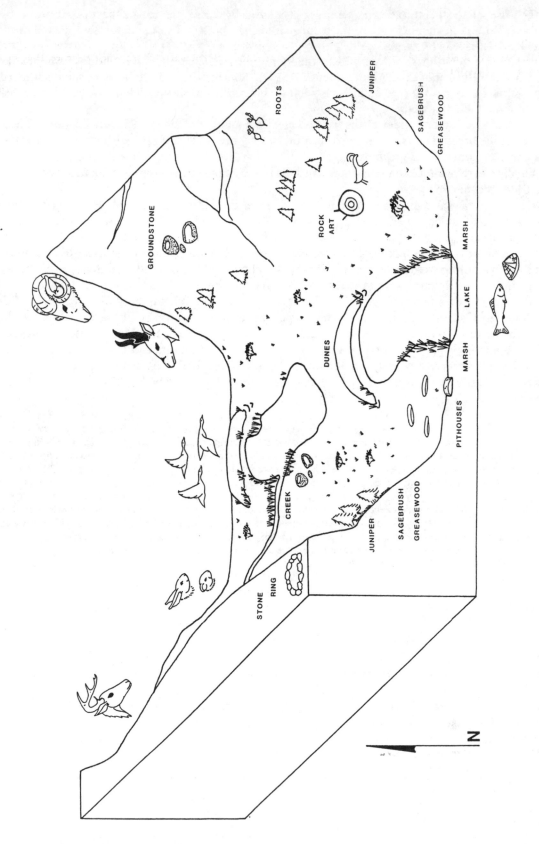

Figure 2. Warner Valley Settlement-Susbsistence Schematic

Acknowledgments

Research in Warner Valley by the University of Nevada, Reno was made possible under cooperative agreements between the university and the Bureau of Land Management Lakeview, Oregon District Office and the U.S. Fish and Wildlife Service, Hart Mountain National Wildlife Refuge. We thank all concerned for their interest and support. This paper is University of Nevada, Reno, Department of Anthropology, Research Report 89–2.

References

Aikens, C., M., and R. Greenspan
  1988   Ancient Lakeside Culture in the Northern Great Basin: Malheur Lake, Oregon. *Journal of California and Great Basin Anthropology* 10(1):32–61.

Bunten, H., W. J. Cannon, D. D. Fowler, E. M. Hattori, and D. Manuel
  1989   Research Design for Archaeological and Paleoenvironmental Investigations in the "TriCorner" Region, California, Nevada, Oregon. Ms. in preparation.

Bureau of Land Management
  1975-89 Site Survey Records and CRM Project Reports, Warner Valley Region, Oregon. Copies on file, BLM Lakeview, Oregon District Office, and Museum of Anthropology, University of Nevada, Reno.

Cannon, W. J., and M. F. Ricks
  1986   The Lake County Rock Art Inventory: Implications for Prehistoric Settlement and Land Use Patterns. Contributions to the Archaeology of Oregon. *Association of Oregon Archaeologists Occasional Papers* No. 3:1–23.

Couture, M. D., M. F. Ricks, and L. Housley
  1986   Foraging Behavior of a Contemporary Northern Paiute Population. *Journal of California and Great Basin Anthropology* 8(2):150–160.

Cressman, L. S.
  1936   Archaeological Survey of the Guano Valley Region in Southeastern Oregon. *University of Oregon Monographs, Studies in Anthropology* 1:1–48. Eugene.
  1937   Petroglyphs of Oregon. *University of Oregon Monographs, Studies in Anthropology* No. 2. Eugene.
  1942   Archaeological Researches in the Northern Great Basin of South-Central Oregon. *Carnegie Institution of Washington Publication* No. 538.

Dansie, A. J.
  1989   Warner Valley Mammalian Faunal Remains. Appendix 1 in *Summary Report of Archaeological Investigations in Warner Valley, Lake County, Oregon, 1987–1988*, by D. Fowler, E. Hattori, and C. Creger. University of Nevada, Reno, Department of Anthropology Research Reports 89–1. Reno.

Fagan, J. L.
  1974   Altithermal Occupation of Spring Sites in the Northern Great Basin. *University of Oregon Anthropological Papers* No. 6. Eugene.
  1988   Clovis and Western Pluvial Lakes Tradition Lithic Technologies at the Deitz Site in South-Central Oregon. In *Early Human Occupations in Far Western North America: The Clovis-Archaic Interface*, edited by J. A. Willig, C. M. Aikens, and J. L. Fagan, pp. 389–416. Nevada State Museum Anthropological Papers No. 21. Carson City.

Fowler, C. S.
  1986   Subsistence. In *Great Basin*, edited by W. L. d'Azevedo, pp. 64–97. Handbook of North American Indians, vol. 11, W. G. Sturtevant, general editor. Smithsonian Institution, Washington, D.C.

Fowler, C. S., and S. Liljeblad
  1986   Northern Paiute. In *Great Basin*, edited by W. L. d'Azevedo, pp. 435–465. Handbook of North American Indians, vol. 11, W. G. Sturtevant, general editor. Smithsonian Institution, Washington, D.C.

Fowler, D. D., E. M. Hattori, and C. C. Creger
  1989   *Summary Report of Archaeological Investigations in Warner Valley, Lake County, Oregon, 1987–1988*. University of Nevada, Reno, Department of Anthropology Research Reports 89–1. Reno.

Greenspan, R. L.
  1989   Fish Remains Recovered from Prehistoric Sites, Warner Valley, Oregon. Appendix 2 in *Summary Report of Archaeological Investigations in Warner Valley, Lake County, Oregon, 1987–1988*, by D. Fowler, E. Hattori, and C. Creger. University of Nevada, Reno, Department of Anthropology Research Reports 89–1. Reno.

O'Connell, J. F.
  1975   *The Prehistory of Surprise Valley*. Ballena Press Anthropological Papers, No. 4. Ramona, California.

Oetting, A. C., and R. M. Pettigrew
  1987   *Archaeological Investigations in the Lake Abert-Chewaucan Basin, Lake County Oregon: The 1986 Survey*. The Cultural Heritage Foundation, Portland.

Pettigrew, R. M.
   1980   The Ancient Chewaucanians: More on the Prehistoric Lake Dwellers of Lake Abert, Southeastern Oregon. *Association of Oregon Archaeologists Occasional Papers* 1:49–67.
   1985   *Archaeological Investigations on the East Shore of Lake Abert, Lake County, Oregon.* University of Oregon Anthropological Papers No. 32. Eugene.
Ricks, M. F., and W. J. Cannon
   1989   Some Thoughts on Prehistoric Settlement and Subsistence in the Warner Valley Region, Southern Oregon. Ms. on file, Department of Anthropology, University of Nevada, Reno.
Weide, D. L.
   1975   *Postglacial Geomorphology and Environments of the Warner Valley–Hart Mountain Area, Oregon.* Unpublished Ph.D. dissertation, University of California, Los Angeles.
Weide, M. Lyneis
   1968   Cultural Ecology of Lakeside Adaptation in the Western Great Basin. Unpublished Ph.D. dissertation, University of California, Los Angeles.
   1974   North Warner Subsistence Network: A Prehistoric Band Territory. *Nevada Archaeological Survey Research Paper* 5:62–79. Reno.
Willig, J. A.
   1988   Paleo–Archaic Adaptations and Lakeside Settlement Patterns in the Northern Alkali Basin, Oregon. In *Early Human Occupation in Far Western North America: The Clovis–Archaic Interface,* edited by J. A. Willig, C. M. Aikens, and J. L. Fagan, pp. 417–81. Nevada State Museum Anthropological Papers No. 21. Carson City.

ABORIGINAL SETTLEMENT IN THE LAKE ABERT–CHEWAUCAN MARSH BASIN, LAKE COUNTY, OREGON

Albert C. Oetting

Abstract

The Lake Abert–Chewaucan Marsh Basin contains a variety of modern wetlands settings. Archaeological investigations have identified over 300 archaeological sites, including many with circular pithouse depressions and rock rings. Analyses of survey and excavation data resulted in the definition of a regional cultural chronology and a reconstruction of aboriginal settlement patterning. Riverine, marsh, and lake–side settings were important to humans throughout the later Holocene and changes in site distributions indicate an increasing focus on wetlands resources through time. Pithouse villages, found in these wetlands settings, began to be occupied about 4,000 years ago but most were used within the last 2,000 years. Late Archaic II settlement patterns, house forms, and specific artifacts suggest these people were culturally affiliated with the Penutian–speaking Klamath. Aggression from Numic speakers, rather than environmental deterioration, may have forced Penutian withdrawal from the basin prior to Euroamerican contact.

Natural Setting

T he Lake Abert–Chewaucan Marsh Basin is in the south-central Oregon portion of the northern Great Basin (Figure 1). Pluvial Lake Chewaucan filled this basin and the neighboring Summer Lake Basin during the Pleistocene (Allison 1982:12). The Chewaucan River, flowing from the uplands west of the Chewaucan marshes, supplied water to this large lake and still connects the sub-basins of Upper Chewaucan Marsh, Lower Chewaucan Marsh, and Lake Abert. The Summer Lake Basin was isolated by late Pleistocene times. The Chewaucan River flows onto the basin floor at the town of Paisley, passes through the marshes, and drains into Lake Abert, a closed–basin saline body of water. These three sub–basins form the region focused on in this study (Figure 2).

The area is typical of the Oregon high desert and the northern Great Basin in terrain and environment, with sharp fault-block relief and arid climate. The Lake Abert–Chewaucan Marsh Basin is part of the Basin and

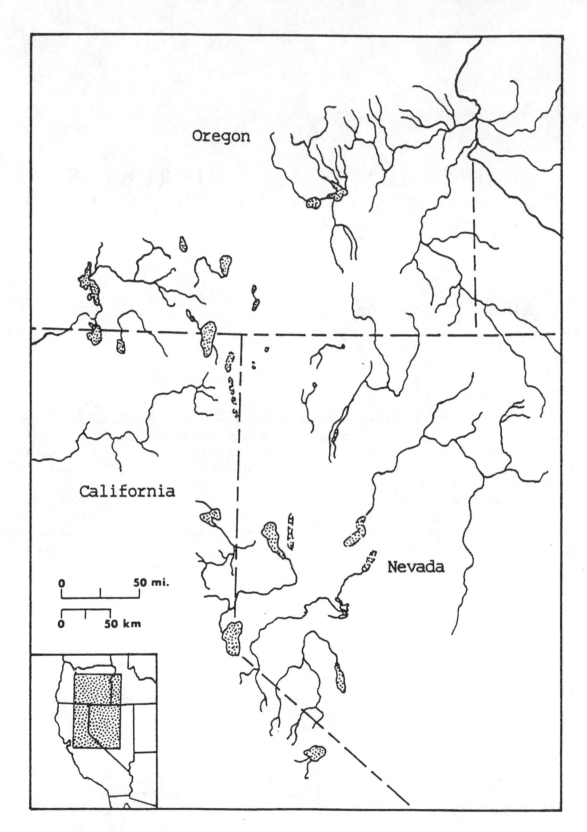

Figure 1. Location of the Lake Abert–Chewaucan Marsh Basin.

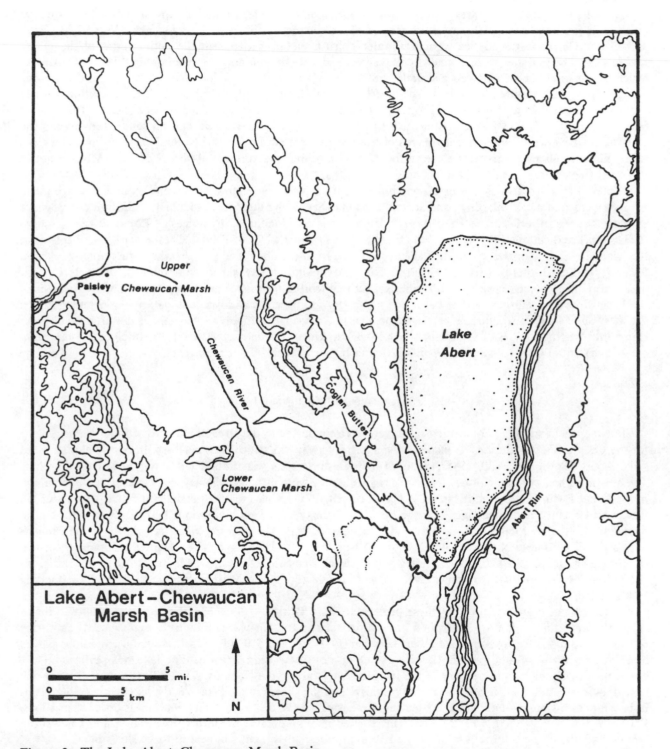

Figure 2. The Lake Abert–Chewaucan Marsh Basin.

Range Geomorphic Province (Baldwin 1981:144). The very flat basin floor consists of two grabens, both filled with lake–deposited silt and bounded by tilted fault–blocks with steep fault scarp rims. Summers are warm and dry with substantial diurnal temperature variation, while winters are cold. Precipitation is sparse and generally comes in winter and spring.

The Chewaucan River, however, provides a reliable source of water to the basin, maintaining two extensive marshes, a mcander/slough floodplain system on the lower reaches of the river, and Lake Abert. The Upper and Lower Chewaucan marshes were freshwater bulrush–cattail wetlands in the bottomlands of the marsh sub–basins. The marshes were drained between 1884 and 1915 by confining the river within dikes and channels. Much of this land is now irrigated and under cultivation. Despite the diversion of irrigation water, the average annual river discharge reaching Lake Abert is equivalent to that under natural conditions, since evapotranspiration from the marshes formerly reduced the river's inflow rate to a significant extent (Phillips and Van Denburgh 1971:B13). Lake Abert is large and shallow, its water saline and alkaline. Other than the Chewaucan River, the only current sources of fresh water around the lake are several small springs along the shoreline and ephemeral streams. The surface elevation of the lake averages about 4,255 feet AMSL, although this level fluctuates since the basin has no outlet.

Wetland resources in the form of marsh and riparian plants, waterfowl, and small to medium size game animals were and are available in and around both marshes, along the river floodplain, and around freshwater springs at the northern end of Lake Abert. These areas are dominated by bulrush (*Scirpus validus*), sedges (*Carex* spp.) and cattails (*Typha latifolia*) (Franklin and Dyrness 1973:245–246). "Chewaucan" is probably from the Klamath term *tcuwakan*, arrowhead place," derived from the abundance of arrowhead or wapato [*Sagitaria latifolia*] gathered there" (Spier 1930:10).   Salt and upland desert shrub communities, characterized by greasewood (*Sarcobatus vermiculatus*) and sagebrush (*Artemisia tridentata*) are present on the drier portions of the basin floor and margins.   The basin hosts a variety of migratory and resident waterfowl, including ducks, geese, swans (Anatidae), and grebes (Podicipedidae) (Greenspan 1985:147). Animals in the area range from chipmunks (Sciuridae), rabbits (Laporidae), and muskrats (*Ondatra zibethicus*) to antelope (*Antilocapra americana*), mule deer (*Odocoileus hemionus*), and bighorn sheep (*Ovis canadensis*).

Archaeological Background

Between 1975 and 1977 archaeological surveys were conducted by the Oregon State Museum of Anthropology for the Oregon Department of Transportation along Highway 395, which runs north-south on the east shore of Lake Abert (Pettigrew 1980, 1985). Thirty-two prehistoric sites were found along the 19 km of shoreline. Twenty–three had surface cultural features suggesting they were pithouse villages, sites considered uncommon in the Great Basin (Heizer and Napton 1970; O'Connell 1975). These features included circular depressions in the ground surface and rock rings of large boulders, both types having dimensions between 3 m and 11 m in diameter (Pettigrew 1980:52-53; Connolly and Pettigrew 1985). The majority were thought to be the remains of houses. The number of these features, over 440, was unexpected and impressive. Limited mapping, recording of surface features, and subsurface testing was done at 28 of these sites in 1977 and 1979 by the Museum (Pettigrew 1985). In 1982 further excavations were conducted by the Museum at five of these sites (Oetting 1988).

Based on preliminary data from these projects Richard Pettigrew (1980:53, 1985:183–194) proposed that a relatively large and sedentary aboriginal population, termed the Chewaucan Culture, made use of lacustrine resources around a freshwater Lake Abert between 3500 B.P. and 500 B.P. Environmental conditions played a major role in this model, both in the rise and demise of Chewaucan Culture. The lake was perhaps 50 feet above its modern elevation, because of the increased moisture of the Neopluvial after 3500 B.P., and lacustrine resources were abundant. Chewaucan Culture thrived on the shores of the lake. As the lake declined, however, it became more saline and alkaline, placing increasing stress on these lacustrine subsistence adaptations. Pettigrew felt that, by 500 B.P., the lake had attained its non–potable modern configuration and Chewaucan people had abandoned the region. Northern Paiute groups subsequently moved in to fill this void.

In 1984 and 1986 archaeological surveys funded by the Oregon State Historic Preservation Office were conducted in the basin, to expand the inventory of recorded sites and to provide the beginnings of a regional data base for comparison and analysis (Oetting and Pettigrew 1985, 1987; Oetting 1989a). These surveys intensively examined 17.6 square miles of the basin lowlands and lower slopes of the valley margins. In all, 280 sites were recorded, including 91 lithic scatters, 146 scatters of flaked lithic debris and ground stone, and 43 "village" sites, sites containing large circular depressions and/or rock rings. As discussed below, the majority of these depressions are considered to be the remains of excavated semi–subterranean pithouses and the rock rings are surface house structures. Thousands of tools, including many ground stone implements, were observed in the field and 1,673 specimens, primarily projectile points, were collected.

The present study describes the regional chronology developed for the basin, examines aboriginal settlement patterns, infers subsistence practices, and explores their change through time. Thus, this paper is primarily culture–historical in nature. Settlement patterns and chronological changes within the basin can then be used to assess the feasibility of the Chewaucan Culture hypothesis. Site distributions and surface data from the State Historic Preservation Office–funded surveys (Oetting 1989a), including surface-collected projectile points and other artifacts, provided the majority of data for the present study. Data from the excavations on the eastern shore of the lake (Pettigrew 1985; Oetting 1988) and from two other small excavations in the basin (Weld 1962; Oetting 1989b) were used to supplement the survey data and to mitigate some of the problems with using surface-collected information.

Chronology

Chronological analyses focused on the large projectile point inventory secured during the surveys. The 1,044 projectile points from the surveys were classified using temporally–sensitive types established for the western and northern Great Basin (Table 1; based on Heizer and Hester 1978; Thomas 1981; Oetting and Pettigrew 1987). The excavations on the east shore of the lake had provided 12 radiocarbon age determinations from cultural components with associated projectile point assemblages (Table 2). The ages ranged from 3480 ± 130 B.P. to 110 ± 70 B.P. and corroborated the temporal periods assigned by cross–dating the point types in the associated assemblages (Oetting 1988:211–217). These excavations also demonstrated that over 80% of the tested sites contained only one temporal cultural component (Oetting 1989a:42) thus, artifacts on the surface of sites in the region should reflect the age of the site's occupation.

Projectile point assemblages from 40 of the survey-recorded sites were seriated using Robinson Index Scores of Agreement and clustered through both average–linkage and complete–linkage cluster analyses (Oetting 1989a:91–107). Each site assemblage contained between eight and 31 points, contributing to a total of 467 specimens. The seriations and analyses revealed site clusters dominated by particular projectile point types, types considered to be chronologically significant. A multidimensional scaling plot graphically portrays these site clusters (Figure 3).

Based on these findings, a regional cultural chronology was defined (Table 3). It contained four named temporal periods, each characterized by a primary point type or combination of types (Oetting 1989a:107–116). Sites were assigned to temporal periods based on the proportions of particular point types present at that site (Table 4). The proportion criteria were defined from the site clusters identified in the various statistical analyses.

The **Initial Archaic** (11,000 to 7000 B.P.) has Great Basin Stemmed points. The **Early Archaic** (7000 to 4000 B.P.) is dominated by Northern Side–notched points. The **Middle Archaic** (4000 to 2000 B.P.) has two phases. The early part, Middle Archaic I, contains Gatecliff Split Stem and Elko series specimens, while the Middle Archaic II is characterized by Elko series points. The **Late Archaic** (2000 B.P. to Euroamerican contact) is also divided into two phases. The Late Archaic I has equivalent numbers of Elko series and Rosegate series points co–occurring and the Late Archaic II is dominated by Rosegate series points. Desert Side–notched and Cottonwood Triangular points, characteristic of the Late Prehistoric in the western Great Basin (Hester 1973:127), were associated with Late Archaic II sites, but formed less than 2% of the overall projectile point collection.

Table 1. Chronological Spans of Lake Abert–Chewaucan Marsh Basin Projectile Point Types, Based on Typological Cross-Dating

Lake Abert–Chewaucan Marsh Type	Great Basin Type	Age[1]
SSN	Desert Side-notched	750 B.P. — historic
UST	Cottonwood Triangular	1000 B.P. — historic
RGS	Rosegate series[2]	2000 B.P. — historic
ES	Elko series[2]	4000 B.P. — 1000 B.P.
GCS	Gatecliff Contracting Stem	3800 B.P. — 2200 B.P.[3]
GSS	Gatecliff Split Stem	5000 B.P. — 2700 B.P.
HCB	Humboldt Concave Base	6000 B.P. — 1300 B.P.[3]
WL	Several[4]	10000 B.P. — 1000 B.P.[3]
NSN	Northern Side-notched	7000 B.P. — 4000 B.P.
LCB	Black Rock Concave Base	11000 B.P. — 7000 B.P.
GBS	Great Basin Stemmed	11000 B.P. — 8000 B.P.

[1]Based on Heizer and Hester 1978, Thomas 1981, Wilde 1985, and Holmer 1986 (see also Oetting 1989a:Appendix C).
[2]Varieties combined (ELK2 type used by Wilde [1985:146-148] not included).
[3]Poor temporal indicators.
[4]Cognates include San Dieguito leaf-shaped bipoints (10,000 B.P. – 8000 B.P.), Cascade (7000 B.P. - 5000 B.P.), Nightfire Island Small Foliate (5000 B.P. - 2000 B.P.), and Cottonwood Leaf-shape/Bipoint (1000 B.P. – historic).

The age spans assigned to each period were based primarily on projectile point cross–dating, but the 12 radiocarbon ages from the east shore of Lake Abert provided local radiometric support for the Middle and Late Archaic periods and their phases (Table 1). Ninety–eight of the survey-recorded sites were assigned temporal periods, including 20 assemblages containing only three or four specimens. In each of these, all of the points belonged to a single type. Of the 98 sites, 20 had mixed projectile point assemblages, representing occupation during two or more periods, while 78 were single component sites with projectile points from only one period. Twenty–six assemblages from the Lake Abert excavations were also placed in this chronology.

Pithouse Sites

Seventy–six sites with circular depressions or rock rings are presently known from the basin. Over 580 depressions and 73 rock rings have been recorded (Oetting 1989a:127). The rock rings are confined to the rocky base of Abert Rim, but depressions were found in many parts of the basin. The 168 depressions recorded during the surveys ranged in diameter from 3 m to 12 m and in depth from 20 cm to over 1 m, but most were 5 m to 7 m across and 40 cm to 60 cm deep. No excavations were conducted at the 43 sites recorded during the surveys, but records of previous excavations conducted **within** such features in the Lake Abert–Chewaucan Marsh Basin were examined (Oetting 1989a:125–163). These included test trenches excavated through two depressions by Luther Cressman in 1939 (Oetting 1989b), amateur trench excavations in two depressions on the west shore of

Table 2. Radiocarbon Ages from the Lake Abert-Chewaucan Marsh Basin, by Chronological Period

Site	Assemblage	Site Location	Age Years B.P.[1]	Laboratory Number
Late Archaic II				
35Lk 542	542LTS	East Shore, Lake Abert	110 ± 70	Beta-6338
35Lk 542	542LTS	East Shore, Lake Abert	170 ± 90	Beta-6337
Chewaucan Cave[2]		Lower Chewaucan Marsh	340 ± 80	GaK-1755
35Lk 534	534	East Shore, Lake Abert	530 ± 160	Beta-6591
35Lk 536	536SU	East Shore, Lake Abert	870 ± 80	Beta-6594
Late Archaic I				
35Lk 542	542LTN	East Shore, Lake Abert	1140 ± 110	Beta-6067
35Lk 536	536MU	East Shore, Lake Abert	1140 ± 120	Beta-6335
35Lk 536	536MU	East Shore, Lake Abert	1170 ± 80	Beta-6066
35Lk 535	535U	East Shore, Lake Abert	1350 ± 80	Beta-6593
35Lk 480	480	East Shore, Lake Abert	1430 ± 140	Beta-6590
Middle Archaic I				
35Lk 536	536ML	East Shore, Lake Abert	2510 ± 90	Beta-6336
35Lk 542	542U	East Shore, Lake Abert	2940 ± 110	GaK-8532
35Lk 494	494L	East Shore, Lake Abert	3480 ± 130	GaK-8980

[1]Based on half-life of 5,568 years.
[2]Date obtained on grass bag containing cache of tools, baskets, snare pieces, and two long nets (Oetting 1989a:293-296).

Lake Abert (Weld 1962), and test pits excavated in 13 depressions and two rock rings during the Museum highway work (Pettigrew 1985; Oetting 1988).

Six of the 17 depressions tested contained definite evidence of floors (three with multiple floors), rims, earthen banks around the depression, or central fire hearths, indicating they were the remains of semisubterranean pithouses (Table 5). Another seven depressions yielded probable evidence of house floors but the excavations in these features were too limited to verify such features (Oetting 1989a:143). Both of the rock rings had internal features suggesting they were domestic structures (Table 5). No superstructure remains or evidence for postholes were found in these tests.

Ten of the definite or potential housepits were assigned to a time period based on radiocarbon ages or associated projectile points (Table 5). Six were Late Archaic II in age, two were Middle Archaic II, and two had at least two periods of occupation, a Middle Archaic component overlain by a Late Archaic component.

The tested depressions ranged in size, but those firmly identified as housepits were among the larger ones (Table 5). Five of the six were greater than 6 m in diameter while the four non–house depressions were all 5.2m or smaller. Depression depths were not available for most of the tested depressions, but HP–1 at the ZX Ranch Site was 30 cm deep and the Lower house at the Weld Site was over 70 cm deep (Oetting 1989a:147–148). All of the Late Archaic II features were 6.0 m in diameter or larger, while three of the four earlier pits were less than 6 m across. The dimensions of the depressions recorded during the surveys compare favorably with the pits identified as house depressions by these tests.

Ethnographic and archaeological data on house structures in the northern and western Great Basin and nearby regions indicated that the Lake Abert–Chewaucan Marsh house remains were most similar to those of the late prehistoric and ethnographic Klamath and Modoc (Table 6; Oetting 1989a:161–163). The Northern Paiute, who claimed the region at contact, generally did not construct buildings over excavated pits, although in western Nevada shallow pits were occasionally dug (30 cm to 60 cm deep) if families wintered in the mountains

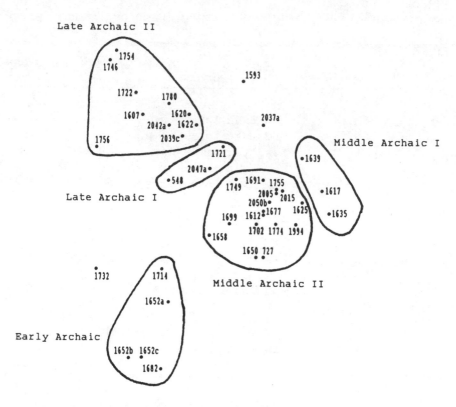

Figure 3. Multidimensional scaling plot using Robinson Index Scores of Agreement.

near pinyon groves (Fowler and Liljeblad 1986:443). Paiute dwellings, both the infrequent pithouses and the common surface brush and pole houses, were between 2.5 m and 4.5 m in diameter. Shallow, saucer–shaped depressions observed at several sites in the northern and western Great Basin (Table 6; e.g., Rodriguez Site, Dirty Shame Rockshelter, Karlo Site) are analogous to the pole and brush houses of the Paiute. The house floors are small (5 m or less in diameter) and the shallow depressions may have resulted from use rather than excavation.

Klamath and Modoc earth lodges were substantial winter structures. These dwellings varied from 3.6 m to 12 m in diameter and their pits were excavated from 30 cm to 1.5 m in depth (Spier 1930:197ff; Ray 1963:146ff). Cressman (1956) excavated several prehistoric Klamath housepits, the majority of which were 6 m to 7 m in diameter and less than 1 m in depth. Similar house remains have been found at several sites in southern Oregon and northeastern California (Table 6; e.g., Big Boulder Village, Border Village, Iron Gate Site, King's Dog Site). Ethnographic Klamath and Modoc structures usually had central posts, but the presence of postholes is variable in prehistoric Klamath examples (Cressman 1956:437). Central fire hearths were common in both ethnographic and archaeological structures (Spier 1930:203; Cressman 1956:436–443). Mat–covered houses, erected over pits 3 m to 4 m in diameter, were sometimes used for winter dwellings by the less affluent Klamath (Spier 1930:202) and may have been common winter houses for the late prehistoric Modoc (Ray 1963:146). The ethnographic Klamath and Modoc often banked earth around the bases of winter structures, forming a low earthen ridge around the excavated pit (Spier 1930:202; Ray 1963:155).

The Klamath occupied the Klamath Lake and Marsh region 40 km west of the Lake Abert–Chewaucan Marsh Basin and their winter villages were located near the many rivers, marshes, and springs in the region. These villages were semi–sedentary permanent sites containing one or more earth lodges (Spier 1930:10–13). A single earth lodge often housed several families. These houses were dismantled in the spring, but the same pits were cleaned and reused each winter. Families moved independently spring through fall taking advantage

Table 3. The Lake Abert-Chewaucan Marsh Basin Cultural Chronology

Period		Associated Projectile Point Types	Age
Late Archaic (I and II)	II:	Rosegate Series	2000 B.P. — Historic
	I:	Rosegate and Elko Series	
Middle Archaic (I and II)	II:	Elko Series	4000 B.P. — 2000 B.P.
	I:	Elko Series/Gatecliff SS	
Early Archaic		Northern Side-Notched	7000 B.P. — 4000 B.P.
Initial Archaic		Great Basin Stemmed	11,000 B.P. — 7000 B.P.

Table 4. Criteria for Classification in the Lake Abert-Chewaucan Marsh Basin Regional Chronology[1]

Period	SSN/UST[2]	RGS	ES	GSS	GCS	NSN	GBS
Late Archaic II	>0%	+50%	≤20%	<10%	>0%	—	—
Late Archaic I	—	25–50%	25–50%	10%	>0%	—	—
Middle Archaic II	—	≤15%	+50%	>10%	—	—	—
Middle Archaic I	—	—	25–50%	25–50%	—	—	—
Early Archaic	—	—	>0%	>0%	—	>20%	>0%
Initial Archaic	—	—	—	—	—	>0%	>20%

[1]Required conditions for classification are underlined.
[2]See Table 1 for type names.

of seasonally available wetlands resources, the focus of Klamath economy, before returning to their winter villages. Villages in particularly favorable locations might be occupied throughout the year (Stern 1966:11).

In sum, the size range (3 m to 12 m), depth (30 cm to 1 m), and arrangement (central hearth, occasional surrounding earth bank) of the Lake Abert–Chewaucan Marsh Basin features suggest closer affinities to the Klamath and Modoc than to the Northern Paiute. The Lake Abert–Chewaucan Marsh pithouse sites, as described below, are found in similar settings near wetlands and are of similar size, ranging from one housepit (at 12 of the 76 known sites) to over 70 house features. Overlapping pits or rock rings were found at some of the larger sites, but in general the features do not overlap. Three of the tested housepits had evidence of multiple floors, indicating reuse of the pit (Table 5). At present then, it seems reasonable to infer that the Lake Abert–Chewaucan Marsh structures and sites functioned like those of the Klamath and that the sites can be considered "villages."

Settlement Patterns

Several settlement pattern analyses involving the survey-recorded sites examined the spatial and temporal distributions of the three primary site types (Tables 7–11). The clearest associations seen were that villages, sites

Table 5. Summary of Tested Circular Features

Site	Feature	Diameter (m)	Floor	Other Features	Debitage Density	Period	House?
Circular Depressions							
35Lk 480	CF–21	4.4	2?	—	200–400	MA/LA I	Yes
35Lk 495	CF–18	9.2	3	rim	220–1260	LA II	Yes
35Lk 497	CF–8	7.0	3?	—	400–1000	LA II	Yes
Weld	Lower	9.1	1	rim	unknown	LA II	Yes
ZX Ranch	HP–1	6.7(9.5)	1	hearth, rim	unknown	LA II	Yes
ZX Ranch	HP–2	6.1	1	hearth, rim	unknown	—	Yes
35Lk 478	CF–13	7.2	1?	—	600–800	—	Maybe
35Lk 481	CF–5	7.2	1?	—	300–700	LA II	Maybe
35Lk 494	CF–8	6.0	1?	—	500–800	LA II	Maybe
35Lk 534	CF–DH10	4.0	1?	—	60–180	—	Maybe
35Lk 536	CF–RP9	4.0	1?	humic soil	1000+	MA/LA I	Maybe
35Lk 542	CF–JAW1	8.0	?	—	400–500	MA	Maybe
Weld	Upper	5.5(9.1)	1?	—	unknown	MA	Maybe
35Lk 483	CF–1	5.0	—	—	100–200	—	No
35Lk 489	CF–5	4.2	—	—	20–60	—	No
35Lk 490	CF–9	3.8	—	—	20–110	—	No
35Lk 496	CF–3	5.2	—	—	50–270	—	No
Rock Rings							
35Lk 495	CF–10A	6.8	1	hearth	200–900	LA II	Yes
35Lk 536	CF–RP1	3.0	1	petroglyphs	1000+	LA II	Yes

with housepits in the basin, were preferentially located near stable, modern water sources (Table 7) and they were generally Late Archaic II in age, that is, less than 2,000 years old (Table 8). Ten of the 15 dated village sites are Late Archaic II in age. If the dated sites from the east shore of Lake Abert are included, 19 Late Archaic II sites are present among the 31 dated village sites. The majority of undated village sites were also found in locations typical of the Late Archaic II and unlike the location patterns of earlier periods.

Lithic scatters were generally small, were often away from water, and were likely to be higher in elevation (Tables 7, 9, and 10). They represent all of the temporal periods and were present in equivalent proportions in the Middle and Late Archaic (Table 8). These sites were probably task specific, short–term use areas and the activities undertaken formed a necessary part of life in all periods.

Ground stone tools were abundant and included equal numbers of manos, metates, pestles, and mortars. These numbers and the carefully finished nature of individual implements, particularly the large mortars, implied large–scale, intensive use of plant resources (and possibly fish) by the aboriginal inhabitants of the basin. Lithic/ground stone scatters were found in most areas of the basin, both near and away from water (Table 7), but were most common at the lower elevations (Table 10). They ranged in surface area (Table 9) and artifact density, suggesting some were short–term activity areas not regularly returned to, but that others probably saw repeated and varied use. Ground stone implements were common at Middle and Late Archaic sites (Table 8).

The overall impression gained from the foregoing distribution analyses was one of a general focus on wetland resources. Village sites were found in close proximity to the marshes, river, lake, and springs. Nearly half of the lithic and lithic/ground stone sites were also located adjacent to perennial or seasonal watercourses. The

Table 6. Summary of House Comparisons

Group or Site	Diameter (m)	Depth (m)	Excavation Pit?[1]	Floor Profile[2]	Post Position[3]	Age	Reference
Ethnographic:							
Klamath: Earth lodge	4-12	<1.0	Y	F/SW	C	Ethnographic	Spier 1930
Modoc: Earth lodge	3.6-10.7	1.2-1.5	Y	F/SW	C	Ethnographic	Ray 1963
Klamath-Modoc: Mat house	3-4	0.3-0.5	O	SS	E	Ethnographic	Spier 1930
North Paiute: Pole & brush	2.4-4.5	—	N	SS/W	E	Ethnographic	Fowler and Liljeblad 1986
North Paiute: West Nevada	3.0-4.5	0.3-0.6	O	SS	E	Ethnographic	Fowler and Liljeblad 1986
Archaeological:							
Lake Abert	4.0-9.2	0.3-1.0?	Y	?	?	3500-100 B.P.	Pettigrew 1985, Oetting 1988
Klamath	6.0-19.0	<1.0	Y	SS&F/SW	V	<1750 B.P.	Cressman 1956
Big Boulder	5	0.5	Y	SS	C	500 B.P.	Mack 1983
Border	8	0.9-1.5	Y	SS	C	500 B.P.	Mack 1983
Iron Gate	4.5-9.0	0.5	Y	SS&F/SW	E	Late Prehistoric	Leonhardy 1967
Nightfire Island	3.5	0.3	Y	F/SW[4]	E	4700-1500 B.P.	Sampson 1985
Blitzen Marsh	?	0.7	Y	F/SW?[4]	?	930 B.P.	Fagan 1973
King's Dog	6.7-7.5	0.7	Y	F/SW	C	+5000 B.P.	O'Connell 1975
Rodriguez	3.0-5.2	0.2-0.5	N	SS/W	E	4500-100 B.P.	O'Connell 1975
Karlo Site	3	—	N	SS/W	E	4500-3500 B.P.	Riddell 1960
Dirty Shame Rock Shelter	5	—	N	SS/W	E	2700-1100 B.P.	Willig 1981
Horse Pasture Village	3.5-4.0	—	N	SS/W	E?	4450-750 B.P.	Clewlow, Ambro, and Pastron 1972
Cocanour	2.4-4.8	—	N	SS/W	E?	6000-3000 B.P.	Stanley, Page, and Shutler 1970
26Pe 67	1.6-3.8	0.1-0.7	Y	SS	E	Prehistoric	Cowan and Clewlow 1968
Humboldt Lake	1.5-4.5	0.2-0.4	Y	SS&F/SW	E?	3200 B.P.-?	Livingston 1986
4LAS 317 I	4-5	0.1-0.3	Y	F/SW	C	1500-700 B.P.	Elston 1979
4LAS 317 II	1.5	—	N	SS/W	E	1500-700 B.P.	Elston 1979

[1]Pit Excavated?: Y = yes; O = occasionally; N = no.
[2]F/SW = flat floor w/ steep walls; SS = excavated saucer-shaped; SS/W = worn down into saucer-shaped.
[3]C = central; E = edges; V = varied.
[4]Floors were clay-lined.

Table 7. Frequency of Sites by Type and Availability of Water

Relationship to Water	Lithic Scatter	Lithic/Ground Stone Scatter	Village Site	Total
Stable Water[1]	20	39	30	89
Intermittent Water[2]	18	31	6	55
Away from Water	50	76	7	133
Total	88	146	43	277

[1]Directly adjacent to river, marsh, or spring/seep.
[2]Adjacent to seasonally–active stream.

Table 8. Frequency of Single–Component Survey-Recorded Sites by Type and Period

Period	Lithic Scatter	Lithic/Ground Stone Scatter	Village Site	Total
Late Archaic II	4	18	10	32
Late Archaic I	3	2	1	6
Middle Archaic II	5	18	3	26
Middle Archaic I	1	7	1	9
Early Archaic	3	1	—	4
Initial Archaic	1	—	—	1
Total	17	46	15	78

Table 9. Frequency of Sites by Type and Surface Area[1]

Surface Area[2]	Lithic Scatter	Lithic/Ground Stone Scatter	Village Site	Total
<4,000	59	54	6	119
4,000–<20,000	24	54	21	99
>20,000	5	38	16	59
Total	88	146	43	277

[1]Survey-recorded sites only.
[2]Square meters.

Table 10. Frequency of Sites by Type and Elevation[1]

Elevation (Feet)	Lithic Scatter	Lithic/Ground Stone Scatter	Village Site	Total
Below 4,280	6	14	6	26
4,280–4,289	27	52	18	97
4,290–4,299	22	31	12	65
4,300–4,309	12	27	3	42
4,310–4,319	6	5	—	11
4,320–4,329	6	8	2	16
4,330–4,339	4	5	—	9
4,340–4,349	3	—	2	5
4,350+	2	4	—	6
Total	88	146	43	277

[1]Survey–recorded sites only.

temporal site distributions, presented below, indicate this wetlands orientation intensified in the Late Archaic II, although wetlands associated sites are present in each of the time periods.

It must be remembered that no excavations were conducted at the survey–recorded sites, so no direct faunal or botanical subsistence data are available. Thus, the role of wetlands resources cannot be demonstrated, but only inferred from site locations and tool assemblages. However, the excavations on the east shore of Lake Abert recovered the remains of several species of waterfowl and three types of fish, along with a variety of terrestrial mammals (Greenspan 1985:156–168; Pettigrew 1985:138–148; Oetting 1988:221–231). One Middle Archaic site and 13 Late Archaic sites contained waterfowl remains, including ducks (Anatinae), geese (Anserini), and grebes (Podiceps). Bones of tui chub (*Gila bicolor*), redband trout (*Salmo* sp.), and speckled dace (*Rhinichthys osculus*) were found at five sites, all Late Archaic in age (see also Greenspan, this volume). Some of the chub and trout bones were charred, suggesting they were economic resources for the human inhabitants of these sites (Greenspan 1985:164). These bones provide some evidence that the Middle and Late Archaic populations were making use of wetlands faunal resources. No botanical remains were recovered during these excavations.

The distribution of sites within each period was examined and is presented in Figures 4 through 6. Information for the Initial Archaic and Early Archaic periods was scanty (Figure 4 and Table 11). The small number of sites from these periods (especially the Initial Archaic) suggests smaller populations before 4000 B.P., but may also reflect the longer exposure to natural factors that may have obscured, buried, or destroyed sites. No distinguishable pattern was noted for the few Initial Archaic sites. Early Archaic sites were primarily found in the lower Chewaucan River area and these sites were largely similar in specific setting and artifact composition. This redundancy in site location and equipment suggests this portion of the basin was repeatedly visited by hunter–gatherers using particular, perhaps seasonal, resources.

The number of sites increased between the Early Archaic and the Middle Archaic and between the early and later parts within the Middle Archaic (Table 11), implying an increase in population and an increase in the time

Table 11. Summary of Significant Cultural and Geomorphic Patterns by Period

Period	Lake Level[1]	Lake Status[2]	River Course[3]	Site Location	Site Types[4]			Settlement Pattern[5]	Subsistence Pattern[6]
					LS	LGS	VIL		
LA II	≤4,260	low	modern	edge of current wetlands	4 12.5	18 56.3	10 31.2	SS	WF
LA I	≤4,270	dec.?	CC	near river and lake	3 50.0	2 33.3	1 16.7	SS	WF
MA II	4,270–4,295	high, fluc.	CC	throughout basin	5 19.2	18 69.2	3 11.5	SS?	D/W
MA I	≤4,280	high, fluc.?	AC	along old channel	1 11.1	7 77.8	1 11.1	SS?	Gen. H/G
EA	dry–4,255?	low	AC	southeast of lower marsh	3 75.0	1 25.0	—	RM?	Gen. H/G
IA	4,265–4,270	dec.?	AC	unknown	1 100	—	—	?	?

[1]Lake level in feet.
[2]Dec. = lake level declining; fluc. = fluctuation in lake level.
[3]CC = river changing course, current floodplain being formed; AC = river flowing in now–abandoned channels.
[4]LS = lithic scatter; LGS = lithic/ground stone scatter; VIL = village; (numbers = site count/percent).
[5]Inferred settlement pattern: SS = semi–sedentary; RM = relatively mobile.
[6]Inferred subsistence pattern: WF = wetlands focus; D/W = diverse with wetlands included; gen. H/G = generalized hunting–gathering.

spent, and resources used, within the Lake Abert–Chewaucan Marsh Basin. Sites were located in most areas within the basin and a great variety in site size and function was seen (Figure 5).

The first evidence of pithouse villages appeared in the Middle Archaic (Table 11). These villages were probably occupied in the winter, but a general sense of residential mobility persists in this period. The number of villages is low when compared with the Late Archaic, and Middle Archaic sites (all types) are found in a wider range of elevations (Table 12). Although similar numbers of sites were recorded during the surveys, only 11.4% of Middle Archaic sites were village sites, while 28.9% of Late Archaic sites had housepits. The range of elevations and the variety of sites seen suggest Middle Archaic people were using many of the basin's plant and animal resources—those in wetland areas as well as those on drier parts of the basin floor and on upland slopes surrounding the basin.

Ten Middle Archaic sites were located along a now–abandoned channel of the lower Chewaucan River and Middle Archaic sites were not found along the edge of the modern floodplain, in contrast with the location of Late Archaic sites (Figures 5 and 6). The presence of these sites near this former watercourse is strong evidence that the river flowed through this channel approximately 2,000 to 4,000 years ago. It is not until Late Archaic II times that cultural activity along the modern course and floodplain of the river is seen. This indicates that the modern topography of the lower Chewaucan River area was developed within the Middle Archaic period or the early part of the Late Archaic and that the basin floor was somewhat higher in elevation prior to this time. This change in the course of the river may have destroyed some Middle Archaic and/or Late Archaic I sites.

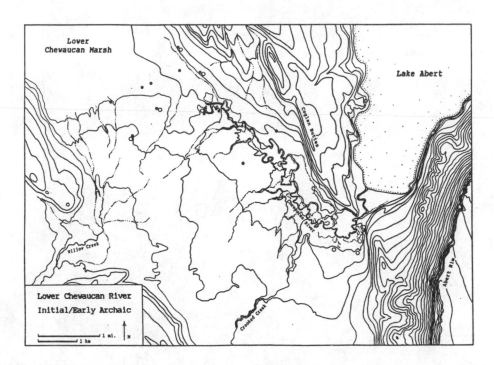

Figure 4. Initial and Early Archaic site locations; open circles = Initial Archaic; darkened circles = Early Archaic.

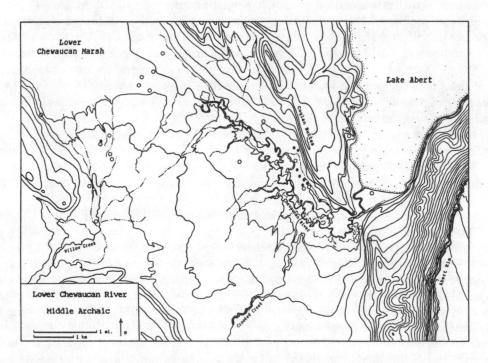

Figure 5. Middle Archaic site locations; darkened circles = Middle Archaic I; open circles = Middle Archaic II.

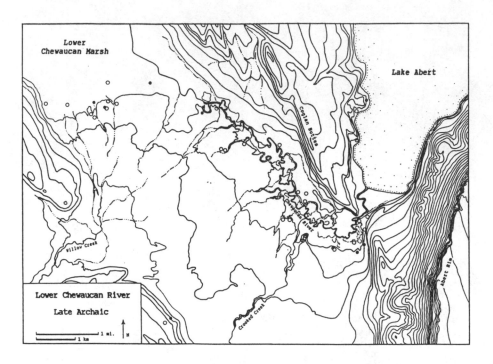

Figure 6. Late Archaic site locations; darkened circles = Late Archaic I; open circles = Late Archaic II.

Considering all Middle Archaic site locations, a somewhat higher lake (and overall water) level is indicated, but the lake may have fluctuated in elevation and size to a significant degree. Middle Archaic sites and projectile points were rarely found below 4,280 feet AMSL, suggesting a lake level about 20 to 25 feet. above the modern lake (which averages 4,255 feet AMSL). The excavations on the east shore of Lake Abert revealed three buried Middle Archaic components, each overlain by beach deposits and a Late Archaic cultural component, at an elevation of 4,275 feet (Oetting 1988:259). The lake was lower than this elevation long enough to allow these occupations, but this beach terrace was inundated for some time before its reoccupation in the Late Archaic. The lake apparently did not rise above 4,290 feet, since no evidence of Holocene lake–deposited sediments was found in excavation units on the terrace at this elevation (Oetting 1988:260).

A generally higher than modern water level may have actually limited the wetlands resources available during the Middle Archaic period, making large portions of the marsh and river areas too deep to support emergent marsh plants. This would limit productive marsh areas to the steeper edges of the Lake Abert and marsh sub–basins, in turn making these marshy areas more vulnerable to water fluctuations. Changes of a few feet in water level could flood or dry these critical narrow edges.

The number of sites recorded for the Late Archaic increased only slightly over that of the Middle Archaic (Figure 6 and Table 11). However, the types of sites and their settings differ from the earlier period. In particular, the number of villages dated to the Late Archaic II or in settings characteristic of this period increased significantly over those of earlier periods (Table 11). The substantial nature of the house features, the density of tools and debitage at these sites, and comparisons with ethnographic Klamath settlement patterns suggest that these villages may have been seasonally re–occupied residential bases, inhabited by semi–sedentary groups. There was also an increase in the number and general size of house features per village site (Oetting 1989a:222), which might indicate an increase in population size.

These pithouse villages were located along the modern course and floodplain of the river, on the south edge of the lower marsh, and at low elevations around Lake Abert. The majority of other Late Archaic sites were found in similar settings, closely associated with modern wetland areas (Figure 6). This spatial patterning of sites

Table 12. Frequency of Dated Sites by Period and Elevation[1]

Elevation (Feet)	Initial Archaic	Early Archaic	Middle Archaic I	Middle Archaic II	Late Archaic I	Late Archaic II	Total
<4,270	1	—	—	—	—	2	3
4,270–4,279	—	—	1	1	—	6	8
4,280–4,289	6	6	8	9	6	20	55
4,290–4,299	9	9	2	3	3	8	29
4,300–4,309	1	1	1	9	—	—	13
4,310–4,319	—	—	—	2	1	—	3
4,320–4,329	—	—	—	3	—	—	3
4,330–4,339	—	—	—	—	—	—	0
4,340–4,349	—	—	—	2	—	1	3
≥4,350	—	—	—	2	1	1	4
Total	13	16	12	31	11	38	121

[1]Survey–recorded sites only (single/multiple component dated sites).

suggests that people of the Late Archaic specialized to some degree in the use of wetland plant and animal resources. Very little use of the higher parts of the basin floor was observed (Table 10) in areas away from marsh, river, lake, or mudflats, but the presence of Late Archaic sites and point styles in the uplands above the basin may reflect hunting and upland gathering.

Site locations indicate water levels were very close to those of modern times, down from the levels suggested for the Middle Archaic. The location of sites along the extant edges of the river and lake suggests that a water regime similar to that of the present was operating by Late Archaic II times. Several large Late Archaic II period village sites on the east and west shores of Lake Abert have housepits between 5 feet and 15 feet above the modern lake edge (Oetting 1989a:195, 222). The consistent placement of sites near the present river and lake margins suggests that changes in water level were smaller and less severe in the Late Archaic. Low water levels would have been conducive to the development and maintenance of more extensive marsh and riparian resource zones, but these zones would still have been very vulnerable if water levels had fluctuated much. It would seem, then, that the most populous and residentially–stable period in the basin occurred within the last 1,000 or 2,000 years, **after** water levels had declined and the lake, marshes, and river had developed essentially modern configurations.

Evaluating the Chewaucan Culture Hypothesis

The settlement patterns identified in the Middle and Late Archaic reflect some agreement with the Chewaucan Culture hypothesis outlined earlier but also indicate significant divergences from this proposal. Following the model developed by Pettigrew (1985:193–194), the following pattern would be expected: initial settlement around 4000 B.P. to 3500 B.P. on the upper terraces of Lake Abert, maximum population and settlement numbers between 3000 B.P. and 1000 B.P. around the lake, but with settlements being found on lower terraces as the lake level fell after 2000 B.P. Population and settlements may have been declining by 1000 B.P. as environmental stresses increased. Settlements would have shifted to alternative freshwater sources as the lake water became undrinkable. However, these alterations were not sufficient to cope with the deteriorating environment and, by 500 B.P., abandonment was complete.

The **observed** settlement patterns are rather different (Table 11). The increased moisture of the Medithermal most likely fostered the Middle Archaic florescence in the region. Pithouse villages were first seen in the Middle Archaic I, about 4000 B.P., primarily on the shore of the lake. The earliest villages were few in number and house remains (along with Elko series broad–necked projectile points) occurred on all terraces, not strictly at the higher elevations. Many Middle Archaic II sites were identified, but only three village sites were found on the east shore and another three pithouse sites were located in other areas of the basin. Middle Archaic II sites were found in more diverse settings than any other period, suggesting a variety of subsistence pursuits. Late Archaic sites, especially those of the Late Archaic II, were closely associated with wetland areas and probably made significant use of these resources. The number of village sites tripled and many more undated village sites may be of Late Archaic II age.

An Alternative Model

The Chewaucan Culture hypothesis cannot adequately account for the observed settlement and inferred subsistence patterns.   Instead, an alternative culture–historical reconstruction for the semi–sedentary, wetlands–using groups of the later Holocene in the Lake Abert–Chewaucan Marsh Basin can be developed (Oetting 1989a:231–236). This model suggests that (1) environmental stress, in general, apparently did not seriously affect prehistoric groups of the later Holocene in the basin, (2) the Middle and Late Archaic inhabitants were Penutian–speaking people, and (3) Northern Paiute aggression forced the Penutian groups out of the basin.

Environmental changes were evidently taking place in the Lake Abert–Chewaucan Marsh Basin during the later Holocene, judging from apparent lake level changes, course alterations of the lower Chewaucan River, and floodplain development. However, these changes appear to have had little deleterious effect on the Middle and Late Archaic inhabitants of the basin. The settlement patterns of these periods exhibit increasing village permanence, increasing focus on wetland resources, and a probable trend of population growth. These patterns suggest an extended period of cultural stability and continuity, which persisted from 4000 B.P. until shortly before Euroamerican contact.

Lake Abert is now an aquatic desert. Its saline and alkaline water is non–potable and supports only a limited variety of plants and animals. The timing of this deterioration is unclear, although the presence of late sites with many housepits along the modern shore and away from other water sources implies that the lake may have retained its freshness into the Late Archaic II. In any case, the reliability of water resources from the river and springs probably mitigated the seriousness of these changes in the lake. In sum, there is no archaeological evidence to suggest that an abandonment of the region occurred because of specific environmental problems.

Pettigrew (1980) suggested that the Chewaucan Culture people may have been related to ancestral Klamath people, Penutian speakers. Aikens (1985) included the Chewaucan groups in a proposed widespread expansion of Penutian–speaking peoples into the western Great Basin beginning about 4,000 years ago, possibly manifested in western Nevada by the Lovelock Culture (Hattori 1982). Over 50 years ago Cressman (1942:140; Cressman, Williams, and Krieger 1940:15) came to similar conclusions on the basis of basketry styles and traditions. These interpretations are supported by the settlement patterns reconstructed above, but can be further developed and clarified.

The use of pithouses suggests cultural continuity between the Middle and Late Archaic periods. Analyses of tool inventories, debitage, and faunal remains from sites on the east shore of Lake Abert demonstrated that the artifact assemblages (other than temporally changing projectile point styles) at these sites were quite similar, suggesting few cultural differences between groups of the Middle and Late Archaic periods (Oetting 1988:187, 274). Thus, people of a single cultural tradition are considered to have occupied the Lake Abert–Chewaucan Marsh Basin since 4000 B.P.

The settlement–subsistence patterns of the Late Archaic II period, the pithouses, and some unique artifacts suggest that groups in the Late Archaic II were, in fact, late prehistoric Klamath people; contemporaneous with and culturally affiliated with the Klamath groups of the Klamath Lake and Marsh region to the west. The settlement locations and inferred subsistence focus recognized for the Late Archaic II parallel those of the ethnographic Klamath as described by Leslie Spier in 1930 and briefly outlined above. Klamath economy centered on wetlands resources. This was reflected by the location of winter villages near rivers, marshes, and springs and in the patterning of the people's annual movements.

From excavations at Kawumkan Springs Midden and other Klamath village sites in the 1950s, Cressman (1956:463–465) felt that the ethnographic Klamath pattern of semi–sedentary pithouse villages near wetlands may have developed between 1700 and 1250 B.P. This coincides remarkably with the inception of the Late Archaic II period. The size, depth, and associated features of the housepit features in the Lake Abert–Chewaucan Marsh Basin, as described above, most closely resemble late prehistoric Klamath houses excavated by Cressman (1956).

Finally, some specific artifact classes suggest Klamath affiliations. Three manos with handles or grips have been recovered from the Lake Abert–Chewaucan Marsh Basin. Two were found in Late Archaic II sites and the third was an isolate from the lower marsh. These are identical to specimens described by Cressman (1956:420–423) for the late prehistoric and ethnographic Klamath and Modoc. Handled manos have not been reported for other groups in the Great Basin, California, or the Plateau (Trygg 1971). These implements are unique to the Klamath–Modoc and, in the ethnographic period, were used in the preparation of *wokas* (pond lily [Nymphaea polysepala]) seeds (Cressman 1956:420).

The large number of mortars, observed at numerous sites during the surveys, also reflect Klamath artifact assemblages. Well–crafted stone mortars, finished on both the interior and exterior, have been found at late prehistoric Klamath sites and were used ethnographically (Cressman 1956:423–425; Spier 1930:177). The Klamath occasionally applied decorations to stone utilitarian items (Barrett 1910; Carlson 1959) and similar practices may be reflected in the pecked decorations found on four mortar rim fragments collected during the surveys (Oetting 1989a:72). Large, well–finished mortars appear to be rare elsewhere in the Great Basin, judging from the lack of references to such items (except in the Carson Sink [Kelly 1983:16–18]), and seem to predate the Numic inhabitants. Surprise Valley Paiute informants claimed their people did not manufacture mortars, but occasionally used archaeological specimens (Kelly 1932:139).

The prehistoric basketry of south–central Oregon was the principal evidence used by Cressman (1936, 1942, 1986) to suggest that Penutian–speaking people were more widespread in eastern Oregon during prehistoric times. Preserved prehistoric basketry from caves in the northern Great Basin is almost exclusively twine–ware and exhibits continuity from the early Holocene to recent times (Connolly 1986). This twined basketry, with a tradition of slanting the pitch of the weft stitch down to the right, was named Catlow Twine (Cressman 1942:34). This style is a lineal antecedent to ethnographic Klamath basketry according to Cressman (1942:45; 1986:123). Adovasio (1986:204; Adovasio et al. 1986:33) is more cautious in suggesting such a genetic relationship, but noted that Catlow Twine was not part of ethnographic Northern Paiute or other Numic basketry techniques, which used coiling and different twining methods (Adovasio et al. 1986:33–34; Cressman 1986:123).

No basketry remains were found during the State Historic Preservation Office–funded surveys or the Lake Abert excavations, but basketry fragments are present in three collections from the basin curated by the Oregon State Museum of Anthropology (Accessions Number 100BA, Number 100II, and Number 263). All of the basketry fragments have been identified as Catlow Twine (Connolly 1986). A cache from Chewaucan Cave, a small shelter overlooking the lower marsh and dated to the Late Archaic II (with a radiocarbon age of 340 ± 80 B.P., Table 2), included two Catlow Twine basketry trays.

In this proposed culture–historical reconstruction, the people of the Middle and Late Archaic were Penutian–speakers on the eastern periphery of an expanded Penutian (Klamath) territory. By Late Archaic II times, the settlement–subsistence patterns seen in the ethnographic period were developing, both in the Klamath heartland and in outlying areas, including the Lake Abert–Chewaucan Marsh Basin. It does not appear that this basin was abandoned by the Klamath because of environmental deterioration, yet it was not occupied by them at contact and the territory was claimed to be Northern Paiute. Early Euroamerican explorers encountered no Native Americans in the basin, although evidence of human activity was noted (Fremont 1846).

Paiute oral traditions in Surprise Valley hold that the Klamath once inhabited southeastern Oregon as far east as Steens Mountain, presumably including the Lake Abert–Chewaucan Marsh Basin, but that the Paiute forced them back into the territory held at historic contact (Kelly 1932). This suggests that Klamath abandonment of the Lake Abert–Chewaucan Marsh Basin was forced upon them by Northern Paiute aggression. No mention of lost territory was made in the Klamath ethnographies (Barrett 1910; Spier 1930; Stern 1966) but the Klamath were continually in conflict with and on guard against "tribes of warlike habit to the north and east" (Spier 1930:24), i.e., the Northern Paiute.

Expansion through warfare by the Northern Paiute and other Numic groups has been documented all along the periphery of their territory at the time of Euroamerican contact (Sutton 1986:76). Northern Paiute oral traditions in western Nevada contain descriptions of warfare with the *Saidukah* or *Saidokado* and their expulsion by the Paiute from the Humboldt Sink (Stewart 1939:140–141; Heizer 1966:245; Sutton 1986:68). The *Saidokado* have been identified by various researchers as Achomawi, Klamath, or Nez Perce (Stewart 1939:141). Northern Paiute warfare is also cited in the displacement of the Maidu (a Penutian group) from the Honey Lake area in eastern California (Layton 1981:135; Sutton 1986:67) and in territorial conflicts with Columbia River groups at the northern edge of Numic territory (Ray 1938; Stewart 1938).

The Paiute apparently wrested control of the Lake Abert–Chewaucan Marsh Basin from the Klamath within the last 120 to 300 years, given the recency of Late Archaic II period radiocarbon dates. This aggression may have been augmented by the formation of predatory bands of mobile, horse–mounted Paiute (Layton 1981:135). The lack of a clearly recognizable Paiute archaeological presence in the basin, however, suggests two alternatives. It may be that the region was still subject to dispute and was not regularly inhabited. Alternatively, it is possible that mounted predatory Paiute bands used a very different settlement–subsistence system, one that may not have left much archaeological evidence in the short time prior to their own displacement by Euroamericans.

Summary and Conclusions

This culture–historical reconstruction suggests that Penutian–speaking peoples occupied the Lake Abert–Chewaucan Marsh Basin from approximately 4000 B.P. until shortly before the arrival of Euroamericans in the region. The appearance of pithouse villages, characteristic of Penutian groups throughout the Plateau and northern California, seems to coincide with the Medithermal climatic amelioration in the Lake Abert–Chewaucan Marsh Basin. Whether these Middle Archaic people expanded into the region from established Penutian–speaking regions to the west or north (Columbia River region) or whether they were indigenous Early Archaic peoples altering their movements and subsistence pursuits (or a combination of these possibilities) is unknown at present.

The site types and settlement patterns discerned for the Middle and Late Archaic period groups indicate that they followed a semi–sedentary lifestyle in which fixed winter villages were re–occupied annually, as exemplified by the ethnographic Klamath. Subsistence pursuits became increasingly focused on wetlands resources through time. Population may have grown and residential stability may have increased as well. The Late Archaic II population can be considered part of an expanded late prehistoric Klamath territory.

Large–scale environmental stress does not seem to have seriously affected people during the Middle or Late Archaic and did not prompt abandonment of the basin. The disappearance of the Late Archaic II people is, instead, attributed to conflict with the Northern Paiute. This aggression forced the Klamath to relinquish much of southeastern Oregon, which included the abandonment of the Lake Abert–Chewaucan Marsh Basin by people of the Late Archaic II period.

References

Adovasio, J. M.
  1986   Prehistoric Basketry. In *Great Basin*, edited by W. L. d'Azevedo, pp. 194–205. Handbook of North American Indians, vol. 11. William G. Sturtevant, general editor. Smithsonian Institution, Washington, D.C.

Adovasio, J. M., R. L. Andrews, and R. C. Carlisle
  1986   Basketry. In *Perishable Industries from Dirty Shame Rockshelter, Malheur County, Oregon*, by R. L. Andrews, J. M. Adovasio, and R. C. Carlisle, pp. 19–50. University of Oregon Anthropological Papers No. 34. Eugene.

Aikens, C. M.
  1985   The Nightfire Island Lakemarsh Adaptation in the Broader Context of Desert West Prehistory. In *Nightfire Island: Later Holocene Lakemarsh Adaptation on the Western Edge of the Great Basin*, by C. G. Sampson, pp. 519–528. University of Oregon Anthropological Papers No. 33. Eugene.

Allison, I. S.
  1982   *Geology of Pluvial Lake Chewaucan, Lake County, Oregon*. Studies in Geology, No. 11. Oregon State University Press, Corvallis.

Baldwin, E. M.
  1981   *Geology of Oregon*. 3rd ed. Kendall and Hunt Publishing, Dubuque.

Barrett, S. A.
  1910   *The Material Culture of the Klamath Lake and Modoc Indians of Northeastern California and Southern Oregon*. University of California Publications in American Archaeology and Ethnology 5(4). Berkeley.

Carlson, R. L.
  1959   Klamath Henwas and Other Stone Sculpture. *American Anthropologist* 61(1):88–96.

Clewlow, C. W., Jr., R. D. Ambro, and A. G. Pastron
  1972   The Horse Pasture Villages. In *The Grass Valley Archeological Project: Collected Papers*, edited by C. W. Clewlow, Jr., and M. Rusco, pp. 69-83. Nevada Archeological Survey Research Paper vol. 3. University of Nevada, Reno.

Connolly, T. J.
  1986   Catalog of Prehistoric Basketry and Other Perishables from Eastern Oregon, vols. 1 and 2. Ms. on file, Oregon State Museum of Anthropology, Eugene.

Connolly, T. J., and R. M. Pettigrew
  1985   Circular Features. In *Archaeological Investigations on the East Shore of Lake Abert, Lake County, Oregon*, vol. 1, by R. M. Pettigrew, pp. 85-100. University of Oregon Anthropological Papers No. 32. Eugene.

Cowan, R. A., and C. W. Clewlow, Jr.
  1968   The Archaeology of NV-PE-67. *University of California Archaeological Survey Reports* 73:195-236. Berkeley.

Cressman, L. S.
  1936   *Archaeological Survey of the Guano Valley Region in Southeastern Oregon*. University of Oregon Monographs, Studies in Anthropology No. 1. Eugene.
  1942   *Archaeological Researches in the Northern Great Basin*. Carnegie Institution of Washington, Publication 538. Washington, D.C.
  1956   *Klamath Prehistory*. Transactions of the American Philosophical Society 46(4). Philadelphia.
  1986   Prehistory of the Northern Area. In *Great Basin*, edited by W. L. d'Azevedo, pp. 120–126. Handbook of North American Indians, vol. 11. William G. Sturtevant, general editor. Smithsonian Institution, Washington, D.C.

Elston, R. G.
  1979   *The Archeology of U.S. 395 Right-of-Way Between Stead, Nevada and Hallelujah Junction, California*. Report submitted to the California Department of Transportation (Caltrans) and the Nevada Department of Highways by the Nevada Archeological Survey, University of Nevada, Reno.

Fagan, J. L.
  1973   *Altithermal Occupation of Spring Sites in the Northern Great Basin*. Unpublished Ph.D. dissertation, Department of Anthropology, University of Oregon, Eugene.

Fowler, C. S., and S. Liljeblad
  1986   Northern Paiute. In *Great Basin*, edited by W. L. d'Azevedo, pp. 435–465 Handbook of North American Indians, vol. 11. William G. Sturtevant, general editor. Smithsonian Institution, Washington, D.C.

Franklin, J. F., and C. T. Dyrness
  1973   *Natural Vegetation of Oregon and Washington*. USDA Forest Service General Technical Report PNW-8.

Fremont, J. C.
  1846   *Report of the Exploring Expedition to the Rocky Mountains in the Year 1842, and to Oregon and Northern California in the Years 1843-1844*. Gales and Seaton, Washington, D.C.

Greenspan, R. L.
  1985   *Fish and Fishing in Northern Great Basin Prehistory*. Ph.D. dissertation, Department of Anthropology, University of Oregon. University Microfilms, Ann Arbor.

Hattori, E. M.
  1982   *The Archaeology of Falcon Hill, Winnemucca Lake, Washoe County, Nevada*. Nevada State Museum Anthropological Papers No. 18. Carson City.

Heizer, R. F.
  1966   General Comments. In *The Current Status of Anthropological Research in the Great Basin, 1964*, edited by W. L. d'Azevedo, W. A. Davis, D. D. Fowler, and W. Suttles, pp. 239–247. Desert Research Institute Social Sciences and Humanities Publications vol 1. Reno.
Heizer, R. F., and T. R. Hester
  1978   Great Basin. In *Chronologies in New World Archaeology*, edited by R. E. Taylor and C. W. Meighan, pp. 147-199. Academic Press, New York.
Heizer, R. F., and L. K. Napton
  1970   *Archaeology and the Prehistoric Great Basin Lacustrine Subsistence Regime as Seen from Lovelock Cave, Nevada.* University of California Archaeological Research Facility Contributions No. 10. Berkeley.
Hester, T. R.
  1973   *Chronological Ordering in Great Basin Prehistory.* University of California Archaeological Research Facility Contributions No. 17. Berkeley.
Holmer, R. N.
  1986   Common Projectile Points of the Intermountain West. In *Anthropology of the Desert West: Essays in Honor of Jesse D. Jennings*, edited by C. J. Condie and D. D. Fowler, pp. 89-115. University of Utah Anthropological Papers No. 110. Salt Lake City.
Kelly, I. T.
  1932   Ethnography of the Surprise Valley Paiute. *University of California Publications in American Archaeology and Ethnology* 31:67-210. Berkeley.
Kelly, R. L.
  1983   *An Examination of Amateur Collections from the Carson Sink, Nevada.* U.S. Bureau of Land Management, Nevada, Technical Report 10. Reno, Nevada.
Layton, T. N.
  1981   Traders and Raiders: Aspects of Trans–Basin and California–Plateau Commerce, 1800–1830. *Journal of California and Great Basin Anthropology* 3(1):127–137.
Leonhardy, F. C.
  1967   *The Archaeology of a Late Prehistoric Village in Northwestern California.* University of Oregon, Museum of Natural History, Bulletin No. 4. Eugene.
Livingston, S. D.
  1986   Archaeology of the Humboldt Lakebed Site. *Journal of California and Great Basin Anthropology* 8(1):99–115.
Mack, J. M.
  1983   *Archaeological Investigations in the Salt Cave Locality: Subsistence Uniformity and Cultural Diversity on the Klamath River, Oregon.* University of Oregon Anthropological Papers 29. Eugene.
O'Connell, J. F.
  1975   *The Prehistory of Surprise Valley.* Ballena Press Anthropological Papers No. 4. Ramona, California.
Oetting, A. C.
  1988   *Archaeological Investigations on the East Shore of Lake Abert, Lake County, Oregon, Volume 2.* Oregon State Museum of Anthropology, OSMA Report No. 88–6. Eugene.
  1989a   *Villages and Wetlands Adaptations in the Northern Great Basin: Chronology and Land Use in the Lake Abert–Chewaucan Marsh Basin, Lake County, Oregon.* University of Oregon Anthropological Papers 41. Eugene.
  1989b   Leftovers from 1939: Testing House Depressions at the ZX Ranch Site, Lake County, Oregon. Paper presented at the 42nd Annual Northwest Anthropological Conference, Spokane.
Oetting, A. C., and R. M. Pettigrew
  1985   *An Archaeological Survey in the Lake Abert-Chewaucan Basin Lowlands, Lake County, Oregon.* Oregon State Museum of Anthropology, OSMA Survey Report 85-5. Eugene.
  1987   *Archaeological Investigations in the Lake Abert–Chewaucan Basin, Lake County, Oregon: The 1986 Survey.* The Cultural Heritage Foundation Report 1. Portland.
Pettigrew, R. M.
  1980   *The Ancient Chewaucanians: More on the Prehistoric Lake Dwellers of Lake Abert, Southeastern Oregon.* Association of Oregon Archaeologists, Occasional Papers 1:49-67. Albany, Oregon.
  1985   *Archaeological Investigations on the East Shore of Lake Abert, Lake County, Oregon, Volume 1.* University of Oregon Anthropological Papers No. 32. Eugene.
Phillips, K. N., and A. S. Van Denburgh
  1971   *Hydrology and Geochemistry of Abert, Summer, and Goose Lakes, and Other Closed-Basin Lakes in South-Central Oregon.* United States Geological Survey Professional Paper 502-B.
Ray, V. F.
  1938   Tribal Distributions in Eastern Oregon and Adjacent Regions. *American Anthropologist* 40(3):384–395.
  1963   *Primitive Pragmatists, The Modoc Indians of Northern California.* University of Washington Press, Seattle.
Riddell, F. A.
  1960   *The Archaeology of the Karlo Site (Las-7) of California.* University of California Archaeological Survey Reports 53:1-110.

Sampson, C. G.
  1985   *Nightfire Island: Later Holocene Lakemarsh Adaptations on the Western Edge of the Great Basin.* University of Oregon Anthropological Papers No. 33. Eugene.

Spier, L.
  1930   *Klamath Ethnography.* University of California Publications in American Archaeology and Ethnology No. 30. Berkeley.

Stanley, D. A., G. M. Page, and R. Shutler
  1970   The Cocanour Site: A Western Nevada Pinto Phase Site with Two Excavated "House Rings." In *Five Papers on the Archaeology of the Desert West*, pp. 1-46. Nevada State Museum Anthropological Papers No. 15. Carson City.

Stern, T.
  1966   *The Klamath Tribe: A People and Their Reservation.* American Ethnological Society, Monograph 41. University of Washington Press, Seattle.

Stewart, O. C.
  1938   Northern Paiute. *American Anthropologist* 40(3):405–407.
  1939   *The Northern Paiute Bands.* University of California Anthropological Records 2(3). Berkeley.

Sutton, M. Q.
  1986   Warfare and Expansion: An Ethnohistoric Perspective on the Numic Spread. *Journal of California and Great Basin Anthropology* 8(1):65–82.

Thomas, D. H.
  1981   How to Classify the Projectile Points from Monitor Valley, Nevada. *Journal of California and Great Basin Anthropology* 3(1):7-43.

Trygg, E. E.
  1971   *A Study of the McLeod Artifact Collection from South Central Oregon.* Unpublished Master's thesis, Department of Anthropology, University of Oregon, Eugene.

Weld, T.
  1962   Testing of House Pits on Ancient and Present Beach Levels, Abert Lake, Oregon. *The Washington Archaeologist* VI(11):1-9.

Wilde, J. D.
  1985   *Prehistoric Settlements in the Northern Great Basin: Excavations and Collections Analysis in the Steens Mountain Area, Southeastern Oregon.* Ph.D. dissertation, Department of Anthropology, University of Oregon. University Microfilms, Ann Arbor.

Willig, J. A.
  1981   *Pole-and-Thatch Structures in the Great Basin: Evidence from the Last 5,000 Years.* Unpublished Master's thesis, Department of Anthropology, University of Oregon, Eugene.

13

PREHISTORIC FISHING IN THE NORTHERN GREAT BASIN

Ruth L. Greenspan

Abstract

This paper examines the role of fish in prehistoric economies of the northern Great Basin, and identifies and addresses some of the problems that may be encountered in the recovery and interpretation of archaeological fish remains. Three internally draining basins in southeastern Oregon were selected for this study: Fort Rock, Harney and Chewaucan basins. Fish bones recovered from prehistoric archaeological sites in each of these basins were examined and interpreted in light of a biogeographic model of fish availability, based upon the distribution, abundance, and seasonal accessibility of different native fishes. The data indicate a different pattern of fish utilization in each of these three contiguous basins.

Introduction

U ntil recently, descriptions of Great Basin subsistence generally emphasized the exploitation of plant foods and mammals in aboriginal economies. The role of fish, along with those of birds and reptiles, was considered supplemental and insignificant, if it was considered at all. One reason for this may be that traditional conceptions of Great Basin subsistence have been derived largely from the work of Julian Steward, who did not consider fish to have been a significant resource outside of Owens Valley, the Humboldt River, Utah Lake, and Bear River (Steward 1938:42–43). As pointed out by Fowler (1982:124;135), Steward's 1938 study did not include data from the rich lacustrine environments of western Nevada, which is likely responsible, at least in part, for his inattention to aquatic resources.

As concerns with Great Basin subsistence issues have increased, and techniques designed to improve recovery of subsistence data have been employed, it has become apparent that aboriginal Great Basin subsistence systems were somewhat different than the original "Desert Culture" models (Jennings 1957) would suggest. What the increased focus on subsistence has made clear is that the variety of resources available to and exploited by aboriginal inhabitants of the Great Basin was, in general, greater than previously thought (Fowler 1982). There could have been considerable variation across space and through time in the particular resources exploited, with little or no change in basic lifeways. On the other hand, in some areas a particular set of resources may have been sufficiently rich and stable to permit a more focal adaptation, and perhaps a somewhat more sedentary settlement system.

Preservation, Recovery, and Quantification

Another reason behind the general lack of consideration given to fish as a Great Basin resource is their apparent scarcity in the archaeological record. Due to their small size and relative fragility, fish remains may be preserved less well than mammal or bird remains. Even more importantly, chubs and suckers, the types of fish most commonly known from Great Basin sites, are relatively small. Their bones, particularly those of chubs, are not likely to be recovered in a one–fourth inch mesh screen, the standard size used in Great Basin archaeology until quite recently.

Experiments designed to quantify the amounts and categories of bone lost through different screen mesh sizes in Great Basin sites have been conducted by various researchers (Thomas 1969; Pettigrew 1985; Greenspan 1985:156–157; Aikens and Greenspan 1988). Not surprisingly, this work has shown that use of smaller screen sizes significantly increases the rate of recovery of fish remains from Great Basin sites. At one site, nearly 10 times as many fish bones were recovered in one–eighth inch mesh as in one–fourth inch mesh screen (Aikens and Greenspan 1988). It is clear, then, that standard excavation techniques employing the use of one–fourth inch mesh screen may not be adequate for the recovery of small fish remains.

In addition, the manner in which fish were processed and consumed may result in their being differentially represented in the archaeological record. Fowler and Bath (1981:185) report that the Pyramid Lake Paiute processed some shiners, chub, and dace by sun-drying them whole, and then grinding them into powder for soup; this would eliminate any trace of them from the archaeological record. Larger fish were filleted before being dried. This practice would result in most of the bones being deposited at the processing site, which might differ from the habitation site. At Hidden Cave, in Nevada, virtually all the recovered trout bones were vertebrae, which strongly suggests that the heads of the fish were removed prior to their being brought to the cave (Smith 1985:171; 176). Fish bones recovered in coprolites from Lovelock Cave (Follet 1970) and several other caves in the western Great Basin (Heizer and Napton 1969) indicate that some small fish were ingested whole, or nearly whole, which would affect both the deposition and the preservation of the bones.

The problem of evaluating the relative importance of various resources represented in archaeological assemblages is a general one. Much has been written on the quantification of vertebrate archaeofaunas and many of the problems have been made explicit (Grayson 1973, 1978, 1979b, 1981, 1984; Casteel 1972, 1976a, 1976b, 1976/77, 1977, 1978). The reader is referred to a thorough discussion and critique by Grayson (1984) of those measures of taxonomic abundance that are commonly used in faunal analyses. This paper is not directly concerned with the relative abundances of different taxa, because it deals essentially with only one taxon. However, quantification of relative abundances involves very real problems, which need to be addressed in any complete faunal analysis. In working with fish remains from Great Basin sites, these problems are magnified by the fact that standard archaeological excavation techniques are frequently not adequate for the recovery of small fish bones, as discussed above.

An Approach to the Study of Great Basin Fish Remains

The original study from which this paper was extracted (Greenspan 1985) involved the analysis of fish bones recovered from prehistoric archaeological sites in three contiguous, internally draining basins in the Northern Great Basin: the Fort Rock Basin, the Harney Basin, and the Chewaucan Basin (Figure 1). Fish remains from each of these basins were examined and interpreted in light of a biogeographic model of fish availability. This approach is conceptually derived from descriptive ecology and is based upon the distribution, abundance, and seasonal accessibility of different native fishes. As pointed out by Schalk (1977), such an assessment of resource structure permits one to evaluate the nature of the resource for a particular area, and provides a basis for comparison between areas. I think this approach has particular importance in the analysis of Great Basin fish

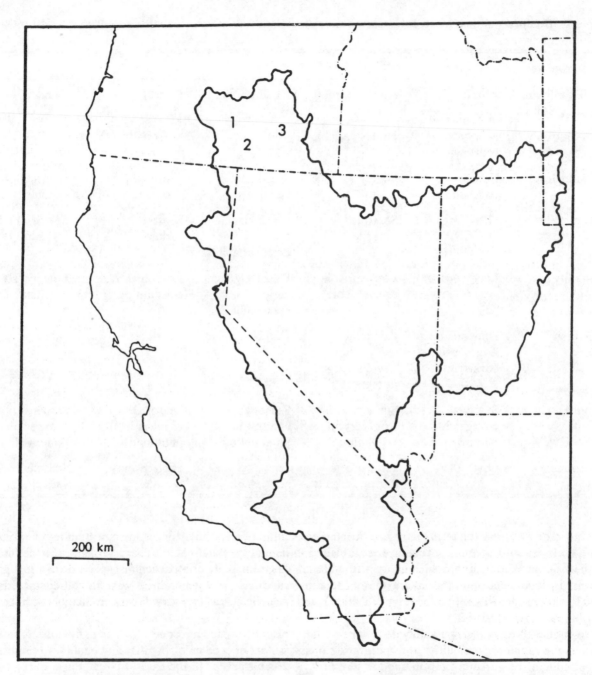

Figure 1. Location of the Study Area in the Northern Great Basin. Key: (1) Fort Rock Basin; (2) Chewaucan Basin; (3) Harney Basin.

remains, which, for various reasons outlined above, tend to be underrepresented in the existing archaeological record, thus making other methods of analysis more difficult.

The topography of the Great Basin, with its considerable relative relief and localized hydrographic conditions, results in a variety of fish habitats, including lakes, streams, springs and marshes. Aquatic ecosystems in deserts are extremely unstable, and fluctuate a great deal (Cole 1981:480). Because the distribution of surface water is subject to fluctuation, fish habitats tend to change in their presence, distribution, and nature over time.

Table 1. Summary of the Generalized Characteristics of Great Basin Fish Habitats (from Naiman 1981:498-499)

Parameter	Spring	Streams	Marshes	Rivers	Lakes
Predominant Water Source	Aquifer	Aquifer/runoff	Aquifer/runoff	Runoff	Runoff
Discharge	Nearly constant	Highly variable	—	Seasonally variable	—
Water level	Nearly constant	Highly variable	Seasonally variable	Seasonally variable	Seasonally variable
Temperature	Often constant	Seasonally variable	Maximum seasonal and daily variability	Seasonally variable	Seasonally variable
Salinity	Low, constant	Low, variable in drying pools	Relatively high, varies seasonally	Low, nearly constant	Low, nearly constant
Oxygen	Depends upon site, usually consistant	Adequate, except during low discharge at night	Highly variable	Adequate	Adequate
Light	Seasonal changes in photoperiod	Some shading from terrain, vegetation	Seasonal changes in photoperiod	Seasonal changes in photoperiod	Seasonal changes in photoperiod
Turbidity	Low	Low, except during freshets	Low	High at most times	Seasonally variable

In order to assess the availability and economic potential of a specific fish resource, a number of variables must be taken into account, including those relating to habitat type and habitat characteristics, the life history of the fish, and the hydrographic history of the basin. The availability of a particular species of fish in a given locality is dependent upon the interaction of the above variables. In a generalized way, habitat characteristics tend to vary predictably with habitat type (Table 1), and life cycle characteristics will vary predictably with species and habitat characteristics.

A model of resource availability does not reveal the extent to which a resource was actually utilized; rather, it limits the range of possibilities, thus permitting an assessment of economic potential and enabling a prediction to be made of resource utilization under a given set of circumstances. In the case of Great Basin fishes, these circumstances may be quite variable, and each case must be assessed individually.

In discussing a resource's economic potential and its availability for human exploitation, it is important to examine not only the distribution and abundance of the resource, but also the cultural factors affecting its exploitation. Available technology, religious taboos and other factors affecting food preferences, as well as the availability of other food resources, are some of the factors that must be considered. In addition, as discussed above, cultural factors may affect the disposition of the bones, and hence the likelihood of their presence in an archaeological site. Bone preservation and archaeological recovery techniques must also be taken into account in predicting the presence or absence of fish remains in archaeological assemblages.

The approach advocated here may be viewed on three analytical levels. The first is empirical and involves information imparted by the fish bones themselves, such as the taxonomic identification of the specimens; the

Table 2. Major Late Quaternary Environmental Intervals in the Great Basin

Interval	Time Period	General Description
Late Pluvial	12,500–7500 B.P.	Greater effective moisture than present; lake levels high, but generally declining from higher Pleistcene levels
Postpluvial	7500–5000 B.P.	Lesser effective moisture than present; generally low lake levels
Neopluvial	5000 B.P. to present	Increased effective moisture; some lake levels higher than modern levels; gradual decline to modern conditions

condition of the bones (whether they have been charred, for example); possibly the size and age of the fish at time of death; occasionally the season of death. On a strictly empirical level it is possible to learn a great deal from the presence and distribution of archaeologically–recovered fish bones.

The second level of analysis is interpretive and involves integration of the empirical data with ethnographic or archaeological information pertaining to fishing technology, and with information derived from the study of modern fish: their life histories, ecology, and habitat requirements. It is then possible to make inferences regarding fish exploitation, such as where and how the fish were caught, whether they were caught in large or small quantities, and what time of year they were caught.

The third level of analysis is predictive. In order to realize the full predictive power of this approach, it is necessary to have detailed information about the habits, requirements, and preferences of particular fish in particular habitats. It is also necessary to be able to reconstruct the paleoenvironment in a fairly detailed way. By further taking cultural and taphonomic factors, and archaeological recovery techniques into consideration, one could then predict the presence of fish remains in archaeological sites.

For the most part, the case studies summarized below (detailed analyses are presented in Greenspan 1985) are dealt with on the empirical and interpretive levels. The predictive level is approached in a general way, but the data required to rigorously test a predictive model in the cases studied are currently unavailable.

The distribution and abundance of fish are dependent upon the presence of suitable aquatic habitats; as discussed above, the presence and nature of such habitats may fluctuate considerably in desert environments. Therefore, environmental data form an important background against which to infer the distribution and availability of fish over time. Local environmental reconstructions are critical to detailed modeling. For the purposes of general discussion, however, a three–part postglacial environmental sequence, following that proposed by Antevs (1948) and refined by many researchers since then, will be followed (Greenspan 1985:29–40). Following Currey and James (1982) the terms Late Pluvial, Postpluvial, and Neopluvial will be used to describe the environmental intervals outlined in Table 2.

Fort Rock Basin

The Fort Rock Basin, in south–central Oregon, is physiographically transitional between the Basin and Range Province to the south and the Harney High Lava Plains Province on the north (Allison 1979:8). It is a broad, flat expanse divided into three sub–basins: Silver Lake Valley, Fort Rock Valley, and Christmas Valley (Figure 2). The divides between the sub–basins are low and fairly subtle. The only present fish habitats in the Fort Rock Basin are in Silver Lake Valley. Within historic times, the distribution of native fish in Silver Lake Valley has been limited to Silver Lake, portions of Paulina Marsh, and the three perennial streams that feed the marsh and the lake: Silver, Bridge, and Buck creeks. These three streams, which originate in the relatively well–watered uplands to the south and west, are the only perennial water in the Fort Rock Basin.

Silver, Bridge, and Buck creeks all support populations of redband trout (*Oncorhynchus* sp.[1]), tui chub (*Gila bicolor*), and speckled dace (*Rhinichthys osculus*). Only the tui chub has been reported in Silver Lake in historic

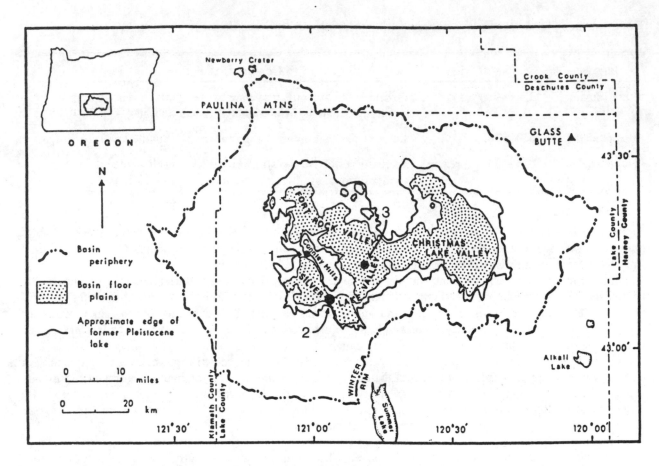

Figure 2. Fort Rock Basin, Oregon. Key to Archaeological Sites: (1) Conley Caves; (2) 35Lk 1013, 35Lk 1016; (3) Thorn Lake Sites.

times; apparently the modern lake has too high a concentration of dissolved solids for trout or dace. The total desiccation of Silver Lake has been reported at various times in the historic past (Phillips and Van Denburgh 1971); chub reinvade the lake when the water conditions are again suitable.

When lacustrine conditions in the Fort Rock Basin are in a transgressive phase, Silver Lake fills up more rapidly than the other two sub–basins, as it receives water from the three perennial streams. Springs, rainfall, and run–off contribute to the formation of small lakes in both Fort Rock and Christmas valleys, but it is only when the water level is high enough to form a surface connection between Silver Lake and the other sub–basins that a major body of water forms in the entire Fort Rock Basin. Within the past 12,000 years this is believed to have occurred at least twice. A large lake existed during the Late Pluvial period at the end of the Pleistocene, and there is evidence to suggest a subsequent, post–Mazama high lake level in the Fort Rock Basin (Allison and Bond 1983). This lake presumably dates to the Neopluvial Interval.

Fort Rock Valley and Christmas Lake Valley do not now contain any waters that are inhabited by fish, and it is probable that both sub–basins were fishless during the mid–Holocene Postpluvial interval when conditions were apparently even drier than at present. In contrast, the presence today of native fish in Silver, Bridge, and Buck creeks indicates that one or more of these streams have been perennial and have harbored fish life throughout the Holocene (Greenspan 1984).

At times when the water was sufficiently high to connect the three sub–basins, as during the Neopluvial interval, some trout, as well as chub and dace, undoubtedly migrated into all three Fort Rock sub–basins. This is demonstrated by the presence of redband trout bones, as well as those of chub, dace, and an extinct form of

Table 3. Fish Remains from Excavated Sites in the Fort Rock Basin

Site	Level with Fish	Dated Level	Date (B.P.)	Reference
35Lk 1016	3, 4, 5	4	1400 ± 70 (DIC 1813)	Toepel and Beckham 1981
Thorn Lake			3045 ± 70 (WSU–2752)	Mehringer 1983
Connley Cave 6	11	7, 4	3720 ± 270 (Gak–2130)	Bedwell 1973
Connley Cave 4B	26	Mazama ash	approximately 6800	
		30	7240 ± 150 (Gak–2140)	Bedwell 1973
Connley Cave 4B	31	30	7240 ± 150 (Gak–2140)	Bedwell 1973
Connley Cave 4B	34	34	9670 ± 180 (Gak–2142)	Bedwell 1973
Connley Cave 5A	26	27	9800 ± 250 (Gak–1743)	Bedwell 1973

sucker, in surface deposits of Fossil Lake (Allison and Bond 1983). Once such a lake began receding, it is unlikely that the trout would survive long after the surface connection with Silver Lake Valley was severed, as they would be cut off from their spawning grounds in the perennial streams. The chub and dace would likely survive somewhat longer than the trout under such conditions, because some chub and dace populations are able to adapt to spawning along the lakeshores, unlike the trout, which spawn only in the streams.

Archaeological Fish Remains in the Fort Rock Basin

Fish remains have been recovered from cave sites and open sites in the Fort Rock Basin. Table 3 lists the major excavated sites in the Fort Rock Basin at which fish bones have been recovered. Associated radiocarbon dates, or other temporal indicators, are included as available. Site locations are shown in Figure 2.

Connley Caves

Fish bones (all identified as tui chub) have been recovered from several of the Connley Caves, which are situated at the northern edge of the Silver Lake sub–basin on the flanks of the Connley Hills at an elevation of 1355 m. Most of these remains are from cultural deposits with radiocarbon dates placing them in the Late Pluvial interval. The earliest are from a level immediately overlying a date of 9800 ± 250 B.P. (Gak–1743), and the latest are bracketed by a radiocarbon date of 7240 ± 150 B.P. (Gak–2140), and by Mazama ash, dating to approximately 6800 B.P. In addition, two elements of tui chub were recovered in an apparently Neopluvial context from one of the Connley caves. These specimens were bracketed by radiocarbon dates of 4350 ± 100 B.P. (Gak–2131) and 3720 ± 270 B.P. (Gak–2130) (Bedwell 1973).

Thorn Lake Dunes

Fish remains have been recovered in association with a radiocarbon date of 3045 ± 70 B.P. (WSU–2752) from a site in Holocene dune deposits located approximately 10 km north–northeast of Thorn Lake (Mehringer 1983) in the Fort Rock Valley sub–basin. All identifiable specimens belong to the cyprinid family; all those identified to the species level are *Gila bicolor* (Greenspan 1985). Three additional sites in the Thorn Lake dune deposits have yielded fish remains. All of the fish represented at two of these sites are identified as *G. bicolor*; at the third site two charred salmonid vertebrae, probably representing redband trout, were identified (Greenspan 1985). A more detailed analysis of these sites is forthcoming (Peter J. Mehringer, personal communication 1989).

Silver Lake Narrows

Tui chub specimens have been identified from two open sites situated in the narrows between Silver Lake and Paulina Marsh. At site 35Lk 1013 a single basioccipital identified as *G. bicolor* was recovered from an undated context. Temporally sensitive artifacts suggest the site was occupied during the Neopluvial interval. At site 35Lk 1016, one km north of 35Lk 1013, 162 fish bones were recovered from a small fire pit radiocarbon dated to 1400 ± 70 B.P. (DIC–1813) (Toepel and Beckham 1981:93). All the identifiable elements represent tui chub (Toepel and Greenspan 1985).

Site 35Lk 1016 is a large open lithic scatter and plant processing site on the floor of Silver Lake Valley, at an elevation of 1316 to 1318 m. Cultural material recovered from this site includes chipped and ground stone artifacts and debitage. Other than 162 fish bones, faunal remains consist of only a few mammal specimens, including antelope, rabbit, hare, and unidentified rodents (Toepel and Beckham 1981).

Because of the site's location near the narrows, and the presence of grinding tools and a hearth as well as a variety of chipped stone tools, the locus is interpreted as a seasonal campsite at which a variety of activities took place. The abundance of grinding tools and the location of the site on the open valley floor suggest that plant procurement and processing were major activities. The presence of fish bones and the site's proximity to Silver Lake indicate that fishing also took place at or near the site. Tool manufacture and the processing of hides, wood, and/or bone are indicated by the chipped stone assemblage. Temporal indicators, including Elko and Rosegate projectile points, and a radiocarbon date of 1400 ± B.P. from the fire pit, suggest that the site may have been occupied from as early as 4000 B.P. until late prehistoric times (Toepel and Beckham 1981:98). The site's location is such that it could have been occupied even during the proposed 1316 m (Allison and Bond 1983) high water level of the Neopluvial interval.

All but one of the fish remains recovered from 35Lk 1016 were found in association with the hearth feature and it is possible that these specimens may represent a single catch of fish. However, the recovery of an additional fish bone from a unit 20 m away and another from nearby site 35Lk 1013 indicates that fishing was not an isolated occurrence in this locality.

From this campsite the nearest accessible source of tui chub is Silver Lake. Silver, Bridge, and Buck creeks support chub populations, but the streams are a considerable distance from the site area, with Paulina Marsh in between. Silver Lake, on the other hand, is nearby, and when it contains fresh water it supports populations of tui chub that would be readily accessible along the shoreline on a seasonal basis.

Lacustrine tui chub populations tend to spend the winter months in the open, deeper waters of the lake. Mature adults move into the shallows to spawn in the late spring and may be found along the lake margins through the summer months. The young–of–the–year will remain in the shallows until the onset of winter before migrating to the open water (Kimsey 1954; Moyle 1976:166–168). Thus, in Silver Lake the tui chub resource would be most easily and predictably accessible from late spring through the summer.

The fish bones recovered from 35Lk 1016 were examined for indications of age. With only a few exceptions, it was not possible to determine the age classes of the individuals represented. The few bones that did have discernible annuli (annual growth marks) were those of mature adults, and all the remains were within the size range of sexually mature adults. The apparent absence of immature individuals suggests that the fish represented by the 35Lk 1016 assemblage were caught in the late spring or early summer when the adults were spawning in the shallows and before the young were hatched.

This would also have been an optimal time for root gathering and processing (Couture 1978:29–30), which apparently were important activities at this site, as indicated by the large number of grinding tools (Greenspan 1981). This abundance of grinding tools and the site's location suggest that plant gathering was probably the major draw of this particular locality, while other activities, including fishing, were more likely of a supplemental and opportunistic nature.

Summary and Discussion: Prehistoric Fishing in the Fort Rock Basin

Current archaeological evidence suggests that in the Fort Rock Basin fish were utilized to some extent where and whenever they were readily available. There is clear evidence of their use in Silver Lake Valley during the Late Pluvial and the Neopluvial intervals and in Fort Rock Valley during the Neopluvial interval. There are presently no available data to firmly place any occupation of the Fort Rock Basin within the mid–Holocene Postpluvial interval. Forthcoming radiocarbon dates and stratigraphic data for the sites in the Thorn Lake dunes will shed additional light on the timing of fish availability and utilization, as well as the reconstruction of Holocene lake levels in the Fort Rock Basin (Peter J. Mehringer, personal communication 1989).

There is no currently available evidence to suggest that fish were ever a major resource in the Fort Rock Basin or that any elaborate fishing complex ever developed there. At 35Lk 1016 fishing appears to have been supplemental to the primary plant processing focus of the site. The fish represented in the assemblage could easily have been caught in the shallows of Silver Lake with little or no advance planning or specialized technology. Although little is known about fishing technology in the prehistoric Fort Rock Basin, many small, flat, slightly notched stones that may have served as net sinkers have been observed in surface contexts in lowland settings throughout the Basin (William J. Cannon, personal communication 1985).

The fish assemblages from two of the sites near Thorn Lake are similar to that from 35Lk 1016 (Greenspan 1985:181–188). As other analyses of these sites are not yet available, it is not possible to describe the sites as a whole or to fully interpret the fish remains at this time.

It is possible that fish were caught in locations some distance from the site at which the remains were recovered, and/or that they were being processed for storage and later consumption. While this practice is ethnographically documented elsewhere in the Great Basin (e.g., Fowler and Bath 1981), it is thought to be quite unlikely in the cases reported here. The ethnographic examples of fish storage are ones in which fish constituted a major resource and involved well–developed fishing complexes utilizing specialized technology. There is no evidence to suggest such a major fishing complex existed in the Fort Rock Basin. Indeed, in most of the Fort Rock Basin the fish resource is not adequate to support such a complex. The analyzed Fort Rock Basin sites where fish have been recovered are in locations where fish would be expected to be available locally during the periods the sites were occupied. It is highly likely that the fish represented in these sites were obtained nearby and during the same season that the site was occupied.

In conclusion, fish remains are known to have been recovered from eight sites in the Fort Rock Basin indicating that fishing, while apparently a minor activity, was widespread throughout the prehistory of the basin. The kinds of fluctuations in the level of Silver Lake that have been observed in modern times no doubt occurred in the past as well. This instability and the relatively depauperate fish fauna undoubtedly contributed to the lack of development of major fishing complexes in the Fort Rock Basin. The only perennial fish habitats in the basin are Bridge, Buck, and Silver creeks, the vicinities of which have not been investigated archaeologically. It is possible that a different type of fishing complex, possibly involving the exploitation of trout, might be identified in streamside locations.

Harney Basin

The Harney Basin is the largest enclosed fault–trough basin in Oregon. Like the adjacent Fort Rock Basin to the west, the Harney Basin lies in the transition zone between the High Lava Plains physiographic province on the north and the Basin and Range province on the south and exhibits characteristics of both regions. It is quite well-watered relative to the Fort Rock Basin and has a rich and varied aquatic resource base, including 11 native species of fish.

Although the Harney Basin now drains internally, it is clearly a disrupted portion of the Columbia River system (Hubbs and Miller 1948:75). The basin's hydrographic isolation resulted from the damming of Malheur Gap by the extrusion of the extensive Voltage lava field, which predates 32,000 B.P. by an unknown period of time (Gehr 1980). The lava dam blocked the drainage of water from the Harney Basin into the Malheur River, which drains into the Snake River (a major tributary of the Columbia), and Pluvial Lake Malheur eventually formed behind the dam. The present distribution of native fish in the basin derives primarily from this earlier connection with the Malheur River (Bisson and Bond 1971).

There is evidence that the Harney Basin overflowed into the Malheur River system at Malheur Gap after the damming of the gap by the Voltage lavas. Russell (1905) and Piper et al. (1939:18) noted an ill-defined drain that could be traced into Malheur Gap. Gehr observed a canyon cut into the Voltage basalt at Malheur Gap and concluded that a stream of significant magnitude and duration flowed through the gap at an elevation of 1,254 m. Gehr obtained a radiocarbon date of 8680 ± 55 B.P. (USGS-461B) on a deposit of snails that was found just below the surface of a wave-cut terrace at 1,255.1 m. This terrace represents the highest observed lacustrine feature in the basin. Gehr interprets this as clear evidence that water in the Harney Basin did overflow and connect with the Columbia drainage after the Voltage lava dam formed and that it did so as recently as 8680 B.P. (Gehr 1980:75-81).

Native fishes extant in the Harney Basin include six members of the family Cyprinidae: redside shiner (*Richardsonius balteatus*), tui chub (*Gila bicolor*), chiselmouth (*Acrocheilus alutaceus*), northern squawfish (*Ptychocheilus oregonensis*), longnose dace (*Rhinichthys cataractae*), and speckled dace (*Rhinichthys osculus*); two members of the Catostomidae or sucker family: bridgelip sucker (*Catostomus columbianus*), and largescale sucker (*Catostomus macrocheilus*); three members of the family Salmonidae: redband trout (*Oncorhynchus* sp.), rainbow trout (*Oncorhynchus mykiss*), and mountain whitefish (*Prosopium williamsoni*); and one member of the sculpin family, Cottidae: mottled sculpin (*Cottus bairdi*).

Archaeological Fish Remains in the Harney Basin

The Harney Basin has a diverse and abundant resource base; this richness is reflected in the archaeological record. More than 1,300 prehistoric archaeological sites have been officially recorded, reflecting human occupation of the area for more than 10,000 years. These sites occur in lowland, upland, and transitional settings. Recorded site types include large and small open sites, habitation rings, rockshelters, burials, pictographs, and petroglyphs. Some of the open sites have been interpreted as probable village locations.

Although very few radiocarbon dates have been obtained from Harney Basin sites, early occupation of the area is evident from the recovery of Clovis fluted points (Newman et al. 1974), Windust points (Fagan and Sage 1974), and Great Basin Stemmed points (Minor and Toepel 1988) from undated surface contexts in the basin. An early lake margin occupation is indicated by a series of sites on the south shore of Harney Lake. Five of these sites are associated with the 8680 B.P. highstand of Lake Malheur. Associated artifacts include Windust or Lind Coulee points, basally-ground leaf-shaped points, crescents, and true blades (Gehr 1980).

More recent intensive occupation of marsh and lakeside environments in the Harney Basin is represented by a number of lowland sites (Figure 3). The Headquarters Site (35Ha 403), located on the south shore of Malheur Lake at the mouth of Blitzen River, is an extensive cultural deposit that is interpreted as a prehistoric village (Thomas 1979; Campbell n.d.; Aikens 1983; Minor and Greenspan 1985; Aikens and Greenspan 1988; Minor and Toepel 1988). The site's lakeside location and the quantities of aquatic resources represented in the faunal assemblages indicate a lacustrine adaptation. A similar exploitation of lake and marsh resources is represented at the Blitzen Marsh (35Ha 9) and Hogwallow Spring (35Ha 8) sites. These sites are both located on the edge of an extensive swamp associated with the Blitzen River. The Blitzen Marsh site has been interpreted as a probable winter village, whereas Hogwallow Spring is thought to represent a repeatedly occupied temporary campsite (Fagan 1974). Site 35Ha 1263 is another locality that may represent a village and at which a significant use of lacustrine resources in indicated. This site is located on the edge of Diamond Swamp in the eastern portion of the Harney Basein (Toepel et al. 1984). All of these sites have fish remains in their assemblages.

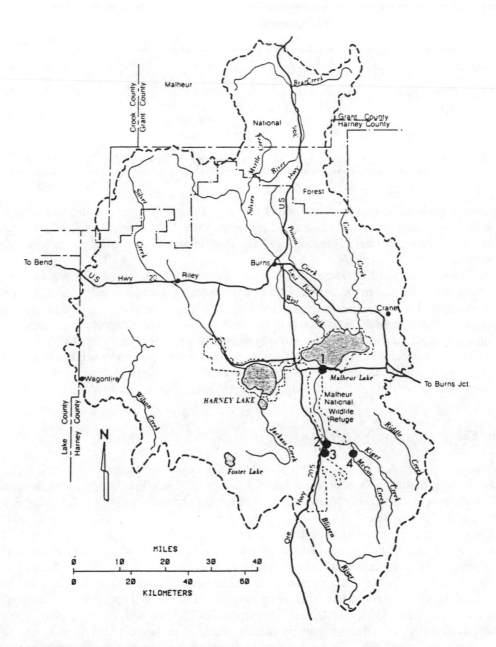

Figure 3. Harney Basin, Oregon. Key to Archaeological Sites: **(1)** Headquarters Site; **(2)** Blitzen Marsh; **(3)** Hogwallow Spring; **(4)** 35Ha 1263.

Radiocarbon dates have been obtained for only two of the above sites. Blitzen Marsh provided a series of radiocarbon dates ranging from 2350 ± 80 (Gak–3302) to 220 ± 80 B.P. (Gak–3296) (Fagan 1974:101). A date of 1480 ± 110 B.P. (Beta–9573) was obtained from 35Ha 1263 (Toepel et al. 1984). Typological cross–dating of temporally sensitive artifacts suggests that occupation at both of these sites may have begun considerably

Table 4. Summary of Archaeological Sites in the Harney Basin Producing Fish Remains

Site	Provenience of Fish	Provenience of Date	Date B.P.
Headquarters Site	Surface–145 cm	none	ca. 4000–500
Hogwallow Spring	Strata 1, 2	none	ca. 5000–3000
Blitzen Marsh	Strata C, B, A	Stratum C	1400–170
		Stratum B	2350–1280
35Ha 1263	Strata 1, 2	between Strata 2, 3	1480 ± 110

earlier, perhaps as early as 7000 B.P. By the same relative dating technique, the Headquarters Site is thought to have been occupied more or less throughout the Holocene (Minor and Toepel 1988), while Hogwallow Spring was apparently used during the last 5,000 years, with the most intensive occupation occurring in the period from 5,000 to 3,000 years ago (Fagan 1974).

Although the prehistory of the Harney Basin is very incompletely known, available evidence indicates that people were occupying lake and marsh margin localities there during much, if not all, of the Holocene. Extensive utilization of marsh and lacustrine resources in the context of a semi–sedentary or sedentary lifeway occurred at least during the period from 3000 to 1000 B.P. and fish were clearly an important resource in that adaptive strategy. Table 4 lists those excavated sites in the Harney Basin at which fish remains have been recovered in sub–surface contexts. Associated radiocarbon dates or other temporal indicators are listed where available. As the data show, there are no radiocarbon dates directly associated with cultural deposits that date from the Late Pluvial or Postpluvial intervals in the Harney Basin, and nothing is known about fishing for those earlier periods.

Headquarters Site

The Headquarters site, at the headquarters complex of the Malheur National Wildlife Refuge, is situated on a terrace just below a basalt knoll, at an elevation of 1,251 to 1,253 m. The Blitzen River flows along the base of the knoll on its west side, entering Malheur Lake just west of the Headquarters site. There is a spring in the northwestern portion of the site.

The presence of prehistoric cultural deposits at the Headquarters site has been known at least since the construction of the refuge headquarters facilities in the 1930s, at which time a variety of artifacts and cultural features, including human burials, was encountered (Campbell n.d.). Although no intensive excavation has occurred at the site, a number of testing projects, as well as controlled surface collection and archaeological monitoring of construction activities has taken place since the late 1970s (Thomas 1979; Campbell n.d.; Aikens 1983; Minor and Greenspan 1985; Aikens and Greenspan 1988; Minor and Toepel 1988). The investigations carried out to date reveal an extensive and intensively occupied prehistoric settlement, with rich and varied artifact and faunal assemblages. Chipped stone tools recovered from this site include projectile points (stemmed/lanceolate, Humboldt, Northern Side–notched, Elko, Rosegate, and Desert side–notched varieties); knives, awls, drills, scrapers, and gravers. Cobble tools include hammers, anvils, choppers, scrapers, and net weights, and ground and pecked stone tools include manos, metates, mortars, pestles, mauls, abraders, palettes, an atlatl weight, and a bola stone. Faunal remains include deer, elk, hare, rabbit, muskrat, squirrels, pocket gophers, birds, and fish.

The Headquarters site has been interpreted as a probable aboriginal village based upon the density and variety of the cultural materials recovered as well as the presence of burials (Minor and Greenspan 1985; Aikens and Greenspan 1987; Minor and Toepel 1988). The site's setting on the edge of Malheur Lake near the mouth

Table 5. Summary of Identified Fish Taxa from the Headquarters Site

Taxon	1985	1984	1978	Totals
Gila bicolor	343	22	11	376
Cyprinidae cf. *G. bicolor*	86	0	0	86
Ptychocheilus oregonensis	3	0	1	4
Cyprinidae cf. *P. oregonensis*	4	1	1	6
Catostomus sp.	61	2	26	89
Cyprinidae	0	13	13	26
Cyprinidae/Catostomidae	0	5	0	5
Other	0	5	22	27
Totals	497	48	74	619

of the Blitzen River affords access to a variety of aquatic and terrestrial resources, exploitation of which is indicated by the artifacts and faunal materials recovered. Although no radiocarbon dates have been obtained from the Headquarters site, the projectile points recovered indicate initial occupation of the site perhaps as early as 8,000–11,000 years ago (Minor and Toepel 1988:33), with more intensive occupation occurring within the last 3,000–4,000 years.

All of the reported archaeological investigations at the Headquarters site have resulted in the recovery of fish remains. Those that have been analyzed are reported in detail elsewhere (Greenspan 1985; Minor and Greenspan 1985; Aikens and Greenspan 1988); they will be summarized here (Table 5).

The fish bones recovered from the Headquarters site indicate a significant exploitation of locally available cyprinids and suckers and no apparent use of the salmonid or sculpin species present in the basin. Although squawfish and chiselmouth are represented in small numbers, the only cyprinid present in significant quantities is tui chub. Dace and shiners were not identified in the assemblages, although some of the smaller vertebrae, which, among the cyprinids, are not generally identifiable on the specific level, may be those of dace or shiner.

The above discussion of *G. bicolor* behavior and accessibility with respect to populations in Silver Lake would be applicable to populations in Malheur Lake as well. Very little information is available regarding the behavior of stream populations of tui chubs. Presumably, like lake populations, stream populations would be caught most easily in the spring and summer months when they tend to congregate in the shallow, vegetated areas.

Suckers, like their close relatives, the cyprinids, occupy a wide range of habitats including lakes, mountain streams, and large, lowland rivers (Moyle 1976:212–213; Sigler and Miller 1963:93). They are, however, more specialized than the cyprinids, being primarily bottom-feeders, and are not quite so highly adaptable. Very little is known about the life histories and behavior of suckers in general and of the bridgelip sucker in particular. Slightly more is known about the largescale sucker. Adult largescale suckers are bottom dwellers and prefer shallow water. They are especially abundant in the mouths of streams entering lakes and are also commonly found in backwaters and along vegetated lakeshores. Spawning habitat is generally in pools or riffle areas of streams with gravelly or sandy bottoms. Occasionally largescale suckers will spawn in lakes, on gravelly shoals, or along the shoreline. Spawning occurs at age four or five in the spring when the water temperature has reached 46–48°F (8–9°C). The newly hatched fry remain in the gravel or on the surface of the sand in the spawning grounds for a few weeks, after which they move to the open water. They stay in midwater or near the surface until they reach roughly 18 mm in length. At that time they move to the bottom and into somewhat deeper water (Wydoski and Whitney 1979:98; Scott and Crossman 1973:545–546; La Rivers 1962:342).

Thus, like the tui chub, the largescale sucker is most readily available for harvesting during the spring months when suckers are spawning. During their annual spawning migrations, large groups congregate in streams or lake margins making them susceptible to being taken with nets or basketry scoops. In the absence of any detailed information about the behavior and life history of the bridgelip sucker, it is assumed that this fish follows the generally known sucker pattern described above. There is some evidence to suggest that it prefers portions of streams with more swiftly flowing currents than does the largescale sucker (Miller and Miller 1948), and that it spawns a bit later in the year (Wydoski and Whitney 1979:101).

At times when Malheur Lake has any significant amount of fresh water in it both the suckers and the chubs would be available in the immediate vicinity of the Headquarters site, possibly on a year round basis, and certainly in the spring and summer, when they would be abundant and easily caught in the lake shallows and in the mouth and lower reaches of the river. They could be easily exploited using nets, traps, or hooks.

Hogwallow Spring

The Hogwallow Spring site is located on the eastern edge of the Blitzen Valley. The spring after which the site is named flows from beneath a low rimrock on the edge of the marsh that forms the western margin of the site. On the eastern edge of the site is a sheltered area formed by a three meter high rimrock (Fagan 1973:81). The site area is fairly circumscribed with the marsh on one side and relatively steep slopes on the others.

Cultural debris recovered from the Hogwallow Spring site includes projectile points, preforms, knives and other bifaces, gravers, scrapers, spokeshaves, worked and unworked flakes, manos, milling stones, bone awls, a bone bead, and other worked bone and antler fragments. Among the projectile point types recovered are Northern Side-notched, Humboldt, Elko, Surprise Valley Split Stem, and Rosegate specimens. Faunal remains include large and small mammals, birds, fish, and freshwater mussels. As mentioned above, no radiocarbon dates were obtained from the Hogwallow Spring site, but the distribution of projectile points suggests that the site was occupied over the last 5,000 or perhaps 7,000 years with the most intensive use in the period from 5,000–3,000 years ago. The site is interpreted as a temporary campsite, repeatedly occupied for the purposes of exploiting the local marshland resources (Fagan 1973:84).

A total of 334 fish bones was recovered from test excavations at the Hogwallow Spring site, representing northern squawfish, tui chub, chiselmouth, largescale sucker, bridgelip sucker, and a third, unidentified sucker that is no longer known from the Harney Basin. Table 6 shows the distribution of fish taxa by strata, as well as the number of fish bones recovered per cubic meter for each of the strata.

The location of the Hogwallow Spring site along Blitzen Marsh and the lower Blitzen River affords excellent access to the various fish species that spawn in the lower reaches of the river. Any of the species of fish that are native to the Harney Basin could be present in this stretch of the Blitzen. The cyprinids, suckers, and salmonids would all be most easily accessible to people at the Hogwallow Spring site during their respective spawning seasons when they would be most predictably and most abundantly present in the immediate site vicinity. Except for the mountain whitefish, which spawn in the fall, all these fish are spring and/or summer spawners.

Neither whitefish nor trout is represented in the faunal assemblage. Both are known to be present in the main stem of the Blitzen River (Bisson and Bond 1971:273) and undoubtedly were in the prehistoric past as well. The salmonids are absent not only from the Hogwallow Spring site, but from all the investigated sites in the Harney Basin. There are several possible explanations for this pattern. Trout and whitefish prefer protected habitats and are thus less accessible to human predation than the suckers and cyprinids. It is also possible that they may have been deliberately avoided or that they were exploited but were processed in such a way that their bones did not get discarded at the sites. On the other hand, given that only a small number of sites have been excavated in the Harney Basin, and that work has been concentrated in the lowland areas, and given that better trout habitats are likely to be farther upstream, this pattern may simply represent an archaeological sampling problem.

In summary, investigations carried out at the Hogwallow Spring site indicate that it represents an intensively and repeatedly occupied camp from which a variety of aquatic and terrestrial resources were exploited. Fishing

Table 6. Distribution of Fish Remains by Stratum, Hogwallow Spring

Taxon	NISP	MNI	N/m^3
Stratum C			
P. oregonensis	4	2	
G. bicolor	1	1	
Cyprinidae	2		
Catostomus sp.	3	2	
Total	9		4.6
Stratum B			
G. bicolor	8	3	
Catostomus sp.	1	1	
Unidentifiable fish	1		
Total	10		12.5
Stratum A			
P. oregonensis	36	4	
G. bicolor	8	2	
A. alutaceus	2	1	
Cyprinidae	8	—	
C. macrocheilus	13	3	
C. columbianus	1	1	
Catostomus sp.	99	8	
Cyprinidae/Catostomidae	33	—	
Unidentifiable fish	114		
Total	315		75.0
Site Total	334		

was a very important part of the subsistence pattern inferred at this site–fish represent 36% of the faunal assemblage (Fagan 1973). The abundance of various cyprinids and suckers suggests occupation in the spring and summer, when these species make mass spawning migrations up the river. They would be very easily caught at this time, with nets, traps, diversionary weirs or dams, or hooks and lines.

Blitzen Marsh

Blitzen Marsh is a large, stratified, open site located in the Blitzen Valley south of Diamond Swamp. The site is situated on a broad terrace above the Blitzen River just east of the point where Blitzen Valley becomes constricted between two basalt knolls and roughly 1.5 km downstream from the Hogwallow Spring site.

Blitzen Marsh is very rich in cultural materials. Features encountered include house pits, living floors, storage pits, hearths, and a disturbed human burial. Classifiable projectile points include Northern Side–notched, Humboldt, Elko, Rosegate, Cottonwood, Surprise Valley Split Stem, and Desert Side–notched types. A wide variety of other chipped stone, ground stone, and cobble tools were represented. Bone and shell beads, a bone flute, and other pieces of worked bone were recovered, as were pipe fragments, pigment, and pigment–stained flakes (Fagan 1974).

Large quantities of faunal remains were recovered and include large and small mammals, birds, fish, egg shells, and mussel and snail shells. The 297 fish bones recovered, representing less than 5% of the faunal assemblage (Fagan 1973), have never been identified and unfortunately have not been available for analysis during the course of this study. The bulk of the fish remains were recovered from Stratum C which, on the basis of radiocarbon dates, obsidian hydration dating, and typological cross–dating of projectile points, has been assigned an age of 3000 to 150 B.P. (Fagan 1973).

Blitzen Marsh is a large and intensively occupied aboriginal settlement. The presence of house and storage pits, and a burial, as well as the density and variety of cultural debris accumulated at the site, indicate that this site may represent a prehistoric village. Its location affords excellent access to river and marsh resources, as well as relatively easy access to nearby upland areas, and the faunal and artifact assemblages indicate that these resources were extensively utilized.

Although the fish remains have not been available for examination, the location of the site is such that the same types of fish available at Hogwallow Spring would be available at Blitzen Marsh. If Hogwallow Spring was occupied only seasonally, and Blitzen Marsh was occupied for most or all of the year, the pattern of fish exploitation might have been somewhat different at these two sites. The apparent differences in period of most intensive occupation, and the differences in site function between these two sites are other factors to consider in comparing them.

McCoy Creek

The McCoy Creek site (35Ha 1263) is located on the southwestern margin of Diamond Swamp. It sits on a bend in McCoy Creek, a tributary of Kiger Creek, which in turn is tributary to the Blitzen River. The site was tested in 1984 (Toepel et al. 1984), and more intensive excavations were undertaken in the Fall of 1988. Analysis of the materials recovered in 1988 has not been completed at this writing (Rick Minor, personal communication 1989) and the following discussion is based primarily on the earlier testing at the site. Although this site is neither as large nor as intensively occupied as the Headquarters site, it did yield a wide variety of artifacts and faunal materials. Classifiable projectile points include Northern Side–notched, Humboldt, Elko, and Rosegate types. Other chipped stone tools include knives, biface fragments, gravers, scrapers, and utilized flakes. Cores and unmodified flakes were also recovered. The chipped stone assemblage was made from obsidian, cryptocrystalline, and basalt raw materials. Basalt ground stone tools include manos, metates, and a cobble hammer. The faunal assemblage includes remains of deer, canid, hares, rabbits, voles, ground squirrels, muskrat, ducks, frogs, and fish (Toepel et al. 1984).

The site is interpreted as having been a likely village location or a heavily utilized base camp. A possible housepit was excavated during the 1984 testing and remains of two wickiups were identified in 1988 (Toepel et al. 1984; Rick Minor, personal communication 1988).

During the 1984 testing at McCoy Creek 42 fish bones were recovered. Only cyprinids were identified and, with the exception of one probable squawfish bone, all the identified cyprinids are tui chub. Many more fish remains were recovered from the 1988 excavations, but these have not yet been quantified or analyzed.

In a study of the modern distribution of fish in the Harney basin, Bisson and Bond (1971) collected redside shiners, speckled dace, and trout in McCoy Creek, and in Kiger Creek they collected those three species plus longnose dace, bridgelip sucker, and mottled sculpin. It is interesting to note that in McCoy Creek, near where the site is located, Bisson and Bond did not collect tui chub or Northern squawfish, the two species thus far identified from the site. It is possible that historic period channelization of area streams in order to drain Diamond Swamp has resulted in changes in fish distribution. In particular, it is possible that during the Neopluvial interval, without the effects of the canals and with increased effective moisture and a higher water table, Diamond Swamp may have supported significant populations of chub and other lacustrine species typical of the Harney Basin lowlands (Carl E. Bond, personal communication 1989).

Summary and Discussion: Prehistoric Fishing in the Harney Basin

The Harney Basin is well–watered and accordingly has a rich aquatic resource base. Archaeological data indicate a well–developed lowland adaptation dependent upon the exploitation of a wide variety of resources in river, lake, and marshside habitats. Upland habitats were utilized as well, although apparently less intensively. The florescence of this pattern seems to have occurred within the last 4,000 to 3,000 years, and to have continued until late prehistoric times. There is evidence of much earlier lakeshore habitation as well (Gehr 1980), although a detailed description of this adaptation awaits further work.

Fish appear to have been a very significant resource for prehistoric people in the Harney Basin, representing more than one–third of the faunal assemblage at Hogwallow Spring, and a large proportion at the Headquarters site. They are present in significant numbers at the Blitzen Marsh site as well, although they represent less than 5% of the excavated faunal assemblage there. It should be pointed out that, with the exception of the 1984 and 1985 testing of the Headquarters site, excavations at these sites involved the use of one–fourth inch mesh screens. Use of one–eighth inch mesh would undoubtedly have resulted in recovery of more fish remains, particularly those of the smaller species such as tui chub.

The Hogwallow Spring site appears to have been a camp from which a variety of resources was exploited, including fish, particularly suckers, squawfish, and some chub (which may well be underrepresented due to the use of one–fourth inch mesh screen). The site's location, the large number of fish bones, and the fact that the fish bones constitute 36% of the faunal assemblage suggest that fishing was one of the primary activities carried out here. The fish represented at Hogwallow Spring are species that make mass spawning migrations and tend to congregate in shallow, shoreline areas in the spring and summer. It is reasonable to think that occupation of the Hogwallow Spring site occurred during this time of year when the fish recovered from the site would have been most easily caught and when other resources, such as edible plants and waterfowl, would have been abundant as well. This is also the time of year in which groups such as the Klamath, who historically occupied territory to the southwest of the Harney Basin, left their winter villages for temporary fishing camps (Spier 1930:10). Although the above scenario remains in the realm of speculation, the seasonal model provided by the biogeography and life history of the fish can serve to guide the formulation of specific hypotheses to be tested.

The Headquarters site, which represents a more extensively occupied settlement than Hogwallow Spring, was probably a village and may have been occupied at least to some extent throughout much of the year. Fish would have been available in Malheur Lake, the Blitzen River, and probably in nearby Sodhouse Spring. The mouth of the river would be an excellent place to harvest suckers and cyprinids during their annual spawning migrations; less intensive fishing could take place throughout the year.

Although fishing occurred at McCoy Creek, it does not appear to have been as major an activity there as it was at Hogwallow Spring, the Headquarters site, and Blitzen Marsh. The McCoy Creek site is not as favorably situated for intensive fish exploitation as the other three sites, being located on a small tributary stream. If this site represents a winter village, it is possible that the people who lived there moved to more favorable fishing locations in the spring and summer much like the ethnographically–documented pattern of the Klamath (Spier 1930:10–11).

Thus far the only evidence of fishing technology known from the Harney Basin is notched stones interpreted to be net sinkers. Three such weights were collected from the surface of the Headquarters site (Minor and Toepel 1988). During a recent survey of sites exposed by erosion resulting from the rapid fluctuations of the lake levels the last few years, more net sinkers were found at sites on two islands in Malheur Lake. At each site a pile of 20–25 notched stones were collected from the surface. In each case, it appeared as though a net had been lost or discarded with the weights still attached, and that eventually the netting disintegrated, leaving only the net sinkers (Rick Minor, personal communication 1989).

Stewart (1941:370–71; 387) reported that the *Wada–dokado*, the Northern Paiute groups whose territory included the Harney Basin, utilized a variety of tools in fishing, including nets, weirs, baskets, basketry traps, harpoons, spears, fish arrows, hooks, and poison. The types of fish represented in the Harney Basin sites could have been caught using any of these techniques. Nets, alone, or in conjunction with weirs, would be a very efficient tool in intensively exploiting the spawning runs.

At present, there is no archaeological evidence of storage of fish in the Harney Basin. The *Wada–dokado* (Stewart 1941:376), the Cattail Eaters (Wheat 1967:63-64), and the Pyramid Lake Paiute (Fowler and Bath 1981:185) all dried fish for later consumption, as did the Klamath (Spier 1930:155) and the Washo (Downs 1966:14). It is likely that if the prehistoric occupants of the Harney Basin were catching fish in sufficient quantities to have an immediate surplus, they were processing some of them for later consumption. The fish resource in the Harney Basin is adequate to support a surplus and, if people utilized large nets or wiers, they certainly would have had access to fish in large quantities.

The data available for the Harney Basin indicate occupation of the basin since Late Pluvial times and that marsh, river, and lakeside habitats have been favored localities for much, if not all, of that time. By 4,000 or 3,000 years ago, intensive occupation of the lowland areas is evident with a generalized subsistence base, including a variety of aquatic and terrestrial resources. The rich and varied resources available in the Harney Basin permitted the development of an adaptive strategy that included major settlements, perhaps not unlike Klamath winter villages. Suckers, and various cyprinids, particularly tui chub, were a significant part of the complex of resources that supported this adaptation.

Chewaucan Basin

The Chewaucan Basin lies within the Basin and Range physiographic province in south-central Oregon. It is separated from the Fort Rock Basin on the north by a series of tilted fault blocks. There is considerable relative relief in the basin, with elevations ranging from 1,263 m on the bed of Summer Lake to 2,549 m at Gearhart Mountain (Allison 1982).

Typical of the Basin and Range province in Oregon, the terrain is primarily volcanic in origin and is characterized by north–south trending fault–block mountain ranges separated by internally draining basins. Within the Chewaucan Basin are four sub–basins, each a down–faulted trough (Figure 4). From northwest to southeast they are: Summer Lake, Upper Chewaucan Marsh, Lower Chewaucan Marsh, and Lake Abert. Summer Lake and Lake Abert occupy the lowest portions of the basin and both sub–basins contain relatively shallow, alkaline lakes. Lake Abert and the Chewaucan Marshes have been treated as one basin, with Summer Lake as another (cf. Phillips and Van Denburgh 1971). Summer Lake and the Abert–Chewaucan basins are now separated at Paisley Flat by a large fan-delta formed by the Chewaucan River during a high stage of Pluvial Lake Chewaucan, and subsequently reworked by wave action during lower stages of the lake (Allison 1982:33).

The Chewaucan River is the primary source of running water in the Abert-Chewaucan basin. It originates in the forested highlands south of the basin, flows through Upper and then Lower Chewaucan Marshes, and enters Lake Abert at the southern tip of the lake. Several ephemeral streams drain into the marshes, but contribute little to the flow of the Chewaucan River (Allison 1982:19). Other sources of water for Lake Abert are precipitation on the surface of the lake, a number of small springs along the lake shores, and ephemeral streams draining into the lake, the largest of which is Poison Creek on the east side (Phillips and Van Denburgh 1971:B12).

Reconstruction of Holocene lake level fluctuations suggests the same general pattern as that observed in the Fort Rock and Harney basins, although unlike the Harney Basin, the Chewaucan Basin appears to have been a fully enclosed basin throughout the Quaternary; Pluvial Lake Chewaucan did not overflow at its maximum level of 1,378 m (Phillips and Van Denburgh 1971:B12). A highstand of Lake Abert at roughly 9,400 years ago is indicated by a radiocarbon date of 9390 ± 45 B.P. (USGS-351) obtained on a tufa–like carbonate crust on beach gravels at an elevation 20–22 m above the present surface of the lake (Gehr 1980:74–75). Gehr interprets this as being apparently coeval with the 9620 B.P. lake he infers in the Harney Basin.

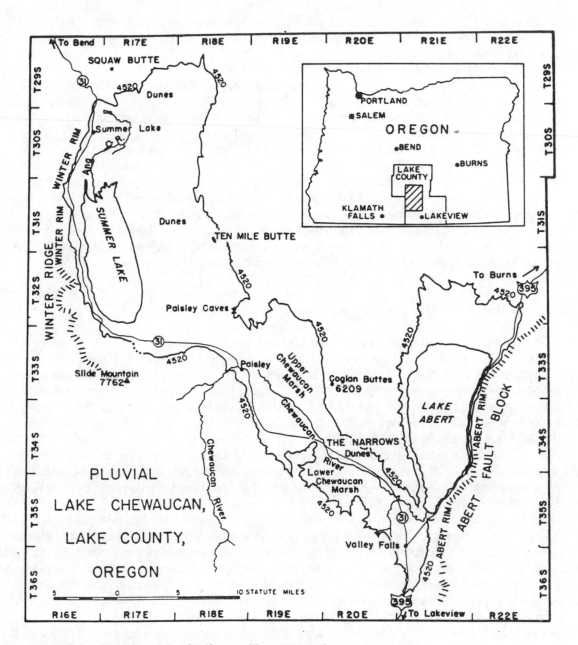

Figure 4. Map of the Chewaucan Basin (from Allison 1982:12).

Allison (1982:69) considers that transverse dunes in the northern part of the Summer Lake Basin were probably formed during the Postpluvial period. He also infers that Lake Abert and Summer Lake became completely dry during that time because the concentration of dissolved solids in the lakes is such that it can be expected to have accumulated within only a few thousand years (cf. Van Winkle 1914).

Allison assigns a Neopluvial age to a wave-cut bank at 1,284 m, approximately 60 feet (20 m) above modern levels of Lake Abert. North of Summer Lake a now-dry beach at 4,190 feet (1,277 m) cuts across Mazama pumice sand dunes and is thus considered of Neopluvial age (Allison 1982:70-71).

Five feet of lacustrine sediment was deposited on the playa north of Lake Abert within the last 5,000 years. This is evident from a radiocarbon date of 4530 ± 250 B.P. (USGS–W–2196) obtained from leached sediments four to five feet under the playa surface (Van Denburgh 1975:C25).

Like the adjacent Fort Rock Basin, the Chewaucan Basin has only three native fish species: tui chub (*Gila bicolor*), speckled dace (*Rhinichthys osculus*), and redband trout (*Oncorhynchus* sp.). With the possible, though unlikely, exception of a few catfish (*Ictalurus nebulosis*) bones whose significance is still unclear (Greenspan 1985:207-9), there is no evidence to suggest that any other species of fish were present in the Chewaucan Basin during the history of Pluvial Lake Chewaucan.

Present fish habitats include the Chewaucan River, Ana River, Ana Reservoir and some of the smaller springs and streams in the basin. Trout are present in the Chewaucan River and some of its tributaries, in Ana Reservoir, and the Ana River. When Ana Springs was free–running, before the construction of the dam that created Ana Reservoir, trout were found in the springs as well. Chub and dace exist in all of those habitats, as well as in some of the smaller springs. XL Spring and Brattain Spring contain only chub.

At times of considerably higher water, when the lakes were fresh and the streams received greater flow, fish were undoubtedly more widely distributed in the basin. Although the lakes are now too alkaline to support fish, they certainly would have done so when the water was fresh.

Archaeological Fish Remains in the Chewaucan Basin

Professional archaeological research in the Chewaucan Basin was initiated by Luther Cressman in the 1930s, and continues today. Much of the work has been oriented towards surface survey and collection (Cole 1969, 1975, 1976; Cole and Pettigrew 1976; Pettigrew and Cole 1977; Aikens and Minor 1977; Cannon 1977, 1978; Pettigrew 1981, 1985; Oetting and Pettigrew 1985, 1987; Oetting 1989; Oetting, this volume); The only reported professional excavations undertaken to date in the Chewaucan Basin have been at Paisley Five Mile Point Caves, southeast of Summer Lake (Cressman et al. 1940; Cressman 1942) and at a series of open sites along the east shore of Lake Abert (Pettigrew 1981, 1985; Oetting 1988). The survey and excavation data indicate that lakeside, marshside, and upland habitats were utilized by inhabitants of the basin beginning at least 8,000 years ago. Major settlements, many with evidence of domestic structures, are common in the lowlands, particularly along the lower reaches of the Chewaucan River and on the shores of Lake Abert (Oetting and Pettigrew 1985; 1987; Pettigrew 1981; 1985; Oetting 1988; 1989).

Archaeological survey and excavations along the east shore of Lake Abert undertaken in the late 1970s and early 1980s resulted in the identification of several large prehistoric settlements. At a number of sites stone rings and circular depressions were found; many of these circular features are interpreted to be domestic structures. Rock art and concentrations of chipped and ground stone tools were also common at these sites. This complex of sites is seen as evidence of prehistoric villages that were supported by the rich lacustrine and terrestrial resources available in the vicinity. Occupation of these settlements occurred at various times within the last 3,500 or even 5,000 years (Pettigrew 1985; Oetting 1988; Oetting, this volume).

These sites show evidence of a broad–spectrum economy based upon the exploitation of a variety of locally available resources. Ground stone plant processing implements, such as manos, milling stones, and mortars, are common at these sites and indicate that seeds, roots, and other plant products were probably significant resources. Faunal remains include a variety of waterfowl, hares and rabbits, various rodents, deer, sheep, and antelope, various carnivores, freshwater mussels, and fish.

Fish remains were recovered from only five of the sites and were found in very small quantities. This may be due, in part, to recovery techniques employed during excavation. During the testing phase of the project the excavated material was passed through one–fourth inch mesh screens. No native fish remains were recovered at the time. When soil column samples were subsequently processed in the laboratory, and material was wet–screened through a Number 32 sieve (approximately 0.5 mm mesh), hundreds of bones identified as *Gila bicolor* (tui chub) and *Rhinichthys osculus* (speckled dace) were recovered from a single column sample taken from 35Lk 480. Although it is not clear whether these specimens are part of the cultural deposit at the site, their recovery in the column sample prompted the use of screens with one–eighth inch mesh during the subsequent 1982 excavations, resulting in the recovery of faunal remains from four of the five sites. Fish bones were recovered from each of these four, resulting in a total of 23 fish bones recovered during the screening process, 17 of them recovered in the one–eighth inch mesh, and only four recovered in the one–fourth inch mesh. The fish remains, and the sites from which they were recovered, are described elsewhere (Greenspan 1985); a more detailed description of the sites is provided by Oetting (1988).

The 23 fish bones recovered during the 1982 season are considered to represent fish that were exploited and consumed by the sites' occupants. Some of the bones appear to have been charred, which is suggestive of their consumption by humans. These bones, though few in number, show that fishing was definitely practiced by the people who lived on the east shore of Lake Abert. The fact that very limited archaeological testing turned up fish bones from four of the five sites tested in 1982 (the fifth site did not contain any faunal remains), suggests that fishing for chub and trout was not uncommon at Lake Abert, though this impression is not otherwise quantifiable on the basis of present evidence.

Presumably the lake was higher and fresher at the time these sites were occupied than it has been in historic times. The presence of major settlements along the lakeshore, plus the recovery of freshwater fish bones from some of these settlements, is suggestive of a freshwater lake, particularly since most of the sites have no other source of fresh water. The evidence for Neopluvial high levels of Lake Abert discussed above fits well with the archaeological evidence.

Assuming the lake was higher and fresher, the fish represented in the faunal assemblages could have been caught in the lake itself, or perhaps in some of the tributary streams, such as Poison Creek. If the small quantities of fish bones recovered reflect a real situation, and not a sampling problem, it is unlikely that methods geared towards the exploitation of mass spawning migrations were being utilized here. It is highly likely that even when the lake was higher than at present, these sites were not situated in favorable locations for mass exploitation of fish. The fish may have been caught near the sites, perhaps using hook and line in the lake; or, they may have been caught in more favorable fishing spots, perhaps the mouth of the Chewaucan River, and some of them brought back to the east shore sites for consumption.

Discussion: Prehistoric Fishing in the Chewaucan Basin

The Chewaucan Basin exhibits a general adaptation quite similar to that observed in the Harney Basin. Major settlements were located along the margins of lakes, marshes, and streams, with a highly diversified economic base. While fishing was clearly a significant aspect of that adaptation in the Harney Basin, current evidence does not reveal a similar dependency in the Chewaucan Basin.

The Chewaucan Basin has only three native species of fish as compared with 11 in the Harney Basin. Furthermore, the Harney Basin, which is larger and better watered than the Chewaucan Basin, supports a more abundant as well as more diverse fish fauna. Another very important distinction is that Lake Abert has no outlet; because it loses water only through evaporation, it becomes quite alkaline during periods of decreasing effective precipitation. Malheur Lake, on the other hand, drains into Harney Lake, and thus periodically refreshes itself. While Lake Abert has not supported fish life during historic times, Malheur Lake has. Undoubtedly, this situation existed at many times during the past as well. While Lake Abert has certainly supported fish life at various times, in the long run, Malheur Lake is a more productive fish habitat.

It is therefore likely that the Chewaucan Basin never supported as rich a fish resource as did the Harney Basin. The resource was certainly never as diverse nor as stable; it was probably never as abundant. This may account, at least in part, for the much lesser reliance on fish observed in the Chewaucan Basin.

It should be pointed out, however, that the sites along the east shore of Lake Abert are in far from the most favorable locations for fishing. The many major sites observed during surface survey along the mouth and lower reaches of the Chewaucan River (Oetting and Pettigrew 1985) are much better situated for the exploitation of fish. The excavations along the east shore of Lake Abert have demonstrated that people in the area did exploit fish; sub–surface investigation of sites along the lower Chewaucan River may reveal a greater use of fish.

Summary and Conclusions

The results of the present study reveal a different pattern of fish utilization in each of the three basins. In both the Harney and Chewaucan basins, reliance upon marsh, river, and lakeside habitats is indicated by the presence of extensive settlements, possibly villages, in those locations. These major settlements date from the Neopluvial interval, and possibly earlier. In the Harney Basin fish were a significant resource contributing to this adaptation. Available data suggest fish were considerably less important in the Chewaucan Basin, which is characterized by less diversity and a more limited distribution of fish than the Harney Basin. However, it is also likely that part of this apparent difference is a sampling problem, as the sites that have been excavated to date in the Chewaucan Basin are not those that are most favorably located for the exploitation of fish.

In contrast to these two basins, there is no indication of any major settlements in the much drier Fort Rock Basin, where fish were utilized as an apparently minor resource beginning as early as 10,000 years ago. Much of the Fort Rock Basin is quite dry; only the Silver Lake sub-basin contains perennial water. The water level of Silver Lake and the size of Paulina Marsh fluctuate considerably. As pointed out by Weide (1976), fluctuating lake and marsh margins may not be very productive environments except at their source areas, e.g., the mouth of a tributary. The relatively small amount of perennial water in the Fort Rock Basin may very well account for the observed lack of substantial settlements like those observed in the neighboring Harney and Chewaucan Basins.

While fishing does not appear to have been a major activity in the Fort Rock Basin, nonetheless, it was a widespread and persistent one. The role of fish in Fort Rock Basin economies may have been similar to that described by Kelly (1932) for the Surprise Valley Paiute, where fish were taken primarily at times when other resources were scarce, making them a minor, yet critical, resource.

Although this study has been limited to three contiguous basins in the Northern Great Basin, fish remains have been recovered from prehistoric sites throughout the Great Basin. These occur in a variety of cultural, temporal, and geographic contexts (Greenspan 1985:174–79). On a regional basis, groups in the rich, lacustrine basins of western Nevada, and those in Utah Valley (e.g., Janetski 1990) show the strongest reliance on fish in ethnographic times. The highly developed technology and social forms (e.g., Speth 1969) used in exploiting fish in these regions suggests that the ethnographic pattern was one of some antiquity. This is substantiated by the recovery of fish remains and fishing gear from numerous prehistoric cave sites in the western Great Basin dating as early as 9540 ± 120 B.P. (UCLA-675) (Follett 1982; Hattori 1982).

Outside of these areas of lacustrine orientation, the role of fish in the Great Basin is less obvious. This study has shown that the importance of fish may vary considerably between and even within three contiguous basins, and that it may vary through time, as well. More research along the lines presented here will undoubtedly show that fishing in the Great Basin was far more widespread and important than previously thought, and that in some areas, under certain conditions, fishing may have played a significant role in the adaptive strategies of the prehistoric inhabitants.

Acknowledgements

This paper is abstracted from my dissertation. Many people and agencies were very helpful to me in the completion of that project. They are individually cited in the dissertation; although I won't list them here, I want again to acknowledge their contributions. This version has benefitted from being subjected to the editorial pens of C. Melvin Aikens, Kathryn Cruz–Uribe, Eugene M. Hattori, Joel C. Janetski, Rick Minor, and Albert C. Oetting.

Endnote

[1]Recently, the Names of Fishes Committee of the American Fisheries Society voted to accept the generic name *Oncorhynchus* for those pacific trouts formerly under the genus *Salmo* (Smith and Stearley 1989). The specific case of the redband trout has not been decided at this writing; it will be proposed that the Oregon redband be named either *Oncorhynchus newberryi* or *O. mykiss newberryi* (Ralph F. Stearley, personal communication 1989).

References

Aikens, C. M.
  1983 Request for Determination of Eligibility to the National Register of Historic Places of Archaeological Site 35Ha1038 (MNWR-98), Malheur National Wildlife Refuge, Harney County, Oregon. Ms. on file, U.S. Fish and Wildlife Service, Portland.

Aikens, C. M., and R. L. Greenspan
  1988 Ancient Lakeside Culture in the Northern Great Basin: Malheur Lake, Oregon. *Journal of California and Great Basin Anthropology* 10:32-61.

Aikens, C. M., and R. Minor
  1977 The Archaeology of Coffeepot Flat, South-Central Oregon. *University of Oregon Anthropological Papers* No. 11. Eugene.

Allison, I. S.
  1979 *Pluvial Fort Rock Lake, Lake County, Oregon.* Oregon Department of Geology and Mineral Industries Special Paper No. 7.
  1982 *Geology of Pluvial Lake Chewaucan, Lake County, Oregon.* Studies in Geology No. 11. Oregon State University Press, Corvallis.

Allison, I. S., and C. E. Bond
  1983 Identity and Probable Age of Salmonids from Surface Deposits at Fossil Lake, Oregon. *Copeia* 2:563-564.

Antevs, E.
  1948 Climatic Changes and Pre-White Man. *Bulletin of the University of Utah* 38:20. Biological Series 10(7):168-91.

Bedwell, S. F.
  1973 *Fort Rock Basin: Prehistory and Environment.* University of Oregon Books, Eugene.

Bisson, P. A., and C. E. Bond
  1971 Origin and Distribution of the Fishes of Harney Basin, Oregon. *Copeia* 2:268-287.

Campbell, S. K.
  n.d. Untitled Report An Archaeological Fieldwork at the Headquarters Site (draft). Ms. on file, Malheur National Wildlife Refuge Headquarters.

Cannon, W. J.
  1977 Cultural Resources Survey of the West Shore of Lake Abert. Submitted to the Lakeview District Office, Bureau of Land Management, Oregon.
  1978 Archaeological Reconnaissance of Upland Depression Lakes. Submitted to the Lakeview District Office, Bureau of Land Management, Oregon.

Casteel, R. W.
  1972 Some Biases in the Recovery of Archaeological Faunal Remains. *Proceedings of the Prehistoric Society* 36:382-388.
  1976a Comparison of Column and Whole Unit Samples for Recovering Fish Remains. *World Archaeology* 8:192-196.
  1976b *Fish Remains in Archaeology and Paleo-environmental Studies.* Academic Press, New York.
  1976-1977 A Consideration of the Behaviour of the Minimum Number of Individuals Index: Faunal Characterization. *Ossa* 3/4:141-151.
  1977 Characterization of Faunal Assemblages and the Minimum Number of Individuals Determined from Paired Elements: Continuing Problems in Archaeology. *Journal of Archaeological Science* 4:125-134.
  1978 Faunal Assemblages and the "Weigenmethode" or Weight Method. *Journal of Field Archaeology* 5:71-77.

Cole, D. L.
  1969 *Archaeological Survey of the Proposed Coffeepot Dam Project in Lake County, Oregon.* Submitted to the University of Oregon Museum of Natural History, Eugene.
  1975 *Survey of the Hogback Summit-Pikes Ranch Section of the Lakeview-Burns Highway for Historical, Archaeological and Prehistorical Sites.* Report of the Museum of Natural History, University of Oregon, to the Highway Division of the Oregon State Department of Transportation. Eugene.
  1976 *Progress Report: Archaeological Research on the Hogback Summit-Pikes Ranch Section of the Lakeview-Burns Highway, Lake County, Oregon.* Report of the Museum of Natural History, Unversity of Oregon, to the Highway Division of the Oregon State Department of Transportation. Eugene.
  1981 Habitats of North American Desert Fishes. In *Fishes in North American deserts*, edited by R. J. Naiman and D. L. Soltz, pp. 472-492. Wiley and Sons, New York.

Cole, D. L., and R. M. Pettigrew
  1976 *An Archaeological Survey of the Proposed Improvement of the Pikes Ranch-Valley Falls Section, North Unit, of the Lakeview-Burns Highway, Lake County, Oregon.* Report of the Museum of Natural History, University of Oregon to the Highway Division of the Oregon State Department of Transportation. Eugene.

Couture, M. D.
  1978 *Recent and Contemporary Foraging Practices of the Harney Valley Paiute.* Unpublished Master's thesis, Department of Anthropology, Portland State University, Portland.

Cressman, L. S.
  1942   *Archaeological Researches in the Northern Great Basin.* Carnegie Institution of Washington Publication No. 538. Washington, D.C.
Cressman, L. S., H. Williams, and A. D. Krieger
  1940   *Early Man in Oregon.* Archaeological Studies in the Northern Great Basin. University of Oregon Monographs, Studies in Anthropology No. 3. Eugene.
Currey, D. R., and S. R. James
  1982   Paleoenvironments of the Northeastern Great Basin and Northeastern Basin Rim Region: A Review of Geological and Biological Evidence. In *Man and Environment in the Great Basin,* edited by D. B. Madsen and J. F. O'Connell, pp. 27–52. SAA Papers No. 2. Society for American Archaeology, Washington, D.C.
Downs, J. F.
  1966   *The Two Worlds of the Washo: An Indian Tribe of California and Nevada.* Holt, Rinehart and Winston, New York.
Fagan, J. L.
  1973   *Altithermal Occupation of Spring Sites in the Northern Great Basin.* Unpublished Ph.D. dissertation, Department of Anthropology, University of Oregon, Eugene.
  1974   *Altithermal Occupation of Spring Sites in the Northern Great Basin.* University of Oregon Anthropological Papers No. 6. Eugene.
Fagan, J. L., and G. L. Sage
  1974   New Windust Sites in Oregon. *Tebiwa* 17:68–71.
Follett, W. I.
  1970   *Fish Remains from Coprolites and Midden Deposits at Lovelock Cave, Churchill County, Nevada.* In *Archaeology and the Prehistoric Great Basin Lacustrine Subsistence Regime as Seen from Lovelock Cave, Nevada* by R. F. Heizer and L. K. Naption, pp. 163–175. University of California Archaeological Survey Report No. 10. Berkeley.
  1982   An Analysis of Fish Remains from Ten Archaeological Sites at Falcon Hill, Washoe County Nevada, with Notes on Fishing Practices of the Ethnographic Kuyuidikadi Northern Paiute. In *The Archaeology of Falcon Hill, Winnemucca Lake, Washoe County Nevada,* by E. Hattori, pp. 178–205, Appendix A. Nevada State Museum Anthropological Papers No. 18. Carson City.
Fowler, C. S.
  1982   Settlement Patterns and Subsistsence Systems in the Great Basin: The Ethnographic Record. In *Man and Environment in the Great Basin,* edited by D. B. Madsen and J. F. O'Connell, pp. 121–138. SAA Papers No. 2. Society for American Archaeology, Washington, D.C.
Fowler, C. S., and J. E. Bath
  1981   Pyramid Lake Northern Paiute Fishing: The Ethnographic Record. *Journal of California and Great Basin Anthropology* 3(2):176–186.
Gehr, K. D.
  1980   *Late Pleistocene and Recent Archaeology and Geomorphology of the South Shore of Harney Lake, Oregon.* Unpublished Master's thesis, Department of Anthropology, Portland State University.
Grayson, D. K.
  1973   On the Methodology of Faunal Analysis. *American Antiquity* 38:432–439.
  1978   Minimum Numbers and Sample Size in Vertebrate Faunal Analysis. *American Antiquity* 43:53–65.
  1979a On the Quantification of Vertebrate Archaeofaunas. In *Advances in Archaeological Method and Theory,* vol. 2, edited by M. B. Schiffer, pp. 199–237. Academic Press, New York.
  1979b On the Quantification of Vertebrate Archaeofaunas. In *Advances in Archaeological Method and Theory,* vol. 2, edited by M. B. Schiffer, pp. 199–273. Academic Press, New York.
  1981   The Effects of Sample Size on Some Derived Measures in Vertebrate Faunal Analysis. *Journal of Archaeological Science* 8:77–88.
  1984   *Quantitative Zooarchaeology: Topics in the Analysis of Archaeological Faunas.* Academic Press, New York.
Greenspan, R. L.
  1981   Analysis of Ground Stone Implements. In *Survey and Testing of Cultural Resources Along the Proposed Bonneville Power Administration's Buckley–Summer Lake Transmission Line Corridor, Central Oregon,* by K. A. Toepel and S. D. Beckham, pp. 207–282, Appendix C. Eastern Washington University Reports in Archaeology and History No. 100-5. Cheney, Washington.
  1984   Holocene Lake Level Fluctuations Inferred from Fish Remains in the Fort Rock Basin. *Tebiwa* 21:50–55.
  1985   *Fish and Fishing in Northern Great Basin Prehistory.* Ph.D. dissertation, Department of Anthropology, University of Oregon. University Microfilms, Ann Arbor.
Hattori, E. M.
  1982   *The Archaeology of Falcon Hill, Winnemucca Lake, Washoe County, Nevada.* Nevada State Museum Anthropological Papers No. 18. Carson City.
Heizer, R. F., and L. K. Napton
  1969   *Archaeology and the Prehistoric Great Basin Lacustrine Subsistence Regime as Seen from Lovelock Cave, Nevada.* Contributions of the University of California Archaeological Research Facility No. 10. Berkeley.
Hubbs, C. L., and R. R. Miller
  1948   The Great Basin, With Emphasis on Glacial and Postglacial Times: The Zoological Evidence. *Bulletin of the University of Utah* 38(20):17–166.

Janetski, J. C.
  1990   Utah Lake: Its Role in the Prehistory of Utah Valley. *Utah Historical Quarterly* 58(1):5–31.
Jennings, J. D.
  1957   *Danger Cave*. University of Utah Anthropological Papers No. 27. Salt Lake City.
Kelly, I. T.
  1932   Ethnography of the Surprise Valley Paiute. *University of California Publications in American Archaeology and Ethnology* 31:67–210. Berkeley.
Kimsey, J. B.
  1954   The Life History of the Tui Chub, *Siphateles Bicolor* (Girard), from Eagle Creek, California. *California Fish and Game* 58(4):285–290.
LaRivers, I.
  1962   *Fishes and Fisheries of Nevada*. Nevada State Fish and Game Commission, Carson City.
Mehringer, P. J., Jr.
  1983   The Stratigraphy and Dating Potential of Holocene Dunes, Christmas Valley, Lake County, Oregon. Report submitted to the Bureau of Land Management, Lakeview District, Oregon.
Miller, R. R., and R. G. Miller
  1948   The Contribution of the Columbia River System to the Fish Fauna of Nevada: Five Species Unrecorded from the State. *Copeia* 1948(3):174–187.
Minor, R., and R. L. Greenspan
  1985   *Archaeological Testing in the Southeast Area of the Headquarters Site, Malheur National Wildlife Refuge, Harney County, Oregon*. Heritage Research Associates Report No. 36. Eugene.
Minor, R., and K. A. Toepel
  1988   *Surface Investigations in the Northwest Area of the Headquarters Site (35HA403), Malheur National Wildlife Refuge, Harney County, Oregon*. Heritage Research Associates Report No. 72. Eugene.
Moyle, P. B.
  1976   *Inland Fishes of California*. University of California Press, Berkeley.
Naiman, R. J.
  1981   An Ecosystem Overview: Desert Fishes and their Habitats. In *Fishes in North American Deserts*, edited by R. J. Naiman and D. L. Soltz, pp. 493–531. John Wiley and Sons, New York.
Newman, T. M., R. Bogue, C. D. Carley, R. D. McGilvra, and D. Moretty
  1974   Archaeological Reconnaissance of the Malheur National Wildlife Refuge, Harney County, Oregon: 1974. Report submitted to the Oregon State Historic Preservation Office, Salem.
Oetting, A. C.
  1988   *Archaeological Investigations on the East Shore of Lake Abert, Volume II*. Oregon State Museum of Anthropology Report No. 88–6, Eugene.
  1989   *Villages and Wetlands Adaptations in the Northern Great Basin: Chronology and Land Use in the Lake Abert–Chewaucan Marsh Basin, Lake County, Oregon*. Unpublished Ph.D. dissertation, Department of Anthropology, Unversity of Oregon, Eugene.
Oetting, A. C., and R. M. Pettigrew
  1985   *An Archaeological Survey in the Lake Abert–Chewaucan Basin Lowlands, Lake County, Oregon*. Oregon State Museum of Anthropology Survey Report No. 85–5. Corvallis.
  1987   *Archaeological Investigations in the Lake Abert–Chewaucan Basin, Lake County, Oregon: The 1986 Survey*. The Cultural Heritage Foundation, Report No. 1. Portland, Oregon.
Pettigrew, R. M.
  1981   The Ancient Chewaucanians: More on the Prehistoric Lake Dwellers of Lake Abert, Southeastern Oregon. *Association of Oregon Archaeologists Occasional Papers* 1:49–67. Albany, Oregon.
  1985   *Archaeological Investigations on the East Shore of Lake Abert, Lake County, Oregon*, vol 1. University of Oregon Anthropological Papers No. 32. Eugene.
Phillips, K. N., and A. S. Van Denburgh
  1971   *Hydrology and Geochemistry of Abert, Summer, and Goose lakes, and Other Closed-Basin Lakes in South–Central Oregon*. U.S. Geological Survey Professional Paper 502–B. Washington, D.C.
Piper, A. M., T. W. Robinson, and C. F. Park, Jr.
  1939   *Geology and Ground–Water Resources of the Harney Basin, Oregon*. U.S. Geological Survey Water–Supply Paper 841. Washington, D.C.
Russell, I. C.
  1905   *Preliminary Report on the Geology and Water Resources of Central Oregon*. United States Geological Survey Bulletin 252. Washington, D.C.
Schalk, R. B.
  1977   The Structure of an Anadromous Fish Resource. In *For Theory Building in Archaeology*, edited by L. R. Binford, pp. 207–249. Academic Press, New York.
Scott, W. B., and E. J. Crossman
  1973   *Freshwater Fishes of Canada*. Fisheries Research Board of Canada, Bulletin 184. Ottawa.

Sigler, W. F., and R. R. Miller
    1963   *Fishes of Utah.* Utah State Department of Fish and Game, Salt Lake City.
Smith, G. R.
    1985   Paleontology of Hidden Cave: Fish. In *The Archaeology of Hidden Cave, Nevada,* edited by D. H. Thomas, pp. 171–178. Anthropological Papers of The American Museum of Natural History 61(1). New York.
Smith, G. R., and R. F. Stearley
    1989   The Classification and Scientific Names of Rainbow and Cutthroat Trouts. *Fisheries* 14(1):4–10.
Speth, L. K.
    1969   Possible Fishing Cliques Among the Northern Paiutes of the Walker River Reservation, Nevada. *Ethnohistory* 16(3):225–244.
Spier, L.
    1930   *Klamath Ethnography.* University of California, Publications in American Archaeology and Ethnology vol. 30. Berkeley.
Steward, J. H.
    1938   *Basin–Plateau Aboriginal Sociopolitical Groups.* Bureau of American Ethnology Bulletin No. 120. Washington, D.C. (Reprinted in 1970 by the University of Utah Press, Salt Lake City.)
Stewart, O. C.
    1941   Culture Element Distributions: XIV, Northern Paiute. *University of California Anthropological Records* 2(3). Berkeley.
Thomas, D. H.
    1969   Great Basin Hunting Patterns: A Quantitative Method for Treating Faunal Remains. *American Antiquity* 34(4):392–401.
Thomas, S.
    1979   Archaeological Test at Malheur National Wildlife Refuge Headquarters Site, MNWR 83, Water Project. Submitted to U.S. Fish and Wildlife Service, Portland.
Toepel, K. A., and S. D. Beckham
    1981   *Survey and Testing of Cultural Resources Along the Proposed Bonneville Power Administration's Buckley–Summer Lake Transmission Line Corridor, Central Oregon.* Eastern Washington University Reports in Archaeology and History, Bonneville Cultural Resources Group Report No. 100–5. Cheney, Washington.
Toepel, K. A., and R. L. Greenspan
    1985   Fish Remains from an Open Site in the Fort Rock Basin. *Journal of California and Great Basin Anthropology* 7(1):109–116.
Toepel, K. A., R. Minor, and R. L. Greenspan
    1984   *Archaeological Testing in Diamond Valley, Malheur National Wildlife Refuge, Harney County, Oregon.* Heritage Research Associates Report No. 30. Eugene.
Van Denburgh, A. S.
    1975   *Solute Balance at Abert an Summer Lakes, South–Central Oregon.* U. S. Geological Survey Professional Paper 502–C. Washington, D.C.
Van Winkle, W.
    1914   *Quality of the Surface Waters of Oregon.* U.S. Geological Survey Water–Supply Paper 363. Washington, D.C.
Weide, D. L.
    1976   The Altithermal as an Archaeological "Non–Problem" in the Great Basin. In *Holocene Environmental Change in the Great Basin,* edited by R. Elston, pp. 174–184. Nevada Archaeological Survey Research Paper No. 8. Reno.
Wheat, M. M.
    1967   *Survival Arts of the Primitive Paiutes.* University of Nevada Press, Reno.
Wydoski, R. S., and R. R. Whitney
    1979   *Inland Fishes of Washington.* University of Washington Press, Seattle.

14

WETLANDS IN UTAH VALLEY PREHISTORY

Joel C. Janetski

Abstract

According to Madsen (1982) prehistoric settlement and subsistence in the vicinity of wetlands remained essentially the same during the Formative (Fremont) and the Late Prehistoric periods in the eastern Great Basin despite a shift from limited food production to a total reliance on wild foods. Archaeological evidence from lake-edge Fremont and Late Prehistoric sites in Utah Valley clearly demonstrates the importance of wetlands resources in the economies of both strategies. The data are not adequate, however, to rigorously test Madsen's conclusions.

Introduction

Round about it (Utah Lake) reside the Indians mentioned (Utes) who live on the lake's abundant fish, whence the Sabuagana call them Fish-eaters. Besides this, they gather the seeds of wild plants in the bottoms and make a gruel from them, which they supplement with the game of jackrabbits, coneys, and fowl, of which there is a great abundance here. They also have bison handy not too far away to the north-northwest, but fear of the Comanches prevents them from hunting them (Warner 1976:60).

This graphic description of the Utah Lake Ute by the Spanish explorers in 1776 stresses the importance of wetland resources in the diet of these hunter-gatherers and suggests a lakeside settlement pattern for the contact period. These impressions are reinforced by the ethnographic and ethnohistoric literature on the Timpanogots (Janetski 1983, 1986, n.d.a; Lowie 1924; Smith 1974, Steward 1938, Stewart 1942) Archaeological research in the valley suggests that this wetland focus was in place by at least the onset of the Fremont era (ca. A.D. 700) and perhaps much earlier.

Research Focus and Review of Previous Work

My own research interests in Utah Valley prehistory are various, but include the fact that the valley offers information about prehistoric cultural systems, both hunter-gatherer and horticultural, that operated in a lacustral setting. Of particular interest here is the impact concentrated wetland resources had on settlement and subsistence choices made by groups practicing apparently rather different strategies, i.e., horticulturalists (Fremont) and hunters and gatherers (Archaic and Late Prehistoric) (cf. Madsen 1982).

Madsen (1980, 1982) and Madsen and Lindsay (1977) have drawn attention to the importance of marsh resources to the horticultural groups (Sevier Fremont) that lived along the relatively well–watered Wasatch Front. Based on this research, Madsen (1980, 1982) has suggested that in the vicinity of wetlands Fremont sedentism was based primarily on marsh resources, and, although domesticates were present, they were a less critical portion of the resource base.

The conclusions of Madsen are intriguing in light of my own research (1986, n.d.a) which suggests that the settlement–subsistence strategy of the non–horticultural Ute of Utah Valley was heavily influenced by the resources of Utah Lake and its associated marsh/riverine systems. Utilizing ethnographic and ethnohistoric data, I described the settlement patterns of the Timpanogots as including long term residential camps located in the valley bottoms close to the lake. In addition, the ethnographic literature on the Timpanogots (Smith 1974, Stewart 1942, among others) clearly establishes the importance of fish and other water–loving animals and plants in their diet. Further, the settlement–subsistence strategies of Late Prehistoric peoples appear to be similar to that of the pre–contact Ute (Janetski 1990). Such a pattern suggests a nearly year around use of these sites and approximates the sedentary pattern and wetland resource focus described for the Fremont by Madsen.

The implication of the work of Madsen on the Fremont and myself on the Ute and Late Prehistoric is that there were few differences in the strategies of Formative peoples and hunter–gatherers in the vicinity of wetlands. Madsen (1982:221), for example, has described the settlement and subsistence patterns around both the Great Salt Lake marshes and Utah Lake as "very similar" throughout prehistory despite the probability of an ethnic replacement of peoples at the end of the Formative. He points out that, although site elevations tend to change through time (higher during the Formative and lower during the late Prehistoric), that change appears to be correlated with lake elevations rather than with shifting strategies. In this, Madsen is, to some degree, echoing the views of Aikens (1966) and Stuart (1981) for the Great Salt Lake and Spencer (1980), Forsyth (1986), and Janetski (1990) for Utah Lake.

The notion that differences in Fremont and Late Prehistoric settlement patterns were determined by lake levels rather than by strategy shifts (from an emphasis, even a secondary one, on horticulture to a complete reliance on wild foods) has really not been tested for either the Great Salt Lake area or Utah Valley. Recent work at the Orbit Inn site (Simms 1987, Simms and Heath 1989), a Late Prehistoric occupation in a marshy context at the northeastern end of the Great Salt Lake, and a reconnaissance survey on the Weber and Ogden River deltas (Russell et al. 1989) have begun to provide useful data for that area, although more systematic work, both excavation and survey, is needed if useful comparisons are to be made.

The intent of this paper is to present what is known of Fremont and Late Prehistoric settlement and subsistence from sites in the vicinity of Utah Lake to test the Madsen hypothesis for this area. Predictions of that hypothesis might include: (1) settlement choice for both Fremont and Late Prehistoric lakeside sites was determined primarily by lake levels, and (2) subsistence strategies for both time periods were characterized by a broad–based exploitation of marsh/lacustral resources.

Implicit in the prediction regarding settlement–lake level relationships is that an advantage, perhaps having to do with access to resources, is gained by situating at some optimum distance from the lake edge. What that distance might be is not really known. Logically, if we are talking about sedentary strategies or year–round settlements, that location would have to be above the expected high water mark for the year. More specifically, if settlement choice for lake or marsh edge sites were determined primarily by the level of the lake, and assuming that the level of Utah Lake was higher (following the Great Salt Lake model) during the Fremont period and lower during the Late Prehistoric, differences in settlement choice should be measurable in terms of site elevation. The tasks here seem quite straightforward: (1) review the data on the levels of Utah Lake for the critical period (A.D. 1200—A.D. 1400) in search of evidence for a drop in elevation, and (2) compare elevations of known Late Prehistoric and Fremont period sites to determine if a significant difference exists. If a drop did occur, we should expect site elevations for the later period to be significantly lower than elevations for the Fremont period. If a drop did not occur and strategies are essentially the same, we would expect numerous multicomponent (Fremont and Late Prehistoric) sites to be present in marsh or lake–edge locations.

The subsistence issue is more difficult given problems incurred when comparisons are attempted using data subjected to differential recovery and analysis (see Grayson 1984 and Sharp 1989 for discussions of such problems). Fortunately, Grayson (1984:161–167) has explored Madsen's hypothesis somewhat utilizing faunal data from several Utah Fremont sites. In essence, Grayson concludes that, if Madsen is correct in his prediction that the Fremont in the vicinity of wetlands were more dependent on wild resources than horticulture, that dependency should be reflected in the faunal data. Specifically, the diversity of the faunal array should be high, reflecting a broad or general exploitation of marsh fauna (Grayson 1984:166). Due to problems with controlling for sample size effects, Grayson restricts his analysis to avian assemblages. The analysis here will attempt to follow Grayson as much as is possible with the data at hand. Methodological details will be provided in the discussion of subsistence.

Valley—Lake Ecology

Utah Valley sits in the heart of the central Wasatch region of the eastern Great Basin (Figure 1). The valley stretches 50 miles from upper Goshen Valley on the southwest to Dry Creek Canyon on the northeast, and nearly 25 miles from Soldiers Pass on the west to Hobble Creek Canyon on the east. It is bounded by mountain ranges, the most impressive of which is the massive Wasatch Front to the east which rises dramatically to nearly 12,000 feet.

The valley bottom consists of fertile alluvial slopes along the east and west sides of the lake. The wider (up to five miles), gentler east slope is cut by several streams issuing from the Wasatch, and broadens into extensive, well–watered flatlands to the northeast, southeast and southwest (Goshen Valley). Extensive marshes are present in Provo Bay on the east and Goshen Bay on the south and smaller marsh communities rim the lake's east shore. The west edge of the valley along the east facing slopes of the Lake Mountains is less than a mile in width and contains no permanent water and rather sparse vegetation.

The dominant geographical feature of the valley is Utah Lake. Covering 150 square miles, it is one of the largest freshwater lakes in the United States west of the Mississippi (Jackson and Stevens 1981). Utah Lake is freshwater due to the presence of a perennial outlet, the Jordan River, which drains into the highly saline Great Salt Lake 40 miles to the north. The lake is fed by several streams draining the Wasatch Front as well as several large, underwater springs. It is shallow, averaging only eight feet deep with maximum depths between 15 to 20 feet (with the exceptions of some spring holes at the north end) (Carter 1969:4). The lake bottom is predominantly mud and organic silt with limited stretches of gravel along the western and southeastern shorelines.

Precipitation in the valley averages 14 inches annually with peaks occurring in the spring and fall. Internally, rainfall is highly variable with the southeastern edge of the valley averaging 18 inches and the northern end of the valley averaging about 11 inches. Frost free days range from 126 at the mouth of the Provo River to 167 near the mouth of Spanish Fork Canyon (Eubank and Brough 1979:227–230).

Utah Valley Resources

The resources of Utah Valley have been detailed elsewhere (Janetski 1986, 1990, n.d.a) so will be treated briefly here. The fauna of Utah Valley is typical of the eastern Great Basin generally. The upland valleys and mountains of the Wasatch Front immediately east of the valley contained deer (*Odocoileus hemionus*), mountain sheep (*Ovis canadensis*), elk (*Cervus elaphus*), carnivores (*Ursus* sp., *Canis latrans* and *C. lupus*, *Lynx rufus*), and many smaller animals such as porcupine (*Erethizon dorsatum*), marmot (*Marmota flaviventris*), rabbits (*Sylvilagus* sp., *Lepus americanus*), ground squirrels (*Spermophilus* sp.), mountain grouse (*Dendragapus tetroanidae, Bonasa umbellus*), and others. Antelope (*Antilocapra americanus*), rabbits (*Lepus californicus, Sylvilagus* spp.), sage grouse (*Centrocercus urophasianus*), ground squirrels (*Spermophilus* spp.), wood rats (*Neotoma* spp.), among

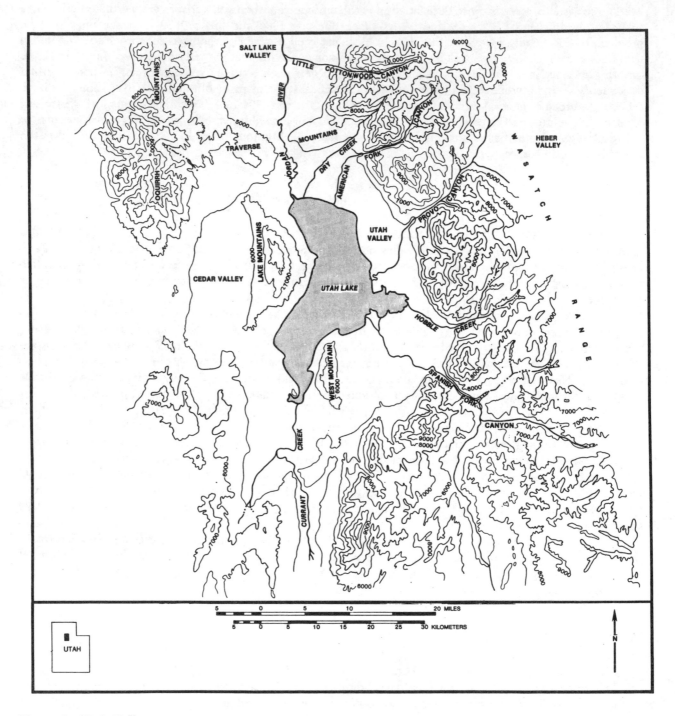

Figure 1. Utah Valley.

others were available in the valley surrounding the lake as well as the drier valleys and lower mountain ranges just to the west. Bison (*Bison bison*) were present in the valley prehistorically.

Lake–marsh related animal resources were abundant in the vicinity of the lake. Pritchett et al. (1981) lists 85 wetlands–oriented bird species that frequent the lake's environs and which were present in great numbers during the spring and fall migrations at the time of European settlement (mid to late 1800s). These include ducks, coots, geese, swans, herons and various wading birds.

Water–loving mammals, especially muskrat (*Ondatra zebithicus*), but also beaver (*Castor canadensis*), and probably mink (*Mustela vison*) and otter (*Lutra canadensis*) (Durrant 1952), were present if not common around the lake. Good numbers of shellfish lived in silty or muddy bottoms in the lake and streams, although only two, *Anadonta* spp. and *Margaritana margaritifera*, are large enough to have been important food items and the latter was usually not eaten (Chamberlain and Jones 1929:29).

The economically significant fish in Utah Lake were the Bonneville cutthroat trout (*Salmo clarki utah*), various suckers (*Catostomus* spp., *Chasmistes liorus*), Utah chub (*Gila atraria*), and the mountain whitefish (*Prosopium williamsoni*). Of the 12 fish species native to the Utah Lake system, 11 are now extremely rare or extinct (Heckman et al. 1981). With the exception of the late fall spawning whitefish, all the native fishes spawned in the spring. Trout spawning began as early as the middle of March while the June suckers spawning activities lasted until early summer. For the most part, spawning occurred in the streams, but all Utah Lake fish populations probably contained both lake and stream spawning forms (Heckman et al. 1981:111).

As with the fishery, the native vegetation in the valley and around the shores of the lake has been drastically altered in distribution and composition due to development, the introduction of exotic plant species, and introductions of exotic fishes, especially carp (Cottam 1926:29). Currently, the dominant plant communities adjacent to the lake are saline meadows and playas covering nearly 10,000 acres (Brotherson and Evenson 1982). In the meadows are extensive stands of saltgrass (*Distichlis spicata*) and lesser amounts of Baltic rush (*Juncus balticus*), alkalai grass (*Puccinellia airoides*), and numerous other salt tolerant species. The playas, evaporative salt pans mostly restricted to Goshen Bay, contain relatively few plant species, but samphire (*Salicornia rubra*) and pickleweeds (*Allenrolphia* spp.) are common.

The marsh community is less extensive than the saline meadows but nonetheless covers several thousand acres in Goshen and Provo bays, Powell's slough (Figure 2), and along the eastern shore of the lake. Dominant here are several species of bulrush (*S. acutus*, *S. maritimus*, *S. pungens*, *S. americanus*), saltgrass, reeds (*Phragmites australis*), and cattail (especially *Typha latifolia*). Limited stands of pondweed (*Potamogeten latifolius*) are found just off shore.

The valley to the east of the lake is broad and grassy, especially in the bottoms, with some sage and bunch grass on the more gravelly benches to the east. Historically, the several streams in the valley were lined with trees, especially cottonwoods (*Populus* sp.) and boxelder (*Acer negundo*) (Colton 1946:64). Modern lake shore vegetation consists of sometimes dense stands of bulrush (both *S. maritimus* and *S. acutus*), reed (*Phragmites* sp.) and cattail.

The uplands to the east contain stands of chokecherries (*Prunus virginiana*), serviceberries (*Amalanchier utahensis*), and scrub oak (*Quercus gambelli*). Pinyon pine (*Pinus monophylla, P. edulis*) is common at the higher elevations in the mountainous areas to the southwest as are other plant resources known to have been important prehistorically.

Previous Archaeological Work in Utah Valley

Recorded archeological observations and field work began in Utah Valley with the Wheeler expedition in the 1870s who described the numerous mounds west of the town of Provo (Severance and Yarrow 1879). This "mound" focus typifies the research in the valley for the next century. Palmer (1876, 1880), Judd (1926), Steward (1933), Reagan (1935) and various other professionals and amateurs into the 1970s focused their attentions primarily on the highly visible mound sites most of which are attributed to the Fremont period (700 to 1250 A.D.). Exceptions include work by the University of Utah in the late 1930s at a Late Prehistoric site (Ut 13)

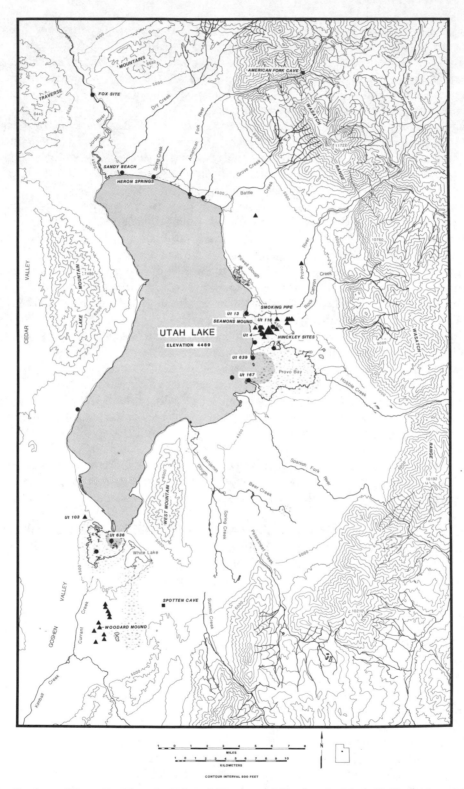

Figure 2. Distribution of Late Prehistoric (●) and Fremont (▲) sites in Utah Valley below 4,600 feet.

at the mouth of the Provo River (Beeley 1946) and excavations at two caves, Spotten Cave at the south end of the valley (Mock 1971) and American Fork Cave in American Fork Canyon (Hansen and Stokes 1941). With the work of myself (Janetski cf. 1986) and Forsyth (1986) during the 1980s, attention has shifted somewhat to hunter–gatherer occupations, especially the Late Prehistoric. The results of both survey and excavation at selected locales within the valley are discussed in more detail below (see Janetski 1986, 1990 and Spencer 1980 for more information on previous archaeological work in the area).

Prehistoric Settlement Patterns in Utah Valley

Information on prehistoric settlement in Utah Valley comes primarily from several reconnaissance surveys carried out by Brigham Young University during the 1960s (Jones 1961, Gilsen 1968, Montillo 1968, Wheeler 1968), although earlier excavations by Steward (1933), Reagan (1935) and Christensen (1946) have also documented several site locations. Spencer (1971) carried out an informal survey of the western shore of the lake. Jones' survey was valley wide in scope while Gilsen focused on Goshen Valley to the south, Wheeler worked in West Canyon in the northwestern corner of the valley, and Montillo looked for sites in the Provo River delta area. More recently, I examined the eastern shore of the lake (Janetski 1988).

As with the early excavations, the overriding interests of the earlier surveys was the Fremont period (see, for example, Montillo 1968:2), consequently prior to 1985 only a few sites dated to the hunter–gatherer Archaic and Late Prehistoric periods had been recorded in the valley. My (Janetski 1987, 1990, n.d.b) research on hunter–gatherers has significantly increased the number of documented Late Prehistoric sites. Archaic sites continue to be elusive and that period is not included in this analysis.

In an attempt to restrict the data to lake edge occupations and control for functional differences, the settlement data used for this study are limited to residential sites in the valley bottom with elevations below 4,600 feet. For Fremont sites, a residential function was assumed if researchers considered structures to be present; Late Prehistoric sites were classified as residential based on the presence of features (hearths, pits, etc.), and/or a combination of diagnostic artifacts such as Promontory ceramics, arrow points, grinding stones, etc. In actuality, every lake–edge site containing undisputed diagnostics of the Late Prehistoric period was included to increase the data set. The elevation limitation was based on proximity to marshes or the edge of the lake. In Goshen Valley, for example, marshlands extend well to the south of the lake apparently following an old channel of Currant Creek well to the east of the existing channel (Richens 1983:17). This limitation effectively eliminates sites in the upland areas such as Kimball Creek and West Canyon which are well back from the edge of the lake and therefore would not be effected by shifting lake levels. Even with this limitations in elevation, some concern exists as to what effect a rise in the level of the lake might have on these sites. Clearly a pluvial of considerable magnitude would have to occur before locations at the 4,600 foot line would be flooded. Nonetheless, if these sites are unaffected by lake levels, but yet are positioned adjacent to marsh habitat, our expectation would be that such sites should contain evidence of both Fremont and Late Prehistoric occupations.

Fremont Settlement

As noted, Fremont settlement data has been gathered, for the most part during the 1960s, via opportunistic surveys. A Fremont affiliation usually was assumed if Fremont style ceramics and/or mounds were present. The latter were formed by the collapse of surface adobe structures. Such mounds have been documented along the various creeks draining into the lake, but especially along the Provo River where the majority of archaeological work in the valley has been done. This region consists of several square miles of flat, fertile land crossed by old meanders of the Provo River. Water from springs and runoff still flows through the few existing remnants of these channels. The high ground adjacent to the channels were places often chosen for prehistoric settlement. The number of Fremont sites formally recorded on the Provo River delta is 20, although this number likely underrepresents the number of mounds in the area. For example, an opportunistic survey by amateurs done in the 1930s documented and located well over 100 mounds in west Provo (Bee and Bee 1934–1966). Montillo

(1968:6) located 38 mounds on the delta, but apparently did not record them beyond casual plotting. The delta region has now been disturbed by a century and a half of farming and housing development, causing significant disturbance of archaeological remains and making relocation of these sites difficult.

Formal surveys include Jones' (1961) valley–wide reconnaissance that recorded 24 Fremont sites, several of which were based on descriptions by locals or previous research rather than field observations. Gilsen's (1968) survey in Goshen Valley did some systematic work along Currant and Kimball creeks, but primarily documented sites referred to him by locals. He recorded 63 sites; 30 of these were classified as Fremont. Wheeler (1968), following up on the work of Jones (1961), recorded two additional Fremont structural sites in West Canyon to the northwest of the lake.

Other areas of mound concentrations apparently also included the lower American Fork River and Dry Fork Creek as well as areas adjacent to smaller streams in the northern part of the valley (Harold Hutchings, personal communication 1985), although none have been recorded here. Mounds were also present along Peteetneet Creek (Palmer 1876, 1880) and Summit Creek (Bee and Bee 1934–1966), in the extreme southeastern end of the valley. Again, none of these has been relocated.

Locations of known Fremont structural sites in the valley bottoms (below 4,600 feet) are presented in Figure 2. These sites tend to cluster along the streams and extend nearly to current lake edge. This streamside preference appears to be true for all drainages with perennial water. Again, the absence of block or systematic sample surveys argues for a cautious use of the settlement data from the valley.

Late Prehistoric Settlement

Understanding Late Prehistoric settlement is severely hindered by the paucity of known sites dating to this period. The earliest information comes from casual surveys of the lake shore by Steward and Reagan in the 1930s who described the remains of prehistoric "Shoshonean" peoples (probably Late Prehistoric sites) well out in the lake bed. The latter researcher describes his findings as follows:

> At a dozen locations on the Utah Lake front, a mile lakeward from the usual shore line, the area being left high and dry due to the drought of 1934, the writer found crude pottery which is neither Basket Maker nor Puebloan. . . . Associated with these are Shoshonean type arrow points and Shoshonean type metates (Reagan 1935:75).

None of these sites were located on maps or excavated. Reagan also reports that a number of the mounds he examined in the Provo River delta area were multicomponent and contained Late Prehistoric artifacts, both pottery and arrow points, overlying Fremont occupations. These findings are supported by Forsyth's (1986) analysis of material remains from Seamons Mound (42Ut 271), also on the delta (Figure 2), which contained both Fremont and Late Prehistoric diagnostics.

Later surveys focused on higher ground and few late sites were documented. Jones'(1961) survey of the valley, for example, describes only two Late Prehistoric sites, 42Ut 13 a large site at the mouth of the Provo River that had been excavated in the late 1930s by the University of Utah (Beeley 1946) and collected by numerous amateurs, and 42Ut 167 near the mouth of the Spanish Fork River (Figure 2). It is not clear whether Jones visited this site, but it has since been revisited by myself and documented as an extensive Late Prehistoric occupation. In Goshen Valley Gilsen (1968) only determined cultural affiliations for sites with Fremont diagnostics, essentially ceramics; all others were classified as unknown. Wheeler and Montillo likewise do not mention Late Prehistoric or Archaic sites.

A survey I carried out in August of 1988 examined the north, east, and south shores of Utah Lake at and just above the 4,486 foot elevation (Janetski 1988). Ten sites were recorded during this survey, five of which contained diagnostics of the Late Prehistoric period, especially Promontory ceramics. Interestingly, no diagnostics of the Archaic or Fremont periods were encountered despite the close proximity of known Fremont sites at several points.

The data available on Late Prehistoric settlement patterns suggest that long term base camps, as evidenced by visible, developed middens, wide artifact arrays (found at the excavated sites and assumed for unexcavated

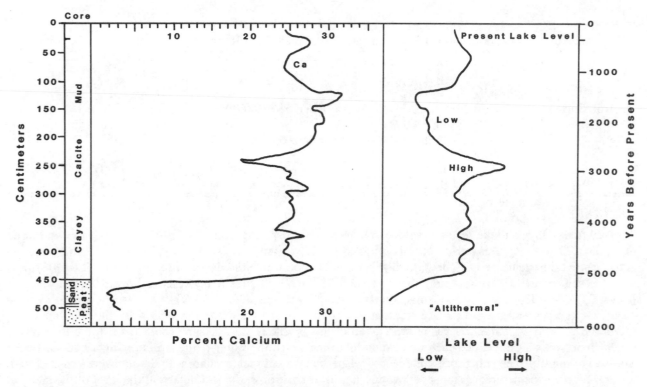

Figure 3. Characteristics of a core sample of Utah Lake sediments. High concentrations of calcium (calcite) are believed to associate with low levels of the lake as compared to recent levels. The same and peat layers below 450 cm are believed to correlate with the altithermal (from Brimhall and Merritt 1981).

sites with similar characteristics), and cache pits, are located close to the lake, usually in close proximity to the mouths of streams. This definition eliminates the Fox Site (42Ut 573) from the settlement analysis as it did not contain either ceramics or cache pits (Janetski n.d.b). The Fox Site located on the Jordan River outlet was excavated in 1985 by Brigham Young University and is discussed in more detail in the subsistence section below.

Discussion

As established earlier, lake level data are critical for this settlement analysis. Did Utah Lake experience a drop between the end of the Formative and the onset of the Lake Prehistoric, ca. A.D. 1300–1400? Unfortunately, data on lake levels are not abundant. Most useful is the work of Brimhall and Merritt (1981) who have generated a relative model of lake fluctuation using calcium carbonate levels as indicators of high and low stands—the higher the percentage of carbonates, the lower the lake. Their analysis (Figure 3) suggests fluctuation of lake levels that correspond rather well with Antevs (1948) model of Holocene environmental change. Temporal estimates are based on the assumption that the sandy/peat level encountered at 4.5 m below surface corresponds with the end of the altithermal at about 4000 B.P. This despite the fact that the peat was dated at 11,400 ± 800 radiocarbon years (Bolland 1974 cited in Brimhall and Merritt 1981). This date is thought to have been contaminated with detrital calcite and is therefore rejected (Brimhall and Merritt 1981:28). Further, their model is relative only and does not attempt estimates of absolute lake levels. Regardless, their reconstruction does suggest that the level of Utah lake was in decline after about 800 years B.P.

Table 1. Carbon 14 Dates from Late Prehistoric Utah Valley Sites Mentioned in the Text

Site	Date in Carbon 14 Years	Calibrated Range	Calibrated Midpoint
Fox Site	250 ± 50 B.P.	1495 – 1800 A.D.	1650 A.D.
	270 ± 60 B.P.	1485 – 1795 A.D.	1590 A.D.
Heron Springs	650 ± 70 B.P.	1255 – 1400 A.D.	1330 A.D.
	440 ± 60 B.P.	1340 – 1485 A.D.	1420 A.D.
	570 ± 90 B.P.	1260 – 1475 A.D.	1370 A.D.
Sandy Beach	450 ± 80 B.P.	1330 – 1636 A.D.	1480 A.D.
	510 ± 70 B.P	1335 – 1435 A.D.	1385 A.D.

Additional data on lake levels have been obtained from the Sandy Beach site (42Ut 592) at the north end of the lake. The Late Prehistoric cultural occupation here is dated to ca. A.D. 1440 (Table 1). Of most interest is the stratigraphy (Figure 4). The basal layer (Level I) upon which the dated cultural deposits (Level II) sit is a coarse sand identical to the sand being deposited on the beach edge today. Above Level II are sterile silts (Level III) likely deposited by aeolian action on exposed lake sediments (Don Currey, personal communication 1987). On the current ground surface is a thin layer of coarse sand deposited in 1983 when the lake inundated the beach. The most parsimonious interpretation of this profile is that the sand (both Level I and the surface sands) represents a period of beach inundation following which the water remained fairly high, but still below the level of the site. The silts represent a period when the lake sediments adjacent to the site were exposed, with water's edge a considerable distance below the site. In other words, the lake fell from the level of the site (ca. 4,488 feet) after the Late Prehistoric occupation (ca. A.D. 1440) and did not rise to that level again until the 1980s.

Both the Brimhall and Merritt and Sandy Beach data tend to support the possibility of a drop in lake levels during the critical period under examination here. This conclusion is consistent with data for the Great Salt Lake as well (Murchison 1989:123). Consequently, if Madsen is correct, then we should see a shift downward in site elevation data for the Late Prehistoric. Data on this topic are presented below.

Comparisons of Fremont and Late Prehistoric valley bottom settlements reveal some interesting patterns. Figure 5 displays all known structural or base camp sites from those time periods in the valley below the 6,000 foot elevation. The upper level (above 4,600 feet elevation) sites are included in this figure for the sake of comparison, but are not included in the statistical analysis. As can be seen in Figure 5, numbers of sites for both time periods are greatest close to the lake. The most obvious difference between the distribution of Late Prehistoric vs. Fremont sites is that the majority of Late Prehistoric sites fall below the 4,490 foot elevation. No Fremont sites have been recorded below 4,490 feet. To determine whether this difference is statistically different an analysis of the means for sites below 4,600 feet was carried out using a t–test (Long and Rippeteau 1974) with the value of t calculated as

$$t = \frac{D}{\sqrt{\sigma_x^2 + \sigma_y^2}}$$

where D = the absolute difference in the mean elevations of Late Prehistoric sites (μy_x, calculated as 4489.38, n=16, σ_x^2 = 4.3), and the mean elevations of Fremont residences (μ_y, calculated as 4502.7, n=34, σ_y^2 = 15.5). The t score of .81 is not significant (df = 48).

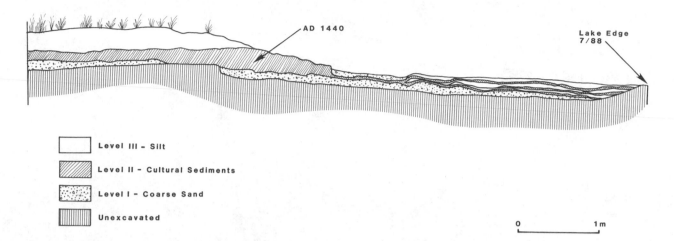

Level III - Silt

Level II - Cultural Sediments

Level I - Coarse Sand

Unexcavated

Figure 4. Stratigraphic profile at Sandy Beach (42Ut 592).

Clearly the statistical analysis demonstrates that, despite subtle differences in site elevations suggested by Figure 3, settlement choice for Late Prehistoric and Fremont peoples were very similar. This suggests that either the lake did not drop enough to have a measurable effect on settlement locations, and/or that settlement location was about the same for both time periods regardless of lake levels. In either case, what we should expect if site location is about the same for both periods is occupation of similar locations by both Fremont and Late Prehistoric peoples resulting in multi-component sites. Are multicomponent sites known in the study area? The answer to that question is, yes, although they are not common. On the Provo River delta, three sites have been documented to contain both Fremont and Late Prehistoric materials. The Seamons Mound (42Ut 271) excavated by BYU in the late 1960s contained significant quantities of both Promontory and Fremont style ceramics (Forsyth 1986:190). Reagan (1935) observed mixed Fremont and Late Prehistoric assemblages at the Jacobson Mound (42Ut 4) and the Marrott Mound (42Ut 116). Of the latter, he states:

> Our excavation in this mound . . . showed that three sets of people had occupied the site. The lower section (third) showed indications of walls, at least on its south side. Pottery of the near Proto-Kayenta type [Fremont] found in this part shows that its occupancy was somewhere near the close of Pueblo II times. The middle third of the mound seems to have been debris, or wrecked edifices, of a people of whom we as yet know little. While the upper third seems to be of much more recent date, probably being recent Ute-Shoshonean (Reagan 1935:71).

Interestingly, Forsyth's (1986) analysis of ceramics recovered by Reagan at the Marrott Mound found no Promontory sherds. Finally, Forsyth also reports that an amateur collection (Bee and Bee 1934–1966) contained mixed ceramics from Bee's Site 1 (Ut 13) and 3 (probably Ut 639), both in the Provo River delta area (see Figure 2). A single multicomponent site (42Ut 103) has been reported in Goshen Valley, although the Late Prehistoric presence consisted of a single "Shoshoni" sherd on the surface (Gilsen 1968:25). All of these multicomponent sites are close to the edge of the lake. It should be added that some Fremont ceramics have been recovered from surface collections at Goshen Island (42Ut 636), primarily a Late Prehistoric site, but the excavated Late Prehistoric sites excavated by the author, Heron Springs and Sandy Beach, were single component and contained no evidence of earlier occupations.

In summary, the settlement data leaves us with many questions, although some impressions can be discussed. First, the fact that some overlap between Late Prehistoric and Fremont site elevations occurs certainly should not be a surprise. A similar pattern is present in the vicinity of the Great Salt lake (Russell 1989:81). As is the case there, the Utah Lake data are deficient for areas below the 4,487 foot elevation as the lake has been too high recently to survey the lower reaches of beach. Clearly considerably more systematic survey and studies of lake levels that include absolute dating is needed.

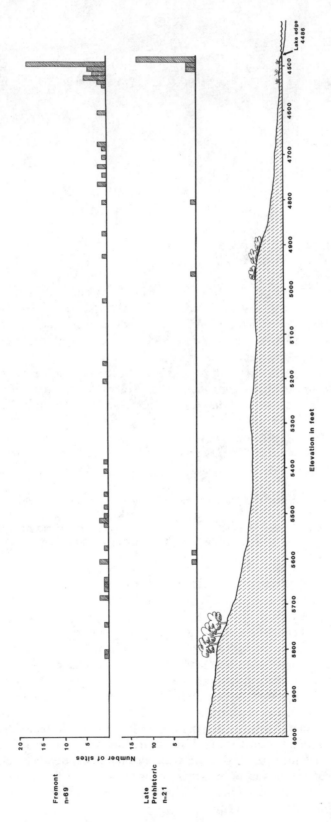

Figure 5. Distribution of Fremont and Late Prehistoric sites in Utah Valley by elevation.

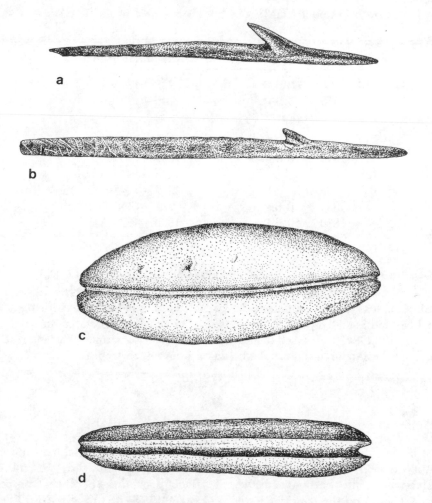

Figure 6. Bone Harpoons (*a, b*) from Woodard Mound and probable net sinkers (*c, d*) from Utah Valley.

As an aside, Figure 5 suggests that survey in the region between ca. 4,800 and 5,500 feet is also of interest to determine if the bimodal distribution of both Fremont and Late Prehistoric sites between 4,480 and 6,000 feet is real (i.e., either functional, temporal or both) or a function of sampling bias.

Prehistoric Utah Valley Subsistence

Useful information on prehistoric subsistence in Utah Valley is scarce. Early excavators either do not discuss subsistence (e.g., Steward 1933, Reagan 1935) or simply provide lists of species represented in the animal bones from sites (e.g., Beeley 1946, Christensen 1946). This pattern continued into the 1970s with several excavation reports either simply making passing references to plant or animal remains (Wheeler 1968, Mock 1971), or listing species of either plants or animals (Green 1961), or not mentioning subsistence data. Gilsen (1968:122), for example, comments on the "great preponderance of fish bones," while discussing the function of grooved stones, perhaps sinkers, from Goshen Valley (see Figure 6c, d for examples of probable Fremont period sinkers from Utah Valley found by amateur James Bee). Presumably the reference to fish bones stems from Gilsen's excavations at Woodard Mound, although this is not clear.

Table 2. Carbon 14 Dates from Fremont Utah Valley Sites Mentioned in the Text

Site	Date in Carbon 14 Years	Calibrated Range	Calibrated Midpoint
Woodard Mound	700 ± 60 B.P.	1235 – 1345 A.D.	1290 A.D.
	670 ± 50 B.P.	1245 – 1395 A.D.	1320 A.D.
	Modern		
Smoking Pipe	350 ± 50 B.P.	1415 – 1645 A.D.	1530 A.D.
	640 ± 70 B.P.	1255 – 1405 A.D.	1330 A.D.
	640 ± 110 B.P.	1235 – 1415 A.D.	1325 A.D.
	770 ± 80 B.P.	1050 – 1345 A.D.	1198 A.D.
	860 ± 90 B.P.	925 – 1305 A.D.	1115 A.D.
	890 ± 50 B.P.	1030 – 1275 A.D.	1153 A.D.

During the 1980s subsistence has been a strong research interest in Utah Valley. Cook (1980), for example, analyzed faunal remains from Spotten Cave (Mock 1971), Seamons Mound (Forsyth 1986), and the Hinckley mounds (Green 1961) to assess the importance of the lake's resources in the prehistoric diet. Richens' (1983) research at Woodard Mound included considerable attention to subsistence related material, both faunal and floral. The work of Forsyth (1984) and myself (Janetski 1990, n.d.b) has continued this interest. The discussion and analysis will focus on the faunal data since the botanical information from the Late Prehistoric sites is not yet available.

Fremont Subsistence

Because the interest in subsistence has been so recent, few data sets are available for the Fremont on this topic. The analysis by Cook (1980) of several faunal collections from Fremont sites is useful in a general way; however, several discrepancies have been noted between his findings and those of others (compare, for example, the species list from 42Ut 111 on the Hinckley Farm in Green 1961:68–70, to the species list for 42Ut 111 in Cook 1980:54). Further, cursory examination of the bones from the sites Cook included in his analysis suggests either errors in species identification or omissions of some specimens; consequently, those data are not useful for this discussion. That leaves two sites, Woodard Mound (Richens 1983) and Smoking Pipe (Billat 1985, Forsyth 1984), for which there is useful subsistence information.

Woodard Mound (42Ut 104) is located in a saline meadow environment in Goshen Valley at the south end of Utah Lake. It was a popular place for excavation by BYU during the 1960s and 1970s with field work being done there in 1966, 1967, 1969, 1971,and 1972 (Richens 1983:17–21). Richens continued the work at Woodard Mound in 1980–81. He located and clearly defined and documented a rectangular pit house with adobe walls, a basin–shaped hearth, a ventilator shaft, a number of trash–filled pits inside and outside the house, and a burial under the southwest corner of the structure. Earlier excavations did not expose complete structures, but did find several smaller features including a pit cribbed over with small timbers (Gilsen 1968:64). The site is carbon 14 dated to ca. A.D. 1250 (Table 2), placing it quite late in the Fremont occupation of the valley (Richens 1983:46). Material culture was typically Fremont with substantial quantities of ceramics, chipped and ground stone tools, and bone implements. Of particular interest here is the recovery of four complete and four fragmentary harpoons (Figure 6a, b). Richens screened sediments with quarter inch sieves and recovered both animal and plant remains. Faunal remains are dominated by fish, muskrat and rabbit (Table 3).

Smoking Pipe is a Fremont occupation located within Fort Utah State Park on the Provo River delta. Fremont deposits were noted here in backhoe trenches in 1968 while archaeologists from BYU searched for remains of the original Fort Utah (Forsyth 1984). Some testing was done in piecemeal fashion between 1980

Table 3. Fremont Faunal Assemblages from Utah Valley Used in this Analysis

Taxon	Smoking Pipe NISP	Woodard Mound NISP
Antilocapra americana		4
Bison bison	1,831	
Canis cf. latrans		1
Canis familiaris	1	
Castor canadensis	1	1
Catostomus ardens	1,327	84
Chasmistes liorus	30	
Dipodomys ordi		1
Erithizon dorsatum	1	
Fulica americana		3
Gila ataria	73	192
Lepus californicus	10	57
Mephitis mephitis	11	
Mustela frenata	1	1
Odocoileus hemionus	42	7
Ondatra zibethicus	15	192
Ovis canadensis		10
Salmo Clarkii	742	4
Spermophilus townsendii		21
Sylvilagus nuttali		79
Thomomys bottae		6
Totals	4,085	663

Total taxa: Smoking Pipe 13
Woodard Mound 15

and 1983. However, in 1983 and 1984 the site was explored more thoroughly and two trash pits were uncovered and defined. No structures were found, but recovered artifacts are characteristic of the Fremont. The dates from the site span several hundred years between A.D. 1100 and 1500. Particularly important at Smoking Pipe are the faunal data. Anticipating the need for finer controls, all sediments were water screened through eighth inch mesh sieves. As a result, thousands of fish bones were recovered in addition to the remains of a number of bison and other animals (Table 3).

To date, four Late Prehistoric excavations have been carried out in Utah Valley: 42Ut 13, the Beeley Site, Heron Springs, Sandy Beach, and the Fox Site (Figure 2). The Beeley site, located on the edge of the lake just north of the mouth of the Provo River, was excavated in 1938 by the University of Utah (Beeley 1946). As only a list of identified species is available, these data will not be included in this discussion.

Heron Springs and Sandy Beach, were tested by myself in 1987 and 1988 respectively and are discussed together because of their similarity. Both are located along the beach on the northern shore of Utah Lake. At the time of excavation Heron Springs was on a beach island bounded by the lake on the south, marsh on the north, and largely covered by dense stands of reed. The site was split by an extinct channel of Spring Creek. Sandy Beach is about a half mile east of the mouth of Dry Fork Creek and two and a half miles west of Heron Springs. The sites are dated by Carbon 14 to about A.D. 1400 (Table 1). Material remains recovered now appear to be characteristic of the early Late Prehistoric period: Promontory pottery (a crudely–made, coarsely–tempered ware made into large mouthed jars), slab metates, two–handed manos, Desert Side–notched and Cottonwood Triangular style arrowheads, and bone tools and beads. Also present is a chipped stone tool unique to Late Prehistoric sites (Figure 7k, l). The function of the tool, which resembles a large shouldered drill, is not known, but may have to do with butchering animals or fish. No evidence of structures has yet been found. Common features, especially at Heron Springs, are pits of varying sizes and small shallow hearths.

Faunal remains at Heron Springs and Sandy Beach were recovered using a water screening method and eighth inch sieves. The recovery process consisted of picking larger artifacts and bone during water screening, then dumping the screen contents or residue onto plastic sheeting to dry. This residue was then taken to the lab and carefully sorted to recover all bone fragments and smaller artifacts. This latter step was taken to insure, as much as possible, comparability between faunal collections. As might be imagined, this process resulted in the recovery of thousands of bone fragments, especially fish, but many mammal bone fragments as well. The faunal material from Heron Springs and Sandy Beach are still being processed, although a 30% sample of the Heron Springs faunal remains and a 15% sample of the Sandy Beach material are used in this discussion (Table 4). Currently, the functional interpretation of these lake edge sites is that they were long term camps likely occupied from fall into late spring.

The third Late Prehistoric site, the Fox Site, is located on the bank of the Jordan River about five miles from the lake outlet (Janetski n.d.b). It is Carbon 14 dated to the early 1600s AD. No features were found here, although this may be due to some surface disturbance of the site (Kay Fox, personal communication 1985). Site sediments were water screened and residue saved as with the Heron Springs and Sandy Beach work. The deposits contained a narrow range of chipped stone artifacts: Desert Side Notched and Cottonwood Triangular arrow points, a number of "beaked" tools (Figure 7n), and large quantities of debitage evidencing tool sharpening and modification, and a few fragments of ground stone. With the exception of a single small sherd of "Fremont" grayware, no pottery was recovered. Fish bone, primarily Utah sucker (*C. ardens*), was abundant with over 100,000 pieces examined (Table 4). Based on minimum number estimates, over 1,000 suckers were represented in the excavated portion of the site. Sucker size, reconstructed through comparison of selected elements ranged from prehistoric examples with modern specimens of Utah sucker (Shiozawa n.d.), was one to two feet in length and one to four pounds. Macrobotanical analysis recovered little of interest other than scattered *Chenopodium* sp. seeds (Young n.d.). The Fox Site contrasts markedly with the lake shore sites described above. It appears to have been a short term, special use site occupied in the spring during the spawning season of the Utah sucker.

Discussion

Comparisons of the subsistence data excavated from Fremont and Late Prehistoric sites is made difficult by differences in recovery technique and, to some extent, analysis. Both Grayson (1984) and Sharp (1989) have dealt with problems of data comparability as they examined faunal assemblges from Fremont sites in Utah, drawing special attention to pitfalls of sample size effects in attempting comparisons of faunal diversity from

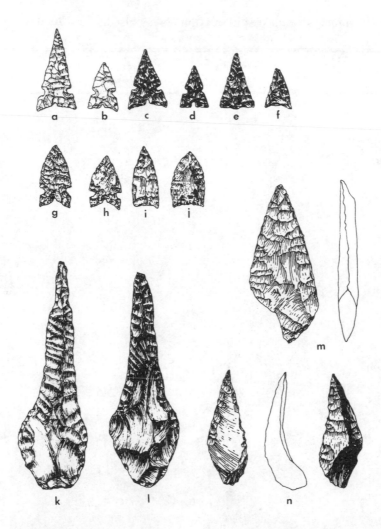

Figure 7. Chipped stone tools from late Prehistoric sites in Utah Valley. Desert Side–notched arrow points (*a–b* Heron Springs, *c–d* Sandy Beach, *g–h* Fox Site); Cottonwood Triangular arrow points (*e–f* Sandy Beach, *i–j* Fox Site); shoulderd drills (*k* Heron Springs, *l* Sandy Beach); biface (*m* Fox Site); beached tool (*n* Fox Site).

assemblage to assemblage. They define diversity (following Peilou 1975) as consisting of both richness (number of species represented) and evenness (the distribution of specimens across species). Sharp (1989), for example, examined Fremont faunal assemblages from various parts of the state and demonstrated that richness tends to be directly related to sample size ($\sum$NISP); in general, the larger the sample the higher the richness value.

Grayson (1984), on the other hand, in presenting research particularly germane to the interests of this paper, analyzed existing Fremont faunal data to test Madsen's hypothesis regarding the basis of Fremont sedentism at marsh–side locations. Specifically, Grayson (1984:166) (restating Madsen's argument) says that "Fremont peoples utilized a wide range of marsh resources in generalist fashion." Such a broad–spectrum use of marshes should result in a highly diverse array of floral and faunal resources being brought to residential bases for consumption and this pattern should be represented in the archaeological record. To test this hypothesis Grayson focuses on measuring the diversity (particularly the evenness) of faunal arrays from Fremont sites in marsh–edge settings and sites in non–marsh environments with the expectation that one should see a less diverse faunal array at sites

Table 4. Late Prehistoric Faunal Assemblages from Utah Valley Used in this Analysis

Taxon	Fox Site NISP	Heron Springs NISP	Sandy Beach NISP
Antilocapra americana		2	27
Bison bison		13	1
Bufo woodhousei	1		
Canis latrans			6
Canis lupus			178
Castor Canadensis		1	
Catostomus ardens	50,276	1,256	1,177
Cerves elaphus		1	2
Chasmistes liorus			9
Dipodomys ordi		2	
Erithizon dorsatum	1		6
Gila atraria	264	215	139
Lepus californicus	1	9	49
Microtus lionus		19	21
Mephitis mephitis		1	
Odocoileus hemionus	3	13	11
Ondatra zibethicus	10	112	333
Ovis canadensis	1	1	1
Rana pipiens	3		
Salmo Clarkii	13	22	47
Sylvilagus auduboni			13
Taxidea taxis		1	
Thomomys bottae	8		1
Totals	50,581	1,668	2,021

Total Taxa: Fox Site = 11
 Heron Springs = 15
 Sandy Beach = 17

Table 5. Values for Fremont and Late Prehistoric Faunal Assemblages from Utah Used in this Analysis

UTAH VALLEY		Σi	$1/\Sigma p_i^2$	ΣNISP
Fremont				
	Woodard Mound	15	4.816	660
	Smoking Pipe	13	2.959	4,085
Late Prehistoric				
	Fox Site	11	1.012	50,581
	Heron Springs (30%)	15	1.713	1,668
	Sandy Beach (15%)	17	2.642	2,015
OTHER				
Fremont				
	Bear River 1	13	1.432	1,859
	Bear River 2	16	1.939	1,121
	Bear River 3	14	1.525	830
	Backhoe	7	4.062	100

removed from marsh settings due to a greater investment of time and energy on horticultural products. Although for various reasons he had to restrict his analysis to avian assemblages, Grayson's conclusions tend to support Madsen's predictions; that is, Fremont peoples living in the vicinity of marshes utilized a broader array of faunal resources than peoples in non–marsh settings.

The focus of this paper is somewhat different, although clearly related to the interests of Grayson. Rather than examining variability in Fremont faunal assemblages, the specific interest here is in comparing Fremont and Late Prehistoric subsistence patterns. Again, based on Madsen's hypothesis that "Shoshonean (Late Prehistoric) subsistence indicates a degree of variation very similar to preceding Archaic and Sevier/Fremont groups" (Madsen 1982:221), we should see similar patterns of diversity in the faunal arrays from Fremont and Late Prehistoric sites, all else being equal.

Before proceeding, it is necessary to explain how the diversity measures presented by Grayson and for the Utah Valley sites were obtained. Grayson utilizes two statistical procedures to obtain first, a measure of diversity and second, to determine, if possible, the extent to which that measure is being effected by sample size. For the first measure Grayson chooses the reciprocal of Simpson's index, $1/\Sigma p^2$, where p_i is the "proportion of the individuals in the total collection that falls in species i" (Grayson 1984:160). Simpson's index is essentially a measure of evenness where "the higher the value, the more evenly distributed the individuals across species" (Grayson 1984:160). He then tested for relationships between the calculated measures of diversity for sample size effects by comparing diversity values with ΣNISP using Spearman's rho (r_s).

Diversity values for the faunal assemblages from Fremont and Late Prehistoric sites in Utah Valley were calculated using Simpson's index ($1/\sum p^2$, again a measure of evenness) and these data are presented in Table 5. The calculations included all data for specimens identified to the species level. Since birds are only identified at some of the sites, Aves data were not included in the analysis. I have included faunal data from the Bear River Fremont sites and Backhoe Village (which are also in marsh settings) to allow calculations of sample size effects and for comparison with the Utah Valley sites. Other marsh–side Fremont sites such as the Levee and Knoll sites (Fry and Dalley 1979) and the Injun Creek sites (Aikens 1967) were not included as only the avian faunas have been analyzed for the former, and the latter may contain mixed Fremont and Late Prehistoric materials (see for example the dates in Aikens 1966). No other Late Prehistoric faunal data for the eastern Great Basin are available as of this writing. The relationships between $\sum$NISP and diversity, both evenness ($1/\sum p^2$) and richness ($\sum i$, i = a taxon in an assemblage) were pursued by calculating Spearman's r_s. These calculations were done using data from all sites (both the Fremont and the Late Prehistoric) and for the Fremont data alone.

The results of these statistical analyses are varied. When all sites were compared, sample size showed a moderate negative correlation with diversity ($r_s = -.517$, $p < .05$). That is, as the assemblage size increased, assemblage diversity tended to decrease. This finding likely stems from the effects of differential recovery techniques: the use of eighth inch screens at the Late Prehistoric sites and either no screening or use of quarter inch screens at most Fremont sites (the exception being Smoking Pipe). However, sample size did not appear to be effecting the richness of the assemblages when all sites were compared ($r_s = -.017$, $p > .20$). When only Fremont sites were compared, no relationship between sample size and diversity was found for evenness ($r_s = +.54$, $p > .20$) or richness ($r_s = -.25$, $p > .20$). In other words, sample sizes at the Fremont sites examined here do not appear to be greatly effecting diversity values. [Footnote: This is in contrast to the findings of both Grayson (1984) and Sharp (1989) who found that when both marsh–side and non–marsh–side Fremont sites are compared: (1) evenness tends to be inversely correlated with sample size (Grayson 1984:162), and (2) that for all Fremont sites richness tends to increase with sample size (Sharp 1989:22). Explanations for this difference in findings likely include the use of slightly different data sets (Grayson was only looking at mammals) and the bias of a limited number of sites]. These findings suggest that, although comparisons among Fremont sites might result in fairly reliable data, comparisons of Fremont and Late Prehistoric faunal assemblages, which is just what I wanted to do, should only be done in a very tentative fashion until data sets recovered in comparable ways are available. The following comments on Fremont and Late Prehistoric subsistence are offered in that context.

The diversity values ($1/\sum p^2$) calculated for the two Utah Valley Fremont sites are somewhat higher than those from the Late Prehistoric sites (Table 5). This difference suggests greater specialization at the Late sites. When values for evenness and richness are combined (Figure 8), this impression is reinforced. In other words, the faunal analysis does not appear to support Madsen's prediction regarding similarity of subsistence strategies. However, the discrepancy may, in part, be explained by differences in site function or season of use. The broad spectrum approach to marsh resources predicted for both the Fremont and the Late Prehistoric hunter–gatherers may be best seen in a suite of sites rather than one or two (David B. Madsen, personal communication 1990). The Fox Site, which is considered to be a specialized fishing camp occupied temporarily in the spring (an interpretation reinforced by the low diversity value), may be a case in point. The lake–edge sites such as Heron Springs and Sandy Beach were probably residential and could perhaps be seen as functionally complementary to the Fox Site, although the temporal and subtle artifact style differences cause some concern. These residential Late sites are likely more comparable functionally to the Fremont sites in the valley. Much of the difference seen betweeen Woodard Mound and Sandy Beach, for example, could likely be explained by differences in recovery technique; it is apparent that screening with eighth inch seives at marsh–edge sites tends to recover many more fish bones which tends to move the diversity values downward. If it is the case that comparable recovery would result in greater similarity in diversity values from both Fremont and Late Prehistoric residential sites, then Madsen's position would be supported.

The tendency for the Bear River sites to plot similarly to the Late Prehistoric sites (Figure 8) is also of interest as it suggests these locales were specialized sites perhaps occupied during particular times of the year. Again, this impression may also be misleading as the un–evenness (lower diversity values relative to other Fremont residential sites) evident here is likely largely a function of the large numbers of bison bones found

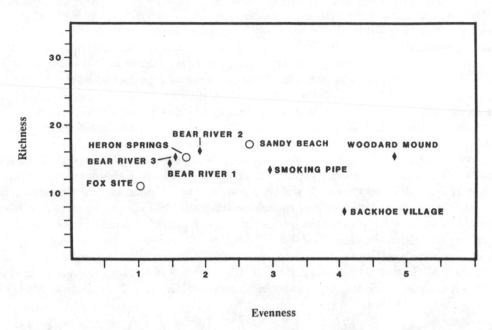

Figure 8. Faunal assemblage diversity at selected marsh-side Fremont (♦) and Late Prehistoric (○) sites in Utah.

(large bones tend to preserve well and are readily recovered) and the exclusion of birds. Regardless, the tendencies seen in Figure 8 are consistent with the conclusions of the excavators of the Bear River sites (cf. Aikens 1966:59) and the findings of Sharp (1989:23). The faunal data from Woodard Mound and Backhoe Village suggest a more generalized strategy perhaps representing their fairly long term use in marsh-side locations.

Conclusions

Conclusions relative to the questions being asked of the Madsen hypothesis are mixed. Although the data do not refute Madsen's position that no shift (other than ethnic) occurred following the Fremont period, they cannot be said to confirm it. The settlement data argue, albeit weakly, for Madsen while the faunal data tend to provide evidence (equally weak) against it. The discussions of settlement and subsistence for Utah Valley and other marsh-side settings along the Wasatch Front have been revealing primarily in that they point to the inadequacy of the data available on these topics. The settlement data for Utah Valley, for example, is seriously biased. It bears repeating that the survey data for Utah Valley were gathered with Fremont sites in mind. This factor, combined with the absence of any other than reconnaissance survey suggests that the settlement data are potentially biased against hunter-gatherer sites. The resolution of this problem will require systematic survey work in those portions of the valley that are relatively little disturbed, for example Goshen Valley.

Well-controlled subsistence information, although improving in quantity and quality, is desperately needed for Utah Valley and elsewhere in the eastern Great Basin (cf. Madsen 1980, 1982, Sharp 1989). Especially critical are standardized recovery techniques and sorting by qualified analysts. The information potential of such data are considerable. An additional subsistence issue demanding attention is the role of plants in both strategies. Madsen's (1980, Madsen and Lindsay 1977) original argument regarding the importance of wetlands in Fremont diets was based on the use of plants rather than animal resources. To some extent the argument for a wild-resource base for Fremont sedentism is founded on the absence of evidence for corn horticulture in sites such as those on the Bear River and the location of those sites in areas not likely to support corn fields (Aikens 1966, 1967, Madsen 1982:218). Madsen, for example, considers the Willard site "unique" in part because it contained charred corncobs (Judd 1926). Interestingly, corn was common (363 kernels, 64 cob fragments and 50 stalk fragments, pollen) at Smoking Pipe (Billat 1985:92) and in the Fremont levels of Spotten Cave (Mock 1971:80–81). Corn (one charred cob fragment and pollen) was also found at Woodard Mound (Richens 1983:115–116). The remains of other domesticates (beans at Smoking Pipe and Woodard Mound, beans and squash at Spotten Cave) were also found at these sites. Although wild seeds, including wetland species (e.g., *Scirpus* sp. and *Typha* sp. etc.), were also present, these findings point to a considerable role of horticulture for the Fremont in Utah Valley. Until this important data set is recovered systematically and reported for both periods, the understanding of subsistence strategies will be incomplete.

The primary contribution of this paper consists of drawing attention to the data needed if our understanding of one of the most interesting problems in eastern Great Basin prehistory, the shift from the Formative to the Late Prehistoric, is to be better understood. It was recognized at the inception that the various analyses would be likely be frustrated by inconsistencies and inadequacies in the data. The value to the author lay in the process of reviewing those data and moving through the mechanics of the analysis. This effort has focused attention on the kinds of data necessary to answer specific question of settlement and subsistence and has shed light on the broader issues of the role of wetlands in prehistoric strategies. The data presented here demonstrate the continued importance of those resources over the last 1,500 years. It is likely that ongoing research will demonstrate that wetlands were fundamental in shaping settlement and subsistence in Utah Valley since man first arrived.

Acknowledgments

I would like to thank Don Grayson for his comments on this paper and for graciously making research data available. Thanks are also due to David Madsen for his useful suggestions. Finally, thanks to Colleen Baker and Jonathan Kau for their work in sorting through the bone from Utah Valley sites.

References

Aikens, C. M.
   1966   *Fremont–Promontory Relationships in Northern Utah.* University of Utah Anthropological Papers No. 82. Salt Lake City.
   1967   *Excavations at Snake Rock Village and the Bear River No. 2 Site.* University of Utah Anthropological Papers No. 87. Salt Lake City.
Antevs, E.
   1948   Climatic Changes and Pre–White Man in the Great Basin with Emphasis on Glacial and Postglacial Times. *University of Utah Bulletin*, 38(20), Biological Series 10(7):168–91. Salt Lake City.
Bee, J. W., and R. G. Bee
   1934–1966 Archaeological Collections, Utah County, Utah. Notes and Ms. on file, Museum of Peoples and Cultures, Brigham Young University, Provo.
Beeley, S. J.
   1946   *The Archaeology of a Utah Lake Site.* Unpublished Master's thesis, Department of Anthropology, University of Utah, Salt Lake City.
Billat, S. E.
   1985   *A Study of Fremont Subsistence at the Smoking Pipe Site.* Unpublished Master's thesis, Department of Anthropology, Brigham Young University, Provo.
Brimhall, W. H., and L. B. Merritt
   1981   Geology of Utah Lake: Implication for Resource Management. In *Utah Lake Monograph*, pp. 24–42. Great Basin Naturalist Memoirs No. 5. Provo.
Brotherson, J. D., and W. E. Evenson
   1982   Vegetation Communities Surrounding Utah Lake and its Bays. Ms. on file, Bureau of Reclamation, Provo.
Carter, D. R.
   1969   *A History of Commercial Fishing on Utah Lake.* Unpublished Master's thesis, Department of History, Brigham Young University, Provo.

Chamberlain, R. V., and D. T. Jones
1929   A Descriptive Catalogue of the Mollusca of Utah. *Bulletin of the University of Utah, Biological Series* I(1). Salt Lake City.

Christensen, R. T.
1947   *A Preliminary Report of Archaeological Investigations Near Utah Lake, Utah, 1946.* Unpublished Master's thesis, Department of Archaeology, Brigham Young University, Provo.

Colton, R. C.
1946   *A Historical Study of the Exploration of Utah Valley and the Story of Fort Utah.* Unpublished Master's thesis, Department of History, Brigham Young University, Provo.

Cook, C. W.
1980   *Faunal Analysis of Five Utah Valley Sites: A Test of a Subsistence Model from the Sevier Fremont Area.* Unpublished Master's thesis, Department of Archeology and Anthropology, Brigham Young University, Provo.

Cottam, W. P.
1926   *An Ecological Study of the Flora of Utah Lake, Utah.* Unpublished Ph.D. dissertation, Department of Botany, University of Chicago.

Durrant, S. D.
1952   *Mammals of Utah: Taxonomy and Distribution.* University of Kansas Museum of Natural History Publication No. 6. Lawrence.

Eubank, M., and C. Brough
1979   *Mark Eubank's Utah Weather.* Weatherbank, Inc., Salt Lake City.

Forsyth, D. W.
1984   *Preliminary Report of Archaeological Investigations at the Smoking Pipe Site (42Ut150), Utah Valley Utah—The 1983 and 1984 Seasons.* Museum of Peoples and Cultures Technical Series No. 84-92. Brigham Young University, Provo.

Forsyth, D. W.
1986   Post Formative Ceramics in the Eastern Great Basin: A Reappraisal of the Promontory Problem. *Journal of California and Great Basin Anthropology* 8(2):80-203.

Fry, G. F., and G. F. Dalley
1979   *The Levee Site and the Knoll Site.* University of Utah Anthropological Papers No. 100. Salt Lake City.

Gilsen, L.
1968   *An Archaeological Survey of Goshen Valley, Utah County, Central Utah.* Unpublished Master's thesis, Department of Anthropology and Archaeology, Brigham Young University, Provo.

Grayson, D. K.
1984   *Quantitative Zooarchaeology.* Academic Press, New York.

Green, D. F.
1961   *Archaeological Investigations at G. M. Hinckley Farm Site, Utah County, Utah.* Unpublished Master's thesis, Department of Anthropology and Archaeology, Brigham Young University, Provo.

Hansen, G. H., and W. L. Stokes
1941   An Ancient Cave in American Fork Canyon. *Proceedings, Utah Academy of Sciences, Arts and Letters* 11:3-13.

Heckman, R. A., C. Thompson, and D. A. White
1981   Fishes of Utah Lake. In *Utah Lake Monograph*, pp. 107-127. Great Basin Naturalist Memoirs No. 5. Provo.

Jackson, R. H., and D. J. Stevens
1981   Physical and Cultural Environments of Utah Lake and Adjacent Areas. In *Utah Lake Monograph*, pp. 3-23. Great Basin Naturalist Memoirs, No. 5. Provo.

Janetski, J. C.
1983   *The Western Ute of Utah Valley: An Ethnohistoric Model of Lakeside Adaptation.* Ph.D. dissertation, Department of Anthropology, University of Utah, Salt Lake City. University Microfilms, Ann Arbor.
1986   The Great Basin Lacustrine Subsistence Pattern: Insights from Utah Valley. In *Anthropology of the Desert West, Essays in Honor of Jesse D. Jennings*, edited by C. J. Condie and D. D. Fowler, pp. 145-168. University of Utah Anthropological Papers No. 110. Salt Lake City.
1987   Utah Lake Archaeology. *Of Human Interest, The Newsletter of BYU Anthropology and Archaeology* 3(2):3.
1988   Lake Margin Settlements in Utah Valley. Paper presented at the 21st Great Basin Anthropological Conference, Park City.
1990   Utah Lake: Its Role in the Prehistory of Utah Valley. *Utah Historical Quarterly* 58(1):5-31.
n.d.a   *The Ute of Utah Lake.* University of Utah Anthropological Papers No. 116. Salt Lake City, in press.
n.d.b   *The Fox Site: A Late Prehistoric Fishing Camp in Utah Valley.* Museum of Peoples and Cultures Technical Series. Brigham Young University, Provo, in preparation.

Jennings, J. D.
1978   *Prehistory of Utah and the Eastern Great Basin.* University of Utah Anthropological Papers No. 98. Salt Lake City.

Jones, C. H.
1961   An Archaeological Survey of Utah County, Utah. Unpublished Master's thesis, Department of Archaeology, Brigham Young University, Provo.

Judd, N.
1926   *Archaeological Observations North of the Rio Colorado.* Bureau of American Ethnology Bulletin No. 82. Washington, D.C.

Long, A., and B. Rippeteau
    1974   Testing Contemporaneity and Averaging Radiocarbon Dates. *American Antiquity* 39:205–215.
Lowie, R. H.
    1924   Notes on Shoshonean Ethnography. *American Museum of Natural History Anthropological Papers* 20:185-314. New York.
Madsen, D. B.
    1980   Fremont/Sevier Subsistence. In *Fremont Perspectives*, edited by D. B. Madsen, pp. 25–34. Antiquities Section Selected Papers 7(16). Utah State Historical Society, Salt Lake City.
    1982   Get it Where the Gettin's Good: A Variable Model of Great Basin Subsistence and Settlement Based on Data From the Eastern Great Basin. In *Man and Environment in the Great Basin*, edited by D. B. Madsen and James F. O'Connell, pp. 207-226. SAA Papers No. 2, Washington, D.C.
Madsen, D. B., and L. W. Lindsay
    1977   *Backhoe Village*. Antiquities Section Selected Papers 4(12). Utah State Historical Society, Salt Lake City.
Mock, J. M.
    1971   *Archaeology of Spotten Cave, Utah County Central Utah*. Unpublished Master's thesis, Department of Anthropology and Archaeology, Brigham Young University, Provo.
Montillo, E. D.
    1968   *A Study of the Prehistoric Settlement Patterns of the Provo Area in Central Utah*. Unpublished Master's thesis, Department of Anthropology and Archaeology, Brigham Young University, Provo.
Murchison, S. B.
    1989   *Fluctuation History of Great Salt Lake, Utah, During the Last 13,000 Years*. Limnotechnics Lab Tech Report No. 89-2. Department of Geography, University of Utah, Salt Lake City.
Palmer, E.
    1876   Exploration of a Mound in Utah. *American Naturalist*. 10:410–414.
    1880   Review of Published Statements Regarding the Mounds at Payson, Utah, With an Account of their Structure and Origin. *Proceedings, Davenport Academy of Natural Sciences* 1876–1878 2:167–172.
Pielou, E. C.
    1975   *Ecological Diversity*. John Wiley and Sons, New York.
Pritchett, C. L., H. H. Frost, and W. W. Tanner
    1981   Terrestrial Vertebrates in the Environs of Utah Lake. In *Utah Lake Monograph*, pp. 125-169. Great Basin Naturalist Memoirs No. 5. Provo.
Reagan, A. B.
    1935   Archaeological Report of Field Work Done in Utah in 1934 and 1935. *Proceedings, Utah Academy of Sciences, Arts and Letters* 12:50–88.
Richens, L. D.
    1983   *Woodard Mound: Excavation at a Fremont Site in Goshen Valley, Utah County, Utah 1980–1981*. Unpublished Master's thesis, Department of Anthropology, Brigham Young University, Provo.
Russell, K. W., M. E. Stuart, J. A. Brannan, and H. Weymouth
    1989   *Archaeological Reconnaissance in the Ogden/Weber River Marshes*. Weber State College Reports of Investigation No. 89-1. Ogden.
Severance, M. S., and H. C. Yarrow
    1879   Notes Upon Human Erania and Skeletons Collected by the Expeditions of 1872–73. *United States Geographical Surveys West of the One Hundredth Meridian*, vol. 7, Archaeology. Washington, D.C.
Sharp, N.
    1989   Redefining Fremont Subsistence. *Utah Archaeology 1989* 2(1):19–31.
Shiozawa, D. K.
    n.d.   Size Estimates of Utah Sucker from the Fox Site. In *The Fox Site, A Late Prehistoric Fishing Camp in Utah Valley*. Museum of Peoples and Cultures Technical Series. Brigham Young University, Provo, in preparation.
Simms, S. R.
    1987   Second Year Excavation at the Orbit Inn Site, Brigham City, Utah. *UPAC News* 5(3):4.
Simms, S. R., and K. Heath
    1990   Site Structure of the Orbit Inn: An Archaeological Example of Inference from Ethnoarchaeology. American Antiquity, in press.
Smith, A. M.
    1974   *Ethnography of the Northern Ute*. University of New Mexico Papers in Anthropology No. 17. Albuquerque.
Spencer, A. C.
    1971   An Archaeological Survey of the Knolls and Vicinity, Utah County, Utah. Paper submitted to the Junior Symposium of Science and Humanities, Salt Lake City.
    1980   Cultural Resources Evaluation: Utah Lake and Lampton Reservoir Area. Prepared for Water and Power Resources Service, Federal Building, Salt Lake City. Ms. on file, Museum of Peoples and Cultures, Brigham Young University, Provo.

Steward, J. H.
    1933   Early Inhabitants of Western Utah. *Bulletin of the University of Utah* 23 (7):1–34. Salt Lake City.
Steward, J. H.
    1938   *Basin-Plateau Aboriginal Sociopolitical Groups*. Smithsonian Institution, Bureau of American Ethnology, Bulletin 120. Reprint by University of Utah press, Salt Lake City.
Stewart, O. C.
    1942   *Culture Element Distributions: XVIII, Ute-Southern Paiute*. University of California Anthropological Records 6(4):231-355. Berkeley.
Stuart, M.
    1981   A Revised Summary of Weber County. Ms. on file, Utah State Historical Society, Antiquities Section, Salt Lake City.
Warner, T. J. (editor)
    1976   *The Dominguez-Escalante Journal*. Fray Angelico Chavez (translator). Brigham Young University Press, Provo.
Wheeler, E.
    1968   *An Archaeological Survey of West Canyon and Vicinity, Utah County Utah*. Unpublished Master's thesis, Department of Anthropology and Archaeology, Brigham Young University, Provo.
Young, S.
    n.d.   Macrobotanical Analysis. In *The Fox Site, A Late Prehistoric Fishing Camp in Utah Valley*. Museum of Peoples and Cultures Technical Series. Brigham Young University, Provo, in preparation.

15

MARSHES AND MOBILITY IN THE WESTERN GREAT BASIN

Robert L. Kelly

Abstract

Archaeological and ethnographic data point to the important role marshes play in sedentary or low mobility foraging societies—societies different from those normally associated with the Great Basin. A simple model is used to discuss conditions under which foragers might become sedentary; the model points to local resource abundance in the context of regional resource scarcity. Storage may also play a role in encouraging sedentism. Archaeological data from the Carson Sink suggest a transition about or sometime about 1500 B.P. from a mobile to a less mobile foraging system. This transition is correlated with a possible decrease in precipitation, making marshes more productive relative to their regional context; a shift to winter-dominant precipitation sometime after 1500 B.P. may have increased the need for winter stores and lowered large game populations. Further modeling efforts are needed to simulate mobility under various conditions, as well as more accurate paleoecological data.

Introduction

For many years, archaeologists assumed that sedentism was a straighforward product of resource abundance, and that "in general sedentary life has more survival value than wandering life to the human race . . . other things being equal, whenever there is an **opportunity** to make the transition, it will be made" (Beardsley et al. 1956:134; emphasis added). This view no longer dominates anthropology, but there is still no consensus on why some hunter–gatherers became sedentary. The issue is of particular importance because it relates to the evolution of hierarchial sociopolitical structures and domestication (cf. Price and Brown 1985). In this paper, I use a simple theoretical foraging model to examine the possible conditions under which hunter–gatherers might become sedentary. I then briefly examine the archaeology of the Carson Sink in western Nevada (Figure 1) in light of this model. The archaeology of the Carson Sink is still poorly understood and at present there is no evidence of year–round sedentism there. However, there may be a change in the way the Carson Sink was used about 1500 B.P. (and perhaps also at 700 B.P.) which bears on our understanding of sedentism.

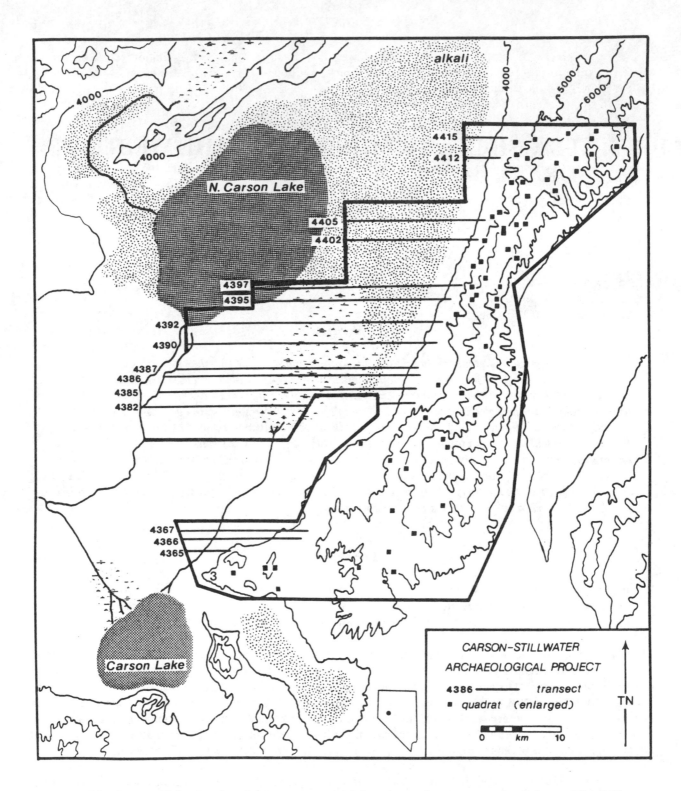

Figure 1. The Carson Sink, showing the survey area with locations of transects and quadrats. The Stillwater Marsh is in the center. Other sites are: (1) Lovelock Cave; (2) Humboldt Cave; (3) Hidden Cave (elevation in feet).

Sedentism

There is substantial disagreement over the concept of sedentism, and most definitions conflate several dimensions of mobility, for example, individual, seasonal, and long-term territorial movements (Eder 1984; Rafferty 1985). This conceptual issue is beyond the scope of this paper. For the present, we will define sedentism as the absence of annual residential movements; consequently, efforts to understand sedentism require that we understand the factors influencing whether or not a group moves from a particular camp.

There are two competing hypotheses in the literature that purport to explain hunter–gatherer sedentism which Price and Brown (1985) refer to as the "push" and "pull" hypotheses. In the first, hunter–gatherers become sedentary when high return rate resources are available in sufficient density throughout the year and from year to year; this is what Binford (1983) has termed (and criticized as) the "Garden of Eden" hypothesis. Binford argues that hunter–gatherers will remain mobile if possible to maintain information about their environment as well as social ties to other groups; this information and these social ties are a group's insurance in times of resource fluctuations. This criticism is countered by the assertion that many environments simply do not fluctuate very much and there is consequently no perceived need for such "insurance." On the other hand, sedentary agriculturalists must also maintain information about their environment as well as social ties with other groups—and they seem to do so without being mobile. It is also true that to be sedentary and not be an agriculturalist, there must be a continual supply of food that can be collected at an energetic gain within the foraging area, or food that can be collected in bulk and stored for the lean period of the year (e.g., salmon on the Northwest Coast). So the presence of continuously available resources of some minimal return rate is a necessary precondition for hunter–gatherers to become sedentary. The question is: is it sufficient to cause a transition from a mobile to a sedentary system? Would hunter–gatherers always exploit the opportunity to become sedentary?

The second hypothesis sees hunter–gatherers becoming sedentary under conditions of "resource stress" when higher ranked resources decrease in availability thus requiring use of lower-ranked resources. This commits energy to resource acquisition and processing, hence mobility must decrease. However, what constitutes "stress" is vague. Is it when people are starving, or just when resource return rates drop below an acceptable level? What variables affect the interplay between the use of less efficiently harvested resources and movement to an area of more efficiently harvested ones?

Obviously, archaeology needs to rethink sedentism (cf. Rafferty 1985). In the first place, sedentism is often conceived of as an either/or situation. Either you are sedentary or you are mobile. This is not a useful way to think of the problem. It is more useful to think about the different components of mobility (cf. Kelly 1983, n.d.a) such as residential movements, individual forays, and territorial shifts, and the variables that affect them. In this paper, we examine only one set of relationships, that between individual foraging efforts and movements of the base camp.

Great Basin Archaeology and Sedentism

The Great Basin usually does not conjure up images of sedentary, village–dwelling hunter–gatherers. What therefore can Great Basin archaeology contribute to understanding sedentism? Ethnographic and archaeological data from Utah (Fremont material), and now from the western Basin as well, suggest that marsh resources figured prominently in some Great Basin hunting and gathering lifeways characterized by reduced residential mobility, and perhaps sedentism. Pithouse villages, indicative of restricted residential mobility (if not year–round sedentism, but we do not know for certain) occur near marshes in western Utah and contain evidence of marsh use but little evidence of maize agriculture (Madsen 1979; Madsen and Lindsay 1977; Madsen 1982). In the western Basin, mobility may have been reduced and greater use made of marsh resources after 1500 B.P. (see below). Therefore, the archaeology of Great Basin marshes, unaffected by the complicating effects of agriculture, can inform us about the nature of hunter–gatherer sedentism.

Unfortunately, there has not yet been a thorough archaeological demonstration of sedentary use of marshes (Janetski 1986), although such an assumption has existed for years. Heizer's (Heizer and Napton 1970) concept of **limnosedentism**, a sedentary lifeway focused on the use of marsh resources in the Humboldt Sink (Figure 1), was based on direct evidence of marsh resource use in the duck decoys, fish hooks, nets, and coprolite contents of the Lovelock Cave caches and on two assumptions: (1) that marsh resources were present in abundance, and, (2) that humans would take advantage of any opportunity to become sedentary. But there were no direct data to substantiate year–round use of the marsh. Livingston's (1986, 1988) research with the Churchill 15 and Lovelock Cave collections has gone far in remedying this situation. Between these two sites, the full four seasons are represented in the avian assemblage, although it is not possible to argue one way or the other whether they indicate year–round occupation of the Humboldt Sink.

The ethnographic literature is not much help either. Zenas Leonard (1904:167) describes the inhabitants of the Humboldt Sink (if that is indeed where Leonard was at the time) as living in shallow, grass and earth covered pithouses, suggestive of reduced residential mobility. The nineteenth century Toedökadö living in the Carson Sink, however, were certainly mobile, with people living at the marsh at the same time that some were collecting grass seeds and hunting in the mountains (Thomas 1985:21–26; Kelly 1985:31–40). Besides the Carson Sink, nineteenth century Toedökadö territory reached as far east as the Desatoya Mountains, while occasional fishing expeditions were made to the Walker and Truckee Rivers. Ethnographic data, however, are potentially biased due to the effects of white immigration. A complete understanding of the relationships between the environment and hunter–gatherer mobility requires an archaeological study. It was for this reason that research was initiated in the Carson Sink (Figure 1), the location of an extensive wetland, the Stillwater Marsh.

Foraging, Residential Movements, and Storage

A reduction in residential mobility requires that people shift more energy to logistical mobility and resource processing. Eder (1984) has shown, for example, that as group mobility of the Philippine Batak decreases, individual mobility increases (cf. Binford 1980). Therefore, sedentism entails a reorganization of, rather than reduction in, energy expenditure. What would lead hunter–gatherers to shift energy expenditure in this way?

As noted in the beginning of this paper, the Garden of Eden argument suggests that resource abundance causes sedentism. We can examine this argument through use of the marginal value theorem (Charnov 1976; Stephens and Charnov 1982) to predict when a forager should leave a resource patch. The question is: considering energetics only (and not information needs) even if it were possible for a forager to remain at a given location for a year, would they do so? Figure 2 shows the relationship between net energy gain and the length of residence in a patch; in the case described below, a "patch" can be thought of as the effective foraging area surrounding a residential location. Net energy gain is initially high when a group enters a patch, but begins to decrease as foragers deplete the patch of resources and increase their search time for resources and/or the travel time to resource locations. Thus, the net energy gain curve in Figure 2 initially rises from 0, eventually levels off and then decreases as more energy is expended than is gained.

The marginal value theorem is used to predict the "moving on threshold", the point along the net return curve at which the forager should move to another resource patch. Charnov demonstrated that a forager attempting to maximize the return rate should leave the patch when the instantaneous (marginal) return rate dropped to the average return rate for the environment as a whole, taking the average returns of other potential patches and travel time into account. The marginal return rate of any point along the curve is the slope of a line tangent to the curve at that point. The "solution" to the problem of when to leave the patch can be discovered graphically (for the mathematical proof, see Charnov 1976). A line with origin = 0 and slope equivalent to the average return rate for the environment as a whole is drawn on the figure with the net energy gain curve (line A in Figure 2). A line drawn parallel to A but tangent to the net return curve (line B) has a slope (return rate) equal to that of the overall environment and therefore intersects the net return curve such that ƀ = the time to stay in the patch. In Figure 2, foragers would leave the patch at time = ƀ, even if they could still make a net foraging gain by remaining in the patch (as suggested by the net energy gain curve). Foragers should not use all the food available to them within their effective foraging radius. Another simulation demonstrates these relationships hold true even in a region of "abundant" resources.

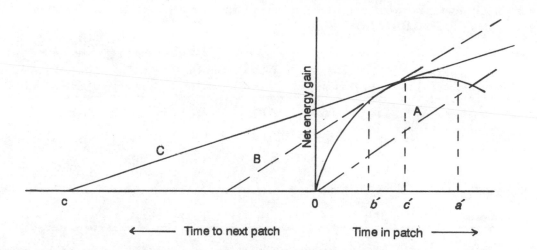

Figure 2. Schematic diagram of Charnov's marginal value theorem. Line A has a slope equal to the average environmental return rate; Line B, with the same slope, intersects the net gains curve such that b́ = the time to leave the patch. As travel costs to the next patch increase (Line C), the length of time the forager stays in the patch increases (ć).

The simulation used here is based on a group size of 25 with a given demographic composition and daily caloric requirements (a total of 42,096 kcal for three families) generated by the Right Byte nutrition program. Walking rate is set at 3 kms/hr and the cost at 300 kcal/hr; walking cost increases by 30% when returning with food (Table 1).

Table 2 and Figure 3 show the result of a simulation in which a group of 25 hunter–gatherers live in an environment where a high return rate resource (4000 kcal/hr) is homogeneously distributed across the landscape[1]. The resource is collected by three active foragers (one per family) who must bring in at least 14,032 kcal/day apiece (minimum return rate of 1754 kcal/hr, assuming an eight–hour workday). The net return rate decreases with increasing foray distance since obviously more time and energy is invested in traveling to and from the resource patch (column 3 in Table 1). Net return, therefore, is:

$$((8 \text{ hrs}-(2 * T))*4000)-((300 \text{ kcal/hr} * T)+(390 \text{ kcal/hr} * T))/8$$

where: T = travel time to the foraging area

The foragers can collect food at a net gain for more than 6 km from camp. We can think of the effective foraging radius as defining the "patch" size; the average return rate for this patch therefore is about 2930 kcal/hr.

We can also compute the return rate if the group were to move to a new foraging area after exploiting the resources within a given radius of the site. In this simulation movements to a new foraging area are equal to the foraging radius, although runs with residential moves equal to the foraging diameter did not produce results significantly different from those reported here. Allowing an hour for camp breakdown and setup[2], the post–move return rate of the individual forager equals:

$$((7 \text{ hrs}-(\text{radius}/3 \text{ km/hr})*4000)-(300 *(\text{radius}/3 \text{ km/hr})))/8$$

The foraging return rate is 4000 kcal/hr on the day of the move as post–move foraging travel costs would be nearly zero (since the area within a .75 km radius is still being exploited).

It is difficult to determine the appropriate time frame or what is to be considered the average return rate for our hypothetical environment as a whole. To do so, we would have to know when foragers leave their

Table 1. Group Demographic Composition and Caloric Requirements Used in the Foraging Simulation (computed from the Right Byte Program)

Member	Age	Height (inches)	Weight (pounds)	Kcal/ day	Number	Total Kcals
Male (active)	25	66	150	3320	3	9960
Male	45	66	160	2341	3	7023
Female (active)	25	62	140	2468	3	7404
Female	45	62	150	2003	3	6009
Children	10	—	—	1300	9	11,700

Note: Childrens' requirements are for a range of ages, although only age 10 was used; the total cost may be underrepresented.

patch—exactly what we are trying to predict here. Note, however, that at the average return rate of 2931 (achieved at a foraging distance of about 2.6 kms), that the after move return rate is higher than the within patch return rate (Figure 3)[3]. Once eating everything within 2.6 km of camp, the foragers would do better to move their families to the edge of the foraged area (3 km) and use a pristine area. Even with moving, the forager would still achieve a higher return rate for that day—and will return to a 4000 kcal/hr rate the following day.

Exactly how long a forager could remain in this patch depends on the density of the food resource (return rate is of course determined in large part by density). If we assumed a food density of roughly .25 post–harvesting/processing kcal/m^2, then this 6 km radius patch could potentially be occupied for upwards of 300 days—(671 days if a complete radius foraging pattern is assumed); but by leaving after foraging within a nearly 3 km radius, the patch is occupied for only 84 days (167 if the complete radius is foraged). Even though the forager could remain in the patch and forage at an energetic gain for nearly a year, they should still leave long before patch depletion occurs if they wish to maintain a high return rate. Therefore, even in a Garden of Eden, and leaving aside other factors that would encourage movement, foragers should still move.

It should also be apparent that if a seasonal resource appeared elsewhere that provides a higher return rate than that currently being experienced, a group should move to that resource's location if its return rate is not effectively diminished by the distance to the new resource. For example, Bellshaw (1978:78) notes that hunter–gatherers along the coast of New South Wales in Australia appeared to move not because of local food depletion, but because of the appearance of other foods elsewhere.

Resource Distribution

Now let us examine how a change in the assumption of homogeneous resource distribution affects the occupation of a foraging patch[4]. Charnov demonstrated that the solution to the question of how long a forager should remain in a patch could also be found by drawing a line from the point along the X axis indicating the distance (or time or energy involved in moving) to the next patch (point c) that is tangent to the net return curve of the currently foraged patch (line C in Figure 2). As is obvious, the further away the next patch is (or the more energy required to get to the resources of that patch[5]), the lower the slope of the line and consequently the longer the forager should remain in the current patch (ĉ). As the next patch becomes more distant, the forager should remain in the current patch for longer and longer periods of time.

If the next patch is sufficiently far away, or requires a sufficiently large investment of energy in order for it to be utilized, and if it is feasible for the forager to remain in the current patch (either because it provides a continuous supply of resources or because a storable resource is present), then the group should become

Table 2. Foraging returns at increasing distance from a camp compared to the returns expected after moving the minimal distance to a new foraging area.

Foraging Radius (km)	Net Return (kcal)	In Patch	Return Rates After Move	(kcal/hr) 2 Days After Move
0.00	32,000	4,000	—	—
0.75	29,287	3,728	3,365	3682
1.50	27,655	3,456	3,231	3615
2.25	25,482	3,185	3,096	3548
3.00	23,310	2,913	2,962	3481
3.75	21,137	2,642	2,828	3414
4.50	18,965	2,370	2,693	3346
5.25	16,792	2,099	2,559	3279
6.00	14,620	1,827	2,425	3212

sedentary. This suggests that in some circumstances **sedentism is a product of local abundance in the context of regional scarcity.**

How do Great Basin wetlands figure into this scenario? If we view marshes in the western Great Basin as isolated, diverse resource patches, then the extent to which marshes are used as the focus of sedentary settlements is a product of the abundance and distribution of resources in areas surrounding the marshes. This perspective is perhaps especially relevant to the western Great Basin. Receiving the full brunt of the Sierra Nevada's rain shadow effect, western Nevada is one of the drier areas of the Great Basin. Yet, because of topographic conditions, the western Basin contains many standing bodies of water: Pyramid Lake, Walker Lake, Lake Winnemucca (before the 1930s), Carson Lake, Stillwater Marsh, and the Humboldt Marsh. These bodies of water are the product of what ecologists used to call "unearned water"—water derived from sources other than local rainfall (Sierran snowpacks for Walker, Winnemucca, Pyramid and Carson lakes, large watersheds in eastern Nevada for the Humboldt Sink). Since desert productivity is tied largely to precipitation, fluctuation in local precipitation would alter the regional context of marshes making them more or less productive relative to the regional resource scene and consequently altering their incorporation into mobility strategies.

Resource Storage

At this point we need to ask how food storage figures into this scenario. Binford (1980) pointed out that resource storage among hunter–gatherers is correlated with seasonality and that storage is a response to seasonal resource availability (see also Keeley 1988). To put up stores, a forager must be able to acquire not only enough food for current needs, but for future needs as well. In effect, the daily "caloric needs" of the group are increased during the period when food is being procured for storage. This in turn can require that a single resource be harvested in bulk (e.g., salmon on the Northwest Coast). If such a resource is not available, then (1) diet breadth must be increased, and/or (2) the harvest rate of a select few resources must be increased so that some percentage of the gathered food might be stored for later use. This second option increases the rate at which a foraging area is depleted and thus, following the above argument, requires higher mobility during the period when resources are being collected. Yet, at the same time, much effort must be devoted to not only

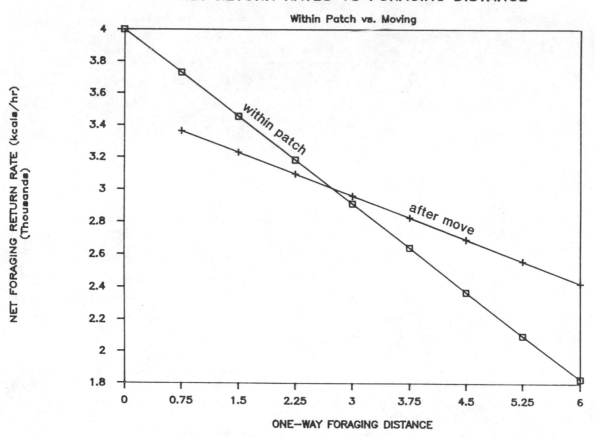

Figure 3. Simulated net return rates at various foraging distances from camp of forager who remains in patch versus a forager who moves to a new location (assuming homogeneous resource distribution, distance to a new patch = the current one-way foray distance). The forager should leave the patch after using the resources within a nearly 3 km radius of camp.

meeting current food needs, but also to the processing of food for storage. Thus, the second option is energetically expensive (although more simulation is needed in this area). Expanding diet breadth might be the more economical solution to food storage in an environment where no single resource is available in bulk. If so, then areas of higher resource diversity should be used more intensively in areas where (or during time periods when) there is a greater need for winter food storage. Such situations would also encourage the use of "secure" food resources for storage; that is, a resource's return rate must be balanced against its anticipated availability[6].

Binford (1980) found that storage practices begin among groups living in environments characterized by an effective temperature of 14-13°C. The Great Basin, with effective temperatures ranging from 14.5 at Las Vegas to 12 near the Snake River (Kelly 1985), is perched on this boundary. Only a slight increase in winter severity is needed to force Basin hunter-gatherers to put extra effort into resource storage for the winter.

Resource storage is a critical issue for Basin hunter-gatherers since ethnographic data indicate that there was no single resource that could reliably be stored in bulk from year to year (Kelly 1985:93-96; Steward 1938:19, 65; Wheat 1967). Piñon was an important stored resource, but ethnographic and botanical data indicate it was not always reliable (Wells 1978:15; Fowler and Fowler 1971:39; Steward 1938:58, 65, 101, 112, 114). Ethnographic data suggest that the Shoshone, Gosiute, and Paiute spent much of the spring, summer, and fall storing a diversity of resources other than piñon for the winter, including seeds, grasshoppers, service berries, yampa, caterpillars, sunflower seeds, roots, fly larvae, dried fish, and rabbit meat. Clearly, inhabitants of the Great Basin faced a winter storage problem. In this regard, how might marshes have been important?

Marshes have high rates of primary production and contain a wide diversity of resources. These resources vary dramatically in their return rates; bulrush seeds, for example can provide up to 1700 kcal/hr while cattail roots provide only about 260 kcals/hr (Simms 1987)[7]. Additionally, all these resources fluctuate on some level, although on different time scales. Like the rest of the desert environment, the productivity of marshes is linked to water. In the Carson Sink, the level of the Stillwater Marsh is controlled by the Carson River (with periodic contributions from the Humboldt and probably Walker Rivers as well). However, the Carson River is by no means constant in its yearly flow (Figure 4a). The plant and animal resources of marshes track changes in water levels (Kelly 1985:Chapter 3) although they track them differently. Depending on the rapidity of the change, shoreline vegetation can disappear, being either dessicated or drowned; decreasing emergent vegetation can increase numbers of aquatic mammals such as muskrat (Figure 4b), as well as waterfowl (Figure 4d), but too little vegetation (or too sudden an increase in water levels) decreases food and nesting material and causes population declines. An increase in water levels promotes fish populations (as it did between 1982 and 1986 in the Stillwater Marsh), but as water levels decline and salinity increases, fish die (as they did in the summer of 1986). Waterfowl density can vary from year to year as well (Figure 4c), partially independent of local marsh conditions. However, while marsh resources can fluctuate, because of their complex trophic structure, there is nearly always some resource available in a marsh; marshes provide something to eat, no matter what the season or how wet or dry the year, although the specific resource available and their respective return rates can be highly variable[8].

An increased need to store resources could have made certain storable resources (such as seeds and fish) of marshes more attractive. One way to cope with winter severity in the Great Basin may have been to locate in an area that could provide some non-stored resources and/or minimize the transport costs of the various resources stored for the winter. Great Basin wetlands are important in this regard because they contain a diversity of resources some or all of which will be available in some quantity all year of every year. In the drier western Basin, where piñon is not abundant, marshes might have been attractive as a location of winter settlements since, as pointed out above, marshes will nearly always provide something to eat, even if it is only minimally nutritional. Madsen (1989), for example, suggests that during the winter, the return rates of marsh resources may be high relative to those of non-marsh resources. Marshes can therefore be important as sources of winter staples, and as the source (and cached location) of winter supplies.

Back to the Hypotheses

At this point we can restate the pull and push hypotheses in light of the computer simulation models and in terms relevant to the Great Basin:

1. Marshes provide abundant, high return rate resources year-round; therefore, we could expect them to have been used by sedentary hunter-gatherers. Both the intensity and sedentary use of marshes should vary with changes in the marsh itself, rather than changes in nonmarsh resources.
2. Sedentism is a product of conditions that increase environmental spatial heterogeneity and/or conditions where the availability of non-stored resources are balanced against the transport costs of stored resources. Since marshes will almost always provide something to eat in any season, they would have become more attractive to people undergoing winter subsistence stress[9]. We can predict that the use of marshes should vary with increasing heterogeneity ("patchiness") of the environment and/or with an increase in the need to store resources.

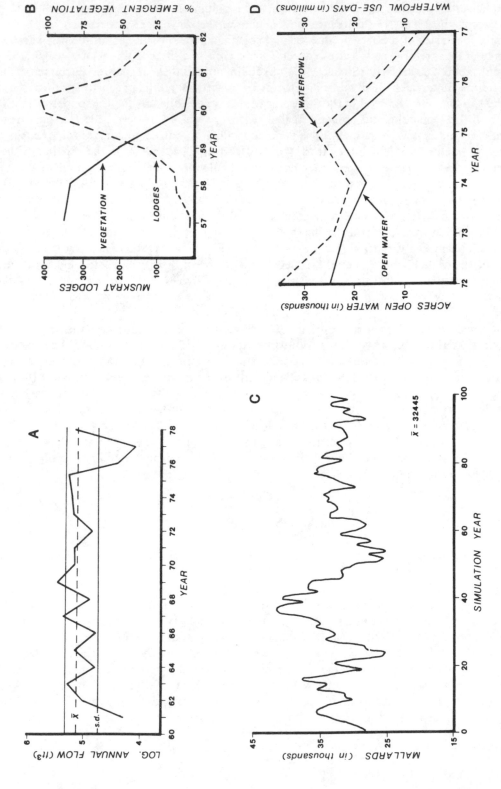

Figure 4. (A) Variation in annual flow of the Carson River, station 312000, from 1960 to 1978 (U.S.G.S. 1978); (B) Response of muskrat population to changes in emergent vegetation cover (Weller 1978); (C) 100-year simulation of Churchill County mallard population; based on Anderson (1975), Munro and Kimball (1982), and Carney and Sorenson (1975); (D) Response of waterfowl to changes in percentage of open water in the Stillwater Marsh (Barber 1978).

Table 3. Cultural Chronology and Time Markers (based on Thomas 1981).

Phase	Temporal Period	Projectile Point Types
Yankee Blade	650 – 100 B.P.	Desert Side–notched Cottonwood Triangular Cottonwood leaf shaped
Underdown	1450 – 650 B.P.	Rosegate
Reveille	3250 – 1450 B.P.	Elko corner notched Elko eared
Devil's Gate	4950 – 3250 B.P.	Gatecliff contracting stem Gatecliff split stem

Sedentism and the Archaeology of the Carson Sink

Neither of these hypotheses can yet be evaluated completely, given the current state of our knowledge of the archaeology and paleoecology of the western Great Basin. However, research in the Carson Sink has begun to shed light on each of these hypotheses. The complete analysis of materials from the Carson Sink (Figure 1) cannot be presented here but will appear elsewhere (Kelly n.d.b, 1988b).

The Carson Stillwater Archaeological Project

The southern half of the wide valley of the Carson Sink is covered by low, partially stabilized sand dunes, with a light cover of greasewood, saltbrush and budsage. The northern half comprises an extensive alkaline plain. The Sink contains the large Stillwater Marsh and formerly contained two lakes that today appear only during years of exceptional winter runoff due to municipal water use and irrigation. There is no stone–tool raw material on the valley floor. It is likely that shifts in stream channels, changes in the flow of the Carson River (produced by periodic stream capture of the Truckee River) and tectonic activity have altered the location of the Stillwater Marsh on the valley floor.

The Stillwater Mountains border the the Carson Sink on the east. A light cover of piñon and juniper grows in the northern mountains at higher elevations; the southern Stillwaters support only an upper sagebrush community. The Stillwaters are not high, but are quite rugged, and contain no streams to speak of and few reliable springs. Projectile point data (using Thomas' [1981] typology[10]) and radiocarbon dates from Hidden Cave suggest an occupation from at least 3700 B.P. (Table 3).

In 1980-1981, I conducted a surface survey of the Carson Sink and Stillwater Mountains as part of the re–excavation of Hidden Cave (Thomas 1985). Fieldwork consisted of survey, intensive surface collections, and limited test excavations (Kelly 1985, 1988b). The valley was sampled with 15 100–m–wide transects, covering 5-7% of the valley floor (256 km total). The northern half of the Stillwater Mountains was surveyed at a sampling fraction of 5% and the southern half at 1% with a total of 57 500 x 500–m quadrats. In total, 161 sites were recorded, 107 of which were on the valley floor; this paper focuses on the valley assemblages.

In 1987, after flooding exposed many new sites and human burials in the Stillwater Marsh, new excavations were conducted by myself and the U.S. Fish and Wildlife Service at several sites (Raven and Elston 1988; Kelly n.d.c). Radiocarbon dates from cultural features and human burials, as well as projectile point occurrences suggest that many of these sites date to the Underdown Phase, 1500 to 650 B.P.

Botanical evidence from Hidden Cave suggests that marshes existed in the Carson Sink at least as early as 3700 B.P. (Thomas 1985). Radiocarbon dates from buried horizons in the Stillwater Marsh date to around 2700 to 3000 B.P. (Raven and Elston 1988; Kelly n.d.c.), while dates on cultural features at sites in the Stillwater Marsh containing evidence of marsh resource use date from 2700 to 800 B.P. (Raven and Elston 1988). At Lovelock Cave duck decoys date to circa 2150 B.P. (Tuohy and Napton 1986) indicating the presence of a marsh in the Humboldt Sink at this time. A sediment core of south Carson Lake taken in 1987 also indicates that a body of water was present here from at least 6000 B.P. (Robert Thompson, personal communication 1989). Thus, it appears that a marsh has been in existence for as long as the valley has been occupied.

If marshes were used because they were the most efficient place for hunter–gatherers to live, then we should see sedentary occupation of the Sink throughout the prehistoric sequence. However, the archaeology of the region points to a major transition in the use of the region around 1500 B.P. (and perhaps at 700 B.P. as well).

The Pre-1500 B.P. Pattern

Lithic analysis of 106 sites on the valley floor shows intriguing patterns in the use of bifacial tools. Prior to 1500 B.P. (Devil's Gate and Reveille Phases), there was a greater number of instances of biface knapping (probably resharpening and maintenance activities) relative to simple flake tool production and other forms of raw material reduction than after 1500 B.P. Moreover, when a bifacial tool was knapped, it produced only a few flakes. We interpret this use of bifacial tools (Kelly 1988b) as being the product of either small, logistical parties operating from a residential camp outside the Carson Sink, or by residential groups occupying the Sink for relatively short periods of time (perhaps seasonally during periods of high resource return rates in the marshes) who had "geared up" for an occupation of the Carson Sink, an area devoid of any stone tool raw material. I suspect that the pre-1500 B.P. biface use pattern described here is more typical of the pre-2900 B.P. occupation of the Sink, but the data are too limited at present for finer chronological divisions.

Caves sites such as Hidden Cave, Lovelock Cave (Heizer and Napton 1970; Loud and Harrington 1929), and Humboldt Cave (Heizer and Kreiger 1956) provide an interesting complement to the pattern in the surface assemblages. These sites contain caches of various kinds of gear, and their primary purpose was as "safe deposit boxes" (Heizer and Krieger 1965:5). There is little evidence the caves were used for habitation (Heizer and Napton 1970:43; Kelly 1985:46-47). Thomas (1985:374), for example, interprets Hidden Cave as having served as a storage location and limited logistic outpost. At Hidden Cave, hunting gear seems to be the predominant cached item (Thomas 1985) while at Lovelock Cave and Humboldt Cave various domestic items and marsh exploitative gear (duck decoys, nets, fish hooks) were cached.

There can be various reasons why gear would be cached in these caves. But all of these point to a periodic (seasonal?) use of the Carson and Humboldt Sinks prior to 1500 B.P. although the age of Humboldt Cave is not clear—there are no radiocarbon dates and some of the points appear to be Rosegates. Interestingly, one is made of metal (Heizer and Kreiger 1956:36). Likewise, the upper deposits of Lovelock Cave that may have contained evidence of post–1500 B.P. occupation were removed by guano miners in the early twentieth century. Lovelock and Hidden Cave also contain caches of human coprolites, although they contain virtually no evidence of occupation as residential sites (indeed, Hidden Cave with its restricted opening would make a poor residence). These coprolites contain unground seeds that could be winnowed from the dried coprolites and reused. Thomas (1985) suggests that these coprolites may indicate a "second–harvest" subsistence strategy (a practice with some ethnographic documentation outside the Basin); if so, they would suggest that visits to the caves were made under conditions when many other higher–ranked resources were not available[11]. Finally, since all of these sites are located some distance from the marshes, they probably do not indicate sedentary use of the Sinks: why cache materials in a cave so far away from home?

The Post-1500 B.P. Pattern

Projectile point distributions and radiocarbon dates from sites and burials in the Stillwater Marsh suggest that the marsh may have been used most intensively between 1500 B.P. and 650 B.P. We must be cautious in making this interpretation, however, since this may be an artifact of geomorphology. Shifting stream channels and tectonic activity have almost certainly caused the marsh to "move" around the valley floor: earlier or later archaeology similar to that exposed recently by flooding may lie buried elsewhere. But what we know now is that most of the sites exposed in the Stillwater Marsh contain Rosegate and Reville Phase points, with the former being dominant (Raymond and Parks, this volume; Tuohy et al. 1987). This mirrors a pattern found in the survey material (Kelly n.d.b).

Analysis of the surface assemblages of the Carson Sink suggests the development of less residentially mobile systems after 1500 B.P.—although exactly when is still unclear. The amount of bifacial material in sites decreases, although an increase in the number of flakes per instance of biface knapping (see above) suggests biface manufacture and maintenance (an activity associated with residences) rather than biface resharpening or use as cores (the pre-1500 B.P. pattern). As the frequency of biface knapping decreases, there is a concomitant increase in bipolar reduction of biface fragments and old cores, as well as an increase in the scavenging of materials from older sites (perhaps many of the Reveille Phase points in the marsh are there due to scavenging by post–1500 B.P. occupants). Such an increase in casual tool production is associated with the appearance of sedentary settlements elsewhere in the New World (Parry and Kelly 1987). It is especially a pattern I would expect to see at residential sites occupied for fairly long periods of time in an area of scarce lithic resources such as the Carson Sink. This parallels Elston's (1982) conclusion that the curation rate of stone tools dropped after 1500 B.P. in the western Great Basin.

The post–1500 B.P. transition encompasses the appearance of shallow houses in both the Carson Sink (Kelly n.d.c) and the Humboldt Sink (Livingston 1986, 1988). Throughout the Basin, the use of small traps (Janetski 1979), perhaps as a way to increase the time utility of hunting excursions, and the use of small, probably arrow points that are nonresharpenable and perhaps more target–specific than previous atlatl dart points (Kelly 1988b) appear after 1500 B.P. Isolated caches (e.g., Hester 1974; Elsasser and Prince 1961) suggest the development of a more logistically organized system (following Binford 1980).

The archaeology of 26Ch 1062 in the Stillwater Marsh manifests a pattern similar to that reconstructed from the survey data. Radiocarbon dates from this site are in the 1300–800 B.P. range. While there are many bifacial tool fragments, there is little evidence of bifacial knapping—and what evidence there is comes almost entirely from obsidian tools. Tools were breaking, but apparently were not being replenished; lithic debris is remarkably small, and consists mostly of shatter and some of the obsidian projectile points bear weathered flake scars, evidence that the points were scavenged from older archaeological sites. There is no evidence of raw material replenishment.

Two features at 26Ch 1062 are probably houses but their microtopography suggests they were open, windbreak–type structures (such as those described by Wright [DeQuille 1963:30-31] and Simpson [1876:85]); large postholes not associated with these structures may indicate the use of ramadas or drying racks.

The sites recently exposed in the Stillwater Marsh also contain numerous circular pits (Raymond and Parks, this volume; Raven and Elston 1988). Those excavated in 1987 at 26Ch 1062 were round, steep–sided, flat–bottomed pits, obviously carefully made, with no evidence of burning. Their structure suggests they were used as storage pits, although direct evidence of this function is lacking as they are filled with midden. Zeanah's (1988) ethnoarchaeological analysis of pit shape and storage length suggests these pits were used for storage on the order of 4 months. Faunal remains at 26Ch 1062 are dominated by tui-chub, various waterbirds and fewer marsh mammals, primarily microtines and voles. There are few artiodactyl remains from the site; only three non–tool pieces were recovered in 1987 while in 1986 the Nevada State Museum recovered bighorn cervical vertebrae in a pit. Site seasonality is at present unknown (but research is ongoing).

Discussion

The surface archaeology of the Carson Sink is an incomplete, and looted, archaeological record, but it is what we have at present, and it argues for change in the way the marshes were used, despite the continued existence of marshes. Such change is not predicted by a model that proposes sedentism is caused by sheer resource abundance. However, we should be cautious. While evidence suggests that the marsh has existed for at least the last 6000 years, more paleoecological data are required to determine if the character of the marsh has changed substantially over this time period. On the other hand, extant paleoecological data point to climatic changes that could have altered the relationships between marsh and non-marsh resources after 1500 B.P.

Current paleoclimatological reconstructions suggest a shift from cool/wet to hot/dry conditions about 1500 B.P. (Davis 1982; evidence is summarized in Kelly 1990); there is also evidence of a shift from a summer dominant precipitation regime to a winter-dominant regime after 1500 B.P., although increasing evidence suggests this did not occur until 650 B.P.

A shift to a hotter and drier environment would have only exacerbated the current rain-shadow effect of the Sierra Nevada. Since the wetlands of the western Basin are not fed directly by local precipitation (see above) they would not have been affected directly by a decrease in precipitation. However, the regional context of the wetlands—plant and animal resources of valley floors, alluvial slopes, and uplands would have been affected, and probably reduced in abundance. A decrease in effective moisture, therefore, could only have made the western Basin more heterogeneous than it already is, altering the relative differences between the return rates of the marsh as a patch and the return rates of other Basin foods. According to our theoretical model, such a change would have encouraged longer occupations of the marsh "patch."

A shift to winter precipitation could have made winter foraging more difficult and increased the need for winter stores, increasing the intensity of resource harvesting during the summer. Increased winter precipitation would have increased winter severity also, which appears to be the primary factor affecting large game population densities, by causing either herd die-offs or long-distance migration (Kelly 1985:59-64; 1990). If large game density decreased, their search costs would have increased. According to the diet breadth model, increasing search costs would have resulted in increased dietary diversity, encouraging use of lower-ranked seeds and, in the western Basin, marsh plants. This is particularly important for, as Simms (1987) demonstrates, even small fluctuations in large game populations can produce dramatic decreases in their return rates by increasing search costs[12]. In a situation of increasing winter severity, marshes could have been the location of stored winter resources, as well as the location of secure resources, no matter how efficient or inefficient their procurement. Thus a change to increasing accumulation of stores could have encouraged decreased residential mobility during the winter (although it may have increased mobility during the summer).

Concluding Comments

The archaeology of Great Basin marshes has a great potential for evaluating hypotheses of hunter-gatherer mobility and diet. But the factors that control hunter-gatherer mobility, especially the decision to remain sedentary for all, or part of the year are clearly complicated. At present, we have many of the questions and have developed some frameworks within which we may propose hypotheses. At this point we know a little bit about prehistoric marsh use, but there is still much we do not know.

On one front we need repeated experimental research with the resources of marshes, especially fish, waterbirds, and aquatic mammals, so that we can determine average return rates for each resource. Also, we need better information on how food resource availability and distribution has changed over time. We know now, for example, that piñon was not always present in the Basin, and that deer are probably recent immigrants. But what about antelope and bighorn sheep? Was the Basin always as game-poor as it was in the historic era? Paleoenvironmental research cannot stop at the reconstruction of cool/wet versus warm/dry periods: such information tells us relatively little about food resources and those are, after all, what hunter-gatherers respond to (see Kelly 1990).

I have made the argument here that we cannot understand marsh resource use without understanding spatial and temporal change in other Great Basin resources. On an archaeological front, more field research in marshes is needed which can document temporal variability in more detail than can be obtained from surface survey data. We need to interpret these sites not in terms of "traditional" categories such as residential or task-specific sites, but in terms of the organization of the system that produced them. Archaeological methodology has only scratched the surface of this topic.

Finally, while the development of optimal foraging models have proved to be an important watershed for understanding hunter-gatherer foraging behavior, we now need to use these as the basis for models of foraging and group movement if we are to understand prehistoric patterns of hunter–gatherer mobility. Jones and Madsen (1989) have made an important first step by developing models of resource transport. Models such as those used in this paper undoubtedly simplify human behavior, but they help to direct research and provide predictions that can be evaluated against archaeological data.

Acknowledgments

Field research in the Carson Sink was supported by the American Museum of Natural History, an American Museum–Lounsbery Predoctoral Grant, the Bureau of Land Management, Carson City District, the U.S. Fish and Wildlife Service, a Rackham Graduate School (University of Michigan) Dissertation Grant, the National Endowment for the Humanities and, in 1987-89, the National Science Foundation (BNS-8704094). None of this field research would have been possible without the support of David Hurst Thomas. This paper was written while the author was a Weatherhead Scholar at the School of American Research.

Notes

[1]Since hypothetical resources are used here, processing costs are assumed to occur in the field. However, the decision to field process a resource is itself a variable worth investigating and an important parameter to consider when modeling the use of specific resources (Metcalfe 1989).

[2]An hour was selected based on discussion with several ethnographers. The point at which a forager should move camp is very sensitive to the camp breakdown and setup time, as well as differences in the cost of walking while moving camp versus the cost of walking while foraging (which are here assumed to be the same, 300 kcal/hr). These will be explored in a later publication (Kelly n.d.a).

[3]This, however, does not prove the marginal value theorem (MVT). Changing return rates from 1000 to 12,000 kcal/hr and holding other variables constant produces no difference in the point where the lines cross (even if, as is true for resources of 1000 kcal/hr, it is only possible to forage at much less than 2.6 kms).

The MVT is imprecise because it does not specify the time period over which return rates are maximized (a day? a month? a year? [cf. Stephens and Krebs 1986:31-32]). Assume that the two day return rate is what is being maximized (see Table 2) and we see that foragers should move even **more** frequently than this simulation predicts. The MVT is also imprecise because the ability to move out of a patch when the instantaneous return rate reaches the average return rate implies that the forager has knowledge of the environment as a whole and violates the encounter–contingency assumption of most optimal foraging models. This latter criticism may be a problem for predators that operate in terms of random encounters, but is not true of human foragers who have knowledge of their environment and who can decide to stay in a patch based on what they expect to find elsewhere. The model used here does assume that resources are homogeneously distributed, and this is not a valid assumption for most environments; it is used here since the modeling process must begin with simple parameters.

[4]Population density can also affect movement. Returning to Figure 2, assume a homogeneous distribution of a particular resource across an infinite plain, such that travel time to the next "patch" is minimal (equal to the foraging radius). As the return rate of this resource increases, the slope of the average return rate line (A) will increase and, using the graphic technique described above, the length of time our forager should remain in the patch should decrease (since the slope of line B also increases, moving the tangential point further "down" the net return curve), leading to the counterintuitive prediction that an increase in return rate should lead to an increase in mobility. This is an intriguing observation, but one we cannot investigate in this paper. Suffice it to say that in an environment of high–return rate and homogeneously–distributed resources, the only apparent reason hunter-gatherers would not move is if there were nowhere to move to, that is, if population density had risen to the point where foraging groups were packed in a region.

[5]This can entail the costs of displacing another resident group through violence.

[6]Once prepared for storage, resources must be cached. In situations where a variety of resources are stored, resources may be cached where they are collected; therefore, the decision to use these resources during the winter is related to the cost of retrieving the cache balanced against the return rate of whatever winter resource is being procured directly (Madsen 1989; Jones and Madsen 1989).

[7]In an earlier work (Kelly 1985), I made a distinction between "marsh" and "terrestrial" resources. Madsen (1989) correctly points out that it is misleading to lump resources into these two categories. There is so much variability in the return rates of either category, lumping them together could mask fine–grained patterns of resource use. However, if one is in a marsh one has obviously made a decision not to go after resources of the piñon–juniper woodlands, and vice versa. Treating marshes as resource patches is a useful characteristic of an **initial** model. Simms' (1987) return rate data coupled with research into resource transport costs (Madsen 1989; Jones and Madsen 1989) may then permit us to make predictions about how specific resources should be used under different conditions as predicted by the model. Such predictions are beyond our capacity at present.

[8]Therefore, we could expect a great deal of variability in the use of marshes over short spans of time that are not archaeologically observable. We must recognize that archaeological patterns, especially in the Great Basin record only gross, large–scale changes in human society.

[9]This trend could be exacerbated by population increase and subsequent territorial packing that would require increased use of any given environmental patch.

[10]I am aware of the criticisms of Thomas' typology by Flenniken and Raymond (1986) and Wilke and Flenniken (1989); while I am convinced that one can resharpen a dart point into what is commonly recognized as a "later" arrow point, I am not convinced that this actually occurred with Great Basin projectile points to such an extent that it leaves projectile points useless as temporal indicators.

[11]It appears safe to assume that the return rate from seeds stored in coprolites would be extremely low and that these would be starvation food. Thomas' interpretation of these coprolite "caches" as starvation foods is not accepted by all, but it must be given consideration as there is ethnographic evidence in support of it.

[12]A change in large game populations may also be indicated by the cessation of stone (i.e., permanent) drive fences and a shift to use of brush fences in the late prehistoric (post–650 B.P.) and ethnographic periods (Pendleton and Thomas 1983; Kelly 1988a; Arkush 1986).

References

Anderson, D. R.
   1975   *Population Ecology of the Mallard V: Temporal and Geographic Estimates of Survival, Recovery, and Harvest Rates.* U.S. Fish and Wildlife Service Resource Publication 125.
Arkush, B. S.
   1986   Aboriginal Exploitation of Pronghorn in the Great Basin. *Journal of Ethnobiology* 6:239-255.
Barber, M. J.
   1978   *Report of Wildlife Management Study, Progress Report 6.* Report on file, Stillwater Wildlife Management Area, Fallon, Nevada.
Beardsley, R. K., P. Holder, A. Krieger, B. Meggers, J. Rinaldo, and P. Kutsche
   1956   Functional and Evolutionary Implications of Community Patterning. In *Seminars in Archaeology: 1955,* edited by R. Wauchope, pp. 129-157. Society for American Archaeology Memoir 11.
Bellshaw, J.
   1978   Population Distribution and the Pattern of Seasonal Movement in Northern New South Wales. In *Records of Times Past: Ethnohistorical Essays on the Culture and Ecology of the New England Tribes,* edited by I. McBryde, pp. 65–81. Australian Institute of Aboriginal Studies, Canberra.
Binford, L. R.
   1980   Willow Smoke and Dogs Tails: Hunter-Gatherer Settlement Systems and Archaeological Site Formation. *American Antiquity* 45:4-20.
   1983   *In Pursuit of the Past.* Thames and Hudson, London.
Carney, S. M., and M. F. Sorenson
   1975   *Distribution in States and Counties of Waterfowl Species Harvested During 1961-70 Hunting Seasons.* U.S. Fish and Wildlife Service Special Scientific Report - Wildlife 187.
Charnov, E.
   1976   Optimal Foraging: The Marginal Value Theorem. *Theoretical Population Biology* 9:129-136.
Davis, J. O.
   1982   Bits and Pieces: The Last 35,000 Years in the Lahontan Area, Nevada and California. In *Man and Environment in the Great Basin,* edited by D. B. Madsen and J. F. O'Connell, pp. 53-75. SAA Paper No. 2, Society for American Archaeology, Washington, D.C.
DeQuille, D. (W. Wright)
   1963   *Washoe Rambles.* Westernlore Press, Los Angeles.
Eder, J. F.
   1984   The Impact of Subsistence Change on Mobility and Settlement Pattern in Tropical Forest Foraging Economy: Some Implications for Archaeology. *American Anthropologist* 86:837-853.
Elsasser, A. B., and E. R. Prince
   1961   The Archaeology of Two Sites at Eastgate, Churchill County, Nevada: II. Eastgate Cave. *University of California Anthropological Records* 20:139-149.
Elston, R. G.
   1982   Good Times, Bad Times: Prehistoric Culture Change in the Western Great Basin. In *Man and Environment in the Great Basin,* edited by D. B. Madsen and J. F. O'Connell, pp. 186-206. SAA Paper No. 2, Society for American Archaeology, Washington, D.C.
Flenniken, J. J., and A. Raymond
   1986   Morphological Projectile Point Typology: Replication Experimentation and Technological Analysis. *American Antiquity* 51:603-614.
Flenniken, J. J., and P. J. Wilke
   1989   Typology, Technology, and Chronology of Great Basin Dart Points. *American Anthropologist* 91:149-158.
Fowler, D. D., and C. S. Fowler
   1971   *Anthropology of the Numa: John Wesley Powell's Manuscripts of the Numic Peoples of Western North America, 1868-1880.* Smithsonian Contributions to Anthropology No. 14. Washington, D.C.

Heizer, R. F., and A. D. Krieger
   1956   *The Archaeology of Humboldt Cave, Churchill County, Nevada*. University of California Publications in American Archaeology and Ethnology No. 47. Berkeley.
Heizer, R. F., and L. K. Napton
   1970   *Archaeology and the Prehistoric Great Basin Lacustrine Subsistence Regime as Seen from Lovelock Cave, Nevada*. Contributions of the University of California Archaeological Research Facility No. 10. Berkeley.
Hester, T. R.
   1974   Archaeological Materials from Site NV-Wa-197, Western Nevada: Atlatl and Animal Skin Pouches. *Contributions of the University of California Archaeological Research Facility* 21:1-36.
Janetski, J. C.
   1979   Implications of Snare Bundles in the Great Basin. *Journal of California and Great Basin Anthropology* 1:306-321.
   1986   The Great Basin Lacustrine Subsistence Pattern: Insights from Utah Lake. In *Anthropology of the Desert West: Essays in Honor of Jesse D. Jennings*, edited by D. D. Fowler and C. Condie, pp. 145-168. University of Utah Anthropological Paper No. 10. Salt Lake City.
Jones, K. T., and D. B. Madsen
   1989   Calculating the Cost of Resource Transportation: A Great Basin Example. Current Anthropology 30:529-534.
Keeley, L. H.
   1988   Hunter-Gatherer Economic Complexity and "Population Pressure": A Cross-Cultural Analysis. *Journal of Anthropological Archaeology* 7:373-411.
Kelly, R. L.
   1983   Hunter-Gatherer Mobility Strategies. *Journal of Anthropological Research* 39:277-306.
   1985   *Hunter-Gatherer Mobility and Sedentism: A Great Basin Study*. Ph.D. dissertation, Department of Anthropology, University of Michigan. University Microfilms, Ann Arbor.
   1988a Bighorn, Pronghorn, Lagomorph, Rat: Great Basin Hunting Patterns and Their Bearing on Sedentism. In *Diet and Subsistence: Current Archaeological Perspectives*, edited by B. Kennnedy and G. LeMoine, pp. 80-85. Archaeological Association of the University of Calgary, Calgary.
   1988b The Three Sides of a Biface. *American Antiquity* 53:717-734.
   1990   Late Holocene Climatic and Cultural Change in the Western Great Basin. In *Reconstructing Climatic Change and Variation and Their Effects on Human Adaptations in the Western United States*, edited D. O. Larson and J. C. Michaelson. Plenum Press, New York, in press.
   n.d.a Hunter-Gatherers: Economy, Ecology, and Society. Ms. in possession of author.
   n.d.b Archaeological Survey of the Carson Sink and Stillwater Mountains, Nevada. *Anthropological Papers of the American Museum of Natural History*, in preparation.
   n.d.c Archaeological Excavations in the Stillwater Marsh, Nevada. Ms. in possession of author, in preparation.
Leonard, Z.
   1904   *Adventures of Zenas Leonard, Fur Trader and Trapper, 1831-1836*, edited by W. F. Wagner. The Burrows Brothers Co., Cleveland.
Livingston, S.
   1986   Archaeology of the Humboldt Lakebed Site. *Journal of California and Great Basin Anthropology* 8:99-115.
   1988   *The Avian and Mammalian Faunas from Lovelock Cave and the Humboldt Lakebed Site*. Ph.D. dissertation, Department of Anthropology, University of Washington, Seattle.
Loud, L. L., and M. R. Harrington
   1929   *Lovelock Cave*. University of California Publications in American Archaeology and Ethnology No. 25. Berkeley.
Madsen, D. B.
   1979   The Fremont and the Sevier: Redefining Agriculturalists North of the Anasazi. *American Antiquity* 44:711-722.
   1982   Get it Where the Gettin's Good: A Variable Model of Great Basin Subsistence and Settlement Based on Data from the Eastern Great Basin. In *Man and Environment in the Great Basin*, edited by D. B. Madsen and J. F. O'Connell, pp. 207-226. SAA Paper No. 2, Society for American Archaeology, Washington, D.C.
   1989   Transportation, Seasonality and Storage Among Mid-Latitude Hunter-Gatherers. Paper presented at the 54th Annual Meeting of the Society for American Archaeology, Atlanta.
Madsen, D. B., and L. W. Lindsay
   1977   *Backhoe Village*. Utah Division of State History, Antiquities Section Selected Papers No. 4. Salt Lake City.
Metcalfe, D.
   1989   A General Cost/Benefit Model of the Tradeoff Between Transport and Field Processing. Paper presented at the 54th Annual Meeting of the Society for American Archaeology, Atlanta.
Munro, R. E., and C. F. Kimball
   1982   *Population Ecology of the Mallard VII: Distribution and Derivation of the Harvest*. U.S. Fish and Wildlife Service Resource Publication No. 147.
Pendleton, L. S. A., and D. H. Thomas
   1983   The Fort Sage Drift Fence, Washoe County, Nevada. *Anthopological Papers of the American Museum of Natural History* 58:1-38.

Parry, W., and R. L. Kelly
  1987   Expedient Core Technology and Sedentism. In *The Organization of Core Technology*, edited by J. K. Johnson and C. A. Morrow, pp. 285-304. Westview Press, Boulder, Colorado.
Price, T. D., and J. A. Brown
  1985   Aspects of Hunter-Gatherer Complexity. In *Prehistoric Hunter-Gatherers: The Emergence of Cultural Complexity*, edited by T. D. Price and J. A. Brown, pp. 3-20. Academic Press, New York.
Rafferty, J. E.
  1985   The Archaeological Record on Sedentariness: Recognition, Development and Implications. In *Advances in Archaeological Method and Theory 8*, edited by M. B. Schiffer, pp. 113-156. Academic Press, New York.
Raven, C., and R. Elston
  1988   *Preliminary Investigations in Stillwater Marsh: Human Prehistory and Geoarchaeology*. Report Prepared for the U.S. Fish and Wildlife Service, Region 1, Portland Oregon. Intermountain Research, Silver City, Nevada.
Simms, S. R.
  1987   *Behavioral Ecology and Hunter-Gatherer Foraging: An Example from the Great Basin*. British Archaeological Reports, International Series No. 381. London.
Simms, S. R., and K. L. Heath
  1988   Site Structure of the Orbit Inn: An Archaeological Application of Inferences from Ethnoarchaeology. Paper presented at the 21st Great Basin Anthropological Conference, Park City, Utah.
Simpson, J. H.
  1876[1983]   *Report of Explorations Across the Great Basin of the Territory of Utah for a Direct Wagon-route from Camp Floyd to Genoa, in Carson Valley*. University of Nevada Press, Reno.
Stephens, D. W., and E. L. Charnov
  1982   Optimal Foraging: Some Simple Stochastic Models. *Behavioral Ecology and Sociobiology* 10:251-263.
Stephens, D. W., and J. R. Krebs
  1986   *Foraging Theory*. Princeton University Press, Princeton.
Steward, J. H.
  1938   *Basin-Plateau Aboriginal Sociopolitical Groups*. Bureau of American Ethnology Bulletin No. 120. Washington, D.C.
Thomas, D. H.
  1981   How to Classify the Projectile Points from Monitor Valley, Nevada. *Journal of California and Great Basin Anthropology* 3:7-43.
  1985   *The Archaeology of Hidden Cave, Nevada*. Anthropological Papers of the American Musem of Natural History No. 61. New York.
Tuohy, D. R., A. J. Dansie, and M. B. Haldeman
  1987   Final Report on Excavations in the Stillwater Marsh Archaeological District, Nevada. Nevada State Museum Archaeological Service Report to the U.S. Fish and Wildlife Service, Portland Regional Office.
Tuohy, D. R., and L. K. Napton
  1986   Duck Decoys from Lovelock Cave, Nevada, Dated by C-14 Accelerator Mass Spectrometry. *American Antiquity* 51:813-816.
United States Geological Survey
  1978   Surface Water Supply of the United States, 1976. Geological Survey Water Supply Paper 1314. Washington, D.C.
Weller, M. W.
  1978   Management of Freshwater Marshes for Wildlife. In *Freshwater Wetlands: Ecology and Management Potential*, edited by R. E. Good, pp. 267-284. Academic Press, New York.
Wells, H. F.
  1978   Historical Accounts of Grass Valley 1863-72. In *History and Prehistory at Grass Valley, Nevada*, Monograph 7, edited by C. W. Clewlow, pp. 11-34. Institute of Archaeology, University of California Los Angeles.
Wheat, M.
  1967   *Survival Arts of the Primitive Paiutes*. University of Nevada Press, Reno.
Zeanah, D.W.
  1988   Pit Features and Food Storage Strategies in the Great Basin. Paper presented at the 21st Great Basin Anthropological Conference, Park City, Utah.

16

ON SOME RESEARCH STRATEGIES FOR UNDERSTANDING THE WETLANDS

David Hurst Thomas

Introduction

T he editors asked me to make a few comments about the various contributions in this volume. I am pleased to do so because I like the direction of many papers published here. Over the past year, two other very important wetlands publications have appeared, preliminary results from excavations in the Stillwater Marsh (Raven and Elston 1988) and Catherine Fowler's (1989) long-awaited compilation of Willard Z. Park's ethnographic notes on the Northern Paiute. We further anticipate that several additional wetlands studies will be published in the near future, including Madsen's long-term, innovative investigations around the Great Salt Lake. By Great Basin standards, this is a virtual avalanche of information relevant to the long-neglected lacustrine adaptations, and the present volume contributes some very useful baseline information.

The "Either/Or" Strawman

In other words, I like this collection of papers very much. But I must immediately distance myself from statements made in the Introduction (Madsen and Janetski, this volume). The editors are to be congratulated for instigating this important inquiry—and for bringing the papers to publication. But I feel that they have misrepresented the nature of previous inquiries into wetlands archaeology in the Great Basin.
This book begins on a curious and precarious premise. Let me quote directly from the first paragraph:

> The Great Basin is, as many pointed out, a land of extremes. Lake, river, and marsh environments supplied with 'free' water from high mountain ranges, contrast sharply with the desert conditions of intermountain valleys and lower foothills; a contrast made more dramatic by a lack of intervening environmental setting. This physical diversity has long been mirrored in the contrasting nature of Great Basin anthropological debates. Specific arguments and their associated terminology have changed with time, but the structure of the debate has not. Prehistoric and ethnographically known Great Basin groups are argued to be either generalists or specialists; they were either limno-mobile or limno-sedentary; they either lived in a 'Garden of Eden' or they lived a life of stress and deprivation. All are arguments which can be characterized as "either/or" polemics (Madsen and Janetski, this volume; emphasis added).

What a bizarre equation: Not only is the Great Basin environment hostile and extreme, but so are the archaeologists who chose to work there!

With this sweeping condemnation, the editors single-handedly condense and revise the history of Great Basin anthropological thinking on the wetlands into a series of simplistic, black/white contrasts. Somebody must point out that this is simply not so. Whereas the environments may be sometimes unforgiving, and some of the scholars "colorful," it is a absurd to suggest that Great Basin wetlands anthropology can be characterized as an "either/or polemic."

The editors follow with another odd statement, informing the reader that "the history of these often contentious debates is covered elsewhere in this volume." Having read the other papers rather closely, I found the discussions to be phrased in precisely the opposite fashion. Catherine Fowler and Don Fowler, in their "A History of Wetland Anthropology in the Great Basin" did not find a pervasive and destructive "either/or polemic." In fact, their review of this literature employs terms like "heuristic devices to trigger an ongoing discussion . . .," and "salutary effect of causing us to consider in detail. . . . " No "either/or polemics" here. Other contributions by C. Fowler, Janetski, and Rhode also deal with the history of wetlands inquiry, but I find no evidence of an "either/or" syndrome. In fact, phrases like "these often contentious debates" and "decades old interpretive dichotomy" crop up only in the editors' own introduction.

An impartial reading of the literature contradicts the editors' claim at every turn. Should the reader find this curious—as I do myself—let us return to a few of the original sources (which the editors do not cite). One major point in the introduction is that the terms "limno-sedentary" and "limno-mobile" are prime offenders in the "either/or polemic." Although the limnosedentary notion has been with us for decades, the term limnomobile was introduced by me in the Hidden Cave monograph, which contained the following explicit caveat:

> We can, for heuristic purposes, identify polar positions regarding the lakeside adaptation. One posture [is] termed the limnosedentary hypothesis. . . . The antithesis [is termed] the limnomobile hypothesis. . . . We cannot distinguish between these alternatives at present. . . . But Hidden Cave does point up the bankruptcy of the extreme limnosedentary and limnomobile positions (Thomas 1985:18, 390 emphasis added).

Does this sound like a "decades-old polarization" or "the darkness of 'either/or'?"

The editors continue to lament another alleged example of polarized thinking, claiming that:

> The continuing confusion generated by this either/or approach has been exacerbated in the last decade by contrasting foragers with collectors and by associating foragers with residential movement and collectors with logistical movement. This additional either/or contrast seems entirely inappropriate to us . . .

And yet, when we look at the original sources—in this case when Lewis Binford's notion of foragers and collectors was transplanted to the Great Basin context—we find no evidence of such "either/or" propositions. These concepts were presented merely as "extreme positions along a strategic continuum, along which various hunter-gatherer mobility and subsistence patterns can be scaled" (Thomas 1983:10a; see also Thomas, Pendleton, and Capannari 1986).

Later on, in the same volume, I selected three protohistoric Great Basin groups to illustrate the impressive degree of variation in adaptive strategies: "The Kawich Mountain Shoshone were a residentially mobile foraging society; the Owens Valley Paiute lived in nearly sedentary band villages and were collectors; the Reese River Shoshone followed a fusion-fission settlement pattern, embodying characteristics of both foraging and collecting strategies" (Thomas 1983a:27). Elsewhere, these same concepts were amplified this way:

> Collecting strategies can take many forms—depending on the quality, quantity, and geographical location of consumable resources . . . Foraging ("mapping on") and collecting ("logistic") strategies may merely represent polar extremes along an adaptive continuum; any given group of hunter-gatherers can be characterized as residentially mobile, logistically mobile, or as some mix of the two. These structural poses are not temporally fixed either, since ecological requirements sometimes are such that a given group must shift seasonally and/or annually along the foraging-collecting continuum (Thomas 1985:17).

Having already pointing out "the bankruptcy" of extreme limnosedentary and limnomobile postures, we interpreted the significance of the Hidden Cave excavations this way:

This site would have been of little use to foragers; there is simply too much preplanned storage and recycling to fit with a model of extreme residential mobility. But on the other hand, Hidden Cave surely does not reflect a lacustral Garden of Eden; there is too much evidence pointing toward logistic mobility and backup planning. The limited regional data from Hidden Cave reflect the multiple strategies of fission-fusion settlements—neither pure foragers nor pure collectors. . . . The Hidden Cave story is undeniably complex (1985:390-391, emphasis added).

Here, I have cited only my own writing. But I am unaware of cases in which others have distorted these basic concepts into a "focus on extremes" or a "simple either/or dichotomy."

I submit that the "either/or" model is a poor characterization of past discussions about Great Basin wetlands; the dialogue simply did not unfold this way. It is an insult and a disservice to those involved to suggest that we were so simple-minded. The "either/or" model is a fictive strawman conjured up as a foil to bolster the editors' claims for a "more balanced and integrated view." Fortunately, none of the other contributors to this volume employs such "either/or" thinking, and I suspect that the reader will avoid that trap as well.

An Unexpected "Either/Or" Boosterism

Given their aversion to the "either/or dichotomy," it is doubly curious that the editors then advocate a posture for future research that itself sounds strangely "either/or." The perspective of evolutionary ecology is strongly pitched as the solution to the problems of Great Basin wetlands: "We believe that hunter-gatherers (indeed all people) tend towards those behaviors that maximize reproductive success. That is, we view a natural selection paradigm as the one most likely to be productive in understanding human behavior generally and Great Basin peoples specifically . . ." (Madsen and Janetski, this volume). Is the debate already solved? What about some diversity of opinion? What do the other participants in the volume think? Could this be ultimate "either/or" dichotomy: Either you pledge allegiance to the tenets of evolutionary ecology or you will never "creep out of the darkness of either/or."

Fortunately, this is another phony "either/or" dichotomy that the rest of us can live without. Evolutionary ecology should not be an "either/or" proposition, and nobody need accept the premise that foraging theory is an intellectual litmus test—either you believe or you do not.

Steven Simms (1988:420) has recently emphasized the important, and often overlooked point that optimal foraging theory is not really a theory at all; it is a research strategy (sensu Harris 1979:Chapter 1). As Marvin Harris (1987:107-111) clearly spells out, a research strategy is what advocates believe best conforms to the canons of acceptable scientific explanation. For decades, Harris has advocated the principles cultural materialism because he believes that this research strategy produces better explanations than those available from any other research strategy; many archaeologists would agree.

But such agreement derives not from a rote recitation of personal belief systems, but from the rather lengthy succession of specific cultural materialistic explanations marshalled by Harris to back his claim: among them are explanations regarding the origin and evolution of sex and gender roles, reasons why warfare is so prevalent, arguments regarding the origins of dietary patterns of food avoidance, plus inferences about numerous settlement pattern and demographic trends. This is an impressive list. Although many cultural anthropologists disagree with the explanations derived from the cultural materialistic research, the onus is upon them to provide better explanations.

The potential of foraging theory for archaeology was clearly overstated by early proponents; we prefer the more seasoned approach, such as that of O'Connell and Hawkes (1981), who present more balanced views of both costs and benefits. But, given the editors' enthusiastic endorsement of the O'Connell, Jones, and Simms (1982) call to arms, one is forced to ask the whereabouts of the list of superior explanations emanating from optimal foraging theory? I can find no list—at least not yet.

If Simms is correct that optimal foraging theory is really a research strategy, then it follows that the efficacy of that research strategy can only be judged upon the basis of results produced—not on a priori extrapolations speculating about why foraging theory "ought to work." If optimal foraging theory is to command serious attention in Great Basin archaeology, then OFT must be capable of providing explanations superior to the alternative. The jury is clearly still out.

My point here is not to demean the potential of foraging theory or optimization as a potential source of insight. Elsewhere, I have evaluated OFT and concluded on a fairly upbeat note (Thomas 1986:258; 1989:Chapter 15). Rather than bend to the "either/or" way of thinking, I suggest viewing OFT as an additional source of good ideas, as one of several research strategies that may (or may not) lead to fruitful lines of inquiry.

Linking the Conceptual to the Archaeological

So how do we judge the effectiveness of a research strategy? Results are critical, of course, and until a solid list of achievements is in hand, no single research strategy can or should attempt to claim victory. This is the first basic criterion.

This raises a second important issue: any research strategy worth its salt must articulate directly with the kind of empirical data involved: that is, research strategies must be falsifiable. Before any theoretical projections can be brought to bear on archaeological data, it is necessary to infer past behavior from the archaeological record and also to infer past environmental states from the paleoenvironmental record. Both records are static, and all dynamics must be inferred through establishing middle-range linkages.

Projections from optimal foraging models—whether they provide good explanations or not—make very heavy demands of the archaeological record. As archaeologists, we must be able to provide comprehensive cultural and paleoenvironmental chronologies, an accurate picture of (1) who lived where (and when), (2) what plants and animals were (or were not) available for inclusion in the diet, and (3) what people actually ate.

Ten or fifteen years ago archaeologists were quick to offer such answers. But more recently, Americanist archaeology has emerged from its Age of Aquarius. We now require better-reasoned associations to establish reliable estimates of seasonality and annual round. We no longer live in the if-wishing-would-make-it-so euphoria of the new archaeology of the 1960s and 1970s.

Grinding stones, for instance, were once routinely considered to be isomorphic with (1) women and (2) seed collection, but we can no longer assume such a relationship. Projectile points once meant "men went hunting," but we now realize that the relationship among subsistence, gender, and technology is considerably more complex. We now recognize that the mere presence of bones and seeds at an archaeological site is no longer considered to be valid evidence of human consumption. Rather, we must adequately document the procurement and processing strategies applied to these resources: how the seeds are processed and how evidence for such processing will appear in the archaeological record.

While research on seasonality, size sorting and intrasite patterning, tool kits and activity areas, regional variability, taphonomy, and postdepositional modifications proceeds apace, such progress carries with it the sober realization that archaeological data are more intractable than was appreciated fifteen years ago. Generating such fine-grained data is a tall order, but technological advances in archaeology—such as accelerator C-14 and stable isotope analysis of human skeletal remains—may eventually be able to help fill the bill.

These are not shortcomings in research strategy—foraging theory or any other. These are uniquely archaeological problems emerging from the specifics of the past and the immaturity of our methods of understanding. Optimal foraging models may prove to be an effective bridge for archaeologists to use to pass into the realm of general theory. But such a passage should not require that archaeologists retrogress into another Age of Aquarius, when we relied on simplistic assumptions about the way the archaeological record works. Such assumptions were fun—they often made for a "good story" —but we now know they are incorrect.

A Lesson from the Stillwater Marsh

In 1980 and 1981, Robert Kelly undertook his survey of the Carson Desert. This was a time of drought, and Kelly found that sites could usually be found only in large deflation basins. But between 1983 and 1986, the Stillwater Marsh was inundated by floods and as the water receded, dozens of previously-invisible archaeological sites appeared. Several contributions to this volume document this extraordinary new archaeological evidence, some coming to rather different conclusions than those offered by Kelly.

Substantive issues aside, the recent events at Stillwater dramatically underscore another point—the extent to which the archaeological record is a contemporary phenomenon. The facts of archaeology are contemporary observations made on the material remains of the past. Sometimes, as in the Stillwater Marsh, the physical condition of the archaeological record itself can change dramatically—rendering the invisible suddenly visible. But let us not deceive ourselves into thinking that what showed up after the flood somehow represents a more "real" archaeological record.

Stillwater Marsh contains numerous archaeological records; the one visible in 1980 is very different from that available in 1986. While both have stories to tell, neither is the "bottom line." Given enough time, there is every reason to expect that subsequent archaeological records will also emerge there. In fact, I would wager that an imaginative application of today's remote sensing technology would also produce some rather unexpected finds in the Carson Desert.

But regardless of how we get our facts—from flood waters or proton magnetometers—these facts are incapable of speaking for themselves. Archaeologists working at Stillwater have encountered various samples of the material remains left from the cultural systems that once operated there. But what do these facts—contemporary observations made on an equally contemporary archaeological record—tell us of past behavior? In order to make sense of these data, it is necessary for archaeologists to breathe behavioral life into the objects of the past. Both archaeologists and geologists rely on the doctrine of uniformitarianism: The processes that now operate to modify the earth's surface are the same processes that operated in the geological past. It is necessary to understand the ongoing geological processes in order to provide the bridging arguments necessary to assign meaning to the objects of the geological past. One must have, for instance, a knowledge of contemporary glaciers in order to interpret the glacial features of the remote past.

Precisely the same issues face contemporary archaeologists when they attempt to interpret the material remains of past cultural processes. Archaeologists also must frame hypotheses to account for the formation and deposition of these physical remains and so require bridging arguments to translate the general hypotheses into specific outcomes that can actually be observed in the archaeological record.

Properly formulated, these bridging arguments will link our ideas about the world to the world itself, and it will attribute meaning to our empirical observations. Middle-range research dictates the way that we perceive the past and is quite different from the research used to explain that past. In this case, defining middle-range relationships requires that we also define the precise relationships between concepts and an appropriate class of empirically observable phenomena. Such a linkage has been extremely important to both past and contemporary Americanist archaeology. But archaeologists have only begun to direct their efforts toward such middle-range understanding.

Donald Grayson has done archaeology a great service by pointing up the severe linkage problems that exist between the zooarchaeological record and the inferences we make about the past (e.g., Grayson 1979, 1984, 1988). Some of this research has been hard to swallow (especially for me because it cut some of my neat faunal interpretations to the quick). But, without question, Grayson has effectively demonstrated that we cannot do some of the things with fauna that we once thought were possible. Still, it is better to learn the lessons the hard way than not at all, and it is gratifying to note that several of the authors in this volume have indeed taken his message to heart.

Janetski's analysis of data from the Utah Valley wetlands is a case in point (Janetski, this volume). Acutely aware of the importance of controlling for the effects of differential recovery and sample size when assessing diversity in the faunal remains, he has carefully worked through his faunal data, attempting to control for the formation processes involved. Such step-by-step analysis of the complexities involved in taxonomic diversity, differential preservation, and taphonomy are now becoming standard fare when analyzing fauna recovered from archaeological sites in the Great Basin sites and elsewhere.

But these biases are not restricted to faunal remains and for whatever reasons, the implications for material culture are still under appreciated—in the Great Basin as elsewhere. Precisely the same interpretative problems plague our analysis of attributes, artifacts, assemblages, and settlement patterns as well.

Consider the everyday problem of variable sample sizes. For years, archaeologists tended to interpret larger, more diverse assemblages as residential (base camps), the smaller, less diverse collections as resulting from short–term, task–specific behavior (extraction locations). But we now know from various studies of sample size effects, that larger assemblages will almost always be more diverse; smaller assemblages will almost invariably contain fewer artifact types—regardless of what artifacts are present and irrespective of what behavior actually produced the assemblages (e.g., Leonard and Jones 1989; see also discussions in Thomas 1983b and 1988).

Some of the papers in this volume seem well–aware of the assemblage size/assemblage diversity problem. Janetski, for instance, is quite cautious in assigning specific function and occupational intensity to the Utah Valley materials. Raymond and Parks refrain from assigning behavioral categories to their complex survey data from the Stillwater Marsh; Rhode shows similar caution. By contrast, the papers by Cannon et al. and Oetting seem considerably more inclined to assign "site types" to their data, but the specific criteria for such assignments are not discussed in much detail.

Linkage problems even hamper our elemental efforts at chronology. Most of us believe that the two best time–markers in Great Basin archaeology are projectile points and potsherds. But even if the temporal duration of each type were known perfectly—and most ranges are still pretty rough—how do we actually translate these temporal types into archaeologically useful information?

David Rhode, for instance, conducted an innovative regional survey attempting to link the Walker River wetlands with the neighboring upland regions. His probabilistic tract survey produced a number of surface projectile points, among other artifacts. Granted that many Great Basin projectile points provide serviceable time–markers, how many diagnostics does Rhode need assign his surface assemblages to a temporal phase? Is one point enough? What about ten? Or twenty–five? We cannot tell from reading the papers by Rhode, Cannon et al., or Oetting how such assignments were made. But we do see from their Table 4 that Raymond and Parks require only a single point to derive their "Period Arrow" and "Period Dart" assignments. We now know from statistical analyses of such temporal assemblages that such single–point finds are meaningless; in fact, there are cases when two or three dozen time–markers are still insufficient to allow accurate temporal assignment from surface materials (see Thomas 1988, Chapter 9).

Let me clearly state that I am not arguing against the development of general theoretical models. Progress is being made along the evolutionary ecology front, and I would urge investigators to consider alternative research strategies as well. But in the rush to general theory, let us not overlook the importance of developing the necessary models at the middle–range level as well. Without these linkages, we will enjoy an abundance of empirical data and a deluge of elegant theory—but no way of articulating the two.

References

Fowler, C. S. (editor)
    1989   *Willard Z. Park's Ethnographic Notes on the Northern Paiute of Western Nevada, 1933-1940*, vol 1.   University of Utah Anthropological Papers, No. 114. Salt Lake City.
Grayson, D. K.
    1979   On the Quantification of Vertebrate Aarchaeofaunas. In *Advances in Archaeological Method and Theory*, vol. 2, edited by M. B. Schiffer, pp. 199–237. Academic Press, New York.
    1984   *Quantitative Zooarchaeology: Topics in the Analysis of Archaeological Faunas*. Academic Press, Orlando, Florida.
    1988   Danger Cave, Last Supper Cave, and Hanging Rock Shelter: The Faunas. *Anthropological Papers of the American Museum of Natural History* 66(1):1–130. New York.
Harris, M.
    1979   *Cultural Materialism: The Struggle for a Science of Culture*. Random House, New York.
    1987   Cultural materialism: Alarums and Excursions. In *Waymarks: The Notre Dame Inaugural Lectures in Anthropology*, edited by K. Moore, pp. 107–126. University of Notre Dame Press, Notre Dame.
Leonard, R. D., and G. T. Jones (editors)
    1989   *Diversity in Archaeology*. Cambridge University Press, New York.
O'Connell, J. F., and K. Hawkes
    1981   Alyawara Plant Use and Optimal Foraging Theory. In *Hunter-Gatherer Foraging Stategies: Ethnographic and Archaeological Analyses*, edited by B. Winterhalder and E. A. Smith, pp. 99–125. University of Chicago Press, Chicago.

O'Connell, J. F., K. T. Jones, and S. R. Simms

1982 Some Thoughts on Prehistoric Archaeology in the Great Basin. In *Man and Environment in the Great Basin*, edited by D. B. Madsen and J. F. O'Connell, pp. 227–240. SAA Papers, No. 2. Society for American Archaeology, Washington, D.C.

Raven, C., and R. G. Elston

1988 *Preliminary Investigations in Stillwater Marsh: Human Prehistory and Geoarchaeology*, volumes 1 and 2. U. S. Fish and Wildlife Service, Region 1, Cultural Resource Series No. 1. Portland.

Simms, S. R.

1988 Some Theoretical Bases for Archaeological Research at Stillwater Marsh. In *Preliminary Investigations in Stillwater Marsh: Human Prehistory and Geoarchaeology*, vol. 2, edited by C. Raven and R. G. Elston, pp. 420–426. U. S. Fish and Wildlife Service, Region 1, Cultural Resource Series No. 1.

Thomas, D. H.

1983a *The Archaeology of Monitor Valley: 1. Epistemology*. Anthropological Papers of the American Museum of Natural History 58(1). New York.

1983b *The Archaeology of Monitor Valley: 2. Gatecliff Shelter*. Anthropological Papers of the American Museum of Natural History 59(1). New York.

1986 Contemporary Hunter-gatherer Archaeology in America. In *American Archaeology Past and Future: A Celebration of the Society of American Archaeology 1935-1985*, edited by D. J. Meltzer, D. D. Fowler, and J. A. Sabloff, pp. 237–276. Smithsonian Institution Press, Washington D.C.

1988 *The Archaeology of Monitor Valley: 3. Survey and Additional Excavation*. Anthropological Papers of the American Museum of Natural History 66(2). New York.

1989 *Archaeology*. Holt, Rinehart, and Winston, Inc., New York.

Thomas, D. H. (editor)

1985 *The Archaeology of Hidden Cave, Nevada*. Anthropological Papers of the American Museum of Natural History 61(1). New York.

Thomas, D. H., L. S. A. Pendleton, and S. C. Cappannari

1986 The Western Shoshone. In *Great Basin*, edited by W. L. d'Azevedo, pp. 262–283. Handbook of North American Indians, vol. 11, W. G. Sturtevant, general editor. Smithsonian Institution, Washington, D.C.

17

REPLY TO THOMAS

David B. Madsen

T his is wonderful; marvelous! I considered the possibilities of a long reply detailing Jennings/Heizer, Steward/Stewart, Madsen/Kelly etc., but I ultimately decided David Thomas's comments need no reply since they speak for themselves. Had I tried, I could not have invented a better way of proving our major point—that the history of Great Basin Anthropology is rife with contentious and polarized debate and that a more synthetic focus conducted in a more congenial atmospherc is sorely needed. One could almost conclude that Thomas agrees with us. It would be defeating our own efforts were I to reply in a similar vein. Besides, Thomas does a better job in making our case than we did.